Social History of Africa

"WE SPEND OUR YEARS AS A
TALE THAT IS TOLD"

SOCIAL HISTORY OF AFRICA
Series Editors:
Allen Isaacman and Jean Hay

BURYING SM
The Politics of Knowledge and the Sociology of Power in Africa
David William Cohen and E.S. Atieno Odhiambo

COLONIAL CONSCRIPTS
The Tirailleurs Sénégalais *in French West Africa, 1875–1960*
Myron Echenberg

CUTTING DOWN TREES
*Gender, Nutrition, and Agricultural Change in the
Northern Province of Zambia, 1890–1990*
Henrietta L. Moore and Megan Vaughan

LAW IN COLONIAL AFRICA
Kristin Mann and Richard Roberts (editors)

THE MOON IS DEAD! GIVE US OUR MONEY!
*The Cultural Origins of an African Work Ethic,
Natal, South Africa, 1843–1900*
Keletso E. Atkins

PEASANTS, TRADERS, AND WIVES
Shona Women in the History of Zimbabwe, 1870–1939
Elizabeth Schmidt

"WE SPEND OUR YEARS AS A TALE THAT IS TOLD"
Oral Historical Narrative in a South African Chiefdom
Isabel Hofmeyr

WOMEN OF PHOKENG
Consciousness, Life Strategy, and Migrancy in South Africa, 1900–1983
Belinda Bozzoli
(with the assistance of Mmantho Nkotsoe)

WORK, CULTURE, AND IDENTITY
Migrant Laborers in Mozambique and South Africa, 1860–1910
Patrick Harries

"WE SPEND OUR YEARS AS A TALE THAT IS TOLD"

Oral Historical Narrative in a South African Chiefdom

Isabel Hofmeyr

HEINEMANN
Portsmouth, NH

WITWATERSRAND UNIVERSITY PRESS
Johannesburg

JAMES CURREY
London

Witwatersrand University Press
1 Jan Smuts Avenue
Johannesburg
2001 South Africa

Heinemann
361 Hanover Street
Portsmouth
NH 03801-3959
United States of America

James Currey
54b Thornhill Square
Islington
London N1 1BE
England

Published in South Africa by Witwatersrand University Press 1993
Published in the United States of America by Heinemann 1994
Published in the United Kingdom by James Currey 1994

ISBN
Witwatersrand University Press 1-86814-216-7
Heinemann   (cloth) 0-435-08099-7
                 (paper) 0-435-08951-X
James Currey   (cloth)0-85255-661-6
                 (paper) 0-85255-611-X

Library of Congress Cataloging-in-Publication Data

Hofmeyr, Isabel
        "We spend our years as a tale that is told": oral historical narrative in a
South African chiefdom / Isabel Hofmeyr.
                p. cm. – (Social History of Africa)
        Includes bibliographical references and index.
        ISBN 0-435-08099-7. – ISBN 0-435-08951-X (pbk.)
        1. Ndebele (African people)–Folklore. 2. Ndebele (African people)–History.
3. Sotho (African people)–Folklore. 4. Sotho (African people)–History. 5. Oral
tradition–South Africa–Transvaal. 6. Tales–South Africa–Transvaal. I. Title II. Series.
DT1768.N42H64   1994   93-33815
968.2--dc20   CIP

British Library Cataloguing in Publication Data
Hofmeyr, Isabel
        We Spend Our Years as a Tale that is Told: Oral Historical Narrative in a
        South African Chiefdom. – New ed. – (Social History of Africa Series)
        I. Title II. Series 398.20968

        ISBN 0-85255-611-X (James Currey Paper)
        0-85255-661-6 (James Currey Cloth)

Printed and bound by Creda Press

For
my mother and father
Syrith and Haldane Hofmeyr

CONTENTS

ILLUSTRATIONS

PREFACE AND A NOTE ON THE TEXT

The title of this book comes from the Book of Psalms, a collection of poetry that has much to say about words and their effect in the world. One of the statements on this theme appears in Psalm 90, verse 9: "We spend our years as a tale that is told," a sentence that reflects on the ways in which we imagine the passing of time through the aid of narrative. This idea is, of course, common to much literary and cultural criticism which has sought to teach us how much of our sense of the past and of ourselves is shaped by story.

It is the same theme that this study explores by examining oral narrative and one of its subsections, historical narrative, in a Transvaal chiefdom that, like many similar communities, has been radically transformed by colonialism and capitalism. In such a community, the relationship of story to history is particularly complex. Not only do historical narratives refer to the past and mediate an understanding of the past through their form, the stories and their tellers also pass through time and are shaped by its often precipitously changing circumstances. Stories, then, comment on the passing of time and times past; they also enfold fragments of the past in themselves while they simultaneously transmute under the pressures of a changing social climate. Like its title which gathers up these concerns in itself, this study attempts to encompass something of these processes.

If one's concern is with the spoken word, then, as any number of studies have shown, one has to exercise great caution in the way these words are represented in writing. However, in undertaking this task, one is drawn in two different directions: either to facilitate reading or to reproduce the interview as accurately as possible, something that often involves, as Bauman says, "loading down the printed text with so much formal furniture that it is inaccessible to the reader".[1] A great deal has, of course, been written on the printed representation of oral texts[2] and, as Bauman points out, "it is incumbent upon anyone who publishes oral texts to be explicit about the presentational format employed".[3]

In determining a format that best suits the nature of the material, the needs of the book and the interests of the reader, I have divided interview material into two categories: that which conveys information and that which is narrative. The

xi

conventions governing the latter have been those that apply to written texts, and where an elision of either the speaker's words or the translator's words has occurred, this has been represented by three dots. In all instances, such elisions are slight and involve either words of assent from the translator or repetitions or stumblings on the part of the speaker.

As regards renditions of narrative, the conventions have been as follows:

Three dashes ——— represent a pause on the part of the speaker.
A single dash – means halting or abrupt cut-off.
Three dots ... represent an elision of speech within the 'turn' of an informant.
When an entire 'turn' has been elided this is marked by three dots in square brackets. [...]

Words or explanations in square brackets signify different things. First, they can be 'stage directions' indicating some action on the part of the speaker, for example [She indicates the size with her hands]. At times such explanation indicates words that are inaudible or an interruption from a bystander. In other instances, the word in brackets is my explanation of a word or a set of circumstances. For example, in one instance an informant refers to Dromaleya, the 'Sotho-ised' pronunciation of the farm Drummondlea which is then inserted in square brackets. As the context will make clear which case is being used, I have not differentiated the convention for representing these different categories.

At times, a second, and, in one instance, a third voice is introduced into the narration. This second voice is always the translator, either giving translations, asking points of clarification or saying 'Mm', 'Yes' or some other single-syllable word of assent and/or encouragement. The third voice is either myself or someone else present at the interview. Most of this interaction has been reproduced except where it severely retards the flow of the narrative. However, I have introduced as much as possible to give a flavour of the interaction. In such multi-voice extracts, the speakers have been identified by their initials.

Unless otherwise stated, all interviews and the excerpts from them quoted in the text have been translated from Sesotho or Sindebele. In the few instances where interviews were originally conducted in English, I have indicated this in the notes to quoted excerpts from these interviews. Where non-Sesotho words have been used in a Sesotho or Sindebele passage, such words have been italicised. Similarly, a non-English word has been italicised in an English passage. The text also contains translations from Dutch, German and Afrikaans. Again, where quotations have been translated, this has been indicated. On a few occasions I have taken the unusual step of translating book and article titles from the Afrikaans and German since a title can often add an interesting nuance to an understanding of a particular issue.

In the appendices, extended verbatim extracts of four interviews are given. These have been included not only so that the full texts of the narratives analysed in Chapter 6 can be examined but also to provide some idea of the nature and feel of the interviews. Some readers may expect a more standard collection of oral narratives of the type that habitually appear at the end of scholarly works. As this book attempts to explain, however, historical narrative is a genre that is seldom performed today. Furthermore, it is a fluid form that comprises a shifting repertoire of plot units. Since these stories were collected in an interview and not a performance situation, these units were often not packaged into tight performance-type units and tended to emerge in looser clusters. Extended narrative units could, of course, be extracted from the interviews and then presented as a series of narrative texts. Such a strategy, however, would not faithfully reflect the circumstances under which the material was gathered.

ACKNOWLEDGEMENTS

In undertaking any research work, one turns oneself into a vagrant, forever dependent upon the goodwill, both intellectual and material, of many people. Since this book has a strong historical bent, it is as well to start at the beginning with my parents Haldane and Syrith Hofmeyr. They have not only sunk considerable sums of their money into educating me, they have also continued to assist me in a thousand ways, not the least of which was translating extensive passages of Dutch and German texts for this book. My sister, Elise Tait and her husband, Kevin, provided me with friendship and accommodation in Pretoria on my trips to the archives. Their children, Brian, Cathy and Carol, were wonderful playmates who graciously agreed to humour their aunt in endless games of hide-and-go-seek and froggy-froggy-may-I-cross-your-golden-river.

One major theme of this study is how oral literary forms are inductively and informally learned. Much of my learning has occurred in this way and has been absorbed from my colleagues in both the Department of African Literature and the History Workshop. From other people, I have learned in a more structured way. The first and most important of these is my supervisor, Tim Couzens, a teacher and friend from whom I have gleaned my most valuable academic lessons. As many academics from Beijing to New York know, the door of Tim and his family is always open to intellectual vagrants, and I have been one of the many who have drawn on his, Diana's and young Raymond's capacious hospitality. Another person to offer support to international vagrants is Shula Marks. I was fortunate to have studied with her and to have had contact with her over the years. Much of my historical understanding derives from her teaching, although as with Tim, the guest's incompetence cannot be laid at the host's door.

At the University of the Witwatersrand, many people have helped me in specific ways. Deborah James, despite an exacting schedule, kindly agreed to read the drafts of some of these chapters. Jane Starfield provided both friendship and numerous insights into questions of narrative and history. Ulrike Kistner was also always ready to share her considerable knowledge of literary theory with me. Debra Nails, from the start, offered enthusiasm, interest and encouragement for this project. My thanks as well to Dick Rayner who arranged, often at some inconvenience to himself, a number of trips to Makapansgat. Santu Mofokeng at very short notice agreed to come and take his extraordinary photographs and, with exceeding good grace, put up with one so visually illiterate as I. Rasi Peter Sekibakiba Lekgoathi for several years worked as a transcriber, translator and interviewer for me. Without his meticulous and professional assistance, this book would certainly never have been done.

No acknowledgement would be complete without mentioning the numerous librarians without whom research would be unthinkable. To those at the State Archives in Pretoria and to those at the Africana, Wartenweiler, Government Publications and the Church of the Province libraries at the University of the Witwatersrand, my thanks. In the same category as librarians, and just as helpful and patient, are the members of the University of the Witwatersrand Computer Centre; my special thanks to that great computer-smith Patrick Pearson.

In doing field work in the Northern Transvaal, I cast myself upon the goodwill of many different people. Felix Malunga and Edwin Nyatlo, despite terrifying work loads, not only took an interest in this project, but also helped to locate informants and translate at interviews. In addition, they arranged for the Mokopane College of Education in Mahwelereng to host me for the three months of field work which I did at the beginning of 1990.

At the college, I met many fine teachers who not only made me feel at home but also involved themselves in this project. While many people helped in this regard, I am particularly grateful to Rose Lephondo and the Lephondo family. Helen Maime also extended her considerable generosity and friendship to me. Her grandmother, Morongoa Kgosana, welcomed me on many occasions and never tired of discussing storytelling. Babygirl and Nico Mabusela helped with interviews and, together with their daughter Ollie, extended many kindnesses to me.

Hanna Schulze also took a great interest in this project and arranged for me to stay at the Makapanspoort mission where Heinrich and Lena Stern and their family bore the full brunt of my vagrancy. I learned a great deal from their kindness and without them this project would never have been done. At the mission, Joe and Jacobeth Ramupudu donated both their time and friendship towards this project. Another person without whom I would not be writing this is Jacob Mthembu. He not only interested himself in the project, but also arranged transcribers and introduced me to informants. Both he and the Khaas family went well out of their way to induct me into rural life in the Northern Transvaal. Sidney Maaka, Jane Letsebe-Matlou and Peter Kekana also kindly assisted with interviews, while the enthusiasm and help of Alwin Puka and John Kgole was invaluable. I was also extremely fortunate to encounter a local historian, Boyboy Maboya, whose knowledge of the region provided the basis for many fascinating conversations.

My greatest debt, however, is to my eloquent informants who put up with the imposition of interviewing; my woefully limited knowledge; and my inarticulate questions. I hope that the written word of this book can do some eloquent justice to the spoken wisdom they so readily shared with me.

The financial assistance of the Centre for Science Development towards this research is hereby acknowledged. Opinions expressed in this book, and conclusions arrived at, are those of the author and are not necessarily to be attributed to the Centre for Science Development. Funding was also provided by the University of the Witwatersrand.

An earlier version of Chapter 2 appeared under the same title in *Journal of Southern African Studies* 17:4, 1991. It is reproduced here by permission of Oxford University Press. Sections of Chapter 3 appeared in an article, "'Nterata': 'The Wire': Fences, Boundaries, Orality, Literacy", in *International Annual of Oral History, 1990* (New York: Greenwood Press, 1992), and permission from Greenwood Publishing Group to reprint is acknowledged. Small parts of Chapter 6 appeared in "No Chief, No Exchange, No Story", *African Studies* 48:2, 1989, and permission from Wits University Press to reprint is acknowledged. Parts of Chapter 7 appeared in "Popularising History: The Case of Gustav Preller", *Journal of African History* 29, 1988, and they appear here with the permission of Cambridge University Press. The aerial photographs, Plates 3 and 10–14, are reproduced under South African Government Printer's copyright authority 9657 dated 9 August 1993.

Introduction

As a growing number of scholars have pointed out, the study of oral performance has for some time been crippled by a situation in which literary and historical concerns have been separated from each other.[1] This gulf manifests itself both in the disciplinary division of labour that separates oral literature from oral history and in the·extent to which studies of oral literature and performance ignore questions of historical context. Under this dispensation, literary studies tend to pursue questions of the phenomenology of performance and formalist textual analysis often with little reference to historical context or change. Oral historical studies, by contrast, sidestep questions of literary form and attempt instead to make testimony render up cores of historical 'fact'. Karin Barber summarises the situation:

> On the one hand, literary critics and folklorists have taken up a stance which combines a limited contextualisation (the emphasis being on 'performance' and the immediate conditions of performance) with a formalist analysis of texts (with the emphasis on the incidence of wordplay, repetition and other literary devices): thus ignoring by and large what the texts actually *say*. Historians, on the other hand, seem increasingly to be regarding oral texts either as raw material, which, subject to a certain amount of processing, will yield historical information; or as the unmediated voices of an alien past. The 'Let the texts speak for themselves' approach tacitly denies the properties of a text *as* a text.[2]

In the field of cultural studies, this fusion of literature and history has for some time been common. Indeed, tendencies like the 'new historicism' and the 'new cultural studies' have substantially blurred literary and historical boundaries.[3] This fusion has also been apparent in the study of certain oral forms, particularly analyses of oral testimony and life history. Yet, in the study of oral literature proper, a certain rigidity has prevailed. There has, of course, been a strong theoretical commitment to interdisciplinary ventures. The practice, however, has seldom matched the intention. Where cross-disciplinary work has occurred, it has been with anthropology that oral literary studies has most frequently rubbed shoulders.

1

This situation has been changed by two recent texts – Barber's *I Could Speak Until Tomorrow* and Vail and White's *Power and the Praise Poem* – whose writers have done much to shift the nature of debate in oral literary studies.[4] The methodologies and rigour of their work not only offer a model to others in the field of oral literary studies, but could also teach much to the 'new historicists' who, as Elizabeth Fox-Genovese has observed, tend to pass "thick description" off as historical analysis.[5]

This book follows the path that has been cleared by scholars like Barber, Vail and White and attempts to heed Barber's advice that what is required is to acknowledge "simultaneously the historicity and the textuality of texts" and to combine "a sociology with a poetics of oral literature".[6] This book has tried to implement these ideas by investigating three related areas: oral storytelling, literacy and historical narrative. The initial aim of the research from which this work is fashioned was to investigate oral historical narrative. It soon became evident, however, that if one wished to pursue both sociological and aesthetic questions, this issue could not easily be separated from a broader family of concerns. The first 'branch' of this family had to do with the wider context of oral storytelling from which oral historical narrative derived its techniques and stylistic characteristics. The second related to the politics of orality and literacy which, in this book, has become the entry point for exploring questions of oral literature and historical transformation. Oral literature is always changing, and during the nineteenth and twentieth centuries oral forms in Southern Africa have altered drastically. Any serious study of oral tradition is obliged to take cognisance of such transformation.

Like most troikas, however, such a tripartite study presented a number of difficulties. Within the realm of Southern African studies, for example, only oral storytelling has attracted systematic attention. The other two areas – literacy and historical narrative – remain largely unexplored. Within the broader field of African studies, on the other hand, all three topics have been more frequently addressed, but not in the form attempted here. African oral literary scholarship has had a great deal to say on oral literature but has been comparatively silent on oral historical narrative which, because of disciplinary boundaries, is generally left to Africanist historians. This group has, of course, produced a great deal of research on oral historical tradition, and they have devoted some attention to understanding the governing literary conventions and procedures of historical narration.[7] Yet their commitment remains to the historicity of tradition rather than its literary properties which have, as a result, not been consistently studied. As regards anthropological research within the field of African studies, certain practitioners have turned their attention to historical traditions and have produced much fine work on the symbolic dimensions and conceptual presuppositions of historical narration. However, when it comes to issues of how and why such traditions change, the anthropological, historical and literary material could offer relatively little guidance.

Since there is no ready-made framework for dealing with oral historical narrative, I have had to draw selectively on oral literary scholarship, oral historical research and anthropological work on historical traditions to construct one. At the same time, as I explain below in more detail, I have also turned to the many fine histories of literacy elsewhere in the world which all contain illuminating insights into the mutually shaping influence that orality and literacy exercise on each other, and consequently on the ways in which oral forms change.[8] Like many other attempts to study oral testimonial forms, this book has had to position itself at a disciplinary crossroads, and we turn now to examine in more detail how the respective disciplinary ingredients have been selected and combined.[9]

I

Because a major aim of the book is to understand oral historical narrative as a literary form, much of the critical apparatus used here has been drawn from the study of African oral literature. However, given that much oral literary scholarship is sceptical of the idea of oral historical narration, this borrowing has presupposed some modification which in turn requires some explanation.

The reservations about oral historical narrative have been most clearly set out by Ruth Finnegan. Directed mainly at historians who from the 1960s and 1970s were energetically collecting oral traditions in Africa, Finnegan's comments warned that such testimony could not simply be read off as an indigenous literary form. In many parts of Africa, she cautioned, oral historical narrative is not a "specialist literary type". Indeed, extensive and elaborate historical narratives are rare outside large, centralised societies or those polities influenced by Arabic culture. Furthermore, the oral narrative collected by oral historians is often an elicited, rather than a 'spontaneous' product which lacks the clear generic and linguistic conventions commonly associated with oral literary forms such as praise poetry. The question also arose whether historical narrative, if not elicited by outsiders, was ever performed. If it was not performed, could it even be said to be oral literature? Summing up the situation, Finnegan says, "... there seem in fact to be relatively few specifically historical formal narratives in Africa".[10]

While Finnegan in no way repudiated historical narrative and continued to see it as a genre that required further research, her reservations none the less have potentially far-reaching implications as regards the status of historical narrative as African, as oral and as literature. First, its status as an indigenous genre, that is its 'Africanness', is potentially in jeopardy. Secondly, its low performance visibility brings its oralness into question. Thirdly, its lack of obvious literary conventions and clear generic boundaries weakens its status as literature. While this case against oral historical narrative is starkly put, it does capture the major misgivings about the form which could be described as being neither particularly oral nor especially literary. Instead, could it not simply be a type of passive, general knowledge rather than part of an active performing repertoire?

This question held particular relevance for me since it soon became apparent that the oral historical narratives that I had been collecting in a Northern Transvaal community as a pilot project had no performance life. If asked when last they had told the story just narrated, people would shake their heads ruefully, frowning as they attempted to locate something that had long since sunk, like a stone, to the bottom of their minds. Yet some of the stories I heard remained coherent and animated. The situation presented a dilemma. Here was a tradition that still had some vigour, but at the same time it had no performance locale. What was one to do? Disqualify the material as oral literature, throw away the tapes, begin again and do yet another performance study on praise poetry or the oral story?

As much evidence from other parts of Africa strengthened the reservations outlined above, there seemed to be something of a case for the garbage can option. Compared to genres like praise poetry, oral historical narrative is indeed, as Cohen has pointed out, "loose and weakly-structured".[11] There is also much evidence from the rest of Africa to suggest that oral historical narrative is both less frequently and less spectacularly enacted than other forms.[12] As regards the issue of indigenous genre definition, a lot of research has emphasised that many 'traditional' societies foster a non-formal and loosely institutionalised view of the past which is extremely difficult to capture, unwittingly burdened as we are in the academy by a more contemporary, highly institutionalised, text-bound, linear and chronological understanding of history.[13] Further evidence of this generic fluidity lies in the fact that most small-scale societies do not have a special word for historical narration. Instead, it is often included under a more general word meaning 'affairs' or 'happenings' while in other instances it falls under the broader heading 'story'.[14] This generic porousness is further exacerbated by the fact that commentary on the past is not only expressed in narrative form but can be embedded in praises, genealogies, prayers and songs. If African oral literary scholarship had paid little attention to oral history, then these considerations perhaps explain why.

None the less, I was still determined to take the road less travelled. Warnings one would certainly heed, but they remained just that – warnings. They certainly told one what *not* to do but had little by way of positive, methodological advice. Clearly I had to turn elsewhere for guidance, and it was in the scholarship of Karin Barber that I found it.[15] What her work did was to provide historiographical insight into the existing state of African oral literary criticism. As Barber shows, much of this scholarship had been moulded by the presuppositions of New Critical thinking that had dominated African literary studies from the 1950s.[16] Largely because of its inherently literate bias, this research tended to fixate on notions of balance, wholeness and unity. In relation to genre, this tradition often favoured forms with clear generic outlines, possibly because its implicit points of reference were written. Guided by these criteria, much oral literary scholarship had been attracted to forms with apparently stable generic boundaries like praise poetry and oral stories.

It might, of course, be countered that these forms were indigenously nominated rather than sought out by unwittingly literate critics. However, while this point certainly has some validity, it cannot alone explain the narrow generic focus, particularly in Southern African studies of oral literature. A further objection to Barber's position also arises since there are a number of disting-uished academics whose work would seem to contradict this idea of generic rigidity.[17] Indeed, the work of scholars like Finnegan, Scheub and Okpewho can, in fact, be said to have pioneered our understanding of oral literary genres as fluid and as having a "structural looseness of narrative composition" that tended more towards accretiveness than Aristotelian unity.[18] In fact, one weakness of an article like Barber's "Popular Arts in Africa" is the absence of these scholars from her footnotes.

However, despite this stated methodological commitment to looseness rather than unity, *in practice* the attention of most scholars fell on well-defined forms while their interpretation of forms inherently tended to seek out order rather than contradiction.[19] Anything more ramshackle, such as oral historical narrative, was difficult to bring into analytical focus if one's fundamental orientation was towards unity and order. Indeed, as Barber argues, a whole range of performance genres cannot easily be trapped in this type of grid. Instead, as she explains, popular oral performance, shaped always by political pressures and crafted from an ever-changing pool of cultural resources, is constantly shifting, and while such oral forms may imply their own categories of analysis, these are "fugitive" and more difficult to pin down than some analyses allowed for.[20]

Overall, then, Barber's insights remain lucid particularly in understanding, as I wished to do, the prevailing emphases of much oral literary scholarship. In addition, her work is extremely useful in introducing a clear sense of political and social struggle as a key determinant in African oral literature. A sense of struggle is absent from the work of people like Finnegan and Scheub, a point that Beidelman has made in relation to the former some time ago.[21] Her arguments not only helped to explain the recurrent preoccupations of much oral literary scholarship, it also opened up the possibility of dealing with oral historical narrative in a sympathetic light. Overall, the idea of analysing a diffuse type of literariness became more manageable.

Having cleared some conceptual space for the analysis of oral historical narrative, the next step was to devise an appropriate methodology and form of analysis. And, since oral historical narrative was closely linked to other forms of oral storytelling, the starting point for such an undertaking was Scheub's outstanding analysis of the Xhosa *ntsomi*. The system of core clichés or images that Scheub described as lying at the heart of the Xhosa storytelling system was also apparent in the oral historical narrative with which I was dealing. Consequently, it is his model of a repertoire of core elements which a teller uses in varying combinations that informs the analysis of oral historical narrative in the second half of this book. However, since the oral historical narrative with which I was dealing is more diffuse than the forms Scheub analysed, there are other traditions of scholarship that have also contributed towards the approach I have adopted here. The methodology that Barber has evolved to deal with Yoruba *oríkì* (a type of praising) and the narratives (*ìtàn*) that on occasion accompany them was useful in this regard. In showing how these forms are not governed by the sense of an ending but are instead a "concatenation of fragments from different times", her analysis suggested ways of approaching the baggy and rambling form that historical narrative often takes.[22]

In addition, other traditions of scholarship have informed the way I have approached historical narrative. These include speculation on the literary qualities of oral historical traditions undertaken by historians;[23] analyses of historical discourse executed by symbolic anthropologists;[24] sociologically inclined investigations into life history and personal testimony;[25] and literary and linguistic examinations of everyday narrative and storytelling.[26] In addition, the so-called narrativist school within the philosophy of history also had much useful guidance to offer in the area of decoding forms of historical consciousness through the literary convention in which the former is almost invariably embodied.[27] In relation to the world of myth and mythical composition, Lévi-Strauss, in his concept of the capacious repertoire of bricolage, has made much the same kinds of points.[28] Together these strands of scholarship suggest fertile ways for analysing apparently non-literary and weakly structured forms of discourse.

So much for analysing the narrative itself. What of the problematic performance status of oral historical narrative? The question was one with far-reaching implications since, if a particular form was not enacted, could it qualify as oral literature? Living as we do in a post-Parry and Lord world, the answer must of course be 'no', since in terms of the classic definition, any piece of oral literature worth its salt must be composed in performance.[29] While some critics have been prepared to forgo the stress on composition, the element of performance remains crucial.[30] Yet, what was one to make of a tradition that had some coherence but lacked a visible performance context in which the necessary skills could be transmitted? It soon became clear that the answer had to be historical since at some point the stories must have had a performance life which had now terminated. But, in turning to the standard contemporary work on African oral literature, there was, with a few notable exceptions,[31] very little to be learned about this problem. Eloquent on every aspect of performance, this scholarship was silent on why and how such performance underwent change. In other parts of the world, the issue of active and passive traditions had been studied in more detail, and from the work of someone like Dégh, for example, it became clear that one must turn not only to the dynamics of transmission but also to a wider historical and sociological consideration of the community and its history.[32]

It was this sociological set of ideas which illuminated another problem presented by the recordings I had done, notably that most of the informants to whom I was referred were men. Within this group, those who were generally the most proficient historians and narrators were senior men of royal standing in the ruling Kekana lineage. This situation raised two questions: what types of stories did women tell and how did commoners' narratives compare with royal tellings? In this book, it is the first question that has assumed primacy, a situation that can be ascribed to two factors. First, as other Southern African studies have shown, there is often a gendered division of genre whereby men tend to tell 'true' historical stories while women specialise in fictional narratives.[33] Hence, if one wishes to come to terms with historical narrative as a genre then it is gender that will be most useful in defining its boundaries. Secondly, in speaking to informants, it soon became apparent that storytellers themselves frequently conceptualised narrative in gendered terms.

For these reasons, this book takes gender to be the decisive division in storytelling, and it is around this axis that I attempt to come to terms with male and female traditions of storytelling. This is not to say that other divisions, like that of royal and commoner, have no importance. Indeed, as other research has shown, each of these groups transmits differing male historical traditions.[34] However, while these may differ markedly in *content*, in all other respects, like style and place of performance, they are similar. As regards female storytelling, the differences between royal tellers and commoners is, as far as I could see, non-existent.

In relation to oral storytelling, then, the most analytically useful distinction is between men and women, and consequently in this book the major emphasis is on gender while differences of royal and commoner are referred to but not consistently followed through. Yet it must be stressed that this attempt to get to sociological grips with cultural production can at best be blurred since oral storytelling depends crucially on talent and creativity, qualities that do not respect established social boundaries.

In pursuing the issue of gender and storytelling, I undertook a second set of interviews with female narrators from which it emerged that women mostly told fictional stories that were often similar in technique to the predominantly male historical narratives.

How did the two traditions interact? To answer this question, I had, of course, to investigate where and how people acquired storytelling skills. From these questions it became clear that such acquisition had occurred in households strictly divided by gender and that such different gender 'spaces' served to differentiate what were, in effect, cognate narrative skills.

Parenthetically, this definition of gender by genre and space throws some critical light on debates of gender and literature in African studies which tend by and large to take an ahistorical view of women's oral traditions. Such studies rightly point to the importance of such traditions for contemporary novels, but tend to conceptualise these traditions as primordial. Crucial questions of how women writers 'reinvent' tradition or use it as a form of legitimation are obscured. For example, many contemporary women writers colonise the production of children's books on the grounds that it is 'traditional' for women to tell stories to children when in fact such perceptions grow partly out of missionary infantilisation of oral narrative. Such issues are seldom probed and instead it is assumed that there is an unproblematic shift from the oral to the written.[35]

Part of this book's intention, then, is to demonstrate the vast changes that oral traditions undergo, and one route through which it does this is to examine changing household shape. One of the major factors impinging on rural households has been forced removals which compel families to move from cluster-style homesteads to grid-plan villages. This shift has implications for the organisation of space, and this work tries to understand how and to what extent male and female traditions of storytelling have transplanted to the new post-removal environment.

These forced removals are but one example of the massive transformations that have assailed South African rural societies in the last two centuries. Against this background, one might have expected some analysis of oral storytelling and historical change. Yet, when one turns to the research of the last four decades, there is, with a few noteworthy exceptions, very little.[36] For a country that had experienced perhaps the most profound transformation in the continent, this silence was indeed a strange one. One of the reasons for this state of affairs has to do with the successive critical apparatuses that scholars have imported to analyse local oral literature. Each model, of course, asked slightly different questions but none had been actively concerned with issues of historical change.

The first set of ideas to influence academic research in South Africa into what was then called 'folklore' was the motif analysis of the historico-geographic school. Concerned more with the geographical spread of particular motifs than with historical change, this school, at least in the way its ideas were applied here, produced works that focused almost exclusively on tale types.[37]

While this approach enjoyed some support in the 1950s and 1960s, by the early 1970s, it was issues of performance and structuralism that came to predominate. In terms of performance, Scheub's pathbreaking work under-standably became the model, and many followed in his footsteps. Through this work we now have a sophisticated understanding of the composition tech-niques, transmission and performance styles of a number of South African oral narratives. In terms of structuralism, a large number of studies involved themselves in the debate over what the appropriate 'chunk' or unit of analysis for oral narrative should be. This work, too, made a contribution to our understanding of oral narrative in South Africa.[38]

However, if one wished to ask questions about how and why storytelling in South Africa had changed or was changing, there was little succour to be had from the existing research. Scheub's work in its exquisitely detailed consideration of the transmission of craft certainly laid down some of the preconditions for answering such questions, but if one was looking for more detailed guidance there was literally nothing.

This lack of historical emphasis may be partly attributable to the time at which much of this research was done. When figures like Marivate and Scheub began work in the late 1960s and 1970s, the significant developments in South African historiography which were subsequently to promote a vigorous local tradition of scholarship were only just beginning.[39] Since then the field of Southern African studies has produced a rich body of social historical material that enables one to raise historico-literary questions in a way not possible twenty years ago. However, subsequent research into oral narrative has continued to follow people like Scheub and Marivate with an often grim conscientiousness that has paid little heed to the potentially exciting develop-ments in other academic spheres.

While Southern African historiography could be of assistance to the study of oral narrative, the relationship could well be reciprocal. One of the major thrusts of recent Southern African studies has been culturalist in orientation and has sought to understand the formation of popular consciousness and its impact on historical processes.[40] However, within this project, the consideration of cultural factors has not always been as sophisticated as it might. Furthermore, there are significant gaps in the material on culture and consciousness, the most notable of which concerns orality. One central feature of much popular consciousness is its formation in predominantly oral communities. This situation has powerful implications for questions of social transformation but, apart from work by Sitas and Cronin, there is again a yawning gap in the literature.[41]

Yet another gap in this literature concerns popular understandings of history itself. As in all nationalist climates, history in South Africa since at least the nineteenth century has become a significant political resource and symbol. Today it is a fiercely contested area and is a source of much political idiom and vocabulary. Yet, against this background, there has been very little academic attempt to come to grips with what popular views of history might be and how these have changed. While there has been a lot of work that is based on oral historical information, this scholarship has tended to mine testimony for its 'facts' without paying much attention to the forms of interpretation and intellectual traditions that inform these 'facts'.[42] It is this absence that has provided part of the rationale for doing this book.

II

In dealing with oral historical narrative in the Transvaal, it is the broad set of concerns described above that has guided the research on which this book is based, and a brief outline of its contents will perhaps indicate the way in which I have solved some of the problems outlined thus far.

The starting point of the book is to reconstruct the form that an active storytelling tradition may have taken in Mokopane or Valtyn, a Ndebele–Sotho chiefdom in the Transvaal close to Potgietersrus (see Fig. 1) in which research was conducted.[43] As the historical material on the area was relatively sparse, an account of this once-active tradition had to be constructed from interview and ethnographic material. This subject forms the focus of Part One of the book which sets out a model of oral storytelling in the chiefdom. Rooted in the household, storytelling was divided by gender. Within the cluster-style housing that characterised nineteenth-century Sotho–Tswana and Ndebele towns and villages, female storytelling was associated with the hut area, while male storytelling found its performance venue in the courtyards or *dikgoro/ makgundla*[44] that united the various households. In general, women tended to tell fictional stories, while men told historical stories, although this division was never watertight. This difference in content aside, the two traditions shared many similarities. They were, for example, often subsumed under one word, *nonwane*, meaning 'narrative', 'tale' or 'story'. In technique and style, they were similar, and in terms of the plot segments from which they were constructed, they belonged to one intermingling, swirling universe. What enabled people to distinguish the two spheres was their place of performance and the gender of their tellers.

Today, however, such a situation no longer exists. Female storytelling still continues, but male historical storytelling has almost entirely disappeared. Accounting for this change forms the substance of Part Two of the book. The three chapters in this second part comprise a series of case studies that explore the influence of literacy as purveyed by mission and school; the impact of colonial government; and the consequences of forced removals on patterns of storytelling. At the same time, these chapters attempt to convey a history of the community in which the research took place by emphasising three crucial

PLATE 1   A view of the chief's capital in the 1880s, taken from the base of the hill, Sefakaola. The central figure is Mokopane. The oral traditions surrounding him are discussed in Chapers 5 and 6 (T.A., T.A.D., 16219)

PLATE 2   The chief's capital in the 1980s, taken from virtually the same spot (Photograph by Santu Mofokeng)

thresholds of change through which the polity has passed in the last hundred years (see Plates 1 and 2).

The first stage in this process relates to the conversion of what had previously been a chiefdom into a rural location in 1890.[45] This transformation was wrought by the South African Republic Location Commission which travelled through the Transvaal either dispossessing chiefdoms entirely or penning them into absurdly small areas of land. The chiefdom of Mokopane suffered the latter fate with the result that migrancy, which up until this point had largely been voluntary, became more of a necessity.

While this dispossession affected the chiefdom in profound ways, its internal affairs remained largely untouched by direct intervention from white political authorities. From the 1930s this situation began to alter, and it is from this period that I date the second threshold of change to affect the chiefdom. From the middle of this decade, the Native Affairs Department went on a campaign to intervene more directly in the internal organisation of rural African societies in a vain attempt to alleviate the effects of chronic land shortage. This intervention was largely directed at altering established patterns of agriculture and land use which departmental officials saw as 'wasteful'. Instead, they favoured a rigid reordering of communities into arable, grazing and residential areas. As a prelude to this reorganisation, the department conducted anti-soil erosion schemes, veld reclamation activities and fencing projects. This bundle of measures and the policy underlying it was knowns as 'betterment'. However, partly because of the exigencies of a war economy and partly because of resistance to betterment schemes, the policy was haphazardly and half-heartedly instituted.[46]

By the 1950s, with the National Party in power, this administrative faintheartedness began to disappear as coercive social engineering in the countryside was speeded up. These changes, which were to have far-reaching consequences, ushered in a third threshold of transformation for the chiefdom. In addition, as part of its ambitious policy to tighten and restructure controls over the black population through rigid influx control and the creation of so-called homelands, the National Party government increased the degree of policing and repression quite drastically. In most homeland areas, these changes registered themselves in alarming population increases as more and more people were endorsed out of 'white' South Africa and dumped into homeland areas.[47]

Like many other rural societies in South Africa at the time, Valtyn felt the full force of this state policy when in the 1960s it was declared a betterment area in terms of which removals were to occur. These relocations required people to move from cluster-style settlements into grid-plan villages. The consequences in most areas of life were devastating but there was one particular toll that concerns us here: oral narrative. While traditions of female storytelling could transplant reasonably well, the *dikgoro* struggled to reconstitute themselves in the new layout. Migrancy had, of course, wreaked considerable havoc with patterns of male storytelling, but it was, so this book argues, the removals that finally changed male storytelling from an active to a passive tradition. Parenthetically, this relocation was accompanied by another forced removal when the location that had been adjacent to Potgietersrus was swept a few kilometres

down the road, out of white view and into the borders of the officially
designated Nothern Sotho homeland, Lebowa (see Figs 1 and 2). The place to
which this location was moved fell within the chiefdom's already pitifully small
territory.

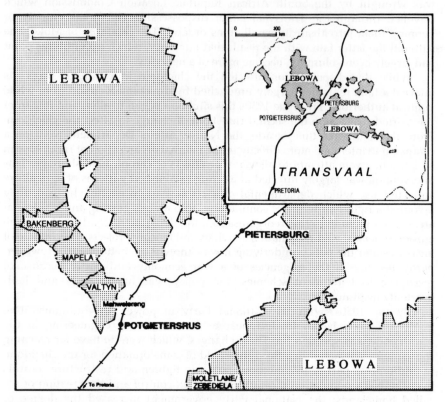

FIG 1   Lebowa and the Northern Transvaal

The case studies in Part Two take these three thresholds as a background
against which the interaction of orality and literacy is explored. While broadly
chronological, these case studies are not strictly so since, as many historians of
literacy have pointed out, the interaction of orality and literacy cannot be
imagined as a straight, evolutionary line in which the written eventually
triumphs over the spoken.[48] Instead, the interaction of these two technologies of
the intellect is jagged, unpredictable and uneven, and in attempting to indicate
this, a contextualist rather than a chronological approach has been adopted.

If there is one principle that this discussion of orality and literacy
establishes, it is that the two areas can never be neatly separated. As Brian Stock
points out in his study of medieval literacy, "The change ... was not so much
from oral *to* written as from an earlier state, predominantly oral, to various
combinations of oral *and* written."[49] In keeping with this idea, the case studies in
Part Two attempt to illustrate the permutations that this oral/literate mix can

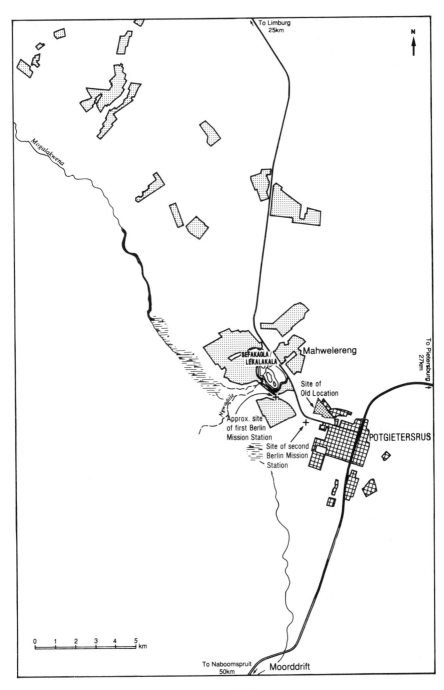

FIG 2 Valtyn, its villages and surrounding vicinity

take. In the initial confrontation of orality and literacy, it is, in fact, the former which transforms the latter, rather than the other way around, as common-sense wisdom would lead us to anticipate. In this process of transformation, a predominantly literate religion – Lutheranism, which arrived with the Berlin Mission Society in the area in the 1860s – becomes 'oralised' in its confrontation with African society, so that instead of being a religion of the printed word, it becomes a religion of the image and the spoken word. Similarly, a literate and bureaucratic colonial government is forced to resort to rule through personal audience, oral message and public meeting. However, particularly in a context of colonial coercion, literate government and schooling do have powerful effects. Schools, for example, write down and institutionalise oral literary forms and so change their meaning and significance. Literate bureaucracies also see the countryside as a blank sheet on which they must write their authority, and this political 'literacy' has a range of consequences. These concerns are also woven into the case studies which attempt not only to illustrate the interdependence of orality and literacy, but also to show that such interaction must always be understood as part of a particular set of political and social struggles into which these two cultural resources are subsumed.

It is this idea of orality and literacy in context which informs Parts Three and Four of the book. As their titles suggest, these latter parts are designed to parallel the first two and, accordingly, Part Three examines examples of oral historical narration that deal with an episode in 1854 in which the Boers, in retaliation for a series of murders, besieged the polity in question for about three weeks. Estimates of deaths range from 1 000 to 30 000. Known in Afrikaans and to a certain extent in English as the siege of Makapansgat, the event, in Sesotho, is known as the *taba ya legolo la Gwaša*, the 'story of the cave of Gwaša'.[50] Chapter 5 analyses the repertoire of basic units from which tellers draw in their narrations of the siege episode. Chapter 6 examines two skilled tellings to illustrate the principles by which the basic units are combined into a longer sequence. By and large, the principles governing these combinations are drawn from the intellectual traditions underpinning chieftaincy, and the chapter argues that the two stories are complex investigations into the meaning of chiefship as a system of political authority and as a symbol of an entire social order.

In order to illustrate that this story and its style of narration have formed part of a wider context, Part Four examines the interaction of the oral and written accounts of the siege. Chapter 7 begins this task by examining how the siege event came to be written up and to be incorporated into the historical mythology that was constructed around Afrikaner nationalism. Yet these two traditions of chief and settler were by no means separate entities and they influenced each other in significant ways so that a neat distinction between chiefly/oral and settler/written is not possible. Since Afrikaner society during the nineteenth century was largely paraliterate, there is little extant documentation of the siege. Hence, somewhere along the line, most written documents were based on oral testimony gained either from Boer informants or from a class of servants and mission converts who acted as the go-betweens for Boer and African societies. Equally, chiefly versions of the story appropriated into themselves fragments from the written accounts. In terms of their implicit forms of interpretation, the two traditions also intersect in interesting ways, and part of the analysis examines how and speculates why both chiefly and settler accounts arrange themselves around similar legendary episodes that, for example, involve saving or bringing back the body of the leader. The concluding chapter turns to examine some of the changes that oral historical narrative has undergone. The most obvious change to this style of storytelling concerns its shift from an active to a passive tradition. However, such attrition is not the only way in which historical traditions have been transformed. Orality, after all, is an extremely tenacious cultural resource, and, in some instances, historical tellers continue to produce capacious accounts despite the changes that have assailed their world. This loquaciousness is not surprising since, as Lévi-Strauss has shown, much oral historical narrative feeds quite indiscriminately on a wide range of forms and information[51] and can reproduce itself easily by using, for example, narrative ballast from radio serials, school text books and local rumour.[52] Another factor promoting the continuation of oral historical narrative is the fact that its form and skills of telling can be acquired via the cognate craft of female storytelling. A few households continue to convey these latter skills as do schools that from an early date appropriated storytelling into their syllabuses.

However, while these factors promote the proliferation of oral historical narrative, other factors militate against a coherent reproduction of the tradition. Broadly put, the processes of dispossession and fragmentation that the polity has undergone mean that a coherent sense of chiefdom no longer pertains. Since this notion forms the centre of gravity for much historical narrative, it is, I argue, increasingly difficult to produce historical narrative that is coherent. Add to this situation the destruction of the *dikgoro*, one crucial institution of 'traditional' historical education, and you have a type of bricolage gone so mad that it often approaches farce. It is in this light that some examples of oral historical narrative are examined.

III

The ideas set out above form the basis of this book. The area in which they have been implemented comprises a cluster of communities in the Northern Transvaal. Shoehorned into the corner of a homeland, Lebowa, that reaches the outskirts of the town, Potgietersrus, these communities appear to merge into one another to make up one of the many rural slums that typify the Transvaal countryside (see Plate 3). However, within this apparently seamless configuration, there are significant divisions. The first of these is an urban/rural divide that separates the 'town' of Mahwelereng from the villages. While the latter falls directly under the administration of Lebowa, the villages are subject to the authority of the chief and Tribal Authorities. Like many other bantustan towns, Mahwelereng came into being in the 1960s when the location next to Potgietersrus was swept back into the borders of the homeland, Lebowa (see Figs 1 and 2). Again, like other homeland towns, it lacks any real economic base and the settlement was intended primarily to serve the needs of white

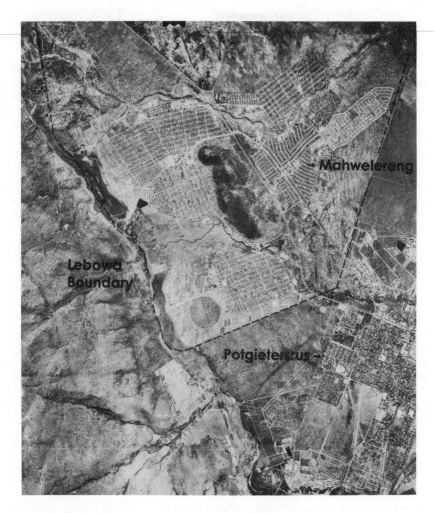

PLATE 3   Aerial survey of part of the chiefdom and Mahwelereng, 1987 (Department of Surveying and Maps, Job 909, Strip 3, No. 2083. Scale 1:50 000)

Potgietersrus.[53] Alongside this township lies the chiefdom, known officially as Valtyn. However, it, as well as the surrounding vicinity, is more popularly referred to as GaMokopane (Sesotho) or KaMugombane (Sindebele) after the famous nineteenth-century chief. As the term Mokopane encompasses a person, chiefdom and wider vicinity, I have generally preferred the term Valtyn to avoid confusion.

While the physical distance between Mahwelereng and the chiefdom is negligible, the social differences between the two are more considerable. From the chiefdom's point of view, the town was an unwelcome intrusion on to much-needed land and, after its establishment, popular feeling against Mahwelereng and its residents ran high. For years afterwards, people under the chief still called it by the name *Anthande lekeišeneng* (we don't like the location).[54] However, it was not simply the loss of space that angered the chiefdom. Like all urban locations, Mahwelereng was seen as the symbol of white control that threatened to engulf the limited independence that the residents of the chiefdom enjoyed from direct white interference. At the same time, the township was seen to embody an ethos of modernity that challenged the prevailing traditionalism of Valtyn. From the vantage of the chiefdom, those in Mahwelereng are apostates who have deserted the cherished world of chiefly tradition. To leave the chiefdom for Mahwelereng is to go into a kind of wilderness or exile where one becomes *lekgolwa/likgolwa*, 'a person who lives in a foreign place for a long time'.[55] Interestingly, the word also means 'a believer' and by extension 'a convert', a person from the mission station, a precursor, in many people's eyes of white-controlled institutions like the location.

Exact demographical statistics for these areas are hard to come by. However, from the available material one can arrive at some sort of estimate. According to 1985 figures, Mahwelereng had a population of 17 915 living in 1 957 houses, an average of 9,2 people per house.[56] As regards an occupational profile, the data is again limited. However, if one takes the Lebowa average as some indication, then 60,8 per cent of the potentially economically active population would be unemployed. Of the employed sector, about one quarter would earn their living as agricultural labourers while another quarter would be production workers. About 18 per cent would work in the service sector while 13 per cent would be in professional, clerical or managerial positions. The remaining 18 per cent work in jobs that are 'not classifiable'.[57] According again to official statistics, 56 per cent of these workers travel beyond the homeland borders to their places of employment. Of this figure, 40 per cent are migrant workers who spend protracted periods away from home. The remaining 16 per cent commute to and from work on a daily basis. However, since these figures were collected at a time when influx control was still in force and many people worked illegally in town, the percentage of migrants must undoubtedly be higher.[58]

In relation to the chiefdom there are no population figures. All that we have is statistics on the number of houses per village. In the biggest village, Mošate, there are 2 548 dwellings. These are broken down into four categories, and the size of each helps to give some sense of the sociological profile of the community. The smallest category of "well-constructed, privately built houses that, by outward appearances, accommodate the more affluent members of the community" comprises 110 dwellings. Thereafter comes a second group of 259 "less pretentious, privately built houses". The third category comprises 645 self-built houses that are defined as being slightly better than the final grouping of 1 534 traditional mud houses.[59] Using the Mahwelereng estimate of nine people per household, the population of the village would be 22 932. Taken together with the other eight villages that fall under the authority of the chiefdom and reckoned on a similar basis, the population estimate reaches 66 483.[60] When the population of Mahwelereng is added in, the figure rises to 81 464. These people live in some 200 square kilometres of land. In the 1960s and 1970s some had access to arable plots. However, these have long since run out and for most people landlessness prevails.

For an area that is supposed to be rural, the population figure is quite staggering and it attests clearly to the violently coercive role that apartheid social engineering has played in places like the chiefdom which has been coerced into its present overcrowded shape by a sustained policy of forced removals. Perhaps less visible but hardly less influential have been the political interventions which have accompanied this forcible rearrangement of the countryside. These political measures were inaugurated in 1951 by the Bantu Authorities Act – the first step on the road to the homeland system. In terms of this legislation, existing governing councils were to become the first tier, or "Bantu or Tribal Authority", in the government of the homeland structure while the chief was to become a state functionary with extended powers which he was expected to use in policing the movements of his subjects. While most areas around the chiefdom had accepted the provisions of the Act by 1954, the chiefdom held out until 1963.[61]

Obviously these coerced demographic and political changes have heightened political tension and fragmentation within the chiefdom. As regards relations between the ruling lineage and the populace, the betterment removals generated much ill will and while no overt dissent was apparent there was clearly a degree of popular discontent.[62] With regard to relations within the ruling lineage, the imposition of the Bantu Authorities Act exacerbated political feuding to such an extent that the Tribal Authority was often paralysed.[63]

However, while this present fragmentation had largely been precipitated by the implementation of apartheid policy in the countryside, it was often conducted in the idiom of much older fractures. One of these stretched back to 1890 when the South African Republic Location Commission penned some 10 000 residents into 12 726 hectares. This dramatic dispossession precipitated massive internal dissension within the chiefdom, and after a succession wrangle the incumbent regent, Ntata Willem Kekana, was forced into exile with a substantial following. However, the chief who then assumed office, Lekgobo Valtyn Mokopane, an alcoholic, proved to be somewhat tyrannical, and perhaps for this reason the exiled faction was invited back again. Whatever the situation, this division has continued to simmer within the polity and has in addition grafted itself to a split between migrants and the incumbent chiefly lineage.[64]

These growing tensions do not, however, mean that members of the chiefdom have abandoned their allegiance to 'tradition'. Indeed, on the contrary, both royals and commoners alike continue to cherish this small area of control that lies partially outside the world of white authority.[65] For most senior members of Valtyn, this attachment to the chiefdom expresses itself as a deep sense of 'Ndebeleness', a sentiment that helps in some measure to provide coherence in an otherwise fragmented sense of tradition and chieftaincy. However, the existing literature has not paid sufficient attention to the character of this ethnicity, and most accounts presume that all Northern Transvaal Ndebele communities are virtually completely 'Sothoised'.[66] In terms of this literature, the Transvaal Ndebele, who migrated from present-day Natal during the 1500s and 1600s, are divided into the Northern and Southern Transvaal groupings.[67] While the Southern Transvaal Ndebele who occupy the central

Transvaal region are portrayed as being 'flagrantly' ethnic, the Northern Transvaal Ndebele are said to all intents and purposes to be Sotho. While this view may in certain respects be true, it does not distinguish sufficiently between the various Northern Transvaal Ndebele chiefdoms. In some of these, like Mapela and Bakenberg which lie adjacent to Valtyn (see Fig. 1), the Ndebele population sinks as low as 18 per cent. By contrast, Valtyn's population comprises 53 per cent Ndebele, 29 per cent Sotho and 17 per cent Tsonga. Apart from Zebediela which has a 55 per cent Ndebele population, Valtyn has virtually the highest Ndebele component out of 13 Ndebele Tribal Authorities in the Northern Transvaal.[68] In this instance, the major marker of ethnic distinctiveness is language, and Valtyn is one of three groupings that still speak Sindebele Semathombeni, the language peculiar to the Northern Transvaal Ndebele. Within this language enclave, the people of Valtyn speak a distinctive dialect.[69]

Even if fixed in language, ethnic categories are not rigid, particularly in the nineteenth-century Transvaal where constant interaction among societies ensured a fluid sense of ethnic definition. However, within this shifting world, the aristocracy of Mokopane clearly retained a tangible sense of being Ndebele, and people recall that early this century the chiefdom comprised linguistically divided villages. Informants also recall that in the past many old women could speak no Sesotho, a situation quite unimaginable today.[70]

Senior spokesmen for the chieftaincy also derive a sense of ethnic distinctiveness from their long-standing defiance of a series of colonisers. They were, they will tell you, never defeated by the major nineteenth-century regional powers, namely the Pedi and the Boers.[71] The other colonisers of the nineteenth century, Mzilikazi's Ndebele, also made their presence felt within the chiefdom although to what extent is not clear. One tradition indicates that the invaders were outwitted and passed on their way without much ado. Another tradition holds that the polity was defeated and had to retreat. As the society probably experienced Ndebele attacks on more than one occasion, both stories possibly have some validity.[72] Whatever the case may be, many people today believe themselves to be descendants of a remnant of Mzilikazi's Ndebele that remained behind. As this view is taught in primary schools, it has wide purchase and is used to claim a link to the Zulu kingdom whence people derive a militaristic sense of ethnicity that grows out of popular perceptions of 'Zuluness'.

Overall, however, this sense of Ndebele identity has become defensive, particularly since the chiefdom is inserted into a Sotho-controlled homeland. There are also historical factors that have promoted this defensiveness. One of these is the arrival of missionaries who did all their proselytising and teaching in Sesotho. Most commoners were Sotho and it was they who filled the schools from an early date and so gained an advantage over the aristocratic Ndebele who were quite firmly set against missionaries.

One long-term result of this mission intervention was a gradual marginalisation of a once-powerful chiefly caste. Add to this their insertion into a Sotho-dominated homeland, and one has a case of a capsized group, turned from a powerful and royal majority into a precariously poised ethnic minority. In recent years the chiefly lineage has attempted to remedy their situation by requesting incorporation into the central Transvaal Ndebele homeland, KwaNdebele, but such pocket-handkerchief nationalism was too small, even for that arch-ethnicist, the South African government.[73]

Taken as a whole, the history of the chiefdom, particularly in the last few decades, has been one of marked and often visible transition. Its geographical setting – likewise one of contrast – provides an appropriate equivalent for this historical saga. As regards its situation, the chiefdom is located along the eastern bank of the Mogalakwena or Nyl River (see Fig. 2). To the west of this river, a range of hills rises by some 700 metres marking the start of the Waterberg Plateau that ascends gently through a series of parallel valleys and ridges. Compared to this plateau, the chiefdom lies in low, flat bushveld country at an elevation of 1 067 metres. However, unlike the area further eastward, the chiefdom experiences a relatively good annual rainfall of between 50 and 62,5 centimetres. In addition, towards the southern end of the chiefdom, the river, which traverses very flat terrain, widens into swamp and marsh areas that can reach about 800 metres in width. The grassy glades of the river banks provide palatable grazing and the alluvial soil is noted for its fertility.[74]

Moving eastward from the lowlands of the chiefdom, the countryside rises gradually, gaining elevation through a series of concentric ridges. It is in one of these that one finds a series of dolomite caves that bear both on the parochial saga of the chiefdom and on a much broader story of human history itself. As regards the local saga, the caves have significance as it was here that the nineteenth-century chief, Mokopane, and his followers were besieged in 1854 by two Boer commandos and their Kgatla auxiliaries. Few survived the three-week siege that followed and this event, as Chapter 5 of this book explains, was to become a legend both in Boer and African society.

This historical legend, however, was to be outstripped by a tale of far larger proportions. Concerned with the origins of the human species, this story began to emerge in the 1940s. By this stage, it became clear that the rich fossil deposits in caves adjacent to the siege cavern included humanoid bones. These fossil finds had first come to light in the 1920s when the travertine lining of these caves had been scraped out for use in a gold extraction process. This palaeontological evidence formed the basis for extensive research, some – but obviously not all – of which generated various strands of myth-making. Largely authored by Raymond Dart, these myths held that since the human remains were surrounded by an embarrassment of animal bones, our early ancestors must have been mighty and brutal hunters. From the evidence in these "blood-bespattered, slaughter-gutted archives of human history", as Dart described the cave, he speculated that human genesis was embedded in killing, cannibalism and warfare.[75] Or, as Bruce Chatwin who himself visited the caves, wrote, "the Weapon had fathered the Man". The theory soon became a popular one and, as Chatwin goes on to point out, Dart's disciple, Robert Ardrey, ranked Dart's work alongside *The Communist Manifesto* in its influence.[76] However, as subsequent research showed, the animal bones had not been dragged in by mighty hunters. Instead, when the caves had not been used for human habitation, the bones had arrived there via the agency of floodwater, porcupines (noted as bone hoarders), scavenging hyenas and so on.[77]

Yet, however wrong-headed Dart's work might have been, it none the less refocused attention on the question of human origins and on the cave system as one of the earliest sites in this evolution. When one adds the more recent historical siege of 1854 to this older history, the series of caves in which these events occurred have themselves become the object of popular fascination, and in 1938, on archaeological, palaeontological and historical grounds, they were declared a national monument.

The research presented here was partly prompted by an interest in the popular mythology surrounding the caves. However, there were also more strictly academic reasons for choosing the siege event that occurred in these caves as a major theme for the book. Apart from the fact that a concentration on one episode would give the research a manageable focus, there was also a clearly defined written tradition which could be contrasted with the oral accounts. The collection of such accounts was done through interviews, carried out with the help of people who lived in the area and acquired informants who were said to be well versed in the history of the region. These local people also interpreted for me at the interview and, at my request, gave only brief and summarised translations to allow people to narrate their stories or story chunks at length.

The interviews fell roughly into two parts. In the first part, informants were asked if they knew the story of the cave siege and, if so, they proceeded to narrate their accounts with both the translator and me asking questions or requesting clarification from time to time. Thereafter, I asked a series of questions about where, how and why they had learned the story just narrated, and finally I asked them for a synopsis of their lives. Interviews were done in English, Sesotho or Sindebele, depending on the informant's choice. The tapes were then transcribed and translated by a number of students. The Sindebele used in these interviews is a dialect peculiar to the region, and in all instances these interviews have been transcribed by speakers from the area. The first set of interviews, which turned out mainly to be with men, was done in a series of day and weekend trips undertaken during the period 1987 to 1989. The second set of interviews, which focused mainly on female storytelling and followed the same format and procedure described above, was conducted during a continuous three-month stay in the area at the beginning of 1990. I stayed on a local mission station and was given an office at the Mokopane College of Education in Mahwelereng where I also did some teaching.

There is, of course, a host of methodological problems swarming around this interviewing technique. As Finnegan has pointed out, when dealing with oral literature one needs to know the status of both the teller and the text since a recording may represent a number of different things that could include

> a fixed and memorized text, a unique and perhaps one-off performance never repeated in similar form, a version by an experienced specialist who, despite minor verbal variations, has gone through many similar performances often in his career, an experiment by a young poet still in his apprenticeship, or a gallant try by a willing but inexperienced non-specialist in response to a foreign researcher's proddings.[78]

Since the tradition of historical storytelling which I encountered was no longer performed and so was largely passive, the possibility for making these kinds of distinctions is limited. However, on the basis of what others said of tellers, what they themselves said, and from an evaluation of their stories, this book has divided tellers into different categories. These include talented narrators who at one time in their life were active performers and whose gender authorised them to learn and perform historical tales; competent but less skilled 'authorised' performers; talented but 'unauthorised' female tellers; and less skilled, 'unauthorised' tellers.

Another problem with the interviews concerns language, and it is self-evident that dealing with the material in translation is not entirely satisfactory. It is also for these reasons that I have veered away from a performance approach and shifted the emphasis in a more historical direction. I have a limited speaking and slightly better reading ability in Sesotho, but without being fully intimate with a language, one is not able to grasp the meaning and nuance of performance. However, as I have attempted to indicate in the first part of this Introduction, there are a number of pressing historical questions that need to be answered, and I hope that in combining literary and historical strengths with imperfect language skills, this book may, none the less, arrive at some useful conclusions. It is, of course, very much a case of making a virtue of necessity, yet, thus far, much of Southern African studies has proceeded in this way and has produced results which have both vigour and insight. By locating itself in this tradition and emulating much of the work produced in it, this book strives to reproduce at least some of that vigour and insight.

PART ONE

Telling Tales

1

"Stories Go Hand in Glove with Building a Man and a Woman"

Household, Gender and Oral Storytelling

One of the most enduring stereotypes in Southern African oral literary studies is that of woman-as-storyteller. Almost invariably a grandmother, preferably seated in the vicinity of a fire, this figure has dominated virtually all local research into oral narrative. As one study of the Xhosa *ntsomi* notes, "That the woman in particular keeps folktale traditions alive is attested to by various researchers amongst various cultural groups." Yet, not a page later, the same study states that men often volunteered enthusiastically to relate stories for the researcher.[1] In some respects this study by Neethling is typical of many others which all note a preponderance of women narrators but simultaneously report a consistent, if small, presence of male performers.[2]

This predominance of women storytellers in Southern Africa, both now and in the past, has been so widely and consistently noted that it cannot, of course, be without substance.[3] Yet in all the years that this situation has been observed, no one has thought to subject the stereotype to any form of critical scrutiny. Have women always predominated as storytellers? If so, how does this institutionalised speaking relate to the institutionalised silencing that characterises women's subordination in precolonial Southern African societies? What, if any, have the traditions of male storytelling been? How, if at all, do male and female storytelling interact? These questions have never really been broached. Instead, the fact that women should tell stories is often taken as self-evident, an assumption that in turn effectively obscures a number of crucial questions about male traditions of storytelling and the politics of gender in oral literature.

Since this study aims to examine historical storytelling, a form of cultural production generally associated with men, it is necessary to locate male and female performance traditions in relation to each other, and also to understand how this one strand of male oral performance relates to others. In order to start with the general and then move to the specific, we will begin here with the first task of considering the relationship of male and female performance traditions. The second task of examining historical storytelling as one male genre among many will be deferred until the second half of the book. This chapter will attempt a broad, predominantly sociological, overview of oral performance that will bring both men and women into view simultaneously. The initial step in such an analysis is to take an overview of gender relations in precolonial Southern African societies. Thereafter we turn to examine the household since it was here that most forms of male and female storytelling emerged and resided. Finally, we dissect some aspects of female storytelling in more detail.

In taking a sociological view of storytelling which addresses *inter alia* the socialising and educational function of narrative, this chapter may seem to fly in the face of much contemporary study of oral literature which emphasises performance and aesthetic issues. Indeed, to stress pedagogic themes in relation to oral literature probably seems both boring and old-fashioned. Also, in underlining the educational and socialising role of storytelling, it may appear that one is re-dooming it to the nursery, and in so doing, damning its tellers by association. Large numbers of nineteenth-century amateur collectors made this mistake and it has taken a great deal of scholarly work to undo the damage. However, if one wants to probe issues of historical change in oral literature, then a return to these wider themes is necessary. To continue with the phenomenology of performance or a structural reading of content would not serve my purposes, as the Introduction has already indicated.

However, in returning to the relationship of oral literature and its wider function, I am by no means implying that, because the stories were seen to be for socialising the young, this class constituted the sole audience or *raison d'être* for oral narrative. Particularly in the case of outstanding tellers, part of their skill resided in their ability to make a story cater for different age groups simultaneously. Also, my focus is not on education *per se*. Rather, it is raised in the context of gender division which separated life into two rigid spheres. These spheres, in turn, were associated with two streams of education which people often identify as the context to which storytelling properly belongs.

In putting across this interpretation, I have relied on three types of source. The first comprises oral literary studies from Southern Africa mainly, but also from the rest of the continent; the second is comparative ethnography from neighbouring Transvaal societies; interviews make up the third source. I have used these sources because the existing ethnography for Valtyn as well as its nineteenth-century historical record is frugal. As a result, this chapter amounts to a speculative model of how oral performance and oral storytelling functioned before the advent of large-scale forced removals.

I

As an increasing number of studies are beginning to show, the ordering force of gender in precolonial Southern African societies was profound and far-reaching.

(Guy has even gone so far as to suggest that gender was "*the* social feature upon which society was based".[4]) While these studies vary in the degree of precedence they allot to such gender division, they all agree that central to the operation of these societies was the subordination of women. Focusing on issues related to the control and appropriation of the productive and reproductive capacities of women, these studies have set out some of the key features of female subordination. These include the appropriation of women's agricultural labour which largely underwrote the household, the basic unit from which all societies were made. Lacking independent access to land except through husbands, fathers or sons, women were at a life-long disadvantage. In the rigid division of labour, controlled by household heads, women assumed responsibility for cultivation, while men controlled cattle keeping. Cultivation necessitated long hours of labour and produced an unpredictable surplus that women could never dispose of entirely as they wished. Largely barred from access to stock, the major form of storable wealth, women could never really accumulate wealth nor trade in the products of cattle.

Alongside these economic constraints, women from an early age were subject to ideological controls. Initially these took the form of a gender-specific education, backed up subsequently by an initiation process that aimed to make women into obedient wives, ready to donate their fertility to producing more people. This ideal of female obedience was also reflected in their virtual exclusion from political and legal forums, from which they were often barred or permitted only as spectators. Overall, then, a picture emerges of women who experienced both economic and intellectual forms of subordination. Prevented from accumulating wealth or ever gaining complete economic independence, they were equally cut off from controlling the major intellectual resources and media of their society.

The limitations that circumscribed women's lives were nowhere more apparent than in the area of speech and performance. As Kinsman points out in the case of Tswana women, they were expected to mind their own business "and leave the *mahuku* [words] to men".[5] Women could, of course, 'speak' through storytelling, praising, dancing and singing, yet, compared to the wide range of performance skills available to men, this female repertoire was limited. Women's major business, as Comaroff makes clear, was to take care of the physical subsistence of society. Men, on the other hand, dominated its media and intellectual resources. They controlled words, ritual skills like sacrifice, and judicial proceedings through which they could influence the representation of the world. Through this representation men, and the agnatic lineages into which they were grouped, became models of society, history and permanence (all ancestors, for example, were male). By contrast, women were seen as temporary and, as Comaroff puts it, they were associated with "unstable and repetitive transformations, with seasonal production, feeding, birth and death ...."[6]

Yet, as Guy stresses, because of their standing as producers and potential or actual mothers, women did enjoy forms of status, independence and security. Indeed, these features often made women, particularly older ones, fierce defenders of their societies. In certain spheres of social life, particularly religion, women could also gain prominence. Another such activity was storytelling.

This pastime probably contributed much to the informal power of women, an attribute that many analysts have seen as crucial to an understanding of women's position in pre-industrial society.[7]

Yet, compared to the intellectual resources at men's disposal, these areas like religion and storytelling were small. None the less, these patches of control, like the limited control over production, could attract certain forms of recognition and status and so, not surprisingly, women often defended these minor cultural prerogatives as well as the wider social order on which these cultural resources commented.

Within the space of a chiefdom, then, there were clearly demarcated spaces for men and women. This separation marked all aspects of life, particularly the household, the space in which storytelling most frequently occurred.[8] Within a polygynous homestead or family group (*kgotla, kgoro* or *motse/muti*), composed of individual huts or households (*malapa/tighodlo*), the female area was associated with the huts that housed the wives and children of the homestead. In some instances, these households were divided into a male area in the front and a female area that took in the hut and the yard behind it. The area that united the various households was also a public, male space which included various byres for the homestead's animals as well as a male gathering place (*kgotla/nkhundla*). Each homestead was, in turn, united into a larger unit, the ward (*kgotla, kgoro* or *mmoto/mmunru*), which, like its smaller counterparts, had a public, central, male arena from which men directed activities such as joint work parties that gave the homestead economic definition. Wards formed the local administrative and political units of the chiefdom and it was through this institution that fields were allocated to household heads.[9]

Within this divided space and unequal world, women generally pursued their storytelling skills in the vicinity of the household. Male storytelling occurred in the various courtyards that dotted Transvaal settlements. For women, the staple genre was the *nonwane/ntsomi*, a story generally but misleadingly referred to as a 'folktale', a term that not only diminishes the craft of this tradition by its overtones of quaintness, but also implies that the genre dealt only in make-believe.[10] In fact, the term *nonwane/ntsomi* did not only include imaginary stories; it could refer to non-fictional accounts touching on topics like local history and appropriate social conduct for girls and women that went under the rubric *megkwa le melao*, a complex phrase meaning law, duty, right, virtue, customary observance, order, justice and so on. Riddling and proverbs also featured as part of the storytelling event as did songs, jokes, gossip and conversation. Storytelling sessions, then, comprised a fluid galaxy of forms and, for many, the term *nonwane* embraced a sense of the entire occasion, not merely its storytelling core.[11]

As regards performers, they were, by all accounts, middle-aged to older women whose audiences were drawn from the homestead and ward in which their household was located. At times these spectators were young children – both boys and girls – up to the age of about eight, but older children as well as adult women (and by some accounts, men) could also participate. As with all performance events, the audience's contribution was crucial to shaping the occasion. Through the question-and-answer formulations of riddling, through the songs both in and outside the stories, through the frequently intoned response *keleketla/kunne* that encourages the teller and indicates that the listeners are awake, the audience, along with the teller and her gestural and dramatic skill, co-operated in making the event a multi-dimensional performance. Storytelling typically occurred in the evening after supper but stories could also be told on an *ad hoc* basis, often to make a point to unruly children.[12]

Male storytelling, by contrast, generally occurred in the courtyard or *kgoro* of either the homestead or ward depending probably on the size of the ward. If it was extremely large, storytelling would probably take place in the homestead; if smaller, in the *kgoro* of the ward. In this symbolically central place as opposed to the peripheral women's area, men congregated to discuss and resolve issues, perform certain types of work and direct the activities like communal labour and the transfer of cattle that linked households into homesteads and homesteads into wards.[13] Another factor integrating households and homesteads was the storytelling that men performed in the *kgoro* in the evenings. Boys above the age of about eight, on returning from their day's herding, would foregather, each having brought a piece of wood for the fire.[14] After supper, they would participate in storytelling sessions which, like the women's events, included songs, jokes, riddling and stories on hunting, war and male custom.[15]

Alfred Lesiba Kekana (see Plate 22), recalling his experience of storytelling as a child and an adult said, "At the *kgoro*, men taught boys the law, obedience, not to fight, stories of their forefathers, what happened in wars, family and kin relations."[16] While these storytelling sessions, like their women's counterparts, were made up from a variety of forms, some of which were lighthearted, these stories are remembered as having a serious edge to them. Their performance, for example, mostly excluded audience response, and was generally more restrained than the stories told by women.[17] The *kgoro* could also host daytime storytelling and, during seasons when work was not demanding, men would sit doing the kind of 'quiet' labour like braying skins, making rope and carving objects that, as others have pointed out, facilitates storytelling since one can tell or listen without having one's work interrupted.[18]

Overall, then, the craft of storytelling was ordered by the major divisions of gender that characterised Transvaal societies. Or, as Lucky Kekana explained, "After eating supper ... the old men remain by the fire at the *kgoro* ... the boys also remain with the old men at the *kgoro*. We girls stay with the old lady in her hut at the fire."[19] Another woman who grew up in Giyani in the North-eastern Transvaal recalled being told stories "in huts where fathers didn't go".[20] The spatial division of storytelling has been noted by others and was, in all likelihood, a feature of all Transvaal and probably Southern African societies. Marivate, for example, who did research into Tsonga storytelling in the late 1960s and 1970s reported that while men and older boys gathered around one fire to tell stories of hunting, women and younger children clustered around another. Lestrade, talking of Sotho societies generally, describes an analogous situation. On a related point, Scheub, too, has pointed out that as far as oral narrative goes, there is a general, but not absolute, division of labour between male historians and female storytellers. Parenthetically, these comments bear out an observation of Ben-Amos who has noted that "hypothetically it would be possible to assume an African society in which women tell stories to children, whereas men narrate them to each other".[21]

II

Yet this division by gender was much more than simply a matter of who sat where. What is at stake is the very nature of storytelling itself which, for many people, is permanently embedded in sexual division. Or, as Lucky Kekana put it, "... stories go hand in glove with building a man and a woman ... stories cannot be separated from men and women."[22] The depth of this gender divide as well as the belief and investment in it are crucial to grasp since in talking about storytelling people frequently predicate its function and meaning on these two separate streams of life.[23] Male storytelling, for example, is often seen as being directed at boys of about ten to eighteen, and is identified as a stage of male socialisation that prefaces initiation, circumcision and marriage. This storytelling is also perceived as being linked to the practical 'veldcraft' education which boys receive from their elders.[24] In discussing storytelling, people often talk about it as part of a gendered stream of experience through which boys become men.

Much the same goes for female storytelling. It, too, belongs to a parabola of experience that passes through childhood, initiation, marriage and childbirth. While the content of *dinonwane* is by no means as obviously gender-specific as the male stories of warfare and hunting, the skill of telling this type of story is seen as essential to the female craft of socialising very young children, both male and female. As with male storytelling, *dinonwane* are seen to be age-graded and, after about eight, the content of stories that girls hear is more gender-specific and also linked more closely to forms of women's work. This strand of storytelling is often seen to continue like a thread into the world of initiation where the business of gender instruction is most visibly institutionalised.[25]

Yet despite the huge gulf that seems to separate these two streams of storytelling, their craft and skill, as Chapters 6 and 7 will explore in more detail, are virtually the same. In terms of plot and content, too, as Doke has suggested, the area of 'folktale' and 'legendary history' merge and overlap in significant ways.[26] What actually separates these two traditions – the place of their telling and the gender of their tellers – is, from one point of view, quite negligible. Never the less, seen from the viewpoint of participants in the society, these related distinctions were so powerful that they could confer differential meanings on what was essentially the same set of skills.

In terms of this differential definition, female storytelling inevitably suffered. Despite their acknowledged importance in education, women's stories were often regarded as a rather frivolous pastime that dealt with the imaginary and fictional. Male storytelling, on the other hand, was seen as more important, partly because of its content which dealt with the 'real' world, partly because of its more sober performance, but also because it was enacted in a prestigious, public, male space and concerned itself with the socialisation of men. Considered within the complete range of oral forms open to men, like praising, praying, invocation, judicial pleadings and so on, historical storytelling was a relatively minor genre. Yet because it belonged to the glamorous world of public male power, and because it formed part of the serious male business of institutionalising and handing on the past, it basked in a kind of reflected glory that outshone the substantially similar storytelling of women. Or, as one informant, Dikgopana Rampula, explained, "the grandfathers were the senior lecturers of the kraal".[27] Yet, as with all social divisions, this one was never impermeable. Men could tell fictional stories, women could narrate local history. Those who probably crossed these boundaries most frequently were the ones with most talent. A good storyteller would always attract an audience, and part of his or her appeal and excellence would be a wide repertoire which, in all probability, drew from both 'real' and imaginary traditions. However, as in all societies, talent is rare, and the majority of more pedestrian tellers plodded their separate gender routes.[28]

Its second-class status notwithstanding, women's storytelling remained a cherished skill. As one of the few public-speaking venues open to women, it probably represented a form of limited cultural power that could attract recognition and status, particularly to those regarded as expert performers. Part of this status was 'borrowed' from age, which conferred its own prestige, and it was largely the middle-aged or older who were performers, perhaps, as Lucky Kekana suggested, because they had more time to tell stories. Recalling her grandmother, she said, "Because she was old, she could not stand up, she could not work. That is why she told us stories."[29] Another informant, Morongoa Kgosana (see Plate 4) observed, "... young people cannot always tell [stories]. But when one gets old, one wants to tell them."[30] However, talent is not tied to age and younger women could also excel and so accrue recognition.[31]

PLATE 4   Morongoa Kgosana (Photograph by Santu Mofokeng)

PLATE 5   Helen Maime (Photograph by Santu Mofokeng)

In so far as storytelling was a resource that could attract minor forms of status, it can be viewed as a type of 'cultural capital' that women inherited from their mothers and grandmothers. It was a form of 'capital' that young brides could use to lighten their way in their new and often difficult circumstances, if only by supplying the household with some new plot lines.[32] Perhaps for this reason, women today often talk about stories in terms reminiscent of inheritance. Informants stressed to me again and again that their mothers and grandmothers had 'passed on' and 'handed down' the stories they knew, and very few people identified their affines as the source from which *dinonwane* had been acquired. Along the same lines, one informant observed that the stories of men and women differed because "they come from different places". In other words, your repertoire of stories and style of telling are shaped by the place you come from rather than the place into which you marry.[33]

This view of storytelling as 'cultural capital' could go some way towards explaining the emphasis on storytelling as

PLATE 6   Sophie Lekgoathi
(Photograph by Santu Mofokeng)

secret and private which one often encounters. Twenty years ago Scheub observed this phenomenon, and it is still apparent today.[34] Lucky Kekana, for example, explained how grandmothers were upset when riddles (like *dinonwane*) made their way into primary school syllabuses. Children were asked to recite riddles and, in this way, some grandmothers felt that their secret store would be stolen or at least diluted.

Another reason why storytelling could confer some status on women was its importance in an educational system that entrusted the minds of the youngest to those of the oldest.[35] This status, of course, accrued to both men and women as storytellers, but to this day women's stories are accorded a special place as agents of socialisation. As one analysis of Zulu stories observes:

PLATE 7   Naomi Teffo
(Photograph by Santu Mofokeng)

> Folktales have served as the mainstream of African education. Folktale images are readily remembered, and the lesson driven home remains attached to narrative cores which are not easily forgotten. The performer of tales fires the child's imagination, and produces an emotional involvement.[36]

One factor illustrating the importance of this narrative education was its universality, something that David Livingstone noted more than 150 years ago in his observation of Tswana society. "The knowledge of some of these parables," he wrote in a letter, "is universal, and if we can believe testimony it was so of old."[37]

Since then others have made similar observations which indicate that storytelling was an essential grace to possess if one was to be considered well-educated, cultured and good-mannered.[38] Those who could not tell stories were often ridiculed, since, as Mbiti puts it for the Akamba case, one "is unable to do the most elementary thing in life".[39] As with African societies elsewhere, storytelling, along with other arts like praising, was, in theory at least, a popular skill.[40] In the words of Naomi Teffo (see Plate 7), a crèche principal who because of her role in education has a great interest in *dinonwane*, "I remember at my home [near Pietersburg] where I was born, ah, everybody used to tell [stories]." Lucky Kekana remarked, "I don't believe there was anyone who was unable to tell stories."[41]

As we shall see in subsequent chapters, this universality is something that no longer pertains, and for this reason it is worth pausing briefly to outline some of the factors that ensured the widespread transmission of stories. The first of these concerns the participatory nature of oral performance in general and oral storytelling in particular. Not only did audience members shape the performance event through their presence and participation, each person was also an informed observer. Or, as one critic phrases it, "... since everyone is a potential performer, everyone is also a budding critic".[42] One way to think about this informed participation is to liken storytelling to a popular spectator sport like soccer. Since most soccer audiences have played the game at some time in their lives, the match becomes accessible in a way that elite art forms can never be.

Informed participation and the high incidence of storytelling which it propagated was also ensured by the emotional involvement and enjoyment of both the teller and audience. This emotional investment, evoked both by the content and style of the story as well as its often intimate family setting, ensured a high degree of participation and attention.[43] This informed participation or 'active' listening, as Bill terms it, also means that the audience exercises certain forms of power in the performance, as bad tellers have no doubt discovered to their cost.[44] If bored or displeased, audiences can fall asleep or leave, a factor that Scheub so admirably builds into his analysis of storytelling as a type of struggle between teller and audience.[45]

Another aspect that promoted popular and widespread participation was a sense of belonging to a hospitable, capacious tradition in which everyone had a share. When asked how she would rank three different tellings of the same story, Sophie Lekgoathi (see Plate 6), turned the question back on me. Strict evaluation, she explained, belonged to the world of formal education and the classroom where some passed and some failed. In storytelling, "everyone passed".[46] Her comments do not mean that performances are not subject to evaluation and assessment, a topic that has attracted much attention in oral literary criticism.[47] As a tradition based on informed participation, *dinonwane* were obviously subject to constant forms of evaluation. However, such evaluation was never rigid and was in keeping with the fluid world of oral performance in which storytelling belonged. In talking about why they enjoyed stories or how they evaluated them, other informants mentioned factors like fluency, suspense, surprise, humour, clarity (both of delivery and 'message') and logical arrangement.[48]

Yet, in coming up with these categories, the people concerned had to think long and hard. As other research into the evaluation of oral narrative has shown, this situation could be attributable to a number of factors including the questions asked; the general inability of interviewing situations to key into the informal discourses that can surround particular genres; the absence of a specialised vocabulary for discussing aesthetic issues; and the fact that categories of evaluation can be embedded in the story itself.[49] Also, as an inductively learned skill, narration seems a bit like breathing and hence so self-evident as to require no evaluating comment. However, over and above these factors, I would suggest that in keeping with the baggy and capacious tradition that constitutes storytelling, its forms of evaluation are correspondingly and generously *laissez-faire*. Just as the rigid and hierarchical demarcations born of highly literate preconceptions may blind us to the 'fugitive categories' of oral performance, so, too, may they obscure the equally fugitive categories of evaluation.

Yet another factor ensuring the universality of oral storytelling was the fact that it resides in a range of everyday cultural skills that could be inductively and informally learned. These skills would include singing, dancing and gesture, the latter being acquired along with speech.[50] Through a complex combination of listening, observation, imitation and practice, as Scheub has shown, these skills could be acquired.[51] Furthermore, as in the rest of Africa, storytelling utilised everyday language and so did not require a specialised vocabulary.[52]

These inductively learned skills could, of course, be acquired from both men and women. Yet, if one can detect any traces of a more formalised, codified narrative learning, then it is in female storytelling that this is most apparent. As Lord has pointed out, the major apprenticeship in oral performance involves mastering the skill of producing the fundamental units or formulas from which a particular genre is elaborated. Or, as he puts it, "... the period of training is pre-eminently one of learning to produce lines."[53] As already pointed out, female storytelling has a much higher incidence of the internal responses (*keleketla/ kunne*) which the audience shouts out to encourage the teller and assure her they are awake. One function of these responses is to mark off narrative 'chunks', thereby not only promoting participation, but also acquainting younger members of the audience with the shape of appropriate narrative units.[54]

However, any status that women might win as educators and performers of a type of popular sport was always ambiguous, for despite the popularity and importance of stories in socialisation and instruction, there was and still is a view that belittles oral storytelling as a slightly risible pastime. Both Nguni and Sotho languages equate the term for 'folktale' with ridiculous tall stories. So, in Sotho, *go bolela dinonwane* (to narrate stories) can also mean to tell tall tales. This relegation of women's creativity to the questionably fanciful casts an interesting light on their wider exclusion from the weightier languages needed to discuss the 'real' world.

Yet it is clear that many women did not share this view, and instead saw storytelling as an important and potentially powerful cultural resource from which status could be wrung. Some critics have also suggested that stories could be a source of subtle subversion through which women could articulate and comment on their social position. Such an assertion depends a lot on the reading one gives *dinonwane*, but, even superficially, there is a great deal to support such a view. Most *dinonwane* can, indeed, be construed as subversive and unsettling accounts in which all known social categories and boundaries are upset. Men become women; animals become human; women fall in love with animals; people eat one another. The stories are also characterised by hallucination, vision and illusion that undermine 'realistic' ways of seeing. As a whole, the body of stories that make up the *nonwane* tradition are fantastic, grotesque, humorously scatological and powerfully erotic. They teem with swallowing monsters, one-legged cannibals, four-mouthed monsters, bees nesting in an inverted man's anus, and witches with phallus-like tails that embody every form of excessive appetite.[55] To make this overpowering fantasy even more bizarre, all stories are unequivocally rooted in the quotidian world.[56]

This subversive potential of fantasy is strongly written into the very nature of oral storytelling itself and, as some have argued, the fantastic resides at the centre of oral memory which best organises information around the memorable and monumental.[57] David Bynum puts a similar if stronger argument by insisting that the essence of oral storytelling resides in "the truth of wonderfully implausible things". Elsewhere he says:

> Whereas plain narrative recounts genuine facts, or at least facts typical of reality, fable depicts these same facts together with others that are fused or disjoined in ways which exist only in imagination. Conflation (or sunderance) of real facts into fantastic combinations is fundamental in fable-making.[58]

In the telling of the tale, however, these inversions, ambiguities, transgressions and hallucinations generally survive only until the end of the story where the accepted moral order is unequivocally reinstated. None the less, in upsetting social order and dissolving dominant ways of seeing, if only temporarily, these stories have a manifestly subversive potential that would be available to the teller should she require it.

This view of these narratives as possessing oblique power emerges indirectly in a number of other ways. Among Tsonga speakers, for example, tellers feel it necessary to 'spit' the tale into the fire at the end of its telling so that it will be 'burned' or 'killed'.[59] One does not know, of course, the earnestness with which this is carried out. But, even if done in jest, it betrays a certain wariness regarding the storytelling world.

This quality of magic and miracle that many have noted as being a hallmark of the oral narrative often seeps into more widespread popular perceptions and understandings. As Kuper has pointed out, "The world of the folktale is a simplified, specialized version of more elaborate cosmologies which are generated in other domains of cultural life." This 'folktale' perception which is most clearly codified in the stories that women tell, often spreads out into areas like historical understanding. Kuper, for example, interprets the widespread nineteenth-century reports of cannibalism in the subcontinent as a response to demographic disaster and massive social transformations by conceptualising them in literary terms.[60] It is a tendency that has been noted in other parts of the world. Robert Darnton, for example, in talking of medieval France says:

> By abandoning their children in the forest, Tom Thumb's parents were trying to cope with a problem that overwhelmed the peasantry many times during the seventeenth and eighteenth centuries – the problem of survival during a period of demographic disaster.[61]

As regards its content, women's storytelling was an important source of wider perceptions and beliefs. In form, too, it was the template from which other storytelling styles could be generated. Yet, overall, women's storytelling was a marginalised and patronised craft, relegated to the distinctively lesser sphere of a separate women's world. Operating in this circumscribed way, women's cultural work can be seen as analogous to their labour elsewhere. Like their agricultural endeavours, women's cultural work was located in the household which was the unit in which stories were performed and learned, produced and reproduced. Despite being similar to male storytelling, women's narrative labour was less valued, just as their cultivation work could never match the glamour and prestige of male cattle keeping. Yet, as Guy has pointed out, women's cultivation underwrote the household unit and the entire social organisation that rested upon it. In exactly the same way, it was female narrative skills that lay at the base of all other storytelling.

Today, these patterns of storytelling are no longer intact. The courtyards that hosted male storytelling have disappeared with the large-scale forced removals of the 1960s. The skills perpetuated in these courtyards have, as a consequence, undergone huge permutations. Female storytelling, too, has changed substantially. In the chapters that follow we turn to examine some of the factors that have precipitated these changes.

PART TWO

The Three Rs: Reading, Writing and Repression

2

Jonah and the Swallowing Monster
Orality and Literacy on a Berlin Mission Station

In dealing with issues of how oral storytelling changes, it is, of course, the theme of literacy that looms large. However, over the last few decades the question of how one conceptualises the interaction between orality and literacy has become increasingly complex.[1] In providing an overview of the debates within this field, Brian Street has clustered the available scholarship into two 'camps' which he terms the 'autonomous' and 'ideological'.[2]

The first set of ideas tends to see literacy as a value-free skill which is largely autonomous from social context and is acquired in more or less the same way with roughly equivalent consequences by all. The second set of approaches has challenged the universalistic assumptions of these ideas and has instead stressed that the acquisition of literacy is subject always to the constraints of the circumstances in which it occurs. As a result, the attitudes to, perceptions of and meanings attributed to literacy will vary enormously. Furthermore, these arguments stress that people do not simply passively absorb literacy but mostly actively appropriate it in accordance with pre-existing forms of knowledge and patterns of communication.

If one wishes to implement this second set of ideas, then one must address at least two related areas: first, the context and set of circumstances in which literacy is encountered, and secondly, the ways in which individuals appropriate aspects of this technology according to indigenous forms of understanding. Furthermore, in a colonial situation, the relationship between context and the way in which people respond to literacy is crucial since, under colonialism, reading and writing are often introduced brutally and swiftly, a situation ensuring that struggles between orality and literacy will have critical political dimensions.[3]

Within the confines of this study, however, the question that arises is how the unit of context is to be defined, since in the Northern Transvaal literacy was first introduced more than 150 years ago, a period that is too unwieldy to consider as one 'context'. Instead, all one can do is to 'reduce' this wider period to key thresholds that encapsulate both the major co-ordinates of colonial power as well as the forms of resistance and accommodation that they precipitated. Part Two of this book focuses on three such 'moments': the advent of missionaries and the literacy they brought; the institution of literate bureaucracies in the form of the Native Commissioner's office; and the intrusion of white political authority into the heart of the chiefdom, something finally effected by a series of forced removals in the 1960s.

Each of these three thresholds forms the basis of a chapter which sketches a background political context as a means of exploring aspects of the interaction of orality and literacy. In each case it is intended to show how the communicative repertoires of both chiefly and colonial societies were crucial resources used in the wider political struggles that were waged. In this process, the communicative resources of each community confronted and transformed one another, and it is the details of this interaction that these three chapters wish mainly to illustrate. Since much conventional wisdom often imagines such cultural interactions as a 'walk-over' for the institutions of colonialism that are often thought simply to have wiped out all indigenous cultural forms in their path, these chapters have tended to stress those instances where the reverse is true, and where the communicative strategies of a predominantly oral community transformed the literate procedures of colonialism by forcing them to come to terms with the demands of popular taste.[4]

While aspects of storytelling and the changes it undergoes will be specifically addressed, these chapters are also intended to suggest a broad background of cultural interaction, struggle and transformation against which the issue of changing oral forms can be imagined.

I

In much of the Northern Transvaal today there is a deep-seated ethnic stereotype which portrays the Ndebele as 'hard-headed', poorly educated country bumpkins. By contrast, the Sotho are seen as go-ahead and well educated.[5] While this view has much to do with the minority position of Ndebele communities in the officially designated 'North Sotho' homeland, Lebowa, the stereotype also arises out of the historical circumstances in which Northern Transvaal Ndebele communities confronted the initial agents of literacy and education – Boers and missionaries. In the case of Valtyn, this history included a series of violent confrontations with the Boer polity followed by the arrival of the Berlin Mission Society which pursued all its business in Sesotho, the language of commoners. Largely because its first exposure to writing was deeply associated with Boer violence, the chiefdom, or at least the royal lineage, resisted the notion of literacy from an early date. The fact that missionary activity was undertaken in the language of the lowly simply strengthened the feeling against literacy. With the advent of formal education at the turn of the century, this resistance to literacy kept many people away from schools and the skills for social advancement which they offered. As 'late starters', many Ndebele found themselves marginalised and marooned, a position that in turn promoted the growth of the stereotype.

However, to 'read' the stereotype as betokening simply exclusion and powerlessness is to grasp only half the story. Considered historically, the Ndebele resistance to literacy, at one stage, represented significant forms of power and initiative. Thus the history of literacy and orality in Valtyn can be seen as paradoxical. The oral performance culture of the chiefdom can be both strong and weak in its interaction with a literate culture which equally has areas of strength and failure. In order to grasp this admixture, this chapter begins by considering the advent of literacy through tracing the arrival of its agents – Boers and German missionaries. Thereafter it turns to examine the mission in more detail by focusing on the ways in which an oral performance culture, in a situation of restricted literacy, was able to transform the institutions of a literate religion. However, the power of this oral culture did not go unchecked, and the chapter finally discusses the effects of one particular mission undertaking – the printing of *dinonwane* in school reading books.

II

While the violence that characterised the initial interaction of Boer and Ndebele communities in the Northern Transvaal was not inevitable, there were a number of factors ensuring that the two societies came into confrontation. Mokopane's chiefdom was situated alongside one of the major routes to the ivory-rich Northern Transvaal. The chieftaincy therefore found itself occupying strategic terrain that the Boers, who began arriving in the area from the 1840s, were keen to control. From the early 1850s the Boers established themselves astride this highway in a small settlement that was subsequently to be called Pietpotgietersrust, a name that would be shortened to Potgietersrust by the turn of the century. From here they were well placed to launch cattle and slave raids which fell most heavily on the chiefdom nearest them, which was that of Mokopane (see Fig. 3). But this chiefdom, which enjoyed considerable regional prestige, was not to be trifled with, and in 1854 Mokopane teamed up with his neighbour "to pull out the nostril hairs" – as one version put it – of the local commandant, Piet Potgieter.[6] Together the two chiefs ordered an attack on the Boers, and in three separate incidents, 28 Boers were killed. The object of the attacks was to frighten the Boers back to Pretoria. Far from decamping, however, the Boers called up a commando that besieged Mokopane and his followers in an episode that will be more fully examined in Chapter 6.[7]

After the siege, the Ndebele chiefdom shifted its capital further westward

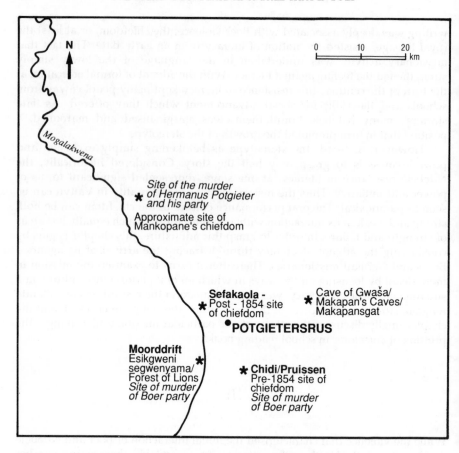

FIG 3   The site of events pertaining to the cave of Gwaša/Makapansgat siege

but still remained close to the Boers (see Fig. 3). Mutual cattle raiding continued, but the Boers, despite their earlier victory in the siege, lacked the numbers and military resources to impose their authority in any significant way. As Paul Kruger said in 1890 when visiting the region, "... these Makapaners have stiff necks which do not gladly carry a yoke".[8]

Against this violent background, it is hardly surprising that the chiefly lineage would have nothing to do with Boer culture, and in 1864 one of the chief's emissaries told two visiting German missionaries that the polity rejected the idea of missionaries and literacy out of hand. Or, as the emissary is said to have put it, "Writing is Boer business." The emissary explained further to the missionaries, "I thought you had come to sell us something. If you want that, we can discuss it. I do not want to learn, and there is not a single one in our tribe who wants that. If you have nothing further, you can go now."[9] The missionaries themselves had come with a view to establishing a station at Mokopane's chiefdom, and in 1865 under pressure from the government of the South African Republic, the chief capitulated and allowed the Berlin Mission Society to establish itself at the foot of the hill, Sefakaola, on whose summit his capital rested (see Plate 8 and Fig. 2).[10] While coercion no doubt played a large part in explaining Mokopane's permission to establish the station, he, like other Transvaal chiefs, perhaps wanted the missionaries for political and diplomatic ends, particularly since he had for some time been embroiled in a low-level war with the Boers. Indeed, it was often as a messenger and emissary that Mokopane used the first missionary, W. Moschutz.[11]

PLATE 8   A drawing of the first Berlin Mission Station at the base of the hill, Sefakaola (Wangemann, *Eine Reise-Jahr*, 461)

The missionaries, however, were not quite as biddable as Mokopane had hoped and they energetically pursued their own agenda of religious conversion and literacy. Their initial attempts, however, met with only limited success. The chief was generally hostile to the mission and his ire only increased as the station began to attract a few of the society's malcontents and the chief's political enemies. The malcontents included women and ethnic minorities, in this case Sotho and the generally despised Tsonga. In addition, from an early date, returning migrants, who had encountered the ideas of Christianity and literacy in industrial centres in the south, formed the central core of what missions rather fancifully liked to see as 'their' converts. The increasingly heavy and irritating chiefly exactions drove some of these migrants towards the mission. As in other Transvaal societies, the byzantine complexities of succession politics ensured that there was always one royal faction that adopted the mission as a resource in its dynastic feuding.[12]

In the 1860s, however, these strands of support were as yet faint and faltering, while the mission itself lived a tenuous existence. In 1868, in the midst of a war between the town and chiefdom, Moschutz was forced to abandon his station to the Boers who used the church to fire on the chief's capital. When the Boers left the station, the inhabitants of the chiefdom tore down what remained of the battle-scarred buildings. The missionary subsequently reoccupied and

PLATE 9   The mission house on the second Berlin Mission Station (Photograph by Santu Mofokeng)

rebuilt the station, but as the war began to turn in the chief's favour, so his interest in the mission waned. By 1870 the white inhabitants of Pietpotgietersrust had abandoned their village under the combined effects of fever, military resistance, a collapsing ivory trade, drought and locust plagues. During this period, the chief pursued a policy of repossession, and a number of Boer farms were reoccupied by their erstwhile owners. Such a climate of flagrant independence was not one in which mission work could flourish and in 1877 the station was also abandoned under pressure from the chief who feared that the Boers would continue to spy on him through the missionary.[13]

Despite its destruction, the mission left behind both material and cultural reminders of its presence. The chief's new iron-roofed house, built with material from the destroyed mission, stood out starkly against a background of thatched huts (see Plate 1), while pomegranates and syringas marked the site where the mission garden had once stood. Culturally, and specifically in terms of literacy, the mission had provided a focus for those who had encountered the written word in the urban centres further south. It had also established writing and reading as a source of power and fascination. Whatever his earlier rejections of writing may have been, the chief, as early as 1872, had felt it necessary to drive the ten or so converts from the small mission church in an attempt to establish who 'exercised authority' – he (the chief) or 'the Book'.[14]

By 1890 the chief in the iron-roofed house was dead. His eventual successor, Lekgobo Valtyn, adopted a more pragmatic approach to literacy. Entirely illiterate himself, one of the first things he did on taking office was to hire a secretary who could write impeccable Dutch and English. This secretary came to the attention of the authorities in 1893 when he and the chief were accused of intercepting and opening official letters intended for the Assistant Surveyor, a figure whose ominous importance was becoming increasingly apparent to those whose boundaries he measured. Lekgobo clearly recognised that literacy was to become a crucial resource, and not surprisingly he attempted to control it in his own interests as best he could.[15]

Such control became considerably more difficult to exercise, however, particularly since the Berlin Mission Society had returned in 1890. This time the mission was established some distance from the chief's capital (see Plate 9 and Fig. 2) and closer to the village of Pietpotgietersrust which had begun to re-emerge at much the same time. The atmosphere for the expansion of both town and mission was much more propitious than in the 1870s, largely because the repressive resources behind white authority had expanded in scope and sophistication. To begin with, the postal, railway and telegraphic communication networks linking the previously remote Northern Transvaal to the south had been dramatically increased, often with the express purpose of quelling African dissent. The Kruger government had also begun to move with some conviction against African communities in the Transvaal. In 1883 the Location Commission began its work of dispossessing Transvaal chiefdoms which were variously denied any land at all or penned into absurdly small areas. In 1890 this commission visited Mokopane's chiefdom and limited its area to 12 726 hectares. The police force was considerably beefed up at this time both to protect the commissioners and to monitor violations of the boundary rulings they determined. In 1893 the first station was established at Pietpotgietersrust.[16]

Against this background the level of colonial interference in the everyday life of African communities increased, causing one exasperated official to remark, ''It is common knowledge that the people and officials of Pietpotgietersrust interfere too much with the natives in the area and that this has in the past caused a great deal of unpleasantness and trouble.''[17]

Yet, as the chiefdom lost land, so the newly established mission gained followers. When it opened in 1890 the station attracted a band of four converts. By 1893 this number had swelled to an astonishing 156. Six years later in 1899, 393 people filled the considerably extended church, while as many as 600 people could attend big festivals like Christmas and Easter.[18] This increase of converts was temporarily halted during the South African War when white authority in the countryside suffered a number of setbacks. Much farmland was repossessed in the Northern Transvaal by its former owners, and at the mission, too, this climate of independence took hold. During the war the resident missionary Daniel Heese was killed near Elim hospital by some Australian soldiers. Parenthetically, their court martial become the focus of international attention and ensured Heese a minor role in the historical drama that was recently filmed as *Breaker Morant*. Without a white missionary present, residents on the station rapidly relaxed the arduous rules that governed all Berlin Mission stations.[19]

This freedom, however, was short-lived. The wake of the war brought a host of zealous Milnerite officials intent on reconstructing the Transvaal countryside in the image of British order. In Potgietersrus a newly appointed town council began surveying, fencing and assisting white settlers to start farming. In addition, the council established a location close to the town while assisting the new Berlin Society missionary to restore order. By the end of the first decade of this century, the mission had become a permanent institution that continued to attract members.[20]

In accounting for this growth, one must turn initially to the internal politics of the chiefdom since it was these local struggles and tensions that often propelled chiefly followers toward the mission. As we have seen, some groups like women, ethnic minorities and migrants had long been structurally predisposed to discontent, and they continued to make their way to the mission in a steady trickle.[21] However, from the 1880s a series of political struggles broke out, shattering the chiefdom internally and augmenting the flow of people to the mission precinct.

The first of these struggles was a war with a neighbouring chiefdom that considerably weakened the polity. In the wake of this conflict, a major schism within the royal lineage threatened the chieftaincy with civil war, and no sooner had these cracks been papered over than a succession dispute broke out, with the loser being acrimoniously banished from the area. In addition, the chief, in the grip of both severe alcoholism and interventionist white authority, began behaving in an increasingly desperate and high-handed way. While the object of his anger was clearly the white authorities in Potgietersrus who sent numbers of policemen after him and his subjects, the chief often turned his fury against his own subjects, particularly women. Well-known to the Department of Native Affairs for his incendiarism, the chief burned two villages and some twenty individual huts between 1900 and 1904 in an ostentatious exercise of the traditional punishment for treason.[22]

Both among commoners and within the royal caste itself, then, there existed cause for dissatisfaction against the ruling lineage. One way to express this discontent was to enter some form of association with the mission. For commoners, the mission and its schools – which used a lot of Sesotho – remained a source of attraction, and it is no coincidence that the mission acquired itself a Sotho name, *GaMoneri*, the place of the *menere*, the Dutch – and subsequently Afrikaans – word for gentlemen/teachers. By 1903 the mission had thirty houses occupied variously by members of the royal family, converts from the original mission, and 'Basotho' and 'Maguamba' from local communities and further afield.[23]

Alongside these factors propelling people out of the chiefdom, the mission itself held a number of substantial attractions. Apart from the converts made as a result of the enormous energy of certain missionaries, especially Heese, others were attracted to Christianity, particularly those who had encountered it elsewhere, either while working as indentured servants on Boer farms or as migrants to the towns of the south. In addition, Christianity itself became increasingly commonplace as more and more churches established themselves in the chiefdom, and by the 1920s there were ten registered churches with eighteen branches that probably involved about a fifth to a third of the chiefdom's residents in some kind of attachment to Christianity. Furthermore, most missions provided certain material benefits and, in the case of the mission station known also as Makapanspoort, it offered opportunity for trade and barter, employment, health facilities, carnivalesque spectacle and new fashions that amounted to a type of subcultural style.[24]

However, there was one thing which almost everyone who came to the mission professed a desire for and that was 'to learn'. Not surprisingly, as literate Christians the missionaries inevitably deciphered this phrase as a wish to become fully literate and possibly to become converted.[25] Literacy, however, does not have the uniformity or monolithic quality that literates often associate with it.[26] On the most simple level, reading and writing, for example, do not automatically go together, and each can be disaggregated into a range of subsidiary skills and activities. Furthermore, as residents of the chiefdom had no need for literacy in their everyday lives, they lacked the inducement that generally dragoons large numbers of people toward a more comprehensive degree of functional literacy.

In such a situation, literacy was entirely voluntary, and so, hardly surprisingly, people 'customised' their literacy requirements in ways that seem unusual from the perspective of the hopelessly literate. Some visitors to the mission, for example, simply wanted to learn the new oral forms of hymns and prayers. More regular churchgoers often wanted to learn to recite and/or read either the whole or parts of the fairly extensive Lutheran catechism. Beyond this, there existed other possibilities for recitation, memorisation and reading. These included Sesotho primers as well as the Bible and prayer books. One could also, if one wished, extend one's speaking and perhaps one's reading skills to English, Dutch and German. Those who were particularly ambitious could learn to write, in one or several languages, but relatively few people did so as writing was initially considered a difficult and tiring pastime.[27] In terms of the opportunities for learning these skills, one could attend a weekly confirmation class, two daily prayer meetings and any of the three Sunday services. There were also daily school classes in which several standards were clustered together. In 1891 ten children attended the school while some of their parents attended on an *ad hoc* basis. By 1897 this number had increased to 34. Tuition was in Sesotho and English, and in later decades this crystallised into a policy of teaching the first four grades in vernacular and thereafter switching to English.[28]

It is important to stress this diversity of skills and differential demand as missionaries often misread any interest in literacy as a sign of religious feeling and a commitment to the values of the mission world. Coming as they did from a highly literate training as well as a mission society that defined itself through the adherence to certain key printed texts, these missionaries made an assumption that is entirely understandable.[29] The idea of disciplined communion with the sacred (and printed) word was, after all, essential to nineteenth-century Protestantism in which texts became the kernel of a religious identity.[30] Small wonder, then, that in their work missionaries hoped to foster the kind of consciousness and sense of an inner life that some would argue is heavily associated with saturated literacy in general and private reading in particular.[31]

Working in a world rooted in spectacle, festival and performance, these Lutherans soon had to abandon their more obvious literate preconceptions in much of their day-to-day practice. Yet, despite the realities of this daily routine, few missionaries ever entirely shattered the mould of their literate thinking. At a time when Heese had only a handful of converts, he continued to look for signs of 'inner participation', decorum and discipline from his congregants. Such traits are most likely to be found in communities saturated with literacy as well as its frequent companion, industrial work rhythms. Many of the notoriously strict rules that characterised Berlin Mission institutions aimed to reinforce this ideal of inner discipline. On Makapanspoort and neighbouring stations these laws were equally severe, and at various points congregants were either excommunicated or punished in other ways for beer-drinking, 'sexual offences', marrying heathens, dagga smoking, and having 'too little earnestness and decorum'. Well might Heese have preached, "Go ye through the narrow gate". In the mission view of things, such discipline aided one in the journey towards sanctification, and although the missionaries probably would not have seen it this way, the disciplines of literacy, particularly silent reading, were an essential precondition for the successful completion of this journey.[32]

For a long time, however, the missionaries were simply unable to implement their understanding of literacy as congregants and visitors to the mission continued their selective appropriation of the written word. As regards church services, these were appropriated by popular taste which helped to dictate the form and style of holy worship and other mission activities. These almost invariably relied on orality, performance, festival, spectacle and image, or, in other words, the central resources of African culture.

This transformation of an avowedly literate religion into a predominantly oral one is evident in a number of spheres. To begin with, in the Northern Transvaal at least, an iconoclastic Lutheranism was forced to become a religion of the image. Pictures of all sorts were very popular, and to this day the interiors of black Lutheran churches in the area are heavily adorned with Catholic decorations.[33]

The seeds of such an 'oralising' impulse had fertile ground on which to fall as the oral roots of much Christianity are never far below the surface. The eucharist, for instance, with its mnemonic objects, originated in an oral age, as did the idea of the sacrament whose original meaning was oath or earnest commitment.[34] The oral impulse of the Bible is always apparent and, hardly surprisingly, Bible stories proved consistently popular in church and school. It was often their similarity to *dinonwane* that accounted for their appeal. One woman, for example, especially liked the story of Jonah and the whale – or, 'big fish', as the original terms it – the Biblical variant of the swallowing monster motif that frequently crops up in *dinonwane*.[35]

In certain instances, missionaries themselves appropriated storytelling as a technique, and on one occasion Heese tried to impress some pig farmers with the story of the Gadarenes. In other instances, missionaries (and government officials) rather hamhandedly attempted to incorporate references to 'folktales' and oral forms of speech in their disquisitions.[36] This popular taste for storytelling may also go some way to account for the rather lurid genre of death-bed conversion stories to which missionaries often referred. Such stories, which found popular favour, invariably tell of last-minute conversions and injunctions to descendants to heed the word of God. Ironically such stories return to the original oral meaning of the word 'will', which signified a final and spoken wish. Such oral wills are still highly respected today.[37]

Yet in transforming a literate Lutheranism it was undoubtedly the pulse of performance and festival that was felt most strongly. Every Christmas the mission was inundated with people coming to see the decorated tree and hear the brass band whose martial strains, interestingly enough, represented a vague and thoroughly militarised memory of Prussian popular culture.[38] Other elements of performance like hymn singing and storytelling played a crucial role in 'oralising' Lutheranism, and these two activities took up the second half-hour of catechism class. Reading occupied the first.[39] The pressure of popular taste also shaped the substance of a literate religion by partly determining which material was translated and printed. Heese, for example, wanted to translate one set of stories called the *Small Treasury*. But as a trial translation of the book proved unpopular, he had to opt for other texts.[40]

In bringing their everyday cultural resources to bear on the literate edifice of Christianity, people were not simply trying to make a relatively strange religion hospitable. They were also trying to protect a way of life and a system of representation. Coming from societies dominated by the politics of performance, most people were accustomed to carnivalesque cultural activities in which the body played a central part. Missionaries, by contrast, came from a world where the repression of this culture of physical carnival was recent enough to have left a climate of distaste and disgust for the things of the body. In Europe this carnival world had been repressed by the forces of industrial revolution and religious reformation and, some would argue, by the spread of printed prose which supplanted carnival as a form of leisure. Hardly surprisingly, then, in their work, missionaries strove to institute the quiet, apparent incorporeality of text above the robust, physical displays of oral performance.[41]

In attempting to institute a textual view of the world, then, the missionaries were, of course, doing more than simply bringing in primers and printed Bibles. They were equally repudiating a wider system based on the culture of the social body. It was largely this culture that people defended, if only through the force of habit. Part of this defence had to do with asserting the dignity of the body and its various performances against the attacks of mission disgust. Another part of the defence was to give body to what the missionaries decorporealised and, like their medieval counterparts who faced growing literacy, to reimmerse the book and the text into the corporeal stream of carnival and spectacle.[42]

In this climate the content of written documents often became irrelevant. Instead what mattered was the book as a concrete object, and from a relatively early date many citizens of the chiefdom considered books to have ritual power which people often attempted to borrow by simply handling them. So, for example, in one neighbouring polity, a chief whose literacy was fairly uncertain demanded the right to preach and read a chapter from the Bible. He also ran his own Bible study at which he was said to have blasphemed against the idea of baptism.[43]

While today such struggles may seem trivial, the stakes were in fact high, since what was at issue here was a, if not *the*, key cultural institution of colonialism. Its enforcement could not be left to chance, and instead the institutional weight of schooling was summoned to dampen the oral energies of a performance culture and insinuate the constraining effects of a literate, documentary culture. One apparently lowly agent in this bigger campaign was the school reader on to whose pages the performance craft of oral storytelling was translated. This act of cultural appropriation precipitated a range of effects, and it is to these that we now turn.

III

As Heese pointed out in the 1890s, one of the major problems facing any mission schooling was a lack of suitable reading material. The well-known series of *Royal Readers* had been available since the 1860s, but as regards African languages there was very little in either the secular or religious realm. So, like their counterparts in other areas of Southern Africa, German missionaries in the Northern Transvaal began producing Sesotho school readers from the 1870s. Most probably modelled on German school and children's literature as well as primers that had already been produced by Lutheran missionaries in Tanganyika, the first of these books made up the *Padišo Series*. Like similar readers in Zulu, these books contained a range of forms which included *dinonwane*, Bible stories, prayers, hymns, proverbs and essays on a range of topics including social conduct, geography, agriculture and biology.[44]

Within the chiefdom the books were first used in the Makapanspoort mission school that Heese started in 1890. By the turn of the century the number of schools in the area had swelled, since the Anglicans and Baptists had also established both missions and schools and, some two decades later, the Roman Catholics had followed suit. These mainstream churches were the only ones to establish registered schools, and by the 1930s they supported five primary schools, three in the chiefdom itself and two on town land. During the 1940s these two latter institutions were taken over by the Transvaal Education Department assisted by the town municipality. There were in addition a number of informal, unregistered schools.

The size of the mainstream schools, let alone the informal ones, is difficult to gauge with any precision. By 1946 the crowded Central School, on town land, had 548 scholars, 231 from the location, 169 from the chiefdom and 148 from surrounding farms. In the same year a post-primary section was added to this school, and between Standards 6 and 8 there were 77 pupils. The mission schools in the chiefdom were not as large and their numbers probably never topped a hundred. Overall, then, the percentage of scholars from the chieftaincy was minute and by the 1930s probably stood in the range of about three to five per cent of Valtyn's population. Yet until the 1930s the demand for schooling was small and the lack of facilities was not acutely felt. By the 1940s, however, the desire for formal education rocketed, and by 1944 Transvaal mission schools were rejecting well over 1 500 applicants per year. This demand for education was finally, but only partially, met in the 1960s when the state's provision of mass schooling, under the guise of Bantu Education, brought five new schools to the chiefdom.[45]

Yet, throughout all these changes in education policy, the use of *dinonwane* remained a standard feature of school life, and in addition African teachers used the performance of *dinonwane* in their lessons. This presence of oral narrative in the classroom is another interesting index of the power of oral culture to assert itself in literate locales. The situation cuts both ways, however, and the influence of institutionalised education on oral narrative soon began to tell. One of the first effects of this absorption of oral narrative into the curriculum was to usurp the role of non-formal education in the household so that to a certain extent school and home competed for the same terrain.[46] This migration of storytelling from the household to the classroom had far-reaching consequences for the style and place of telling; the meaning and definition of the genre; and the status of the teller.

As regards the style and place of telling, the shift to school entailed a range of material changes. The first of these involved a switch from predominantly night-time to daytime storytelling. One of the most obvious losses here was the dramatic impact of the fire and the intimacy of the family setting.[47] Spending time in the classroom also meant that children had less time to observe and imitate the oral forms that they absorbed by apparent osmosis in the household.[48] Whereas in the past learning had occurred *in situ*, education in the classroom was largely out of the context of action.

In addition to a changed set of social relationships now upholding storytelling in school, there were a series of performance implications in this shift of locale. The most obvious of these was that the spoken word now appeared as printed texts, or as one old man, Obed Kutumela, recalled, "Now when we started at school, we found that those things they were telling us at home were in the book." In the most extreme instances, the change was from live performance in the household to silent reading in the classroom. However, the swing was seldom so extreme, and in between there existed a number of possibilities. The first of these was for the teacher or the children to perform stories, but from what people recall, the responses to the story, where they existed at all, became more restrained or more formalised. In addition, the regimented choreography of schools militated against a more intimate sense of interaction.[49]

Another factor influencing performance patterns in the classroom was language. As all schooling was in Sesotho and English, Sindebele and Tsonga speakers would have to translate their stories. In a multilingual community like Valtyn, this task in itself was not hard, but, while the substance of the story could be translated, its songs could not. Through this particular linguistic configuration, a further aspect of performance fell away, leaving the story more staid and mechanical.[50]

While performance in the classroom was mechanical enough, the story when read was even more static. Apart from the range of repressions that written prose involves, renditions of *dinonwane* in the *Padišo Series* suppress any reminders of the original performance situation. There are, for example, no dramatised narrators, no internal responses and no songs. The only pale recollection of the performance situation is the opening formula, '*Nonwane e re*', the story says. That such factors could indeed be introduced is evident from C.L. Nyembezi's *Igoda* Zulu readers which introduce a grandmother as narrator and recreate the storytelling situation in the text.[51]

Written texts also lack the flexibility of oral storytelling which continues to absorb everyday detail and so retain at least a veneer of contemporaneity. In other parts of the continent, critics have noted this tendency – in parts of West Africa, for example, one hears stories of tortoises who attend adult literacy classes. For printed stories such options did not exist and, as time passed, the static stories must have come to seem progressively quainter.[52] In addition, like all printed texts, reading books separate the speaker from his or her speech. This situation confers a further rigidity as the words on the page do not originate with their utterer. Since school texts are often learned by rote, this fixity can confer an almost ritual status on a text as students recite the set and apparently authoritative words that, to all intents and purposes, have a transcendental origin.[53] The net result of this process is to confer a rigid casing on a form that previously lived by fluidity.

As regards the meaning and definition of the stories, their printing in school readers had a range of subtle implications for the way they were evaluated and assessed. Most importantly, reading books established *dinonwane* as things that properly belonged to the realm of primary education and hence of children.[54] The practice of restricting these stories to the reading books for lower grades and phasing them out for the higher ones only reinforced such an association. While storytelling in the household had been strongly associated with children, they had not been its sole audience. Adults, often encompassing three or four generations, frequently went to hear stories which, while ostensibly aimed at children, in fact often referred ironically or obliquely to adult concerns and family politics.[55] Today, however, there is an almost unshakable belief that *dinonwane* are for children, a perception which may be indebted to the way these stories have been institutionalised in primary schools.

In addition to associating the *nonwane* with childhood, school primers, in their choice of stories, reinforced the infantilisation of the genre in other ways. Stories tended firstly to be very short and, like most nineteenth-century collections of 'folktales', primers favoured animal stories above those with human characters (see Appendix 1 for examples). This choice had largely been dictated by the model of the German fable and fairy tale, both nursery genres, and so, by association, the *nonwane* and the society from which it emanated were seen as child-like and insubstantial.[56]

This selection process simultaneously involved forms of bowdlerisation. The nature of much of this excision is predictable and, in their distaste for the body, missionaries left out that which was erotic and scatalogical and, in so doing, bleached away much of the genre's bawdy humour. However, it was not only these predictable areas of sexuality and scatology that were excised. Other, less obvious omissions were made and these concern the bizarre, fantastic and grotesque aspects of stories which were consistently overlooked in favour of the tamer and more realistic ones. It might be argued that animal stories are not realistic in the strict sense of the word, yet considered as a form that favours rationality, clarity and coherence, the animal stories in school readers were intensely realistic (see examples in Appendix 1). As the previous chapter has argued, *dinonwane*, with their emphasis on transgression, inversion, hallucination and disorder, can profitably be read as fantasy. In voting against these qualities, German missionaries and the reading books they compiled, privileged a much more mundane, non-fantastic and ultimately realistic view of the world.

The effects of this emphasis on realism are almost impossible to quantify. Yet as part of a wider set of attitudes inculcated in the classroom, this 'realism' has powerfully insinuated itself to produce a climate that regards forms like *dinonwane* with scepticism and, at times, derision. Today such attitudes are widespread, and many people will tell you that *dinonwane* have lost popularity because children find them implausible and ridiculous. Any discussion of *dinonwane* with students or scholars invariably produces embarrassed giggles – they would probably agree with someone in the Sudan who wrote off oral stories as embodying "a great deal of rubbish which is not relevant to the real world".[57]

One person, Helen Maime (see Plate 5), a great lover of *dinonwane*, explained the shift in attitude as follows:

> Nowadays these children learn many things while they are still very, very young and in the olden days the children didn't see, didn't have experiences like ... people nowadays ... the children now, they go to pre-school, they look at TV and they sort of see reality and you cannot tell them something that is not true, they will tell you, 'This is not true.'

She went on to recall one of her daughters telling a four-year-old nephew a story. No sooner had Thabo, the daughter, begun than the nephew shouted, "No, no, no, you are telling me lies, that cannot happen ... that cannot happen. Eii, Thabo, just get away, you are telling me lies, there is nothing like that."[58] Similarly in Natal one researcher reported that "mothers and grandmothers often complain that their children interrupt performances saying, 'But this cannot be true, grannie. Teacher told us that....'"[59] Such scepticism often exhausts the old. Or, as Morongoa Kgosana, Helen Maime's grandmother, said, "I'm too old ... I'm tired of things I cannot give a reason for."[60]

This shift of perception that diminishes oral narrative also undermines the status that women accrued from storytelling. Overall, it is, of course, formal education which saps much of this status by robbing older women of their prerogative as educators. And, as part of this pattern, women in the household lose the initiative in storytelling which shifts to the school teacher. Old women certainly still tell stories but largely at the instigation of the *misterese* (mistress/teacher). Madumelana Shiloti explains:

> When they come from school, our grandchildren say that teacher said grandmother must teach us stories so that we can go and tell them at school. That is when we begin ... we begin because our grandchildren are at school, when they come [home], they say, 'Teach us stories.'[61]

Another factor that sidelines oral storytelling is a redefinition of time and leisure priorities. This issue, of course, belongs to a much bigger process whereby precolonial work rhythms were retuned to a more rigorous, industrial tempo. By removing children from the household and from forms of family labour, schooling played no small part in this process of recasting time.

This sense of the changing meaning and value of time often crops up in discussions of *dinonwane*. For many old people, members of the younger generation have lost interest in *dinonwane* because they have no time. Sophie Lekgoathi, a women in her eighties, mused, "In the past we were told by our old mother and grannies, they told us stories, but today, you don't have time to listen to our stories." Lucky Kekana expressed a similar view with regard to telling stories about events in the past. "There are not many of these who still want to get history. When we try to teach them about the past, they will say I am coming back just now...." Just as work dictates new priorities and long hours, so schooling sets new prerogatives for the disposal of free time. Homework, for example, has long taken precedence over evening storytelling. Madumelana Shiloti explained:

> We don't say to children, come let's do stories. When they are at home in the evening, we say go and study. Read, tomorrow the teacher wants all the homework done. We chase them from being with us. We say go and do homework ... that's why you see [stories] vanishing now.[62]

Just as the requirements of the classroom invade the home, so, too, do the ideas and images of formal education saturate the way people think about the world in general and storytelling in particular. Very often, women talk about storytelling in the home as though it should emulate storytelling at school. Madumelana Shiloti put it as follows, "At school they use education, so at home the parents teach, teach stories." Morongoa Kgosana explained, "Even these children, they learn stories, they take them like education." Mosiwa Lekalakala maintained that her daughter who had learned storytelling at school was more proficient than she.[63]

While this use of formal education as an analogy or inherent form of explanation is often not conscious, there are instances where people explicitly comment on the hegemonic pervasiveness of institutional, literate schooling and its effects. One aspect of this ubiquity concerns the swamping power of literacy to crowd out memory, the fundamental prop of oral culture. Or, as Madumelana Shiloti explained, "These of the high school, they can forget because ... they read many things ... they make many things in education, so you can forget..." She continued to explain that she herself was not formally educated and for this reason she could still "hold on to stories ... I have got only a little education and so it cannot conceal those stories ... the little education I have of writing cannot conceal these stories."[64]

At the heart of this perception is a view of formal education swallowing up or edging out instruction in the home. This is often an idea that people associate with writing which is also seen to render oral storytelling redundant. For some people writing has an authority that relieves them from the necessity of remembering. "I have forgotten them [stories]," Mosiwa Lekalakala said simply, "They have written them down. They have their books." The same informant spoke about the relationship between oral narrative, writing and schools in terms which give a graphic sense of the twin forces of education and literacy leeching off storytelling and so rendering it marginal and silent.

> At school they [the teachers] want them. They want them. They [the school children] come here and you tell them and then they write in books. They arrive [at school] and read. When they arrive at school they do them.... Yes, at school, they want them. Even the big ones in the higher standards, their grandmothers can tell them stories. They take their books and go in there ... you tell them and they write, write and write....[65]

As part of the process by which formal education dents the prestige and cultural authority of the old, the advent of writing in the context of schooling marginalises older women to a significant degree. This change leaves many old people with a sense of failure in that they have not been able to pass on the cultural skills which they inherited. Lucky Kekana said, "When God asks us what we have taught our children, we are going to be punished."[66]

This sense of failure on the part of the elderly is entirely understandable largely because in migrating from the household oral storytelling has slipped out of their sphere of control. But this is not to say that storytelling has vanished entirely or has withered completely in the face of a literate assault. In certain instances, the introduction of books and writing has stimulated oral storytelling. Or, as one informant put it, "Hear me when I say some people can ... read written documents and then ... make a story."[67] Printed books, in other words, bring in a new stock of plot lines and these could be acquired both at school and elsewhere. Women who worked in domestic service, for example, sometimes brought home the plots which they read to their employers' children. Helen Maime remembers hearing Rapunzel from an aunt who spent time in domestic service. Translated into Sesotho, the story became a firm family favourite. These new plots often became a source of prestige, and when Morongoa Kgosana's granddaughter began to tell a story that the old woman had picked up in domestic service, she interrupted the story with mild indignation, "I know that, it's mine, that's mine, that's mine."[68]

Printed books and schooling also bring in a whole new range of stylistic possibilities and generic classifications. As Makgamatha notes in his study of *dinonwane*, younger tellers with secondary and tertiary education incorporated the techniques of the written short story into their telling and relied a lot on internal evaluation and interior characterisation.[69] In addition, the new stock of generic definitions like fable, essay, recitation, poem, story and history provide further filters of understanding that people could bring to bear on their understanding of present-day storytelling. As we have seen in the previous chapter, indigenous definitions of the term *nonwane* were broad and could encompass a wide variety of forms. Yet, under the steady impact of primers, the meaning of *nonwane* has shrunk until it refers only to imaginary stories and often, as well, only to animal stories.

However, there have been compensations for this shrivelling of meaning: certain English words, have, for example, been conscripted to do service in the redefinition of a changing oral culture. A good example is the word *setori*, the Sesotho for story, which at times seems to have replaced the original more broad-ranging meaning of *nonwane*. Another example is the term *histori* but its discussion belongs to a later chapter.[70]

Until at least the 1940s, most education, apart from being literate, was also religious. As such, the idea of the Bible exercised a powerful and enduring influence on the way that people thought about books, documents and literature, both oral and written. For many people, reading meant reading the Bible, the only manner of printed matter they either encountered or wanted to peruse. In explaining the moral or ethical function of oral stories, one informant referred to them as 'the Bible of the Sotho'. In another instance, Obed Kutumela likened the idea of oral literary creativity to receiving the word of God. Certain tellers, he explained, are born with a special talent which inspires them to use words. This inspiration is like receiving the word of God.[71] In addition to this use of the Bible as a source of metaphorical explanation, more general images of literacy can also be employed to describe the process of oral storytelling. Or, as Ramasela Sema said, in explaining how she remembers stories, "I write them in my heart."[72]

In addition to print, there are other media that inform the way in which oral storytelling is imagined and thought about. Like printed books, the *baioskobo* or bioscope provided people with a new source of plots and a riveting form of entertainment that "brought together every Tom, Dick and Harry".[73] Along with the gramophone, radio and subsequently television, the cinema became a form of leisure that competed powerfully with storytelling. Yet, none of these media entirely supplanted storytelling. Both radio and television gave people new story lines as well as further generic terms, particularly the term 'serial' which is often used in explaining oral storytelling. Furthermore, both radio and television broadcast *dinonwane* in various forms, while storytelling and serials across a range of print and broadcast media attract consistently large audiences and readerships.[74]

Radio and television also insert leisure activities into alternative forms of association and sets of social relationships as people gather for this new form of storytelling at the houses of those who can afford the technology. One informant also claimed that the ethnicisation of radio services reinstituted an interest in oral stories. "Nowadays," she explained, "everyone, even the radio, is back to their culture. That's why they want the return of the things of the olden days." There were also unexpected side effects of radio broadcasting. One man, Moletsi Mahlangu, remembered that when Sesotho broadcasts first started, they ran from five o'clock to six o'clock in the morning and then from half-past nine to ten. Apart from having the effect of waking people up for work, they promoted a new awareness of time, and anyone with a watch was in great demand so that he could tell people when the magic hour of half-past nine had arrived.[75]

The interaction, then, of oral storytelling and the media that attempt to represent it, is convoluted: print, film, broadcasting and oral performance augment and diminish one another in a host of ways. Noting the complexity of this interaction is one thing, trying to assess its scale is quite another. As noted at the beginning of the chapter, Ndebele societies resisted literate institutions, often by eschewing contact with them and their agents. In addition, until at least the 1930s, the demand for schooling was minimal. Furthermore, universal schooling only arrived in the 1960s and, until at least one generation had passed through it, the kinds of changes outlined here could, at best, only nibble at the edges of a powerful oral culture. The fact that the influence of these changes was faint, however, did not mean that it was not persistent, particularly at the level of daily, classroom routine and habit. Here the preconceptions of literacy oozed out of everyday example.

The slow, viral effects of this literate presence on a resilient and tenacious orality are notoriously difficult to pin down. Part of this difficulty, as pointed out earlier, has to do with the technological determinacy that has coloured much debate on literacy and its effects. As Finnegan has noted, these arguments often make universal claims about the cognitive consequences of writing that rarely hold true for a variety of contexts.[76] Instead, as she advises, one should try to be as specific as possible by spelling out the effects of literacy on orality in particular situations. I have attempted to implement this advice by describing both the effects of an oral culture on a literate religion as well as the consequences of printing what was previously performed.

3

The Spoken Word and the Barbed Wire

Oral Chiefdoms versus Literate Bureaucracies

In 1923 the Native Commissioner of Potgietersrus, who was involved in an ongoing feud with Chief Alfred Masibi of Zebediela, wrote to his adversary. "I do not as a rule," he said, "take verbal messages – you must get your secretary to write when transacting government business."[1] A few years later a new chief, Abel Kekana, took office, but in no time the Native Commissioner was at loggerheads with him too. In May 1929 the Native Commissioner wrote to the Secretary for Native Affairs complaining about Kekana's behaviour.

Adverting to my minute No. 2/1 of the 19th ult., and with reference to your No. 27/55 of the 6th inst. in connection with the conduct of the above named chief, I have the honour to submit [a] copy of my letter evenly numbered of the 8th inst. addressed to this chief calling upon him for an explanation as directed by you. To this letter no response was received other than an intimation that he was busy with his circumcision school and would attend to the matter later. On the 16th inst. I attended the Local Council meeting at Zebediela, and there saw the young chief to whom I at once intimated that I was not there to receive his explanation which he could either submit in writing or personally at my office at Potgietersrust. Further that if I received no response to my letter within seven days of the last mentioned date I would submit the matter for further action by you without his explanation. On the 21st inst. attended by his usual satellites who are mainly responsible for his misguided conduct, he presented himself at this Office. He appeared to be very sullen and on the questions contained in my letter of the 8th inst., being put to him he gave his

explanation, which I took down in writing and a copy of which I attach
hereto. His attitude was not at all reassuring, and in the interest of the Tribe
I do urge that he be severely dealt with....I have seen letters addressed to
members of the Royal family urging that this young man be deposed, but
an open expression of their feelings [is] stifled by tradition and sentiment.
However I submit a confidential report sent to me by W.S. Kekana which
clearly reflects the true position....[2]

As the letter makes clear, the conflict between the Native Commissioner
and the two chiefs was conducted through a variety of media and modes of
communication: letters, both public and confidential, public meetings, private
appointments, verbal messages, secret reports and speeches copied down in
writing. From other letters it is clear that telegrams and telephones were also
mobilised in the dispute.[3] It is also clear that the opposing sides attempted to
rely on different kinds of communicative strategies to maximise their advantage.
The commissioner generally wanted things in writing or favoured face-to-face
situations where he was in charge. Chief Abel Kekana, on the other hand,
avoided contact with the commissioner where possible. But when forced to deal
with him the chief engineered an oral interaction while accompanied by his
retinue who evidently exercised a somewhat unsettling effect on the
commissioner.

Both sides, then, tried to determine the form and medium of interaction,
and while the two parties had access to oral and literate resources, both, in a
situation of conflict, tended to turn to the mode with which they were most
familiar. Consequently, in this situation of interaction between ruler and ruled,
both parties presumably felt there was some political edge to be had from
insisting on a particular mode of communication.

This brief sketch of a spat between the chief and Native Commissioner
raises a host of questions about the relationship between forms of
communication and political authority. There is, however, one issue that
emerges particularly clearly and that is the extent to which the forms of
communication are a focus of political struggle. This question of struggle is
important to stress since there have been other studies that assume that those
with authority can unilaterally dictate the forms and modes of communication
between factions possessing unequal power.[4] However, as Fabian in his analysis
of language and colonial power reminds us, we should always consider
"*simultaneously* local, creative response to communicative needs *and* restrictive
intervention from above motivated by a resolve to control communication...."[5]

It is such a bipartite analysis that this chapter aims to implement in order to
consider some of the political dimensions of how orality and literacy interact. In
the previous chapter, some of the cultural implications of these dimensions were
examined. Here, our concern will be more political. The general context for this
chapter will be aspects of the interaction between the Native Commissioner's
office and the chiefdom. In order to consider the first part of Fabian's equation,
we turn to analyse how the chiefdom and its officials responded to and
transformed the communicative procedures with which they were confronted.
The material used in this analysis is the correspondence that passed between the
commissioner's office and Valtyn as well as other surrounding chiefdoms.

In this correspondence, written roughly between the 1920s and 1950s, we can observe various ways in which agents of the chief attempted to bend the language of official correspondence and bureaucracy to meet their particular needs. In transforming this language, it was, of course, on pre-existing forms of discourse, knowledge and understanding that correspondents drew. While it is often difficult to specify exactly what such pre-existing forms might have been, there is one consistent theme that emerges, namely to 'oralise' the written word and make it bear the 'imprint' of the human voices and relationships that necessitated its creation in the first place. Such 'oralising' can be seen in things like an insistence on oral messenger and oral memory; as well as an attempt to subordinate literacy as the medium of ruling to institutions of public assembly, face-to-face government and personal audience. While there may well be a number of ways to interpret these insistences, this chapter construes them as part of the cultural resistance of a community against colonial domination. As in its confrontation with a literate religion, the oral performance politics of the chiefdom challenged the literate institutions of colonial bureaucracy by attempting to 'oralise' them.[6]

As regards the second emphasis in our analysis – what Fabian terms "the restrictive intervention from above" – we turn to consider the Native Commissioner's response to the chiefdom, but on a level far removed from the bureaucratic letter. Instead, our focus will be on a much more overt form of restriction – the fence – or as it was more popularly known, 'the wire'. The fence may, of course, appear unconnected to issues of communication and literacy. However, in so far as literacy and writing provide an important set of vocabularies, idioms and images that can be transferred to other areas of life, and can, for example, be used as an implicit justification of political domination, fencing – which is often imagined as a type of demarcation or 'writing' that fixes white authority in the countryside – can legitimately be considered within this ambit.[7]

In its drive to contain and control the chiefdom, the Native Commissioner's office did, of course, also use quotidian literacy as a more modest means of control, particularly as far as issues of protocol and administrative procedure went. However, while these played a subtle part in the control of the chiefdom, it was, in the long run, more coercive measures that contained the residents of Valtyn. One of these was the fence; and in the second half of this chapter, we examine this political 'literacy' in more detail.

I

In an analysis of the Native Affairs Department during the interwar years, Dubow illustrates the ideological and administrative shifts that it underwent. Heavily influenced by the Transkeian model of native administration, the post-Union department followed a policy of gradualist assimilation but subsequently moved to a more rigid doctrine of segregationism. Administratively, the department initially relied on ideals of government through decentralised paternalism and personal rule. This form of administration was, however, soon supplanted by a much more centralised, purposive bureaucracy.[8]

This shift from local paternalism to centralised bureaucracy probably happened more in theory than in practice. In remote areas like the Northern Transvaal, the Native Affairs Department could never properly institute the full exercise of depersonalised and distant control that a centralised, literate bureaucracy implies. The areas to be controlled were simply too huge, the people in these areas too numerous and too unwilling to be governed. Under these conditions, depersonalised, distant ruling can never take off and instead, Native Commissioners had to rule through a combination of personal audience, public meeting and oral messenger, or, in other words, the cornerstones of oral government.[9]

In this situation, as Sansom has shown, the Native Commissioner's authority – which was in theory extensive – depended on constant negotiation through which the governed gained a measure of autonomy and freedom.[10] The commissioner's office, with its risible staff complement and miserable police contingent, had to tread carefully and could not rile its subjects too deeply.[11]

In this context of contested authority, the conventions of ruling and protocols of interaction become an important focus of struggle. One such form of interaction was the letter which passed frequently between the chief and the commissioner. Mostly concerned with the details of licensing and permits for churches, schools and stores, these letters probably formed the major form of communication between the chief and the commissioner who otherwise only encountered each other for meetings every three months. In between there could, of course, be *ad hoc* gatherings, emergency visits and circuit tours, but since the chiefdom was separated from the commissioner's office in Potgietersrus by a good two-hour walk, and since the town was noted for its hostile racism and complete lack of facilities for black visitors, the chief went to the commissioner's as little as possible.[12] While the commissioner was often more keen to see the chief, the non-existent roads over which he had to drive probably presented some deterrent. Yet, despite these transport difficulties, it must be noted that compared to other chiefdoms in the area, Valtyn was comparatively closer to Potgietersrus and its degree of interaction with the commissioner's office was consequently higher. Overall, however, such interaction was still relatively limited.

For the chief, then, writing letters held several attractions, one of which was that they minimised personal dealing with the commissioner. Another advantage was that by using such correspondence, chiefs could borrow the power of literacy. Like medieval lords who could use their signet rings to 'sign' documents without themselves being fully literate, many chiefs surrounded themselves with the paraphernalia of writing and bureaucracy and paid great attention to things like letterheads and rubber stamps.[13] Through these accoutrements, chiefs announced themselves entitled and authorised to participate in a documentary culture.

Yet, in participating, however indirectly, in a literate universe, the chiefs and their allies were simultaneously changing the meaning and uses of documents. By bathing documents in the stream of orality, they subordinated them to the prevailing practices and procedures of an oral world. An oft-quoted example of the transformative power of orality is the way in which much writing emanating from paraliterate communities mimics speech. This cross-over is generally cited as an instance of a new technology camouflaging itself in the old.[14] Another, slightly stronger, reading of this situation is to think of the practitioners of the old technology forcing the new to conform to their values and views. In so far as a technology of communication is woven into a wider set of cultural and political ideas, this clash between forms of representation has a number of implications.

One of these concerns the way in which oral transactions focus attention on a set of social relationships and a group of actors. Literate technology shifts the emphasis away from the actors towards the text, which progressively tends to be divorced from both its producers and consumers. This alienation is not something that oral communities easily allow, and in many oral situations there is a struggle to keep documents accountable to the circumstances from which they come. As part of the same process, people also try to make documents ring with the human voices that spoke them and the social relationships that necessitated their creation in the first instance.

The first strategy in this struggle was to write as one spoke. While such a style may arguably be entirely predictable, it nevertheless kept alive the idea of a letter or document as part of a conversation that linked people in particular relationships of power and obligation. In keeping with these trends, most letters to the *komosasi* (commissioner) bear the 'imprint' of the human voice. Many of these letters also start *in media res*, a technique which inserted the letter in an ongoing relationship. One such letter began, "My Lordship, allow me please to continue my personal explanation in order to give more light in the matter." Another said, "First of all, I greet you very much. Sir, I went on safely out of Mapela's Location.... My journey took me two days, on account of the scarcity of the buses or that some of the bridges were destroyed by heavy water."[15] Another letter-writer felt it necessary to imply the social network from which he came and so signed off his letter, "I am Jeconias Lebelo. Lebelo's son." Yet another correspondent attempted to remind the commissioner of his obligations by announcing, "I am here to inform the commissioner that I have passed carpentry."[16]

In sending messages, most people still laid more store by the spoken, rather than the written word. Consequently, letters were often accompanied by messengers who would report the substance of the information, embellish the contents of the document they carried, or answer any questions the recipient might have. "Owing to sickness," a headman in Zebediela wrote (or had written on his behalf), "I am sending herewith two men of my section who can give you the whole proceedings of the meeting...." Another writer felt it necessary to apologise for sending a letter, "I am sorry to report this through letter. I wanted to report it personally but unfortunately my bicycle is not in order. Saturday seems too long to come on foot." Letters could also act as dramatic props, and one chief sent a woman who wanted to apply for a store permit with a document that began, "By this letter I say the Government may see herewith a girl."[17]

Another way to embed the spoken voice on the printed page was to reappropriate the written in terms of phonetic spelling. In terms of this practice, one correspondent wrote that "we spek ablcation to make shop". Another asked the commissioner "why you naver ask awar letter" which had been for a "lessense" to "sale soap mill mill and parafin oil". Yet another letter, which like many others relies heavily on the language of supplication and clientship, combines phonetic spelling, direct translation from the Sesotho and the oral, performance language of the church. The letter concluded, "The covernorment he will look for [that is, look after] us. Amen."[18]

The full impact of this 'spoken' writing did not often reach 'the ears of the government' as skilful translation often shrivelled the repetitive and additive style of oral speech into the clipped formalities of bureaucratic English.[19] In expressing their opposition to a new council system, one community wrote as follows:

> With respect Sir Amen I say that everybody at Kamola, they do not like the Council and its power at all. Truly we do not like it. The entire *lekgotla* of Doorndraai they do not like it one little bit. You know that we do not like the Council. We are in a difficult position, we are in difficult position, we do not like the Council. You know that we do not like it.
>
> I remain Johannes Mashishi[20]

A fairly tactful translator got hold of this letter and rendered it as follows:

> Sir, with respect Amen. The residents of Kamola Area are very much against a Local Council. Every body at Dorrondrae. Sir I wish to tell you every body hates a Local Council in this area.
>
> I Remain Johannes Mashishi

Alongside this aural appropriation, many letter-writers also reshaped bureaucratic language to their own ends and according to their own understandings. One typical way in which this conversion occurs is by rendering the abstract, concrete, and many abstract nouns beloved of bureaucracy like 'permission', 'notice' and 'advice', were made to render signal service as concrete nouns or transitive verbs. So, letters frequently requested 'advices', 'a notice' or 'a permission note'.[21] Similarly, chiefs requested Native Commissioners to 'permission' applicants 'to make shop'. The noun 'bearer', which appeared on crucial papers like travel passes in the form 'Allow bearer to...', was often born again as a verb. "I also bearer him as far as I know him as a good man," wrote Chief 'Makapan' in recommending a butchery applicant to the commissioner's office. Elsewhere someone appealed to the commissioner in characteristically concrete terms: "I am going about bearing my complain ... behind my back which I do not know who will take it of from my back."[22]

Another indirect way in which orality affected correspondence was to render the act of writing and authorship visible. Such a process was, of course, often unintentional but it none the less transferred the performative inflections of oral speech on to written discourse where a letter could 'read for itself', a scribe could 'pen off' or end by saying "This comes to the stoppage of my pen". Similarly, one author focused on the physical nature of writing itself when he declared, "I have this opportunity to draw this few line according to my application." The verb 'draw' may, of course, be indebted to a phrase like 'draw attention to', but even if this were the case, its use here focuses attention both on the activity of writing and the concrete origins of the metaphorical phrase.[23]

A further strategy through which people used to keep the authority of orality alive was to rely on oral witness and oral contract. The highest statement of trust was to say that someone 'spoke the judgement from his own mouth', and people frequently repudiated written contracts, particularly those made on their behalf by browbeaten or avaricious chiefs.[24] Confronted with such situations, Native Commissioners were forced to abandon the methods of literate government for face-to-face meeting and, at times, police intervention. One such incident arose in the 1930s over the widely hated tribal levy system whereby people were burdened with extra taxation to buy more land to which the rank and file rarely got access. An irritated commissioner described events as follows:

> They flatly refused to pay the Levy, on the ground that their Headman, Lingana Mabusela, (since dead) did not inform them of it; I pointed out that Lingana actually signed the resolution of 6/9/1929 asking for the imposition thereof, but all argument was of no avail. Ultimately it became necessary to invoke the aid of the Criminal law and some 100 were sent to prison for terms ranging from six weeks to two months.[25]

In defying the previous written agreement, the residents of the Mabusela ward were partly relying on the flexibility of oral contract. As others have shown, much oral contract, despite its claims to traditionalism, was quite contemporary in its ability to erase obsolete or unpopular law which generally dies a quiet death. As Clanchy in his study of medieval literacy says, "Remembered truth was also flexible and up to date ... the law itself remains young, always in the belief that it is old."[26] Such flexibility, of course, cannot withstand the relentless record of written evidence, but the residents of the Mabusela ward made a spirited attempt to do so. Two years after the churlish report by the Native Commissioner they were still repudiating any written agreements and refusing to pay the levy. As the members of the *lekgotla* wrote to the 'magerstreet':

> We shill never pay that the trable leve because we never agreed about it when we where there in the meeting we was face to face we have till every thing about this trable leve that we can't pay the thing.[27]

While literate bureaucrats believed implicitly in the durability and fixity of the printed word, this is probably not how writing must have seemed to many. As Clanchy has pointed out for medieval literacy, in the early stages of writing various forms of forgery flourish. Under such circumstances, it is the malleability and impermanence of the written word that must appear paramount.[28] While the extent of forgery in Transvaal chiefdoms is not at all clear, there is evidence to suggest that there were instances of this 'literate' crime, particularly in connection with the collection of tribal levies. In this regard, literate court messengers often cheated people or bamboozled them with the paraphernalia of receipt books and stamps.[29]

There were other instances in which the malleability of apparently fixed documents emerged. One such instance occurred in 1937 when the self-same Mabusela community hired a lawyer to challenge a levy proclamation in court. As the wording of the levy was ambiguous, it was declared *ultra vires*. It must have been a rather embarrassed Native Commissioner who had to convey this information to the people concerned. At this meeting one apparently ingenuous speaker asked him to explain exactly "how many words were wrong in the last Proclamation".[30] One would give a lot to have heard the tone in which these words were delivered but, like so many bureaucratic genres, minutes of meetings do not allow us such indulgences.

As the Mabusela episode shows, an insistence on orality had powerful political implications. These were further exploited by the tenaciousness with which people clung to any oral agreements made with the Native Commissioner's office. As the Native Commissioner was at times forced to abandon his desk and speak to the chief and people concerned, a lot of agreements in their eyes were oral and, even after years had passed, chiefs or their representatives would continue to insist on various oral promises being honoured. As written records were often lost or burned, and as Native Commissioners changed with great frequency, such requests could safely be embellished or even invented.[31]

While an insistence on orality implied some practical and material advantages, it also offered metaphorical ones whereby the idea and image of the voice became central to much political discourse. People frequently acted on advice spoken to them in dreams (another interesting non-literate form), while the call of the ancestors became a key political metaphor. Again in connection with tribal levies, a group living just north of Pretoria were hit with particularly hefty levy payments in the late 1920s. Some of their more imaginative leaders suddenly recalled that the community had historical links to the chiefdom of Mokopane, which incidentally had much lower levy payments. The Assistant Native Commissioner interviewed the leaders concerned to enquire what had brought this change of allegiance. He reported the interview as follows:

> When questioned by me as to the reason why they now, after this long lapse of years, want to come under the jurisdiction of Barend Makapan, they replied, 'That their father is calling them.'[32]

This stress on the voice as the basis of much political life also took its surreptitious toll on the procedures of the Native Commissioner's office as officials were forced again and again to explain written documents. It was, of course, the sheer number of non-literates who necessitated this verbal glossing of written documents. Yet in these interactions it was their cultural tastes which prevailed as the arcane documents of a literate culture were baptised in living practice by being explained, interpreted and covered with the spoken voice. It was just such a situation that one commissioner encountered when he had to explain a bond to an audience that had no desire to finance the land for which their chief had signed. This is how the peeved commissioner described his encounter in a letter to the Secretary for Native Affairs in which he demanded that the people concerned be forced to apologise.

> I strongly resent the attitude taken up by these natives. The Bond was read over word for word by me in the presence of Mr. Attorney Slabbert to some 400 or 500 natives belonging to the tribe of Jonas Makenna. It was also explained by me thoroughly so that there was no mistake about it – I am thoroughly acquainted with the Sesutto language and the interpretation of the Bond by Makenna was not faulty.[33]

This necessity for oral commentary and exegesis was a task that officials often had to undertake. Another commissioner wrote as follows to his superiors:

The report of the Assistant Director of Native Agriculture and the Senior Chemist of the Department of Agriculture and the map drawn by the Assistant Engineer, Native Affairs Department was explained to the best of my abilities to the meeting.[34]

This enshrouding of the written document in oral commentary formed part of a complex linguistic situation in which the Native Commissioner's office in Potgietersrus operated. While most commissioners could speak Sesotho, they were often not entirely proficient and most letters coming into the office were translated into English. Letters sent to the chief were either in Sesotho or English. However, as the chief's court comprised Sindebele speakers (although most were proficient in Sesotho), one could have a situation whereby letters from the chief to the commissioner could be dictated in one language (Sindebele), written in another (Sesotho), translated, and read in a third (English). Similarly, if a letter went from the commissioner to the chief, it could be written in English, translated into Sesotho and read out in translation in Sindebele. All of this was extremely time-consuming and often formed a source of annoyance to officials.

In their response to the tactics of performance politics, the Native Commissioner's office often behaved as one would expect of a literate bureaucracy. Much of their energy went into trying to promote the kind of literacy that they believed would make people governable. This battle to impose 'orderly government' on the performance politics of the 'theatre state' was waged in joyless campaigns centred on issues of protocol, grammar, procedure and etiquette.[35] In endless letters and meetings, various commissioners at the Potgietersrus office nagged and threatened on how to give speeches and compose letters (*always* with a date, *never* in pencil). Vexed by the apparent flexibility of customary law, Native Commissioners frequently requested that laws be codified and printed. In the end, most chiefs came to request such books which, along with things like date stamps and letterheads, were the few risible performance accoutrements that literate power allows.[36]

Yet, try as hard as they might, the dream of making the subordinate more pliable through literacy was a far-fetched one. Apart from having a hopelessly patchy presence, literacy, if not flatly resisted, was furthermore appropriated and domesticated by the subordinate in selective ways. It was not a situation to encourage the smooth exercise of power. Or, as Benita Parry phrases it,

the fracturing of the colonialist text by re-articulating it in broken English, perverts the meaning and message of the English book ... and therefore makes an absolute exercise of power impossible.[37]

However, the exercise of power depends not only on good grammar, and in its quest for control the Native Affairs Department from the 1920s turned to more coercive and embracing forms. One part of this strategy was to write white authority into the landscape, and from the 1930s platoons of agricultural officers, vegetable garden advisers, prickly pear exterminators, surveyors, bull castrators, engineers, dipping inspectors, soil conservation officials, irrigation

scheme planners, veld improvement officers and forest rangers invaded the
countryside in an attempt to mark and possess it in as many ways as possible.
However, for this political inscription to have any meaning, it required a rigid
'grammar' to keep it in place and it was largely the fence that performed this
function.

II

The story of fencing in the chiefdom properly begins in 1890 when the Location
Commission penned the polity into 12 726 hectares from which about 10 000
people had to subsist.[38] The area was renamed Valtyn's location. The two
adjoining chiefdoms suffered a similar fate and ended up being known as
Mapela's location and Bakenberg location. Together these three chiefdoms lay in
a narrow, solid block, 17 kilometres long and 5 kilometres wide, that housed
some 30 000 people (see Fig. 4).[39]

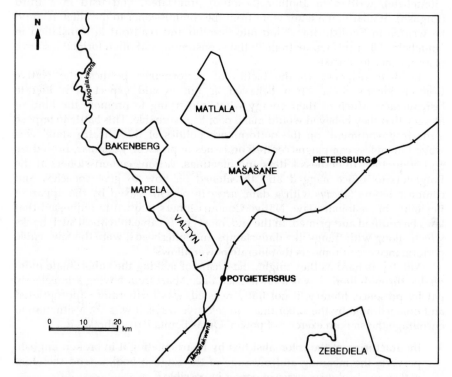

FIG 4   Location boundaries in the Potgietersrus area in the 1940s

In making its decisions, the Location Commission mostly looked at where
people lived and declared this the location. Much grazing and arable land was
consequently lost. In Valtyn this loss was particularly sharply felt on its new
western boundary which after 1890 became the Mogalakwena River. This river
had always been a major source of water and most of the chiefdom's lands were

situated on its banks – most particularly the eastern one but to a lesser extent the western one. Behind this narrow band of fields on the 'west bank', a range of hills rose sharply where cattle were grazed and once a year young boys were sent to be circumcised.

It was on this 'west bank' that the silent fence war began in earnest. While this struggle around fencing often seemed quiet and invisible, the tactical and ideological battle on both sides could become fierce and was often fought quite literally over feet and inches. For the desperately overcrowded chiefdom residents, every scrap of land was crucial. As one old man said, "The Europeans are fond of shifting beacons", so fond, in fact, that when the chiefdom was surveyed in 1936 its surface area turned out to have shrunk from its official size as determined in 1913 of 14 541 hectares to 12 229 hectares.[40] Most white farmers, on the other hand, considered nothing as too much. Indeed, in later years the rabid cry of many farmers in regard to black land was to become 'not an inch more'.[41]

This cry, however, was only to emerge forcefully in the 1920s and 1930s. Back in the 1890s, things did not appear so urgent, largely because the rather vague boundary lines that the Location Commission had ordained remained entirely unfenced and completely hypothetical. Surrounded by company-owned land or unoccupied private farm land, the residents of Valtyn paid little heed to boundaries and carried on with their lives as before. Yet, by the turn of the century, fencing had become more common and, according to both oral and written sources, 'the wire' first came to the Potgietersrus district shortly after the South African War.[42] For those living within Valtyn, their first experience of fencing probably came in 1903, when the Berlin Mission station that straddled town and location land began fencing.

This limited impact of fencing soon began to broaden as improving farmers started seeping into the fertile south of the district, attracted by company land which came on to the market at this time in significant amounts. It was from this point that the first concerted attempts to 'pull the wire' and 'fence the line' emerged.[43] As Valtyn's location lies in the extreme south of the district, it was one of the first areas to witness systematic fencing, and in 1904 an East Coast Fever fence began to make its way along the chiefdom's western boundary.

However, in erecting the fence, it was by no means self-evident where it should go. The old South African Republic Location Commission had left ambiguous records and surveys of the boundaries, while the Mogalakwena River which putatively formed the boundary has a wide, reedy and often marshy bed, not to mention a winding course. Eventually a give-and-take policy was followed whereby the fence, like a kebab stick, skewered the bends of the river.[44]

As all three chiefdoms lay on arable soil similar to the clay and loam of the Springbok flats, some farmers soon began to regard them with avaricious eyes.[45] Other farmers who lived north-east of the chiefdom felt themselves to be trapped in a corridor between two black 'blocks' made up of the three locations 'below' them and two others – Matlala and Mašašane – 'above' them (see Fig. 4). If both groups of farmers could have had their way, all five locations would have been swept further north into marginal bushveld areas, the course of action that they recommended in their evidence to the Stubbs Land Commission of 1918. In 1925 this call for removal was strengthened when the Prime Minister, General J.M.B. Hertzog, paid a visit to the area. Platinum had been discovered near Bakenberg, Mapela and Valtyn, and because of this Hertzog called for the removal of the locations.[46]

His was a point of view shared by the Potgietersrus Town Council and the by growing number of poor whites who congregated in the village in the 1920s and 1930s, many originating from farms bought by the state after 1936 when the area for black occupation was marginally increased. Most residents of this town resented living cheek by jowl with a densely settled town location and chiefdom. At every available opportunity they called for removal in language whose shrill racism increased sharply as Afrikaner nationalist campaigning got under way.[47]

These removals, however, never occurred and, having failed to move people out, farmers had to settle for the next option – fencing in. And from the 1920s farmers began calling for compulsory fencing, largely through their associations that started to appear during that decade.[48] Some of the first farms to be sold to private owners lay on the chiefdom's 'west bank', and it was from here that a renewed offensive was launched to rebuild the East Coast Fever fence. By the 1930s fencing, or attempts to fence, had gone up much of the three chiefdoms' boundaries. In addition to these private schemes, from the mid-1930s the Native Affairs Department launched various anti-erosion and rehabilitation schemes that often brought fencing inside the chiefdom for the first time. By the 1940s the impact of this fencing, both internal and external, had become far-reaching.

The first and most immediate of these changes had to do with over-crowding in terms of land and stock. By 1906 chiefdom dwellers complained of a shortage of land as well as water which the town of Potgietersrus siphoned off in increasing volume.[49] This pressure on land soon began to tell in terms of migrancy and by 1918 70 per cent of men from the Potgietersrus area were said to be working down the mines.[50] By the 1930s overcrowding had become chronic, and Valtyn was likened to the Sahara desert and singled out by betterment planners as 'one of the worst in the Transvaal'.[51] For this reason, Valtyn became one of the first areas in the Transvaal to experience anti-soil erosion measures, veld reclamation schemes and other such projects that clustered under the betterment banner.[52]

In addition to pressure on arable land, internal fencing aggravated the critical shortage of pasture. As far as the Native Affairs Department was concerned, the answer was to cull. However, resistance to such schemes proved so implacable that for a long time other options had to be pursued. One of these involved fencing for 'controlled grazing' which heightened pressure on existing pasture. It was, ironically, a pressure that affected small herd owners more than large ones since those with a lot of cattle generally had the wherewithal to hire grazing from the white farmers who rented out pasture in the area.[53]

By the 1930s most Transvaal locations manifested fairly sharp stratification, and in Zebediela, for example, which lay close by, one man had 171 hectares which he ploughed with eight span of oxen while others worked between a half and four hectares with borrowed cattle.[54] Valtyn was in all probability much the same, and like other surrounding locations possessed a wafer-thin stratum of 'progressive' farmers. It was often this new elite who, together with the old chiefly caste, became the beneficiaries of internal fencing and had privileged access to the land which these fences set aside.[55] In terms of land, cattle holdings and social division, fencing played no small part in reinforcing old cleavages and creating new forms of stratification.

Apart from land and cattle holdings, fencing also interfered in daily life, particularly as far as women were concerned. As was the case with the western boundary give-and-take line, fences often cut off access to water. Apart from often necessitating longer journeys to fetch household water, such fences could also deprive washerwomen who did town laundry for their livelihood.[56]

However, one of the biggest bones of contention remained reeds which often ended up on the wrong side of the fence. A standard item in house building and domestic fencing, reeds also had a wide range of other uses, and apart from being used to construct musical instruments, they also featured prominently in folklore and mythology. Many Nguni traditions, for example, associate reeds with creation, and in the central Transvaal local Ndebele historians identify Mhlanga (a name derived from 'reed') as the first Ndebele chief in the Transvaal. Not surprisingly, given the importance of reeds in everyday life, the act of their cutting, in some Transvaal societies, symbolises one of the founding acts of human civilisation.[57]

Rivers in general are seen to hold mythological power, and in the Transvaal as elsewhere they inspire any number of *dinonwane*. In addition, the Mogalakwena featured in the annual initiation ceremonies in which boys were said to cross over (*go wela*) from boyhood to adulthood. In going to and from the circumcision lodge, it was the Mogalakwena that the young boys crossed.[58] In losing access to river frontage, both material and cultural wealth evaporated from people's lives.

There were other kinds of cultural changes that fencing precipitated. One concerned changes to the power of the chief who traditionally held the right to declare the seasonal start to reed cutting. With the tremendous demand on shrinking reed resources, this was probably one of the first prohibitionary powers of the chief to fall into abeyance.[59] Another cultural change concerned oral history and memory. In addition to the standard items of genealogy and battle history that skilled remembrancers recalled, a memory for beacons, meetings with Native Commissioners, farmers and agricultural officers now became crucial.

In trying to assess the intangible cultural changes that fencing occasioned, it is important to stress that chiefdom residents did not see fencing as a discrete issue. Instead they probably understood it as part of a more general white invasion whose object was to possess the land in as many ways as possible. One aspect of this possession involved marking the land in every conceivable manner, be it with fences, ploughs, bulldozers, graders, pegs, theodolites, boreholes, roads, farmhouses, plantations, contour banks, grass strips and what-have-you. The slightest sign of white activity on the land was seen as presaging imminent land loss.

Fencing, then, in the popular imagination, formed part of a wider net of white control. Small wonder that today at least one old man remembers fencing and literacy as intimately tied.

The issue of fences was brought about by literacy [go bala] ... it was found out that when the Boers claimed land for themselves they did not know how to measure it. The English brought theodolites [dilandmeter] with them.... The Boers never had fences. Even today no-one can say he saw them putting up a fence. They had no skills in putting up a fence. They did not know how to do the corners. [The Boers] did not measure the land. They just used their heads, now they just said, 'This area, from here to that tree ... it is my land.'[60]

Given that many planners often encouraged fencing as it would make herd boys redundant and so force them to school, the old man's perceptions contain much wisdom.[61] His words also illustrate the extent to which views of fencing and boundaries are embedded in certain cultural forms of understanding, a topic to which we now turn.

As any number of studies of colonial culture have shown, settlers almost invariably saw the countryside as a blank page on which they could write their authority.[62] Not surprisingly, many saw boundaries as akin to the written word. Once inscribed on a surveyed diagram, a line, like the printed word, came to represent a supposedly fixed and permanent reality. However, to make a boundary meaningful one requires a fence that both fixes the line and represents it spatially as a thin, sheer wall. This verticalness of the fence is important since it embodies another aspect of colonial understandings of boundaries which are generally seen to sink below the earth's surface and rise above it.

This idea of height and depth was extremely important to colonial understandings of land possession. African agriculture, for example, was considered derisory largely because it was seen as 'shallow'. Colonial farmers, on the other hand, ploughed 'deeply' and so apparently possessed – and earned a right to – the land in a way quite distinct from African farmers. In the perception of the Native Affairs Department, Africans did not 'love the soil' which under their 'scratching' became 'thin'and 'bodiless'. Europeans, on the other hand, practised 'good husbandry'and made the soil 'thick' by adding manure and fertiliser.[63] Alongside this folkloric language, the more scientific vocabularies of geology and surveying also embody notions of possession. Both these disciplines generate the illusion of a saturated knowledge of the earth that stretches both horizontally and vertically. Boundaries were one way of marking such deep possession.

Apart from fixing such boundaries, fences, as far as the Native Affairs Department and their betterment schemes were concerned, played an important demarcation and 'containing' function in that they marked off the various zones set aside for grazing, residence, agriculture and so on. These zones, in turn, formed part of an ambitious scheme to survey, document, change and so control rural societies. Such visions of control were heavily tied up with notions of bureaucratic and documentary order. Central to the implementation of these visions was the fence, which increasingly came to be thought of in quasi-literate terms. Policy documents, for example, frequently included phrases like `maintenance of beacons and proper records', a juxtaposition that says a lot about the close symbolic kinship that boundaries and literate documentation enjoyed in the minds of policy makers.[64]

This cultural perception of fencing was also apparent in the role that boundaries played in marking and maintaining identity. One farmer, for example, wanted to fence not only because the chiefdom's cattle trampled his land, drank his water and inseminated his prize cows, but also because he wanted symbolically to fence off the savage darkness around – and, no doubt, within – him. Or, as he explained it, "I am alone and they are a dark multitude."[65]

These fantasies of possession and demarcation played a powerful role in shaping colonial ideologies. Once on the earth, however, they became much less clear cut. Unlike the printed page, the countryside is seldom smooth or flat, and once one has to transfer the boundary line of the diagram into the reality of the veld there are, of course, rivers, hills, trees and bumps to confound the best-laid plans. While boundaries remain unfenced, such issues do not surface. However, once fencing starts going up, the problems of determining the supposedly fixed boundary become apparent. And as any number of hapless Native Commissioners were to learn, any attempt to solve such problems had to involve at least some discussion and negotiation between both parties, negotiations that furthermore had to be held in the heat of the day, on the spot and orally. These *in loco* inspections or pointing-out ceremonies, as they came to be known, had by the 1930s become a standard feature of rural life.

To the residents of Valtyn who lived in a society where property rights were transmitted, conferred and negotiated by oral testimony and contract, such ceremonies must probably have seemed like simple good manners.[66] However, if the form of the ceremony was familiar, then the idea of a pencil-thin boundary was not. As with most oral societies, the residents of Valtyn did not see boundaries as sharp lines riven into the earth by fencing. Rather, from linguistic evidence, it would seem that indigenous understandings stress the boundary as something that lies lightly on the earth. So, for example, in Sesotho, one puts down a boundary (*go bea mollwane*). As matters finally turned out, this perception had much ironic wisdom. Colonial officials and farmers frequently moved, redirected and simply gerrymandered boundaries. A boundary, then, was indeed something put on the earth that could, like a ribbon, be moved somewhere else.

This loose precolonial sense of boundary does not mean that notions of territory and demarcation were unknown. What was, of course, unfamiliar was the notion that boundaries could be marked in such precise terms. In the past, where boundaries did exist, such as between fields or homes, these were marked with broad bush fences in contrast to which the fence cut an exceedingly stark contrast. It is still this idea of thin harshness that the word *terata/nterata*, from the Afrikaans *draad* (wire), exemplifies. The official and 'polite' Afrikaans word for fence is *heining*, but by popular choice it was the thinness of the wire rather than the fence as a whole that seemed most striking, and it is this idea that popular parlance has preserved.

On both sides of the fence it was generally these unstated ideas that were to guide how people approached the whole issue of boundary disputes. And as the struggles around fencing got under way, it was largely these cultural conventions that people mobilised in their resistance.

In the war of the fences there were a number of crucial steps, and the first of these concerned where the fence would go. Most frequently this procedure began when a farmer whose property bordered on the chiefdom gave notice of his intention to fence. After he had lodged the official papers, the technicalities of where the fence would go and how it would be built had to be arranged. This could happen in a number of ways but generally it involved a meeting of the farmer, Native Commissioner and the chief, accompanied by a retinue of up to fifty followers. Together, they would all congregate at the beginning of the boundary and decide on the exact placing of the fence. Such ceremonies could last for several hours, and on at least one occasion an elderly chief 'sagged out' from exhaustion.[67] In the negotiations, both farmer and chief would indicate where they felt the fence should go, and, in most instances, the Native Commissioner would make the final decision.[68]

From the vantage of the Native Affairs Department head office in Pretoria, the issue of new fencing should have been quite straightforward. Not surprisingly for a literate bureaucracy, the department was deeply attached to the notion of a true and fixed boundary, and in the case of any fencing dispute they would refer authoritatively to the neat lines on surveyors' diagrams which assumed the status of holy texts.[69]

However, as any weary Native Commissioner could tell you, the situation on the ground was sheer heresy. To begin with, much nineteenth-century and early twentieth-century surveying could be charmingly vague, and the possibility of determining boundaries with any exactness only came with the countrywide network of beacons known as primary triangulation. But as primary triangulation only made its way to the Northern Transvaal between 1933 and 1953, the possibility of determining boundaries with any degree of precision was remote.[70] To confound matters further, beacons took a perplexingly wide range of forms that included cement structures, cairns, wooden pegs in the ground and features of the landscape like trees. These objects were variously shifted, pinched, destroyed, ploughed over, stolen for mining pegs and used for target practice, and many officials spent fruitless hours trying to find them.[71] Those that remained were often of an indeterminate status since the untutored eye had little way of distinguishing a boundary beacon from a subdivision beacon. To add to this unholy confusion, the landscape itself often changed over time, and in a wide river bed, for example, the channel of the river could shift by several hundred metres.[72]

Against this background, the idea of a true and fixed boundary could only be a fiction, and it was one that those in the chiefdom often exposed. "The boundary," said one chief, "is unknown. Who knows the boundary and that is it correct? ... We do not trust the Europeans." He continued, "The Europeans informed me some months ago that they had had the line surveyed because they themselves did not know the line." If, as was apparent, the line was indeed unknown, then it became crucial to find it, preferably in a favourable place.[73] Towards this end both sides mobilised all available resources to swing the decision in their favour.

The first such resource that people called on was oral memory. In any event, much of the negotiation on the spot had perforce to be orally conducted, but as the records room of the Native Commissioner's office in Potgietersrus had burned down in 1926 the role of oral memory became crucial. Most often, this memory took the form of competing versions of local history that involved genealogies of previous Native Commissioners and the decisions and determinations that they had made. So, for example, in 1920 one Native Commissioner reported that despite the 'west bank' line having been settled in 1909, a delegation from the chief "persistently st[u]ck to their story that they were told by the late Mr. W.A. King [a former Native Commissioner] that they were entitled to graze their cattle west of the Mogalakwena River and that in a dispute with the owner, King had ruled they were entitled to the ground".[74] Farmers similarly developed their own oral traditions which they passed on by word of mouth to new farmers, often, according to one Native Commissioner, having "'forgotten' or 'inadvertently' pointed out an incorrect line". This quotation, in turn, came from the letter of a previous incumbent of the Native Commissioner's office in Potgietersrus who had been asked to recall – from oral memory – his understanding of the boundary position.[75]

In this business of oral memory, the chiefly representatives were, of course, exceptionally skilled and, in certain instances, people would remember details with extraordinary clarity for three or more decades. However, coming from the powerless, as these versions did, they carried little weight. Furthermore, these oral Nestors now found themselves confronted with a literate bureaucracy whose record keeping undermined the flexibility that much oral memory presupposes.[76]

Even if the chiefdom's residents received an unfavourable decision, they never gave up entirely on the idea of negotiation, and would reopen proceedings at every available opportunity. Such opportunities arose whenever a new Native Commissioner or magistrate took over. One of the first deputations these new officials received invariably concerned the western boundary of Valtyn's location.[77] People also actively created pretexts for reopening the boundary determination, most often by losing or burning the official diagram sent from head office. In requesting a new copy, one could simultaneously broach the issue anew.[78]

Another way to keep negotiation open was to hire one's own surveyor. When a boundary was particularly unclear, either the farmers or often the Native Affairs Department would get in a private or government surveyor. On such occasion the chief would respond by employing his own surveyor, much as one hired one's own lawyer.[79] Wedded as most white farmers were to the notion of a true and fixed boundary, they viewed this action of the chief with great mirth. Any surveyor, the farmers argued, would reach the same decision. The chief, however, knew that there was more than one way to determine a line. The shambolic history of surveying in the Northern Transvaal made every boundary worth checking, and surveyors, often working off different maps, could, indeed, reach different decisions.[80] Also, given the solidarity of white officials and 'conscienceless'[81] farmers, any boundary was worth double checking. Even if the two surveyors' decisions concurred, calling them in usefully stalled the erection of the fence for a while. Finally, people could also resort to more forceful, popular forms of negotiation, and at one pointing-out ceremony, "three to four malcontents made matters difficult".[82] Yet, whatever these *de jure* findings, both sides knew this was simply the beginning of the story. What really counted in the long run was the *de facto* positioning of the fence.

In this part of the battle, the chief and his followers came into their own. Using tactics of determined procrastination, they could often effectively delay or redirect fencing with a tenacity that drove farmers to exasperation. The one major weapon they wielded in this struggle was control of labour. The cost of the fence was, in theory, to be shared jointly, although, according to the Fencing Act of 1912, farmers could borrow the money from the Land Bank. The chief, on the other hand, had by the same law to pay, in some instances from tribal funds and in others from levies. The one small tactic the chief had was to offer free labour to meet the chiefdom's side of the bill.[83]

In most cases this labour would simply not arrive. If challenged by the farmer who would have had to make his way to the chief's capital across extremely indifferent roads, the chief, in immaculately polite and deferential tones, would provide any number of excuses. He was very keen to start the fencing, but a message from the Native Commissioner had instructed him to wait.[84] His people were still unhappy about the position of the fence and he would have to call another *pitso* (general meeting) to discuss the issue. The matter, he would say, requires some thought as he did not wish 'to hurry by mistake'.[85] In some cases the chief literally had no control over the workers who, when confronted with little or no pay, simply went on strike.[86] In other instances, the chief could, sometimes for months on end, be unavailable.[87]

However, should the farmer so much as turn his back, the chief could mobilise a work team with admirable speed. With great precision and efficiency, they would erect the fence in what they understood to be the 'right place'. In other instances, labourers would constantly make 'mistakes' and so require endless close supervision.[88] Farmers, of course, could reply in like terms, and on a number of occasions the work team arrived to find cement poles planted along what the farmer understood to be the 'right line'. All that then remained was for the workers to pull the 'barbert' wire through the fencing poles.[89]

With regard to fencing projects within the chiefdom, the forms of resistance were even more pronounced. Surveying equipment on more than one occasion mysteriously suffered damage.[90] In other instances, internal opposition to the chief manifested itself in resistance to betterment schemes, and in Bakenberg such opposition centred on the Mabusela ward who had previously opposed tribal levies. Following a strongly traditionalist pattern of resistance, the Mabusela leaders said that "they [had] never drunk water from a well and [could] do without it." As a result, expensive borehole machinery frequently seized up because of a few intelligently placed stones.[91]

Once fencing was in place, people responded to it in a number of diverse and creative ways. Mostly and wherever possible, people simply ignored it. Often fencing crossed customary footpaths and pedestrians then either pushed the fence over or wound its strands together so that people could pass underneath. In one instance at least, the Native Affairs Department capitulated to this pressure by erecting stiles and gates.[92] In other instances people not only broke down the fence but stole sections as well. Undertaken with the assistance of sharpened stones, this activity was generally aimed at removing offending bits of wire to "facilitate the theft of grazing" as well as to gain access to game, wood, water and pasture. In other instances, people stole wire for domestic use and snares.[93] By the 1940s officials were complaining of a "veritable epidemic of fence cutting", while in 1937 the Town Clerk of Potgietersrus thought that fencing Valtyn's location a waste of time "as not a strand would remain in place".[94]

The initial state responses to this fence destruction was more in word than in deed. Officials fulminated, farmers cursed, but in practice very little happened. The Fencing Act of 1912 threatened a £75 fine or six months' imprisonment to anyone who "wilfully injures or removes any fence, gate or other appliance or contrivance forming part or serving the purpose thereof", but as police were few and far between, and as people would seldom give evidence against one another, fence destruction often went unpunished. This situation began to change when farmers took policing into their own hands, and many old men from Valtyn have memories of farmers 'arresting' people who crossed their fences. In other instances the farmer leaned on the chief who in turn located the culprits who received thrashings that are recalled to this day.[95]

If there was anything that slowed the rate of fence destruction, then it was undoubtedly such internal policing. As both progressive farmers and the chiefly elite began increasingly to benefit from internal fencing, chiefly retaliation against fence destruction accelerated.[96] Furthermore, given the frequency with which straying cattle were impounded, some cattle owners probably came to see fencing as a mixed blessing. However, in the end there was, and presumably still is, no solution to fence destruction. A symbol and consequence of the nature of social and labour relations in the countryside, fence cutting could only disappear if the character of these relations were to be transformed.

While the most obvious role of fencing is to enforce dispossession and make private property a reality, it does also have a number of cultural functions that are not unrelated to the preconceptions of literacy. The notion of a boundary on a piece of paper, for example, is often seen by literate societies as having the same fixity as the printed text. As the referent of the text, the fence embodies the reality of the boundary and supposedly writes it permanently into the earth. Against the 'literacy' of the fence, the residents of the chiefdom mobilised the resources of an oral performance culture. It was the same set of resources that the chief and his attendants attempted to use in their political interaction with the Native Commissioner's office. At times they successfully forced the commissioner to deal with them on the terms of an oral world. But as the fences surrounded Valtyn, undermining the material base of the life to which people were accustomed, such victories over the commissioner became irrelevant and petty. Overall, it was the barbed wire that caged the spoken word.

4

"Dikgoro tša Kgale" The Courtyards of Long Ago

Forced Removals, Household Shape and the Performance of Oral History

The early 1960s were not good years for the residents of Valtyn. On 6 December 1963 government notice 1881 announced that under the Bantu Authorities Act of 1951 'Vaaltyn Macapaans Location' had become a 'Tribal Authority'. The same government notice also decreed that in terms of proclamation 116 of 1949 the chiefdom had been declared a 'betterment area'.[1] This decree required *inter alia* that the scattered, traditional-style villages within the chiefdom be moved into consolidated grid-plan settlements.

As though this were not enough, some eight months later the chiefdom also lost 376 hectares of much-needed land when the residents of the Old Location just outside Potgietersrus were forcibly moved within the borders of Lebowa (see Fig. 1 and 2). The settlement to which they were relocated was called Mahwelereng, and in August 1964 it was formally opened by the Minister of Bantu Administration, M.D.C. de Wet Nel, or, as he was more popularly known in African communities, 'the storming rhinoceros that cannot be stopped'.[2]

This assault on the territory and internal organisation of the chiefdom was not unusual, and during the 1950s and 1960s many other Transvaal communities were subject to similar onslaughts.[3] This coercive social engineering in turn formed part of a significant shift in the National Party government's strategy to control the black population. Throughout the 1950s the policy of the Native Affairs Department had concentrated on a controlled expansion of an urban African proletariat which would comprise a core of

78

'detribalised' people who were to be recognised as permanent city dwellers. By the 1960s, however, largely as a result of ideological struggles within the Afrikaner political elite, this policy had shifted. In terms of this reformulated thinking, proletarianisation was to be rigorously controlled, if not reversed. In addition, the idea of 'detribalisation' fell from official favour and was replaced by a discourse of 'ethnic self-determination' and 'separate development' in terms of which African residential and political rights were to be anchored in 'self-governing homelands'.[4]

To realise these objectives, the Bantu Affairs Department, as it became known, had to reduce the number of Africans in the city, keep new arrivals out and contain the remainder in 'homelands'. One key aspect in this programme was the influx control system. Another was the homeland structure that from the late 1950s underwent fundamental political and demographic changes to equip the bantustan areas for their impending barracoon role. The prelude for this political restructuring had been the Bantu Authorities Act of 1951. As its name implies, this piece of legislation aimed to set up 'Bantu Authorities' or tribal bodies that were to form part of a triple-decker arrangement of political representation that ended in 'self-governing territories'. This system wiped away the last vestige of indirect African representation in parliament and attempted to divert African political aspiration into bantustans. Each Tribal Authority, as the lowest rung of the edifice was known, was to be headed by a state-appointed chief armed with certain coercive powers that would make him a crucial gate-keeper in the rigorously controlled flow of labour to and from towns. The introduction of the Bantu Self-Government Act of 1959 extended the scope of these measures.[5]

Demographically, the homeland areas experienced quite astonishing population increases as a result of the state's attempt to control urbanisation and enforce territorial segregation. One major strategy in this struggle was mass population relocations. These coerced removals took a number of different forms. Some were removals from urban areas into homelands as locations next to white towns were shunted across bantustan borders. Other removals involved black communities with freehold rights in white farming areas. These were likewise moved into 'self-governing territories'. In addition, thousands of 'non-productive' people were 'endorsed out' of city and town areas, while after 1956 the rate of expulsions from farms increased as new legislation progressively enabled farmers to implement large-scale evictions of tenants.[6]

To accommodate this influx of people, existing residential areas in the homelands had to be radically rearranged. This forcible reshuffling was largely accomplished through betterment removals. As we have seen, betterment policies long pre-dated the advent of the National Party government, but from the 1960s it was the provisions of these schemes which were used to pack an astonishing number of people into the homeland regions. In terms of these schemes, areas were to be divided into consolidated arable, grazing, and residential zones and, in order to institute the latter, people were removed from traditional, cluster-style settlements into grid-style villages.

From the mid-1950s these combined policies of political restructuring and mass relocation were turned, with increasing frequency, against rural societies, but particularly against those with a territorial base that had allowed them some ability – no matter how limited – to keep the interference of the Native Commissioner at arm's length. Betterment and Bantu Authorities enabled a more saturating penetration of white authority that would, as Delius puts it for the case of Sekhukhuneland, "usher the white state into every nook and cranny of rural life".[7] Other aspects of white authority like church, school and wage labour had, of course, seeped into rural societies, but these could be more readily controlled and selectively appropriated. The all-embracing nature of betterment removals, the political restructuring brought about by the Bantu Authorities Act and the forced reshuffling of separate development severely curtailed any latitude that remained to rural communities.

As a growing number of studies have shown, this radical programme of social engineering in the homelands had a number of profound consequences. In general terms, the dramatic population increases have occasioned landlessness, acute overcrowding and increasing impoverishment for the many, while a tiny stratum comprising the traditional political elites, homeland bureaucrats and traders has accumulated a large degree of power for itself.[8] Politically, the introduction of Bantu Authorities brought with it a class of appointed and compliant chiefs who often lacked popular support. In addition, the combined effects of Bantu Authorities and betterment resettlements often precipitated major revolts.[9]

As regards the impact of betterment removals alone, a number of studies have spelled out the economic and social consequences of these schemes which are often held responsible for playing "a major part in finally destroying ... folk culture as a coherent way of life".[10] Economically, betterment generally brings with it land loss, diminution of stock and greater impoverishment. Socially, the relocation of housing tampers with established relationships of kin and neighbourhood as well as the accompanying forms of economic co-operation and social association which they underwrite.

However, relatively little attention has been focused on the cultural consequences of such removals. While this is, of course, a vast and complex task, this chapter will attempt a small part of it by discussing the impact of betterment resettlement in Valtyn on oral storytelling. The focus of the discussion will be on male traditions of storytelling that centred on the *kgoro*. Since the removals entailed a relocation from organic, traditional, cluster-style settlements to imposed grid-style villages, the *kgoro*, as a focus of a circular arrangements of dwellings, could find no exact equivalent in the rectangular world of the betterment settlements, and its demise held out a series of consequences for oral storytelling. The chapter begins by setting out the details of betterment resettlements in Valtyn. Thereafter we consider the *kgoro* as a site of male storytelling before going on to consider the contradictory impact of its demise.

I

As Beinart has illustrated, betterment policies have deep intellectual roots that stretch back to nineteenth-century scientific optimism which in turn promoted a growing faith in technicist solutions to ecological crises. By the 1930s the idea of betterment, which formed part of a wider discourse on conservation, had become bound up with the segregationist imperatives of the state. During subsequent decades, betterment policy underwent various name changes, but the central thrust remained an attempt to 'solve' chronic land shortage and overcrowding in the reserves through technological and 'scientific' intervention in agriculture and land use.[11]

While the detail and emphasis of the policies changed, one of its earliest and most enduring tenets was to divide settlements into rigidly demarcated arable, grazing and residential areas. African agriculture and ecological management, by contrast, had always been flexible, with housing patterns being controlled by the dictates of security and the location of natural resources like wood, water and arable land. In the language of betterment planners, this pattern of settlement was wasteful, while African agricultural practices were destructive and inefficient. Their profligacy needed to be curbed into patterns of 'orderly settlement' and 'rational' land use while officials often believed that "by removing the wasteful practice of scattered kraals", they would miraculously uncover additional land for grazing and arable use.[12]

In terms of the practicalities of these schemes, previously scattered housing was relocated in consolidated grid-style villages, a process that often destroyed the strategic situation of settlement in relation to natural resources like wood, water and fields.[13] After housing had been consolidated, the remaining land was divided into arable and grazing areas. When it came to the parcelling out of arable land, the thinking of the 1930s and 1940s favoured a differential distribution of fields to allow the emergence of at least some viable farming. After 1948, however, land was parcelled out to villagers in holdings of uniform size from which it was impossible to survive. In addition to resettlement and land reallocation, a third prop in the scheme was a programme of cattle culling, although this generally provoked such implacable resistance that it was often dropped. In Valtyn, however, it was carried out.[14]

As the previous chapter has indicated, Valtyn was one of the first Transvaal communities to experience the early stages of betterment which took the form of anti-soil erosion, land rehabilitation and fencing activities. In addition to this reclamation work, plans for dividing the chiefdom into arable, grazing and residential areas had been finalised by the late 1930s.[15] As matters turned out, these plans were only implemented in the late 1960s. Part of the reason for this delay involved the exigencies of a war economy, but the dogged resistance that the reclamation work provoked must also have played some part in stalling these ambitious plans for the physical rearrangement of the chiefdom. This resistance took a variety of forms which included destruction and theft of machinery, strikes and foot-dragging of various kinds. All these slowed the work down, as did the endless number of meetings that officials had to call in an attempt to secure minimal co-operation from the residents.[16]

This popular resistance also exercised a chastening influence on a series of chiefs who left to their own devices would probably have accepted betterment much earlier. However, popular pressure intervened at crucial points to prevent the chiefly imposition of resettlements. One such occasion occurred towards the end of 1949, when the residents of Valtyn were agog with reports that their chief, Gwejela, had sold their land to the government for the purpose of erecting a township. So widespread was the rumour that 'even herdboys' were said to have heard it. The rumour was, incidentally, not entirely without foundation since the Native Affairs Department had finalised plans to shift a shanty town that had grown up on the borders of Potgietersrus into the chiefdom. Understandably, feelings on the issue ran high. Threats were made against the chief who was scared to move out of his home after dark.[17]

While the chief gathered a small handful of supporters around him, the senior men of the chiefdom began pressing the Native Commissioner to depose the incumbent. This they did by invoking the byzantine complexities of succession politics in an attempt to reclassify the incumbent as a regent rather than a 'true' chief. Their invocation of oral memory, however, could not withstand the full bureaucratic weight of the Native Affairs Department which backed the chief to the hilt, largely because he endorsed their betterment policies. In private the Chief Native Commissioner favoured deposition of the manifestly unpopular chief; in public he supported the typically rigid interpretation that government ethnologists had made of Ndebele succession law. "The government," he explained to one of many well-attended meetings, "wants to know the wishes of the people but they should not change from one thing to another every day. The law cannot be this today and that tomorrow." Needless to say, the chief's dynastic credentials, backed by state power, weathered this storm of popular scepticism and he remained in power.[18]

The state response to this show of opposition was to accelerate reclamation activities and as N.J. van Warmelo, the government ethnologist, put it, "to turn on the heat (tax, dog tax, wheel tax, bicycle tax etc) to dispel the prevailing idea that the Government is no longer master in the location".[19] This imposition simply heightened popular opposition, and when the state attempted to introduce Bantu Authorities in 1951 the chiefdom would have nothing of it.[20] By contrast, the leaders of the neighbouring chiefdoms of Mapela and Bakenberg had, by 1954, agreed to the implementation of Bantu Authorities, and by 1959 seven chiefdoms in the Potgietersrus area had accepted the scheme which simultaneously included the implementation of betterment.[21]

Valtyn, however, held out. Ever since aspects of betterment had been implemented in the area, residents had opposed it, an opposition which continued throughout the 1950s and into the 1960s. In addition, by the late 1950s betterment schemes, backed by Bantu Authorities, had become more hastily implemented and coercive, and as these schemes spread to surrounding areas their devastating effects probably stiffened popular resistance in Valtyn. Furthermore, the combination of betterment and Bantu Authorities proved so unpopular in other parts of the Transvaal that major uprisings resulted.[22] As a consequence, the imposition of betterment slowed down slightly as officials began to move more cautiously.

The chiefdom, however, had the one major weakness of its highly fragmented royal lineage which as we have seen had been chronically divided since at least the 1890s. In 1961 Gwejela died, and a fierce succession battle ensued. Filled as it was with a simple-minded heir, allegations of incest and threats of poisoning, this episode would have done any Jacobean tragedy proud. In the end the simple-minded chief was engineered into power, but the factionalism persisted. While the circumstances are not entirely clear, it would seem that by a skilful manipulation of the divisions within the chiefdom's ruling caste the Native Commissioner's office eventually persuaded the simple-minded chief and his supporters to accept Bantu Authorities, betterment and the creation of Mahwelereng within the chiefdom's boundaries. According to one informant, these measures were pushed through in the face of heavy popular opposition with people stoutly maintaining that they would not let their "fatherland be ruled by a commissioner".[23] This opposition to the measures in general and Mahwelereng in particular simmered on for some time and the new settlement acquired the popular name of *Anthande lekeišeneng* (We don't like the location).[24]

As regards the betterment resettlements, the plans took some time to implement and while it is not clear exactly when they began, aerial photographs taken in 1965 indicate that removals had not yet commenced. By 1970 they had been completed (see Plates 10 to 14 and Plates 15 to 20) and the chiefdom had been forcibly rearranged into residential, arable and grazing areas. By this stage, the idea of betterment itself had undergone changes, and any pretence at soil conservation and promoting at least some viable agriculture had fallen away. Instead, plots of uniform size in the newly designated arable area were issued to all.[25] These plots, which were generally a quarter of what was considered necessary for a viable farming unit, could not be used as the sole basis of support, and in any event they soon ran out. This shortage was not surprising since the planning of bantustans in the Northern Transvaal made allowance for the settlement of 40 per cent more residents than there were plots available.[26] By 1987, as the photographs (see Plate 14) illustrate, Valtyn had become a vast rural slum. Arable land had diminished considerably under the impact of massive population expansion, and from a distance there is little to distinguish the chiefdom from Mahwelereng: they have both become overcrowded ghettoes.

II

In their ultimately failed attempts to pressurise their chief to stay clear of officialdom, the residents of Valtyn were, like their counterparts in other chiefdoms, defending the one small but cherished space that remained relatively free of white interference.[27] As we have seen in the previous chapter, the exigencies of indirect rule ordained that the Native Commissioner and his office were 'structurally remote' from the chiefdom and generally had little direct impact on everyday life.[28]

Within the brittle protection of the chiefdom, residents could maintain a degree of control over their everyday lives that was not possible in the more tightly policed town location and the increasingly rigorously controlled white cities where many men and women worked as migrants. A significant symbol of this independence was the traditional, cluster-style housing which differed visibly from the grid-style layout of the town location and the mission station (see Plates 14 to 20). While the houses on the mission station were not entirely regimented but rather loosely grouped around a central road running through the mission precinct, the location was arranged on a strict grid plan.[29] For many, this spatial arrangement, often referred to as *malaeneng* (in the lines), was seen as both a key instrument and symbol of white control that furthermore entailed being administered by a location superintendent. This official had such wide-ranging powers over everyday life that he could even specify the amount of beer that each household brewed.[30]

In the chiefdom, by contrast, the household generally remained beyond the reach of white officialdom, and in it men, as family and homestead heads, enjoyed a degree of authority and control that was often lacking in other areas of their lives. In addition, the household and its leisure activities became a focus of conviviality as well as a crucial cipher of identity. In short, the household and the broader homestead embodied an entire social order rooted in networks of kinship, economic co-operation and cultural association.[31] While increasing migrancy obviously altered these patterns of authority and leisure in the household, it also probably increased attachment to the rural homestead as a symbol of refuge from the alienating experiences of industrial work in white cities.

For many, the set of meanings and social relationships embodied in the household were summarised by the concept of *kgoro*. It is a word with a wide range of meanings, one of which denotes the central courtyard that unites a cluster of households into a homestead. It can also refer to the central courtyard of the ward, made up, in turn, of a number of homesteads. Both these areas are exclusive male arenas and, in addition to denoting the space of these areas, the word *kgoro* can also refer to the people gathered therein. In other instances, the word stands for the entrance to such areas. More generally, it can be used as a synonym for village and as such stands for the idea of a particular type of social organisation rooted in large agnatic clusters.[32]

As we have seen in Chapter 1, the *kgoro* was, in many respects, the nerve centre of social organisation. Here disputes were settled and pressing problems resolved. Here, too, men directed the activities, like communal labour, that linked households into homesteads. The *kgoro* was the place of public gathering and the locale for much ritual ceremony. In addition, and most importantly for our purposes, the *kgoro* was also a place for both literary and historical education. Here, in the evening, men would tell a range of story types that were seen as an important part of male education. Or, as Obed Kutumela (see Plate 21) explained:

> We listened to our grandfathers at night, while seated around the fire as a group. Those who listened carefully would be good storytellers. It is like oration, something learned by word of mouth. They would tell us stories followed by historical narratives. Sometimes they would speak about themselves and their bravery.[33]

Pitje describes a similar situation:

> In furthering ... education, men teach courage and endurance through stories told of tribal heroes. This takes place by the fire-side at the men's place (*kgoroxong*). From actual narration or adult conversation, the boy also learns about tribal migrations, ethnic history, tribal lore, law and custom. In

PLATE 10   An aerial view of part of the chiefdom around the hill, Sefakaola, 1953.
The cluster-style settlements can be seen at the base of the hill (Department of
Surveying and Maps, Job 323, Strip 5, No. 284. Scale, 1:7 500)

PLATE 11   An aerial view of the same part of the chiefdom in 1963. By this stage, Mahwelereng had been established. Removals of cluster-style settlements had not yet begun (Department of Surveying and Maps, Job 495, Strip 6, No. 188. Scale, 1:12 500)

PLATE 12   An aerial view around the hill, Sefakaola, 1970. By this stage the
removals were complete (Department of Surveying and Maps, Job 651, Strip 10,
No.4312. Scale, 1:5 000)

PLATE 13   An aerial view of the same area two years later in 1972. Note that the size of the plots on the periphery of the settlement has halved (Department of Surveying and Maps, Job 684, Strip 4, No. 7230. Scale, 1:5 000)

PLATE 14   An aerial view of part of the chiefdom in 1987 (Department of
Surveying and Maps, Job 909, Strip 3, No. 2083. Scale, 1:12 500)

PLATE 15   A view of the chiefdom in pre-removal days – 1954 (Combrink, *Eeufees*, 23)

PLATE 16   A view of the chiefdom in post-removal days – 1989 (Photograph by Santu Mofokeng)

PLATE 17   A post-removal view of the chiefdom, 1989 (Photograph by Santu Mofokeng)

PLATE 18   A view of the chiefdom from Mahwelereng, 1989 (Photograph by Santu Mofokeng)

PLATE 19   Household shape in the pre-removal chiefdom (Combrink, *Eeufees*, 24)

PLATE 20   Household shape in the post-removal chiefdom. Note the clustering of single-roomed structures (Photograph by Santu Mofokeng)

PLATE 21   Obed Kutumela (Photograph by Santu Mofokeng)

PLATE 22   Alfred Lesiba Kekeana (Photograph by Santu Mofokeng)

PLATE 23   Leka Thinta Mokhonoane (Photograph by Santu Mofokeng)

recognition of this type of training, they say: *'Ngwana'a mosimane o tseya molao kxorong'* (A boy receives his training at the men's place).[34]

One central point to note about this historical education was its universality, at least as far as men were concerned.[35] Women could pick up historical information informally from their husbands, sons and fathers. "Stories of this kind [historical narratives] emanated from discussions around the day-to-day incidents in the community," one woman explained.[36] Using these types of encounters as a source as well as drawing on their own experience, women could include 'true' stories in their repertoires.[37] Through a combination of talent and perseverance, a woman could accumulate enough historical knowledge to become recognised as an expert.[38] Yet, barred as they were from the *kgoro*, the real daily centre of historical education, women were never made entirely articulate in historical knowledge.

Men, on the other hand, were. The foundations of this education were conveyed in the *kgoro* where the skills and crafts of history were performed on a daily basis. Such historical knowledge could on occasion be expressed in forms like praising and song. However, it was undoubtedly narrative that predominated. While the knowledge of such narrative was widespread, the number of skilled and talented performers was obviously much smaller, and one elderly informant, recalling his childhood, put the number of really great male narrators at three.[39] However, as we shall see in Chapters 5 and 6, much of the craft of this historical storytelling presupposed a well-informed audience who could grasp the way in which tellers collocated various story elements.

As regards the content of such stories, this ranged widely, or as Alfred Lesiba Kekana put it, "At the *kgoro*, men taught boys the law, obedience, not to fight, stories of their forefathers, what happened in wars, family and kin relations."[40] Much of this material was not overtly historical and instead focused on instruction in the manly skills of life like hunting. Such accounts often assumed a fairly austere performance style that did not require frequent audience response and had nothing like songs that enlisted active audience participation. At times, the content of such stories could focus on topics like the technicalities of hunting. The content of one such story is summarised by Alfred Lesiba Kekana.

> In the olden days, when one went hunting and killed a big buck or an antelope alone, one would chop a big, thorny tree to cover the buck so that other animals like carnivores should not have access to the dead buck. Then one goes to the kraal to report to the elders about the killing. Then they would bring a sleigh along, uncover the animal and bring it home. If it is a small animal like a hare, for instance, one should sharpen a stick, made from a branch, and tie both the hind and forelegs to either side of that stick. This being done, the hare should simply be taken home. If it is a bird, like a dove, one would not eat it after killing it. Instead, you would take it to the elders. Young men have no right to such food, according to our custom. Then if you killed an animal like a jackal, you would not eat it, you only take the skin to make blankets, which are usually beautiful. We call this *lenaga*, the Sotho call it *lefato*. You get different skins and soak them. This would make a very warm blanket. This is all according to Ndebele custom.

This 'informational' style was by no means the only one, and in other instances instructional material could be encased in a more stylised narrative format very similar to *dinonwane*. Such stories frequently contain the fantastical emphasis of the *nonwane* into which more realistic everyday information is woven. Another story narrated by Alfred Lesiba Kekana which embeds information on hunting and manly behaviour in a legendary setting illustrates the point.

Long ago, there was a man who was travelling with his wife through the forest because there were a lot of beasts. While they were taking their journey, they were attacked by a lion. And it was indeed fierce and caused the husband to run away. He left the woman alone and she cried. Then the lion attempted to pounce on the woman, but she caught it by its tail. As the lion tried to bite her she ran off not letting go of the lion's tail but only screaming, raising the alarm. Then came three men. They were hunters. These men used assegais to kill the lion. After this, they asked her: 'Woman, why do you go in the forest alone?' She said that she was with a man, her husband, who ran away during the encounter. They then decided to take the woman, together with the slain lion, to the chief's kraal. They chief asked where her husband was. She told him where they might find him. They began to search for him. Then the woman said, 'I am no longer in love with this man, because he is a coward. One of the three men who helped me must marry me.' As for that man, he is no good, he is a coward. It is like that, if you are a coward a wife will turn away from you.[41]

Stories like these clearly encompass a variety of themes that could stretch from 'veldcraft'[42] instruction to issues of gender identity, social order and the moral implications of events. Such tales were not, of course, specifically concerned with recording information from the past but they could do this tangentially by, for example, incidentally 'embalming'[43] past episodes.

However, there were other stories that self-consciously set out to record the past, and in doing so these narratives could cover a wide range of subjects that touched on origin, founding heroes, secession, migration, settlement, genealogy and historical narrative that dealt with events within living memory. Junod's description is apposite here:

When you inquire what they [Tsonga informants] know about the past, you find first, a story about their origin which bears a strongly mythical character; secondly, traditions more or less legendary about the migrations of the various clans; thirdly, genealogies of the royal family containing eight to ten names; and fourthly, historical narratives which go back as far as the beginning of the nineteenth century, and which give the impression of true historical facts.[44]

Considered collectively, the historical stories of the *kgoro* comprised a fluid repertoire of subjects and styles that borrowed heavily from the *nonwane* tradition. The different names by which people identify these stories reflects this fluidity. The most frequently used terms are *tiragalo* (occurrence, happening, episode), *taba* (story, affair, incident) or *taba ya kgale* (story/affair/incident of the past), *nonwane*, or *histori* (history). While most people use these terms, one informant, Molalakgori Kekana also suggested *dikanegelo* (narration), *tlhalošo-polelo* (discursive account), *tlhalošo ya setlogo/setšhaba* (account of history/the nation), or simply *polelo* (discussion). This latter formulation of storytelling as a kind of interactive discussion is one that another informant, Alpheus Ledwaba, used.[45] What this range of forms suggests is the fluid nature of historical storytelling whose definition can stretch from a word with relatively clear outlines like *nonwane* to a much more open-ended term like *polelo*.

In terms of their locale, male historical forms were not only restricted to the *kgoro* and could, in fact, crop up in other conversational and work situations. Herding, particularly when it involved long sojourns at distant cattle posts, could provide a context for male storytelling, some of which would be historical. Sedentary work could also promote storytelling among men, and again some of these tales could relate to past events. In any society, storytelling is woven into a number of everyday situations on a basis that is never entirely predictable, and Transvaal polities were probably no exception.[46] Such everyday stories, however, remain fluid and it was undoubtedly the *kgoro* that remained the focus for slightly more formalised and institutionalised telling since it was here that boys gained part of their historical education. This learning did not, of course, end here but continued through initiation and through experience, as with age, men expanded their stock of historical knowledge.

Apart from these evening sessions, the *kgoro* was also the focus for other performances that included marriages, piacular intercessions, ritual occasions, judicial deliberations, funerals and commemorative ceremonies.[47] All these events required the display of historical information which was expressed in a wide variety of forms that included genealogy, praising, beer drink oratory, prayers, ritual intercessions and legal disquisition. These ceremonies were also characterised by a high degree of performance. Part of this performance lay in song, dance, music and mime.[48] But part also lay in the language of ritual which is itself a form of action rather than simply an accumulation of propositional statements.[49] As a focus for these various activities, the *kgoro* became, in Pitje's words, 'an open theatre'.[50]

Within the *kgoro*, then, a range of oral forms was enacted and performed. Together these various parts recorded a sense of the past in different ways and via different mediums. However, within this diversity there was often one common idea by which a sense of the past was both imagined and bracketed into units. This idea related to the notion of chieftaincy. Or, as one informant explained:

> The whole thing [that is, history] came in as a story, tale, something like that. My grandmother says this, and my auntie tells this, my uncle tells that, then this one tells a different story, and that one tells yet another story. When I tell my friend about the chief here, I tell him like this and that, and then this one is going to tell him about the same chief, not the same story, though, a different story. So that's why our chief has many colours.[51]

This quotation illustrates the extent to which the recollection of historical information was packaged into male genealogical chunks which became the major unit for organising a sense of the past and periodising the flow of time.

The archetype for this model was chiefly history which was always arranged in ever-changing, retrospective, regnal units whose endurance in time bolstered claims to political power. Or, as one informant explained such genealogical history, "Since I started narrating this history, you have never heard me talking about a woman ... I speak about a chief after a chief."[52]

From this chiefly model other, lesser histories were constructed. Ward and homestead heads, in ancestral ceremonies, for example, also represented the continuity of their social unit through invoking an ancestral line. All this is not to say that chieftaincy and agnatic seniority were the only *subjects* of historical discourses since, as we have seen, the topics on which historical discourses could touch varied enormously. The notions of male seniority did, however, provide the major historiographical focus around which historical forms of various types could cluster. This genealogical chunking of time in turn comes to represent the continuity of an entire social order. Or, as Paul Connerton phrases it in his perceptive study of social memory, "... an individual's consciousness of time is to a large degree an awareness of society's continuity, or more exactly of the image of that continuity which the society creates".[53]

This agnatic view could, moreover, form the ideological basis of political dissent, particularly in a situation where resistance habitually manifested itself through secession rather than revolt.[54] One major focus for such secession was the ward. An administrative and political unit rather than one based purely on descent, the ward, none the less, expressed its social coherence through the image and idiom of lineage.[55] Under such circumstances, it was lineage history that often provided the means of keeping dissent alive, and on occasions it was this history that could provide part of the motivation for seceding, particularly in the case of commoner or conquered groupings.[56] In response to this potential for dissent, chiefly ceremony often sought to incorporate and so, it was hoped, to contain the history of subordinated groupings, a tactic that frequently took the form of acknowledging, in minor ways, the fact of a conquered group's prior arrival.[57] In Valtyn this appropriation also took the form of absorbing elements of narrative tradition from subordinate lineages. One of these is the Mashishi lineage, often believed to be the original inhabitants of the present-day area of the chiefdom. The story of how a group of intruders tricked the Mashishi by taking their young men hunting and then slaughtering those who remain behind is told by both Mashishi and Kekana informants. In addition, the Mashishi record the fact of their subordination through the story that the ruling lineage took over their habit of eating fish, something the invaders had never done before.[58]

Yet whether used to support or challenge the status quo, the central point to note about this agnatic, patriarchal view of both the past and the present is its power and ability to endure. As a form of social and historical understanding, its hold over the popular imagination has been enormous, and even today many rural communities have an abiding commitment to agnatic rule symbolised in the system of chieftaincy, despite generations of dissolute chiefs.

There are, of course, a number of ways of explaining this phenomenon, not the least of which is that bad chiefly rule is still preferable to direct white authority. However, a full examination of all these factors cannot be attempted here. Instead, there is one less obvious factor which helps to explain the hold of chiefly history that concerns us here, namely the participatory performance that characterised the enactment of history.

Such participation, as Connerton has shown, is one of the most efficient methods of passing on historical memory largely because people perform their parts from what has been termed habit-memory. But, as Connerton argues, most scholars of memory have discounted such habitual recollection as having no cognitive content. Seen, however, from the point of view of political and social memory, habitual behaviour simultaneously recalls and enacts a complex recollection of inherited social relationships and hierarchies. Because these relationships are enacted by the body, they exert a considerable sway over people who habitually co-operate in their repetition and perpetuation. The hold, then, of enacted performance is powerful and goes some way towards explaining the deep-rooted allegiance to chieftaincy and the social order it represents.[59]

III

The performance of history, then, within the *kgoro*, depended on a complex combination of locale, form, performance and participation. What effects did the disappearance of the *kgoro* have on the oral performances that it hosted? Since today female storytelling survives relatively better than male storytelling, one is, of course, tempted to draw a fairly direct link between the demise of the *kgoro* and male narrative traditions. The idea of a kitchen space was, after all, easy to transplant to the grid-style settlements, and with it traditions of female storytelling could transfer themselves relatively well.[60] As regards the *kgoro*, on the other hand, there was no obvious place to which it could relocate, and it is to this changed spatial situation that one is inclined to ascribe the present-day lack of male storytelling. But, while this assertion has some truth, such a one-to-one relationship is oversimplified and there are a number of factors complicating the situation.

Given the centrality of the *kgoro* as an institution, it obviously did not evaporate overnight and, in moving from traditional settlement clusters to *malaeneng*, people reconstituted as much of their world as they could. The architecture on each plot often followed the model of the cluster house, and many households were composed of individual rooms issuing on to a central courtyard rather than a composite, multi-roomed house (see Plate 20).[61] Since the *kgoro* also carried such crucial political and social symbolism, *kgoro*-type meetings were often reconstituted under a tree or at someone's house. The physical space of the *kgoro* may have vanished. Nevertheless, its forms of association, orature and interaction obviously continued in slightly different locales. But as these gatherings often had to be fairly self-consciously reconvened, much of the former fluidity and spontaneity of the *kgoro* withered. Furthermore, the possibility of reconstituting the *kgoro* was open only to a limited number of people who were the first to be resettled. Often members of the ruling lineage, these families had the opportunity to settle with kin. Those who moved later, or arrived subsequent to the removals, had to settle at the periphery of villages among strangers. Under these conditions, families inevitably became more isolated and broke off into their various sub-households which were now located at some distance from one another.[62] In addition, if one lived far from one's kin the possibility of gathering for evening storytelling was remote, and under these circumstances the function of the *kgoro* narrowed as its wider cultural aspects gave way to more pressing concerns with problem-solving and the settling of family disputes.

In such a climate, the function of the *kgoro* as a place of performance and informal learning partly fell away. Lucky Kekana describes her experience of this informal learning that even she as an outsider and girl obtained in the environs of the *dikgoro*:

I know these stories and this history because I was born in a *kgoro*. I am the grandchild of the *kgoro* and I am the child of it. Villages used to have one *kgoro*. There was also only one gate, even when the village was big. We used to play around the gate. When the men in the *kgoro* had finished solving their problems, we used to imitate them. I would pretend to be someone's grandfather, another child would pretend to be someone else's grandfather. Just like that.[63]

Inevitably, the fluidity of these learning patterns could not entirely accommodate itself to the more rigid plan of the betterment villages, and accordingly shrivelled. However, it is not only the issue of informal learning that is at stake here. As we have seen, the expression of chiefly history was synonymous with participatory performance. Once the *kgoro* became more artificial, the frequency of performance decreased. Add to this the effects of mass education that took off in the chiefdom during the 1960s, and one has a further factor diminishing the hold of a participatory, oral performance culture.[64] Since this performance played a crucial role in transmitting chiefly historical memory, the meaning and relevance of chieftaincy was in all probability affected by the disappearance of the *kgoro* as a centre of dynamic and participatory historical enactment.

Another way in which the storytelling context changed was that established gender divisions began crumbling since the new layout of villages could not accommodate the previous sexual division of space. Or, as one person explained, "boys and girls mixed together in the kitchen".[65] As we have seen, the ordering force of gender relations in African societies was extremely powerful, and against this background, the idea of gender 'mixing' amounts to a heresy of considerable proportions.

This image of 'mixing' is one that recurs often in people's recollections of how resettlement affected daily life. In keeping with this image, the disappearance of the *kgoro* and the world it sustained is frequently remembered as a loss of order and purity. As one informant put it, "[The whites] stopped the *kgoro* of long ago. Then they mix us to be one thing." Elsewhere she said, "Nowadays ... we are mixed, because there is no *kgoro*."[66] This 'mixing' that she alludes to concerns both gender, religion and language, and the betterment resettlements are seen as precipitating a chaotic and improper confusion between men and women, Christian and non-Christian, Sotho and Ndebele.

Of course, this 'mixing' had had many dress rehearsals in both the mission stations and town locations, which, by comparison with chiefly villages, were ethnically extremely diverse.[67] Within these two areas, Christian households, in their architecture and gender division, assisted in the erosion of traditional models. One octogenarian informant commented, "... my father wasn't like other men...he was Christian. He stayed with us."[68] Christian households were also noticeably smaller, something that one of Sansom's informants in Sekhukhuneland phrased as follows: "There is no *kgoro*. In the old days everyone lived together and we had cattle. But now we are like the Christians, each man's house is a *kgoro*."[69]

From the point of view of the chiefdom, then, mission stations and locations were sullied spaces that breached propriety. They also lacked the sense of order and proper division, particularly between men and women, that those in the chiefdom saw as essential preconditions for storytelling. This lack of order was, for many, roughly equivalent to the lack of *dikgoro* that symbolised the grid-style layout of areas under white control. Any place without a *kgoro*, or the social relationships that it represented, could only be graceless and uncultured. Or, as Lucky Kekana phrased it, "I believe that the people at the location were unable to narrate stories because there was no *kgoro*."[70]

However, it might be argued that virtually a century of migrancy had already wrought many of these changes, even before the *kgoro* disappeared. For large parts of the year men were away and so missed out on an inductive, informal education and, as Opland points out, the metaphorical richness of migrants' praise poetry often diminishes because of their lack of an ongoing, intimate interaction with chiefly life.[71] Furthermore, particularly when female migrancy gained momentum in the 1960s, the changes to gender relations must have been far-reaching. In addition, migrancy altered the profile of audiences and so tampered with another precondition of storytelling. However, as a number of studies on migrancy and cultural transformation have shown, migrants not only have a high commitment to traditionalism, they frequently reproduce the forms of the countryside in the town. Similarly, they appropriate metropolitan cultural conventions which they 'traditionalise' by subordinating these forms to the precepts of their political world.[72] Furthermore, given that traditional education entrusted the very youngest to the very oldest, the absence of a middle generation could, in fact, be accommodated for some time. Also, extended migrancy is a relatively recent phenomenon that only really became widespread in the 1960s with the advent of labour bureaux that locked workers into one job for many years. Before this time, migrants had much more leeway in job choices and duration of contract, and it was not uncommon for migrants to 'retire' in their thirties.[73] All this is not to say that migrancy had no effects on cultural patterns. Self-evidently it does. Rather, the point is that the impact of migrancy on cultural production is more ambiguous and delayed than one might think.

While the effects of migrancy on male storytelling were ambiguous, there was one effect of removals that was less equivocal. This relates to the disappearance of an everyday, physical world. As Connerton has shown in his study of social memory, one of the most powerful mnemonics we have is the architecture and detail of our daily lives, and it is out of this that most people construct a sense of continuity and time flow.[74] Considered in this light, what the removals in fact did was to rob people of their mnemonic surroundings. Apart from depriving people of their fixed cultural assets, the removals had an added significance since traditional settlements carried a particularly loaded symbolism. In terms of this signification, chiefly villages represented one last, small enclave of independence from direct white authority. In these settlements, residents could maintain a degree of control over their everyday lives that was not possible in the more tightly policed town locations and rigorously controlled white cities. A significant symbol of this independence was the traditional, cluster-style housing with its *kgoro* that differed visibly from the grid-style layout of locations, a spatial arrangement that was seen by many as a key instrument and symbol of white control.

In losing the architecture of tradition, many people simultaneously lost a political symbol and a source of historical memory. Hardly surprisingly, many attribute to the removals a much longer process of change that has assailed rural societies for the past two centuries. These processes are encapsulated in the removals which are often held solely responsible for a perceived demise of tradition. Or, as one man, in talking of removals and oral storytelling, said, "Now, it's all development, man, stories don't work, they don't work any more."[75]

Yet, these demoralising changes notwithstanding, many people have not simply abandoned traditionalism and its cultural practices. Many royal lineages, for example, have a high commitment to traditional skills, and since many of these were the first to settle in new villages, they are in a position to keep alive a vestige of the large, agnatic homesteads that characterised pre-removal settlements and the cultural practices of such groups. And it is largely within these groups that one finds the few remaining practitioners of oral historical narrative. It is to these men that we now turn to examine their historical craft in more detail.

PART THREE

Telling Historical Tales

5

The Craft of Oral
Historical Narrative
The Case of the Siege of Gwaša

As the previous chapter has argued, the basic unit of 'traditional' history is that of agnatic genealogy and it is through this template that a sense of the past is trapped. Or, as Miller phrases it:

> [A]n oral narrator working with epochs defined by kings' reigns can no more imagine an event not associated with a monarch he or she recalls than a literate historian can conceive of something happening outside the comprehensive sequence of calendar years, say, between the years 1640 and 1641.[1]

While this genealogical view of the past colonises the history of all social groupings from the household upwards, it is in chieftaincy that it finds its most elaborate and lengthy expression. The forms through which chieftaincy and its history can be articulated are wide-ranging and include, as the previous chapter has indicated, praising, prayers, songs and narratives.

In this chapter our concern will be with the latter category – historical narrative. One central question in relation to such storytelling, as a number of studies have shown, is how, or indeed whether, notions of chieftaincy can be translated into narrative form.[2] Narrative, after all, is a form concerned with individuals not circumstances, description not analysis, and the particular rather than the collective. Chieftainship, on the other hand, is implicated in much larger political institutions and the aggregates they comprise. To complicate matters further, the history of chieftainship is tied up with complex and massive changes to these various groupings. The initial question that arises, then, is whether narrative has the resources to represent this order of reality. Or, put another way, can these wider social concerns be 'forced' out of narrative with its individual focus? In short, can narrative provide historical understanding?

As so many enquiries into the nature of historical explanation have made clear, the answer to these questions must generally be affirmative. Narrative, with its complex internal arrangements and systems of representation, is, in fact, capable of sophisticated, if subtle forms of social explanation, historical interpretation and cultural exegesis.[3] Translated into methodological terms, these insights suggest that it is close attention to narrative form that will help us to divine historical meaning and interpretation.

Applied to oral historical narrative, this advice requires that we first consider the formal aspects of this storytelling style before we go on to discuss the understanding of chieftaincy which they embody. This chapter will tackle the first task while the second will be postponed for the chapter that follows.

I

As comparative discussions elsewhere have shown, the character of oral narrative is largely shaped by the prerogatives of oral memory and its need to create mnemonic systems.[4] In such a situation, narrative fulfils the task, or more properly, the core images around which both narrative and poetry are elaborated, do so. With its formulaic and rhythmic character, oral narrative is the 'roomiest repository' for information.[5] Or, as Havelock puts it, "... the preferred format for verbal storage in an oral culture will be the narrative of persons in action, and the syntax of the narrative will predominate...."[6]

Emanating from this narrative format will be a number of stylistic features that facilitate recall in performance. These include heroic larger-than-life characters that assist recollection; an episodic rather than a climactic plot that is easier to remember in performance; an additive and copious style that facilitates recitation; and the use of formulaic images through which story segments can easily be retrieved in performance.[7] Other stylistic features of oral narrative include traits like minimal scene setting and switching; two characters to a scene; dramatic dialogue; and use of gestural, performance and phonological resources.[8]

The resources outlined here form the basis of most oral narrative styles and are most obviously apparent in fictional narratives like, for example, *dinonwane*. Hence, as the first chapter has argued, it is with the resources of fictional narrative that oral historical storytellers must go to work.

Yet when it comes to putting across socio-historical rather than fictional concerns, oral narrative would seem to be hobbled by its own peculiar set of limitations. Oral fictional narratives, for example, do not generally deal with large-scale events like wars, catastrophes and upheavals. They are not, as Finnegan puts it, "composed on the grand scale".[9] Furthermore, aspects such as two characters to a scene; minimal scene setting and switching; a stress on heroic characters; and the proclivity of oral narrative to favour sudden rather than gradual change, would all seem to militate against the portrayal of large social institutions like chieftaincy.

For Scheub, this problem is non-existent since for him these epic dimensions come to the surface once several tales are combined.[10] Stitched together, they open up the possibility of epic, a genre that Scheub sees as being defined by the presence of a culture hero. While this approach has much to commend it, it does not probe the details of how the technical 'limitations' of the oral narrative can be transformed to express epic intent.

This is a task that Okpewho, in his examination of epic, has explored in depth. By focusing on both the more obvious aspects of epic such as heroic characterisation, as well as examining the adaptation of more quotidian oral storytelling techniques like humour, phonology, motif, naming techniques and episodic narration, Okpewho illustrates how various performers by dint of creativity and talent have managed to amplify everyday storytelling and musical craft so that it can accommodate the fantastic, larger-than-life figures whose actions in turn come to symbolise significant moments of historical change.[11] While their skill, training, discipline and intellect may well outstrip their less talented peers, performers – or bards as Okpewho prefers to call them – in the end go to work with the same sets of resources as any other teller. In the cases that Okpewho examines, such resources include musical and literary skills, and these are then practised until they can be extended in such a way that they can sustain monumental epic performances.[12]

In Southern Africa, where mammoth-scale empires which traditionally produce historical epic have been rare,[13] the situation is different. Oral historical narratives in the subcontinent rarely attain overtly epic proportions, while the musical or sung dimension that Okpewho sees as central to epic is not generally associated with the relatively subdued and strait-laced style that characterises historical storytelling. If it is scale and the embellished, sung performance of epic that one is after, then it is to praise poetry that one must turn for a more obviously epic sense of dimension and spectacle. Furthermore, as White has shown, praise poetry is the form most frequently used to define and celebrate the epic business of chiefship.[14]

Yet, the differences between the largely West African examples of epic that Okpewho relies on and Southern African historical narrative are not so absolute as to render Okpewho's ideas inapplicable. Southern African historical narrative may well not be entirely epic, but it does certainly manifest epic tendencies, particularly in the 'culture heroes' or founding fathers that inhabit oral traditions.[15] Other epic tendencies, particularly in relation to the use of time and space, can also be detected. Tonkin, for example, has pointed out that in examples of historical narration from south-eastern Liberia, the depiction of space can be made to imply the massiveness of epic scale – and this is indeed a characteristic commonly found in Southern African historical traditions.[16] Similarly, as Henige's analysis of time has shown, the manipulation of chronology and succession can be adapted to imply epic grandeur and continuity, a trait that is again manifest in many Southern African examples.[17] While these epic tendencies may not be of the same order as something like *Sunjata*, the West African epic, there is enough similarity between the West African model and the Southern African examples to ensure that Okpewho's

PLATE 24   A scene of the caves in the 1880s showing the ramparts and skulls
(T.A., T.A.D., 33245)

PLATE 24   M.W. Pretorius (T.A., T.A.D., 4618)

analysis of elaborating historico-epic plots out of everyday storytelling resources can still be used to deal with historical narrative here.

One of the most common of these everyday techniques, as Scheub has argued for the Xhosa *ntsomi*, is the use of mnemonic kernels or what he terms the core cliché, usually a song, chant or saying, into which potential plots or plot segments are distilled. In performance, it is these kernels that are elaborated by the images, details, actions, characters and feelings associated with the core cliché and which unfold as it is called to mind. In responding to varying performance situations and audiences, the teller clusters these units in combinations that are tailored to meet the exigencies of the particular context.[18] In dealing with various oral narrative accounts of the cave of Gwaša siege of 1854, it is with this technique that we will initially be concerned, and we turn now to examine some of the kernels from which various tellers construct their accounts. In the chapter that follows we will narrow our focus on to two narrators in order to learn something of their literary and historical craft. However, before we attempt either of these tasks, it is necessary first to provide an outline of the siege event itself.

II

The cave of Gwaša or Makapansgat siege of 1854 properly belongs to a longer story of growing Boer incursions into the Northern Transvaal from the 1840s. Driven from the Cape by the ending of slavery in 1833, or coming in search of the vicinity's rich game, small numbers of Boers began to settle in the area now known as Potgietersrus. As this spot lay in a break of otherwise continuous mountains through which one of the major routes to the ivory-rich Northern Transvaal went, it had considerable strategic importance. Living on either side of this highway were two polities. To the south-east lay the chiefdom of Mokopane and to the west the Mapela polity (see Fig. 3). The first group fell under the leadership of Setšwamadi or, as he was also known, Mokopane (Sesotho) or Mugombane (Sindebele). The second group was headed by a chief called Mankopane.[19]

Once in the Transvaal, certain Boers aimed to reconstitute the slave society they had left behind, and it was on the polities of Mokopane and Mankopane that they began to prey. One of the most notorious raiders was a man called Hermanus Potgieter, and on this remotest of frontiers his methods were chillingly ruthless. One of his contemporaries reported his operations as follows:

> They [Potgieter and his party] spanned out their wagons at the foot of a rise on which there stood a native village. Presently a couple of natives came down the hill to the encampment and greeted Potgieter. Upon this, he drew out a ramrod and stuck it upright in a neighbouring antheap and pointed to it, but said nothing. The two natives returned to the village and came back presently bringing a couple of slaughter goats. H. Potgieter said never a word but looked sternly at them and pointed to the ramrod. They went

back and fetched an ox. H. Potgieter still pointed to the ramrod. Then they
went and fetched a couple of tusks of ivory and put them down, but the
ramrod remained erect ... Hermanus Potgieter and his men mount[ed] their
horses, r[o]de around the hill and up to the kraal and [shot] some natives.
Presently they came back driving the cattle to the camp and a number of
captured children ... that was the requirement when the ramrod was stuck
upright.[20]

As a result of such raids, the area was soon in a state of undeclared war as
the Ndebele rulers retaliated with messages of mutilation on Boer subjects and
cattle. It was not for nothing that Mankopane's praises called him 'castrator of
the white man's cattle' – and the white man himself, as it subsequently turned
out.[21]

By September 1854 the two allied Ndebele leaders decided to force matters
in an attempt to frighten the Boers back to Pretoria. Hoping to turn the horse
sickness and fever of the impending summer to their advantage, they severely
mutilated and murdered 28 Boers in three separate incidents (see Fig. 3). Hardly
surprisingly, one of the victims was Hermanus Potgieter who was killed and
dismembered at Mankopane's capital. The other two murder episodes were
carried out near Mokopane's capital. The first of these happened at a river
crossing known as the Forest of Lions (*esikgweni sengwenyama*). In subsequent
years it was to acquire the Afrikaans name Moorddrift. Here a party of Boers
was waylaid and murdered. The second set of murders involved a party of men
that had previously separated from those at Moorddrift to go and trade at the
chief's village. On their way, they were murdered.[22]

Since the Boer population in the Northern Transvaal probably numbered in
the hundreds, the death of 28 people was a major blow. A commando was
summoned from Pretoria to strengthen the local force, but as the Pretoria
contingent took some time to arrive Mokopane and his followers had ample
opportunity to seek protection in some caves, a course of action they had
followed in the past when threatened by enemies. The caves lay some 16
kilometres north-east of the chief's capital, and in preparation for the siege
defensive ramparts, which can still be seen today, were erected (see Plate 24).

By late October the commando from Pretoria had arrived, and on the 25th
of that month the two commandos, assisted by some Kgatla allies,
unsuccessfully stormed the caves. Thereafter the Boers tried to blast the roof of
the dolomite caves but this, too, failed. Another strategy was to dump a large
amount of wood in front of the caves and set it alight in an attempt to suffocate
those within, but this produced no results either. Finally, since numbers of
people were reputedly escaping by night, the siege was considerably tightened,
and after about two weeks people in the cave began to give themselves up. The
chief also sent a group of people out to the Boers, but whether as a peace
offering or, as oral tradition claims, to keep the heir to the chieftaincy alive by
sending him into Boer bondage rather than letting him die in the cave, is not
clear.[23]

What is not clear either is whether those in the cave had access to water.
While some accounts claim there was a water source in the caves, others
maintain that the caverns were dry and that many people either died of thirst or

were shot down running to the stream in the valley below.[24] Some versions insist that there was a stream passing through the caves but that the Boers diverted it and so precipitated surrender.[25] Yet others claim that water was in fact plentiful and it was disease that eventually killed people or drove them from the cave.[26]

Whatever the situation may have been, by 17 November Ndebele resistance had almost ceased and Boers could enter the cave without being fired upon. By 21 November M.W. Pretorius, leader of the Boer forces (see Plate 25), "broke open his laager", partly to mount a punitive campaign against Mokopane's ally, Mankopane, and partly because the smell of rotting flesh had become overwhelming.[27] While the extent of fatalities will never be clear, Pretorius reported that 900 bodies lay in front of the caves. He estimated a further 3 000 to be inside.[28] As regards booty, the Boers claimed to have taken 6 300 large and 1 200 small stock from the surrounding area. Together with the people taken as prisoners of war, the stock was divided among the commandos. The Boers also found 450 kilograms of ivory in the cave and this was auctioned off.[29]

While Boer fatalities were minimal, there was one major loss and that was the death of a Boer general, Piet Potgieter, shot from below while peering over the top lip of the cave. As to Kgatla fatalities, no record survives.

Having dealt with Mokopane, the Boers then went after his ally, Mankopane, who fared better on a defensive mountain stronghold from where he and his warriors repulsed Boer attacks. While the Boers by and large remained a relatively weak group, the conflict in the region, none the less, continued to bubble, and in 1858 the Boers mounted another campaign against Mankopane. Ten years later, in 1868, the Boers, led by Paul Kruger, again turned on Mokopane but the chief's forces defeated them and sacked the village of Pietpotgietersrust, as it was then known. The village was abandoned, and it was not until the 1890s that the Boers could claim anything like decisive authority over Ndebele communities in the region.

III

In narrating this set of events today, tellers draw on a variety of core images which they cluster together in various combinations. Trying to specify the number of these core components is both impossible and pointless. No method of storytelling recognises a quota system, and the type and number of units that a teller includes, and the way that these are combined, will in the end be determined by his or her creativity and the nature of the performance occasion and its audience. However, from a sample of twenty-three accounts of the Gwaša siege, it is possible to detect a pool of recurrent elements that most tellers include in their rendition of this event.[30] Trying to identify or categorise these elements is, of course, a difficult business because oral traditions are by their nature flexible and fluid. However, I will attempt to divide these cores into three groupings derived from Scheub's analysis of the Xhosa *ntsomi*. Based as my groupings are on a small sample of twenty-three accounts, they are not intended

PLATE 26   Molalakgori Kekana (Photograph by Santu Mofokeng)

PLATE 27   Madimetša Kekana (Photograph by Santu Mofokeng)

as definitive categories but are simply devices to assist analysis of the testimony collected. Furthermore, historical narratives are generally looser and more baggy than a form like the *ntsomi* and they are consequently more difficult to pin down. For these reasons, and until further research into the historical narrative is undertaken, the groupings put forward here must be seen as having a localised applicability.

The three groupings are as follows:

- relatively stable units arranged around clearly identifiable core clichés or core images that together make up the 'backbone' of the story;
- less stable elements that lack an identifiable core but none the less have some coherence (this category comes close to what Scheub calls the episode cliché, or a set sequence of action, like, for example, a chase scene);
- unstable elements comprising episodes, transitional images, details and motifs that come up frequently but in highly diverse forms.

The object of these groupings is not simply to categorise the material but also to highlight its technique and method since it is through these that we can begin to understand how historical themes and information are forged. Consequently, in each category various examples will be given and then discussed in order to illustrate aspects of their technique and concomitant historical meaning.

As regards the initial category of episodes defined by a core cliché, there are three such units. The first of these concerns the confrontation between Boers and Nbebele. Often, although not always set at the place that came to be called Moorddrift, this episode focuses on how the Boers and Ndebele come to be at loggerheads. Central to the event is a Boer woman whom the Ndebele seize and transform by various methods that include mutilation; dressing her in Ndebele dress; shaving her head; or smearing her with red ochre. The latter two activities are, incidentally, features of initiation procedures for women.[31] After being transformed, the woman is then told, 'Go and tell them [that is, your people] what we have done', a core cliché that characterises all renditions of this episode.

Let us examine an example of this episode as told by Madimetša Kekana (see Plate 27). Parenthetically, his account includes an additional episode relating to the exchange of sheep that occurs in nineteenth-century recordings of the story but is not common today.[32]

What caused that war was, you see, when the Boers, by the way you know them, came here. By the way, they had wagons. When they came here they provoked them, our people. They [the Ndebele] went to fetch sheep. They came with the sheep. When they came with the sheep, they displayed them so that the Boers could see them. They waited there. The *baas* [master] said, 'Are you selling the sheep?' The whites came out, they came out with their women, to see the sheep. They left their guns behind. When they were looking the blacks said, 'Let's kill these whites.' They fell on them, they killed them, and killed them. They took one white woman and cut her breasts, they shaved her head. After they had shaved her head, they said,

'Go and tell the others.' They [the Boers] took their wagons and came this way with them——The Boers were surprised to see a woman dressed in blankets [that is, in Ndebele clothing].[33]

On the face of it, the episode merely seems to portray generalised hostility between Boer and Ndebele. However, when one considers the Boer woman in the episode, it is clear that the account has considerable symbolic depth. To begin with, the woman, in Ndebele terms, is a key signifier of male, political authority. By seizing her, the Ndebele issue a major challenge to Boer political authority. By cutting off her breasts, the Ndebele soldiers degenderise and so neutralise her as a symbol of Boer authority. Having been neutralised, she is then remade or initiated into an Ndebele woman by having her head shaved and by being dressed in blankets. This refashioning of the woman not only challenges the Boer social order, it also proclaims a symbolic suzerainty over them.

Inherent in Madimetša Kekana's account is a strong sense of Ndebele prerogative and control. While similar in content, other accounts give different symbolic emphases and interpretations.[34] In the account of Fred Ledwaba, for example, the woman is transformed by having red ochre smeared on her. Yet in his account, this act is portrayed as one that will protect the white skin of the woman against the harsh sun and wind. However, when the Boers see the red figure in the distance, they think it has been skinned alive and this perception, in turn, accounts for the severity of their reprisal against the Ndebele. This idea of misunderstanding, in turn, is one that informs other accounts where the initial confrontation between Boer and Ndebele is said to have occurred because the two groups could not understand each other's languages.[35]

A second core episode that most tellers include in their accounts relates to the murder of Piet Potgieter. This episode tells how, while standing on a ledge above the cave and peering into it, the Boer general was shot from below by an Ndebele marksman. The core cliché in this instance is the phrase, 'He/they peeped, they peeped', or words to that effect. To give some sense of the variety of styles which people use, I reproduce four versions of this episode. The first, by Molalakgori Madimetša Kekana (see Plate 27), relies on gesture and dramatic enactment and the full sense of the passage can only be grasped bearing this in mind:

MK: Now one day, when they [the Boers] came to this cave, they hid themselves so that they should not be seen. They wanted to find the Ndebele unexpectedly. When they arrived at the cave Potgieter himself, with other Boers, is it not so that he was with the other soldiers? When they arrived at the cave, they——I mean, I heard it rumoured. They arrived at the cave. Now when Potgieter——isn't it he did not see them? When he arrived at the cave, as I hear, when he was peeping into the cave to see exactly where they [the Ndebele] were, peeping like this, peeping like this, only to find he did not realise, here they are, the enemies are lying down, they are waiting and lying. When he, together with his soldiers was seated, the enemies rushed silently towards him.

FM: They wanted to stab him with the spear?

MK: When, when, when one of them saw that he was close enough, he just emerged. When he emerged, his soldiers were ready, they were watching that side where Potgieter was watching, trying to find where these people are hiding. He just felt the descending spear.[36]

The second account by Leka Thinta Mokhonoane (see Plate 23) is briefer and less dependent on enactment:

LM: The Boers did not know where they had run to. The caves were not easy to find as there were things blocking the entrances.
PK: *So as they were in this cave, there was a blockage which they did not see.*
LK: As they were in the cave, they saw a Boer peeping in the darkness. He did not know where these people had gone to. Now one of our people took out a revolver and shot at him. That was the leader of the Boers.[37]

Madimetša Kekana's version runs as follows:

MK: They [the Boers] went after them in the cave while others waited at the entrance. The whites got in and started peeping. Those others [Ndebele] were hiding in the dark. One said, 'Let me shoot at them.' He took a gun and aimed. He got his target which fell right there.
PK: [...]
IH: [...]
PK: [...]
MK: Only to find that they had shot their [the Boer's] leader.
PK: [...]
IH: [...]
PK: [...]
MK: The Boers carried their dead leader out of the cave. When they were outside, they said, 'Heavens, the kaffirs have killed our leader.' Those in the cave said they were going to die of hunger.[38]

The fourth rendition of this episode is by Zaba Maluleke:

When they got here [to the cave], they saw smoke bellowing out. They peeped, when they were peeping, the Matabele shot their leader with a gun, those olden-day guns. They came out with him and they took him there, where they had camped.[39]

What this Potgieter episode most obviously does is to record the memory of one victorious aspect of the siege in which the Ndebele claim the life of a Boer military leader. Since a chief or leader is often seen as representing an entire society, the killing of Potgieter, a Boer chieftain, carries huge symbolic weight. There is furthermore an additional symbolic dimension to the death which revolves around the element of stealth and cunning that the hidden Ndebele exercise in killing Potgieter. In all four accounts, the Ndebele are concealed below in the darkness while the mighty but foolhardy Potgieter sets himself up as a sitting duck for the weapons of the weak. This spatial relationship of above and below, powerful and powerless, is captured in the core cliché, 'he was peeping, he was peeping', a phrase which demands to be acted out. However, in acting out the core cliché and the subsequent death of Potgieter, it becomes apparent that the relationship of powerful and powerless is reversed since it is the mighty who fall and the weak who triumph.

This emphasis on the wiles of the weak is one that often occurs in historical traditions that narrate defeat. One way of saving face is to imply that the conquerors while victorious are stupid and have, in some small way, been outwitted by the guile and wit of the conquered.[40] It is worth noting that this political logic can be detected in the core cliché of the Potgieter episode.

A third and final core episode that also reflects the theme of hoodwinking concerns the fate of the chiefly family in the cave. Sensing that he and his followers face certain death, the chief sends out a group of women and children in the knowledge that the Boers will indenture them as labourers. Included in this party is the legitimate heir to the chieftaincy, and by apparently playing into the hands of the enemy, the chief plans to pursue his own agenda of keeping the dynastic line intact. The young chief does, in fact, survive, and is later discovered by his subjects and returned to his domain.[41] The heart of this episode, or series of episodes as it becomes in the mouths of some tellers, is the scene where some migrant workers recognise the child chief. They ask his name and he replies, 'My name is Klaas.' Since Klaas is the standard name that Northern Transvaal farmers dole out to their servants, it is clear that the chief has lost his identity and has been culturally colonised by Boer society. If this should be the case, then an entire society and dynastic line will be lost since the chief stands for and represents the people. As matters turn out, however, the chief overcomes his amnesia, returns to take up his rightful position and in so doing keeps the dynastic line, and the society it represents, intact.

Stored, then, within this core cliché, 'My name is Klaas' are the central themes of the Gwaša story. Faced with a life-threatening siege, as well as with the experience of indenture, the chiefdom can, by retaining its identity, survive these assaults. Since this episode will be discussed in detail in the next chapter, we will not pursue it here.

Based on an analysis of twenty-three accounts of the story, these three episodes are the most clearly defined and frequently used – partly, no doubt, because they provide a skeleton of beginning, middle and end around which other themes and motifs can be arranged. In addition to these core episodes, there is a second category of episodes that appears frequently but lacks an identifiable core cliché. Let us consider two examples. The first tells of the Boer response to the death of their leader. Outraged by Potgieter's killing, the Boers seek revenge and demand that the chief in the cave be handed over. To assuage these demands, the Ndebele send out a substitute who parades as the chief.

This episode features in an oral account of the siege that was collected during the last century. Recorded in indirect speech, it reads as follows:

> He [the informant] says they [the Ndebele] knew that the Boers wanted Makapan ... in particular, so they killed one of their own number, a man of great size, and pushed his body through the mouth of the cave at night so that the Boers were deceived into thinking that he was Makapan and that he had been suffocated in attempting to escape ... .The native said that the Boers went away rejoicing.[42]

In the 1980s Madimetša Kekana narrated a cognate episode:

MK: When they [the Ndebele] were still undecided, one man said, 'You, the Ndebele, give me the chief's robes. I will go out with the chief's son and one woman.'

PK: Whose woman was that?

MK: She was one of the chief's wives. They dressed him [the man] in the chief's robes saying when the Boers saw him they would shoot him, thinking they had killed our leader.

PK: [...]

MK: At that moment, they came out and the Boers saw them and said, 'Haa! The kaffirs have come out!' They rushed to them and shot at the man thinking they had killed the chief.[43]

A briefer version from Mahula Kekana goes as follows:

MK: After surrendering, the Boers demanded the chief come to be punished.

PK: [...]

MK: Because they [the Ndebele] felt the chief was not responsible for the war, the people agreed that one man should be selected to go and represent the chief and the nation.

PK: [...]

MK: They chose a strong man from the Lamola family to go and die for the tribe. His family would be generously rewarded.[44]

One way to analyse these passages is to subsume them under the theme of hoodwinking and deceit. As we have seen, it was stealth and cunning that claimed the life of Potgieter and it is a similar cunning that prevents his death from being properly avenged. Once again, it is the weak who outwit the mighty. This emphasis on deceit furthermore intersects with another theme: the ability of chieftainship to endure. Threatened by the Boer demand that the chief – the very centre of a society – be handed over, the Ndebele deceive the Boers, and in so doing they keep the heart of the social order intact.

A second example of a recurrent, but unstable, episode deals with the aftermath of the siege. Mahula Kekana phrases it like this:

MK: [After the siege], they came and humbled themselves to chief Mashishi, asking for land.

PK: [...]

MK: They stayed there for a while and then said if the Boers had taken their land, they might as well take it from Mashishi.

PK: [...]

MK: Then they found that Mashishi was strong and also had weapons. They had left theirs behind when they were running away from the Boers. Then they thought of a plan. They thought of a hunting expedition. The young strong men would go while the older ones remained. The aim was that while hunting, they would kill these, while those remaining at home will kill the Mashishi who are remaining. Those on the mountain will light a fire to indicate that the moment had arrived.

PK: [...]
MK: Then Mashishi surrendered and handed the land and power over to them.[45]

In other accounts of this event, the outlines are broadly similar but the names differ. Sometimes it is the Lekalakala who are conquered, at other times it is the Kgobudi.[46] However, no one seems entirely clear and the names will often be changed in the course of a story.[47] To confound matters further, the Mashishi conquest appears elsewhere as an episode that predates both the Mfecane and the siege event.[48] While there is not enough evidence to settle the matter either way, the one clue we have is that the present-day site, Sefakaola, to which the chiefdom relocated after the siege, is also known as Lekalakalaskop. From this one could surmise that if there was indeed a conquest that followed the Gwaša event, then it was most probably directed against the Lekalakala. The Mashishi conquest most probably predated the siege.

However, as other studies have shown, it is not the time sequence of such events that is important. Instead, it is their spatial dimension that is crucial since such episodes of conquest generally signify the relocation of a chief's capital.[49] In relation to the siege event, the chief's capital did indeed move from Chidi, or Pruissen as it is sometimes called after the farm that now covers the area, to the hill Sefakaola. Seen from the point of view of the chiefdom, this move was one of the major consequences of the Gwaša siege and, by including *the idea* of a conquest in their narration, tellers are able to signify this crucial result.

In embellishing the more defined episodes that we have discussed thus far, many tellers rely on a looser set of images, details and motifs. Given the discretionary nature of oral storytelling, it is impossible to list all these. What follows is an account of those that came up most frequently.

Hardly surprisingly for an event where people suffocated from smoke and died of thirst, motifs of fire and water feature frequently. Most accounts focus on the piling of wood in front of the cave and the suffocating effects of the fire. Or, as Zaba Maluleke phrases it, "Then they looked for wood and put it at the entrance, they piled the wood, they piled the wood, the Boers. Even at the other entrance, they piled the wood. Then they lit the fire. They started. Most were killed by smoke. It's like that."[50]

In some renditions, the effects of the fire are played down, and instead the death of many is ascribed to a suffocating disease 'of the breath' that afflicts those in the cave. Molalakgori Kekana describes the disease as follows:

MK: Now there emerged a disease. You shall listen.
FM: Yes.
MK: The disease emerged. It is not the disease that affected the whole world.
FM: Yes.
MK: No. This is the disease that affected only those inside there, inside the cave, inside the cave. To that nation. Do you understand?
FM: Yes.
MK: Now when we look at it, what I've heard, this disease it started, it is caused by the people's breath. The breath was full in that cave, isn't it?
FM: Yes.

MK: Now there is no way out for this breath because there are no windows. Now, this breath started to be restless and boiled until it was contaminated, until it turned into a disease, it caused a perspiring disease. You see now?

FM: Yes.

MK: That is what destroyed Mokopane's nation in there. When it started, no one could cure another or say anything. They– in fact, it became an infectious disease because––it, it was caused––the air was full in there. You see? That's what diminished these people. It was not starvation or what, it is just the air which became contaminated. You see?[51]

As regards water, there are a series of motifs that recur. The first of these tells how the Boers were able to follow the tracks of the Ndebele to the cave, because it had rained and the ground was muddy.[52] Parenthetically, the motif of being betrayed by one's tracks is one that occurs often in historical narrations of this type where footprints in dry soil often reveal the whereabouts of people or alternatively, people are saved by heavy rain that obliterates their tracks.[53]

In other accounts, it is people's desperate need for water that betrays them to the Boers in much the same way as their footprints reveal their whereabouts to their enemies. For one woman, Morongoa Kgosana, her whole memory of the Gwaša siege turned on this axis. All she could recall of the event was contained in the following words:

MK: I do not really know properly because I was still small but my father used to tell me that their aunties–––

JM: Uhu.

MK: They died, they died in there. They told me that they were fighting against the Boers, you see.

JM: Yes.

MK: And then perhaps these Boers, when they [the Ndebele] were hiding in this cave, this cave, by the way, is too big, this cave of Gwaša.

JM: Yes.

MK: They stayed in there, grinding their mealies and ate in there. Now you know, they [the Boers] saw them when they came from the river to fetch water. They recognised them by their going to the river.

JM: They were seen by the Boers?

MK: Yes. They saw where they entered.

JM: Yes.

MK: Now they arrived at the spot and made fire at the entrance.

JM: Yes.

MK: But I know just that, and also that they killed one another.[54]

In the hands of some tellers, this motif of being betrayed by thirst is turned on its head to become an episode where it is, in fact, the Boers who betray themselves by their stupidity. Molalakgori Kekana narrated such an episode:

MK: Now, well our people realised that the motive behind these Boers to erect their many tents here is to lay siege and see where we could fetch water. Then they realised that these Boers are idiots. They [the

Ndebele] came back and the next morning when it was clear, they saw them settled [next to the water] and saw that it's alright. They sent one person to go towards them [the Boers] and climb a huge rock and stand up right. There are these things of– of– of the vegetables with calabashes.

FM: Calabashes, calabashes.

MK: Yes, now you would find a calabash like this– like this———

FM: Yes.

MK: Now they make a hole in there and pour water into it while they cultivated———Now they poured water into that calabash and one person climbed on top of that rock over there so that he could be seen by the Boers [who] took him for an innocent person.

FM: Innocent. Yes.

MK: Well, he sat there and took the calabash and turned it upside down and poured out the water. He said, 'Isn't it those [Boers] are looking?' and saw that he was pouring out water?

FM: Yes.

MK: Now, it was an indication that, 'You do not know what you are doing. You think you are preventing us from getting water but we are drinking here.'[55]

This theme of thirst also manifests itself in the belief that the grave of Mokopane, the chief who died in the cave, is the most powerful sacrificial site in times of drought.[56] The idea that a chief who died of thirst should become the ancestor from whom one requests rain is replete with historical irony. It is also an idea that can be seen as retrospectively mocking the Boer forces who believed they could, by means of a grim and patient siege, conquer those in the cave by thirst. By gaining water from the ancestor who was denied it, people involved in the sacrificial ceremony outwit their historical oppressors, and in one sense it is the victims who have outlasted their persecutors.

Another theme, this time unrelated to water, that also turns on notions of deception, relates to motifs of escape. As we have seen, the story of the child chief being handed over to the Boers is tied up with notions of escape, and there are cognate versions of this episode that tell of men disguised as women who successfully slip through Boer lines.[57]

However, the major motif of escape is expressed through the assertion that the cave itself penetrates deep into the earth, and by making their way through these subterranean passages that eventually emerged, many people were able to survive the siege.[58] All these accounts aver that these passages run all the way to Moletlane, or Zebediela as it is also known, a distance of about 35 kilometres as the crow flies. While the full extent of the caves has never been mapped, and while they do indeed run very deep into the mountains, it is unlikely that they go so far.[59] However, it is the symbolic rather than the geographic dimensions of this story that are important here since Moletlane is the Ndebele chiefdom from which the Mokopane chiefdom originally seceded. Today it remains an important historical point of reference, and the wives of chiefs, for example, are supposed to be obtained there.[60] Since the Ndebele in the caves escape via a long passage that issues forth at the place of their distant kin, it is as if they are saved by the sinews of kinship.

There is, of course, no way of 'proving' such an interpretation but what it does usefully highlight is the way in which one can draw symbolic linkages within and between episodes. Such symbolic linkages are easy to suggest. For example, the notion of the long passage of kinship also resonates with the disease motif: one way to escape both literal and historical suffocation is through the life-giving links of kinship. At the same time, this idea of redemption links up with the imagery of fire, water and the present-day ceremonies at Mokopane's grave. We have also seen how a number of episodes cluster under the theme of hoodwinking and deceit.

One could, of course, continue seeking out such symbolic circuits, but in some sense it would be pointless since we have no firm idea whether these were the kinds of linkages that tellers intended or audiences made. Yet what we can be sure of is that both tellers and audiences made such linkages. Having been trained in the *kgoro*, all men would have a working familiarity with a range of historical episodes, and so any teller could presume that his audience would be well informed. In such a context, much of the teller's skill then depended on the linkages he established between episodes and the kind of associations that his combinations and sequencing could spark within a critical and discerning audience.[61]

At times, of course, the audience could have comprised only young, less well-informed boys, at other times, a variety of ages. However, the flexibility of this storytelling system based in a loose collocation of episodes could cater for such a range, and in some instances only an episode or two could be told. In others, a more complex sequence could be created. An important component of this historical storytelling depended on this ability to tailor the narrative to the situation.

In addition, each teller could vary a performance with other resources like intonation, gesture and the nuances of personal style. Even from the brief, written excerpts given above, the different stylistic emphases of tellers becomes apparent. Madimetša Kekana, for example, relies a great deal on dramatised speech which he often turns to humorous effect, particularly when giving renditions of Boer racism. He is also particularly good at setting an everyday scene against which more historico-legendary events unfold. A technique often used by *dinonwane* tellers, it invests the ordinary with the extraordinary and vice versa. Molalakgori Kekana, on the other hand, uses less direct speech, although he also relies on enactment. His stories are more serious and he enters into more of an active relationship with his audience by indicating, for example, when an episode is beginning and ending and by checking the audience's attention with phrases like, 'Is it not so?' These traits may, of course, have been 'induced' by my presence, but they appear so frequently and regularly in his narration that one can only regard them as part of his stylistic repertoire.

A skilled performer of historical narrative, then, juggles a number of crafts and activities all at once. Central to this craft is the way in which tellers create a network of episodes to meet a particular context. Thus far, all I have done is to catalogue a list of possible episodes and the ways in which they were told to me. In the chapter that follows we turn to examine two sustained tellings in order to understand how two narrators have concatenated various elements in order to convey a view of a social order based on chieftaincy.

6

The Meaning of Oral Historical Narrative

The Case of the Siege of Gwaša

In his discussion of the Xhosa *ntsomi*, Scheub has used the term 'theme' to encapsulate and identify what he sees as the overall meaning of a story. Not surprisingly for a term that encompasses such a wide topic, Scheub's definition is complex.[1] On the most general level, the idea of theme approximates the ideological intent of the *ntsomi* which, in Scheub's reading, strives towards reaffirming and celebrating social order.[2] However, the way in which this overall meaning is created is intricate and entails all levels of the storytelling performance. For example, part of the thematic intent of any performance lodges in the core image which is, in Scheub's words, 'the basic thematic unit'.[3] Theme, however, cannot simply be read off from these kernels, but must also be sought in the way a particular story is actualised in relation to the demands of a specific audience.

> The theme in its various manifestations may shift and alter because of the arrangement of images, and thus cannot be derived from a study of core-images but from an analysis of the total performance, from the arrangement and objectification of the core-image.[4]

While one performance may offer one particular thematic interpretation, it is also the overall tradition that helps to define the ethical and moral concerns that make up theme.

> It is the combination of its many treatments, a complex network found in the series of images brought together to create the individual *ntsomi* performances, which finally determines the meaning of a single work of art and its importance for the theme.[5]

In building up this definition of 'theme', Scheub meticulously accounts for

122

the complex ways in which literary works create meaning. Within each particular work, a creator, responding to a particular context, creates a complex relation of parts which generates a range of effects and meanings that a hearer/reader decodes in a specific situation. These meanings, in turn, hook into other similar works to produce circuits of meaning that hearers/readers bring to bear on their interpretation of the works they encounter.

While there may be problems with Scheub's choice of the word 'theme', his definition of the way in which oral forms create a wider, contextually defined meaning is extremely important and it is this topic that will be explored here. In the previous chapter, we examined a catalogue of parts. Here we attempt to define how two tellers chose to make those parts cohere. We will also briefly consider how this coherence derives from the wider chiefly historiographical traditions of which the narratives discussed here form a part.

However, before we can do so, it is necessary to dwell briefly on the contextual dimension of meaning in oral performance. If, as Scheub and many others have made plain, it is the context that determines much of the work's meaning and effect, then this context must figure in our calculations if we wish to divine something of the larger message of any oral narrative. However, context itself is a complex phenomenon that can be endlessly disaggregated. Apart from the dictates of the immediate environment and audience taste, factors like time, place, talent, audience make-up, pre-existing relationship of teller and audience and experience of both teller and audience, to mention but a few, shape the total meaning of the event.

Since the interviews I collected were not performed, it is impossible for me to discuss these issues. However, if I was denied the opportunity of hearing these stories in a performance setting, then so were the tellers denied the chance of narrating in one. Obviously under such circumstances, everyone has to create a new sense of context which is again multi-dimensional. Much of this new sense of context is, of course, predictable and relates to the dynamics created when an outside, white, female, academic, working with local translators, many of whose first language is Sesotho, interviews old, African, royal, Sindebele-speaking men.[6] Yet the context that operates in such an interview situation is not solely shaped by the sociological profile of its participants, and each of those participants speaks not only to the idea of what they think their interlocutor represents, they talk as well to more familiar groups, to some 'imagined audience' which although absent, provides the shaping horizon towards which they address their dialogue.[7]

In the narrations that I analyse here, I will contend that one such shaping horizon is the notion of chieftaincy which, as already indicated, was the direction in which all historical forms pointed. In reading the testimony in this way, I cannot, of course, 'prove' that this is what they are incontrovertibly about, neither am I maintaining that this is the only interpretation that can be put upon them. Rather, I am suggesting that to read these narratives as complex affirmations of chieftaincy opens up profitable and rich insights into both their craft and meaning.

Furthermore, the dwindling fate of chieftaincy over the last two centuries provides another compelling reason why tellers who still cherish the values of the chiefly world should make it one of the shaping horizons of their narratives.

While the intricate story of declining chieftaincy cannot be told here, the trajectory of this saga, as Schapera has pointed out, involves the winding down of independent ruler to bureaucratic functionary.[8] During the nineteenth century, the assault on chiefship had begun, and in the Transvaal, in addition to the ever-present aggression of natural disaster, came waves of conquerors, first Ndebele, then Boer, then British, each wielding an increasing military might. Under these circumstances, many societies experienced deepened demographic disaster as well as crises of leadership.

During the twentieth century, the pressures on chiefship mounted markedly. By the 1920s legislation that had been accumulating since the 1880s stripped chiefs of their powers to declare war, control foreign policy, judge certain cases and allot land.[9] While this legislation often took time to bite, by the 1940s the bureaucratic erosion of chieftaincy was considerable. The Bantu Authorities Act of 1951 tightened this bureaucratic hold by co-opting the chief as a state functionary.

Throughout the nineteenth and twentieth centuries, then, the institution of chieftainship must have appeared to be under varying degrees of pressure that manifested itself in secession disputes and heightened dynastic feuding within the ruling lineage. While such dynastic politics, as Comaroff has shown, has always played a seminal and shaping role in chiefly life, the pressures of the nineteenth century almost certainly increased the incidence of such chiefly disputes and internal fragmentation.[10]

In retrospect, of course, this deterioration of chieftaincy appears as a continuous and gradual story. Yet it should more properly be conceptualised as a series of thresholds or frontiers that have marked the change of chiefship. The most recent of these thresholds is undoubtedly the advent of betterment and the subsequent imposition of Bantu Authorities which together instituted an unprecedented degree of internal interference in the chiefdom. As others have pointed out, this wave of social engineering precipitated a marked increase in internal chiefly feuding, and it is from across this threshold of massive social change that contemporary informants recall the history of chieftaincy.[11]

Such heightened fragmentation presents particular difficulties for the craft of narrating chiefship. What, after all, does one say of a situation in which a Native Commissioner, appropriately named King, despatches the incumbent chief to a Pretoria lunatic asylum and then takes up residence in the chief's courtyard proclaiming, 'Kgoši ke nna' (I am the chief)?[12] How does one narrate a world in which the thread of chieftaincy, a key metaphor of civilisation itself, can be snapped with apparent ease?

Much oral historical narrative that talks of the nineteenth and twentieth century can be read as a response to this question, and one potentially fruitful way to interpret this testimony is as a series of strategies for keeping the idea of chieftaincy afloat. The narratives that concern us here are drawn from interviews with Molalakgori Kekana and Madimetša Kekana, both men of royal standing with a high degree of commitment to a specifically Ndebele chiefly social order. Their narratives both form extracts from longer accounts that these two men gave of the cave of Gwaša or Makapansgat siege. These extracts, as well as the surrounding material from which they have been taken, are reproduced in Appendices 2 and 3.[13]

The focus of both these extracts is on the capture and indenture of the child chief; his discovery by passing migrants on a farm; and his return to the chiefdom in return for payment of sheep and ivory to the Boer farmer. In analysing them, I will attempt to show that the logic by which they create, elaborate and combine various episodes is rooted in a subtle and rich understanding of chieftainship.

I have chosen to focus on these episodes dealing with the capture and subsequent redemption of the child chief since they are unique to the Mokopane chiefdom. Neighbouring groups who have some link to the siege event still carry the memory of the siege in their historical repertoire.[14] However, none of their accounts refer to the child chief, and when questioned, none of their informants had ever heard of the story. It is, in other words, a story peculiar to the ruling lineage in Valtyn and, as I will attempt to show, it has gathered into itself much of the history peculiar to the chieftaincy of that lineage.

I

In narrating the story of the kidnapped chief, Molalakgori Kekana arranged events as follows. Threatened by disease in the cave, the chief sends out a group of children in the hope that the Boers will take them captive and indenture them and so ensure their survival. Included in the group is the legitimate heir to the chieftaincy. When the siege is over and life has returned to normal, the surviving peers of the child chief reach the age when they must be initiated. Three men are summoned to go and search for the kidnapped chief. Traditional doctors are called and they advise the men on which direction to travel. The men set off and stop at a Kgatla chiefdom where they request assistance. The Kgatla leader knows where the kidnapped chief resides and the three men are taken to a Boer farm. Here, one of the men, Lehlabapele, the young chief's uncle, recognises his nephew.

Most of the men present favour abducting the young chief by force, but one person insists that they have to speak to the Boer farmer. Since the others are too scared to approach the farmer, the man in question sets off alone. He encounters the 'coloured' foreman of the farm who takes him to the Boer who at first threatens to shoot the visitor. When the Boer's wife hears that they are harbouring a chief, she intervenes and persuades her husband to listen since there may be some material benefit that they can gain. The Boer demands a ransom of sheep. The men, who were too scared to speak to the Boer initially, now approach, and just to check that they do indeed know who the young chief is, the Boer arranges a test whereby they have to identify the kidnapped chief.

Leaving the newly discovered chief behind on the farm, the men return home to collect the ransom and stop off briefly at the Kgatla chiefdom. At home they apprise the incumbent chief of their find, and sheep are collected. Langa, the chief of the neighbouring Mapela chiefdom, adds ivory to the ransom. The men return to the Boer who is delighted with the ivory. His wife feeds the men and they, along with the released chief, are sent home with the advice to travel by night lest they be seized by hostile Boers. This message is conveyed to the party by the 'coloured' foreman who also guides them on part of their journey.

Just before entering the chiefdom, they stop at the Forests of Lions, or Moorddrift, as it is now known. The message is conveyed to the chief that the heir has returned. Celebrations ensue and for a short while the young chief is secluded in an enclosure made of branches. Thereafter he is initiated, gets married, becomes the new chief and produces an heir, Valtyn, who in time himself becomes chief.

From even a brief summary, it is clear that this story is an exploration into chieftaincy and its meanings. If one wishes to understand more about how this exploration into the concept of chieftaincy is built up and sustained, then it is to the details of the story we must turn. For, after all, as Havelock has pointed out, much oral historical narrative creates its meanings through a "panorama of happenings not a programme of principles".[15] As the major happenings in this tale concern how a chief is lost and found, it is worth considering the methods by which this process occurs.

The first point to note is that the event which sparks the search is the need to begin initiation, or, in other words, one of the key institutions of chiefly life. It is another key institution – this time the intellectual resources of traditional doctors – that helps the men to undertake their journey. To fulfil their journey and locate the object of their search, the men are assisted by the wider political and diplomatic linkages of their chiefdom, and it is by stopping over at the Kgatla chiefdom that the men discover the whereabouts of the kidnapped chief. Hence, in instituting the search, and making their way through strange and hostile territory, it is on the institutions, wisdom and networks of chiefly society that the men rely.

However, standing between the men and the person they seek is the Boer farmer. While some favour abducting the kidnapped chief in the same way that the Boers initially seized him, one man pushes for the more subtle and intellectual path of negotiation. He alone has the courage to approach the Boer and it as though he is the only one who has the faith to continue with and trust in the chiefly resources that have propelled them all thus far. Trusting in the intellectual resources of his society, the man crosses the 'frontier' into Boer territory. In crossing this boundary, the man finds himself being guided up the hierarchy of farm (and the wider Boer) society as he passes from 'coloured' foreman, to the Boer's wife, to the Boer himself.

In his confrontation with the Boer, the first stage involves the threat of violence. However, after a while the Boer agrees to listen. The passage in question goes as follows:

Suddenly, the Boer entered the house. He took the gun. When he rushed to the wagon with the gun, the lad——the woman said, 'Hey father! No, no, no. No, no, no, no. No, no, no, no. No, no, no, no. Don't do that! You must never do that! My husband, forget the jealousy of your own folk, man. Don't. You see, you hear, my husband? Despise the jealousy of your own folk. You—— [the Ndebele man], isn't it you are saying that this person is a chief?' 'Now! You——you [the Boer] prevent wealth from entering into this house? Demand wealth so that it can enter into this house, man! Because he is a chief!' Indeed the man returned and put down his gun.

In this passage, the Boer, via the agency of his wife, comes to recognise that the erstwhile labourer is a chief and that chieftainship may hold out certain benefits. Because of this, the Boer agrees to listen and negotiate, and in so doing he falls under the sway of the intellectual resources that the man has carried with him from the chieftaincy. Having been precipitated on a journey by the needs of chieftaincy, and having been guided by its resources, the man now carries and transplants some of that wisdom into another society.

In returning home to convey the news, the party is again assured safe passage via the diplomatic and political networks that link chiefdoms. It is the same links to the neighbouring Langa chiefdom (incidentally the home of Mokopane's ally, Mankopane) through which ivory is obtained. When presented to the Boer, it becomes a key symbol and turning point in the story. The Boer, entirely delighted with the tusks, remarks, '... you know what ivory means in our culture? ... You have offered me eternal wealth with these things, man! I am already a chief [with this ivory] even if you exclude this wealth [the sheep].' In receiving the ivory that represents the links between chiefdoms, the Boer comes to recognise the value of chiefship as a social institution.

It is also at this point that chiefship as the controlling intelligence in the story becomes apparent. Both the Boer and the kidnapped chief have been in a state of ignorance since they have been part of a plot of which they have no knowledge. The Boer does not know he harbours a child chief and the young chief is not aware of his true status. Both the Boer and the child are ignorant of chieftaincy, the key institution of Ndebele society, and so they must be ignorant of civilisation itself.

As this is a story, both the Boer and the child chief exchange their ignorance for insight. The Boer comes to recognise that he does in fact harbour a chief and he then comes to accept the wider value of chieftaincy. Having been ignorant of Ndebele society, he has now unwittingly become 'Ndebeleised'. Indeed, the absorption of Ndebele cultural ideas has been implicit in the story all along. By capturing the child chief, the Boer not only recalls the historical memory of indenture, he also enacts a motif that in other Transvaal traditions symbolises notions of cultural transfer.[16]

If the Boer has been 'Ndebeleised', then the child chief is 're-Ndebeleised'. He sheds his servant name Klaas and miraculously overcomes his amnesia.[17] The possibility that the young chief could be reluctant to leave the comparative familiarity of the farm to go off with a bunch of strange men, as one nineteenth-century account implies, is something that this style of story will not contemplate.[18] The child chief is rigorously subordinated to the design of chieftaincy to which he and all others become mere passing facts.

Having 'exported' the benefits of chieftaincy, the party can now return with the young heir. Their safe passage is ensured by the Boer who has been brought within the ambit of the chieftaincy and so can find them a safe path through hostile country. They are, in addition, assisted by the 'coloured' foreman, in all likelihood the descendant of an indentured African. What this pattern of assistance – and indeed the course of the story – implies is that a reciprocal link now stretches from the Boer, to his wife, to the foreman, to the migrants, and from there to the chief himself. Along this line, the current of chiefship flows, reaching into the heart of Boer society.

On returning to the chiefdom the party pauses at the Forest of Lions before entering the chiefdom. There are two ways to interpret this episode. The first one is to bracket it into the whole siege episode since Moorddrift is the site where one of the Boer parties was murdered, an event which in turn precipitated the Boer attack and siege. By pausing at this point where the siege saga started, it is as if the entire event and its consequences are overcome and a new start is made. However, as we shall see when we reach Madimetša Kekana's narrative, there is a second interpretation that relates more to the internal history of the chiefdom. In terms of this history, the Forest of Lions forms part of a geographical sequence of places that marks the historical movement of the chiefdom from its original seat at Chidi (now called Pruissen after the farm which covers it) to its relocation after the siege to the hilltop, Sefakaola.

While it not clear which meaning is intended, particularly since Molalakgori Kekana himself briefly confuses the sequence of settlement sites of the chiefdom, both interpretations do point to the same idea of going back to the beginning and starting afresh.[19] This idea is made explicit in the chief's progress. First of all, he goes into seclusion and undergoes purification. Thereafter he emerges to take up and complete the broken cycle of initiation with which the story commenced. Once this event has occurred, his marriage follows and thereafter a new heir, Valtyn, is born.

Throughout the story, then, the force of chiefship flows strongly, shaping and controlling the reaction and destiny of characters while subordinating them to its larger designs. Not only is it portrayed as a powerful force, it is also one of great subtlety and persuasiveness that can imprint itself on those societies with whom it has contact. Superficially this contact may seem only to involve economic and military exchanges in which the Boers enjoy superiority. However, beneath these more obvious relationships flow others concerning more subtle forms of cultural and intellectual exchange in which the Ndebele enjoy the upper hand.

As we have noted in the previous chapter, deception is a common motif in oral traditions dealing with societies at war. In terms of this David and Goliath motif, the weak through their guile and intelligence outwit the brute ignorance of the strong. In his rendition of this kidnap saga, Molalakgori Kekana gives a particularly subtle, intricate and complex rendition of this theme. Not only are the Boers taken in by the wider designs of chieftaincy, but its intellectual and cultural resources prove so powerful that they can seep into the lives of their erstwhile enemies and convert them to allies. A more enduring and subtle victory one could not wish for.

II

While Molalakgori Kekana's account relies largely on building up a symbolic network through which an interpretation of chieftaincy and its wider significance is gradually augmented, Madimetša Kekana's narration relies on slightly different methods and stresses slightly different aspects of chieftaincy. The outline of his story, which can be read in full in Appendix 3, is as follows. Some migrants returning from the diamond fields stop at a dam to request a drink of water from some herd boys. One of the migrants recognises one of the herders as the kidnapped chief, Mokopane. The following day they return to the dam and speak to the young chief, asking him where his original home might be. On this very farm, the boy replies. The migrants continue on their way and at the chiefdom go to report the news of their discovery to the chief. However, before they can do this, they each must hand over a tribute of £5 to the chief's intermediary. A pair of shoes is also included with their gift of money. They are then entertained with beer and tobacco and finally the chief is called. The migrants ask him if a child has been lost. Indeed, the chief confirms, this is the case. A meeting is called and the citizens of the chiefdom are informed that the kidnapped heir has come to light. All who once knew him as a child are despatched with the migrants to retrieve him. They set off and return to the dam where they initially found the herders. Here, they ask the herders their names. 'My name is Kleinbooi,' replies the first. 'My name is Swartbooi,' answers the second. The kidnapped chief says, 'I'm Klaas.' The migrants reply, 'You are Klaas who?' The answer comes, 'Nothing. I'm just Klaas.' 'Are you not Klaas Mokopane?' the migrants enquire and to this the kidnapped chief agrees.

The migrants then approach the farmer who initially refuses to release him. However, in return for a ransom of thirty sheep and some ivory, he agrees to free the young chief. With this information, this party returns to the chiefdom, pausing first at the Forest of the Lions. To the sound of a horn, they enter the chiefdom and cross the Ngwaditše River, after which they ascend a hill to the chief's capital. As they do so, the kidnapped child's mother comes looking expectantly for her son but she is disappointed.

Some messengers are despatched to Langa's chiefdom to collect ivory, and Langa, in turn, sends them to a neighbouring chief, Molekoa, who hands over the ivory. The sheep are obtained from another chief, Makhujisa. With the sheep and the ivory, the party returns to the Boer who hands over Mokopane. On the final return journey, the party again stops at the Forest of Lions and they then proceed to cross the Ngwaditše River and ascend a hill to the chief's capital. The young chief is hidden behind a curtain of leaves and branches until his mother comes to meet him.

At a ceremony of celebration, cattle are slaughtered and meat sent off to all the chiefs who helped with the ransom. After some time, the young chief is initiated and eventually the incumbent chief Makute, with rather bad grace, hands over the reigns to Mokopane.

In terms of its style, this account relies heavily on extensive circumstantial detail derived from everyday life. Examples of this include the descriptions of how the migrants approach the chief through an intermediary, hand over tribute, and are entertained with beer and tobacco. Since it is still largely this procedure that pertains when approaching a chief, the scene could well be a present-day one. Another example relates to the descriptions of farm life which all have a contemporaneous ring. The account of the migrants approaching the Boer farmer, for example, would be a scene familiar to any rural dweller.

They went to the white man at his own house. They heard a dog barking, 'Hou! Hou!' While standing on the veranda of his house, the white man said, '*Hey you!*' He went to those men and they said, 'Master, master, master!'

It is into this framework of everyday detail that Madimetša Kekana weaves his socio-historical themes. There are two that concern us here. The first relates to the role of the migrants, the second to topographical references.

As regards the first theme, it soon becomes clear that the migrants play a crucial role in defining the meaning of the story. To begin with they are subordinated to the wider authority of chiefship both in the tribute they offer to the chief and in the role they play in finding and bringing back the kidnapped child.[20] In shuttling between the world of the chiefdom and the white world of farm and town, they carry the virtues of chiefdom with them to those who have been lost in the wilderness of white control. So, for example, it is the migrants who help the kidnapped chief remember his true home and real name. It is also the migrants who go out into the neighbouring chiefdoms to collect the ransom of ivory and sheep. Overall, the migrants act as the vassals of the chief and it is they who extend the sinews of chiefship into the wider world.

The migrants also play another crucial role, this time in relation to the topographical points of the story, since it is they who move through a sequence of places as they enter the chiefdom. As with Molalakgori Kekana's account, the first of these is the Forest of Lions/Moorddrift. Thereafter they pause at the Ngwaditše River, after which they make their way to the chief's capital on the hill top, Sefakaola (see Fig. 2). This sequence is repeated twice, first when they report the news of the discovery of the kidnapped chief, and again when they finally bring the chief himself.

The sequence of points that the migrants pass through is significant in so far as two of them – the Ngwaditše River and the hill, Sefakaola – represent the historical movement of the chiefdom from their pre-siege site at Chidi to their post-siege site on the hilltop. It is a sequence of movements commemorated in a song whose words go as follows:

> We come from MmaChidi/We come from MmaChidi/And reach Ngwa-ditše quite well/We come from MmaChidi/We come from MmaChidi/And reach Ngwaditše quite well/Sefakaola has already arrived/Sefakaola has already arrived/Sefakaola has already arrived/At Mokopane's place/Sefa-kaola has already arrived/Sefakaola has already arrived/Sefakaola has already arrived/At Turfloop, at Ngwaditše.[21]

While the Forest of Lions does not form part of this topographical sequence, within the confines of the story at least, it would seem as if we are required to see it as such. It is furthermore a sequence specifically and significantly enacted by the migrants who retrace the order of an older chiefly history. By this enactment, two levels of time and experience – 'traditional' chiefly history and the more recent process of migrancy – are overlaid, and the theme of migrancy is embedded in or written into an older template. In this way, the historical experience of migrancy is subordinated to the designs of chieftaincy, something which the migrants' role as vassals and messengers further reinforces. It is also the migrants who bring the young chief to his mother, and in returning him to his origins, they assist in the process whereby chiefly history can again resume. The chief has been purified, the period of contamination is over and the story can proceed as before. The question that arises at this point is why the migrants play such a pivotal role in the story. To answer this question we must turn briefly to the historical context of Valtyn where, as in so many other Southern African societies, migrancy precipitated a range of generational antagonisms.[22] Within Valtyn itself, migrancy dates back at least to the 1860s, and by the 1890s the missionary Daniel Heese was reporting evidence of tension between the chiefly aristocracy and returning migrants.[23] It was also during this decade that the Location Commission dispossessed the chiefdom, and this in turn precipitated a major schism within the chiefly family. This schism has persisted and has in addition become overlaid with tensions between migrants and the incumbent chiefly caste.[24]

Migrancy and migrants, then, have for some time constituted one of the central political tensions within Valtyn. And, hardly surprisingly, the theme of migrancy and its relation to chieftaincy becomes one of the horizons shaping Madimetša Kekana's account. In portraying these antagonistic relationships, the story domesticates and controls dissent by subordinating the experience of migrants to the pattern of chiefly succession and relentless regnal units that become the driving force behind historical change. All historical themes are absorbed into and imagined through this framework, so that chieftaincy appears as the author of all experience.

However, the technique through which Kekana embodies and encapsulates these concerns is a complex one. To begin with, he establishes a setting that relies heavily on familiar detail, and in this everyday world a set of historico-political concerns is then enacted. The historical themes of migrancy and chieftaincy that Madimetša Kekana takes up are ones that lie at the heart of the chiefdom's development over the last centuries. This cluster of issues is scooped into the story and by being encased in a familiar setting it becomes believable, immediate and accessible. The historical is bathed in the contemporary and the contemporary is made historical. Through this complex process of interweaving the social tensions around migrancy are muted and then projected back into a past which is simultaneously glossed with the trappings and detail of the present.

III

Taken together, these two stories vindicate the idea of chieftaincy in a number of ways. Most obviously, both celebrate the continuity of chiefly authority despite both internal and external threats to its survival. On a more subtle level, the stories portray chieftaincy as a pervasive cultural influence that can both contain internal dissent as well as reach beyond its boundaries into surrounding societies. Both tales also show chieftaincy as a powerful diplomatic force which can control and order the exchange of ideas and goods between societies. Overall, a picture emerges of a chiefdom that not only deals with the world on its own terms but also subordinates other societies to those very same terms, not through crude violence, but through intellectual and cultural prowess.

In addition to these more general themes, both tellers, in narrating an episode that began in 1854, garner into their stories a set of historical concerns that have unfolded since that time. These concerns relate to local experiences and memories of indenture, Boer (and subsequent English) overlordship, migrancy and the politics of chiefship. As with all historical traditions, the extent of their truth is difficult to establish but, as other studies have suggested, there is one direction in which one can look – that is towards the most formalised and conventionalised parts of the narration which have the highest probability of containing some 'possibly historical matter'.[25]

One such conventionalised part of the story is the core cliché which in the case of the story of the kidnapping of the child chief reads, 'My name is Klaas.' As I have already indicated, this core which speaks of indenture and its threat to cultural identity economically preserves the key themes of the episode. However, there is also some evidence to suggest that the kidnapping of a chief, or some occurrence like it, may have happened. In his military despatches, Pretorius mentions that the chief in the cave did indeed send out a group of hostages.[26] Furthermore, in the late 1870s, Sarah Heckford who visited the chiefdom reported that Mokopane, the incumbent ruler, had as a child been kidnapped from a Boer farmer.

> Makapan, or rather Clas Makapan, for the latter is only his surname or family name, is the son of a chief who, after a fearful massacre of the Boers, was at last reduced to submission by them. Clas was taken as hostage, and brought up in a Boer family. When his father died the Kaffirs determined to get the child back, and, fearful that the Boers would not give him willingly, they stole him one night, and having got him, made peace with the Boers by paying for him in cattle. One of the old Kaffirs told me that the little Clas had been very much frightened when he found himself a prisoner amongst the Kaffirs, and had cried and kicked to get away.[27]

Thomas Baines, who passed through the area and met Mokopane, reported that he spoke fluent Dutch, an indication that he must have spent some time in contact with Boers.[28] Taken together, this evidence could be construed as indicating that an heir to the chieftaincy may have been indentured after the siege. However, it is so fragmentary as to pre-empt any firm conclusion and instead simply opens up the possibility for a range of unverifiable interpretations. Why, for example, was the chief retrieved at all? One possible explanation is that his discovery was engineered by a faction who wished to unseat the incumbent, Makute. Alternatively, the story could also be a retrospective invention to cover the suspect origins of an upstart chief,[29] given that Madimetša Kekana's portrayal of Makute as slightly reluctant to hand over office would indicate that the ascendency of Mokopane was marked by some type of struggle. However, since no detailed extant records remain, it is impossible to draw any firm conclusions.

Overall, then, the story cannot really be verified. However, in so far as it encodes the memory of a chiefly class, the story is a faithful historical record that preserves the major issues of Boer incursion, land dispossession, indenture and migrancy that confronted the chiefdom during the nineteenth century. As such it is an historical record replete with symbolic truths.

Yet, as with Scheub's idea of theme, these symbolic truths do not rest solely in one story or set of episodes. Rather, as he points out, it is to the wider tradition of which the one story forms a part that one must also look. In this instance, such a tradition would be the corpus of narrative which together makes up the historiography of the chiefdom. Since this historiography assists in conferring a meaning on its separate parts, we turn, in conclusion, to examine the way in which the Gwaša episode is located in this wider tradition.

There are, of course, a number of difficulties that present themselves in the discussion of the historiography of the chiefdom. First, historiography requires the analysis of two areas: a corpus of texts as well as the principles by which they have been constructed. In relation to the chiefdom, whose oral historical record has not been extensively documented, it is difficult to specify of what this corpus would be composed. Furthermore, as an oral tradition, such a corpus has no fixed form and is instead realised in different contexts, each having its own determining constraints. Because of this fluidity, the principles by which historical performances are constructed can vary widely.

Since the historical recording of the chiefdom's traditions is limited, many of these questions can never be dealt with satisfactorily. However, within this limitation, and bearing in mind the difficulties listed above, one can but summarise the available material and speculate on what some of its guiding principles may be. Very often the only principle of which one can safely speak is that of summary and generalisation since much oral historical tradition, and particularly that which falls beyond the ambit of living memory, undergoes radical generalisation as the time depth increases. By attending to what the principle of such summarising may be, we can gain some insight into one of the axioms governing the production of oral historical performance. In relation to accounts that fall within the range of living memory the detail is more extensive, and one can accordingly speculate more freely on the principles governing the construction of the narrative. In the account that follows I will briefly survey 'ancient' traditions and then look more carefully at the placing of the Gwaša episode.

As with most Transvaal Ndebele origins, surviving accounts of the chiefdom's history begin in the 1500s or 1600s when an Nguni group moved away from present-day Natal.[30] Once in the Transvaal, a major split occurred within their ranks. One section under Manala remained in the vicinity of present-day Pretoria, another under Ndzundza moved further east. From this latter branch, the Kekana lineage split off and settled at Moletlane/Zebediela. A secession dispute then arose, and the unsuccessful faction moved away to found the present-day chiefdom at Chidi/Pruissen.[31]

The principle of summary that operates in these accounts is a teleological one governed by the ideal of chiefly coherence and control which unfolds through a series of key nodes of secession and migration. While some of these nodes are still encrusted with a cluster of narratives, the attrition of detail is high, and all that remains is a parsimonious account of chiefs' names, places and geographical reference points in which the memory of these traditions is anchored. However, when the historical record comes within reach of a three-generation memory, its detail and scope expand considerably. As regards the nineteenth century, most accounts focus on a series of onslaughts, first from Mzilikazi's warriors, then the Pedi armies and finally the Boers.[32] In dealing with these attacks, traditions follow the path of either magnifying or minimising defeat. Where defeat is amplified, the logic of the account operates as an implicit homage to chieftaincy and its ability to survive.[33] Where defeat is downplayed, an attack is presented as no more than a minor inconvenience that disturbs the smooth flow of chieftaincy hardly at all.[34]

It is this latter model that governs how the Gwaša episode is placed in a wider sequence. In order to illustrate this, let us examine two accounts that include the siege episode in a longer string of events. The first such account was given in 1929 by Frans Nuku Kekana, a major historian of and spokesman for the polity, to a Native Commissioner, one of whose scribes translated the testimony using rather erratic capitalisation and punctuation.

> I am the Chief headman of the Makapan Ndebele tribe and reside in Valteins Location, Potgietersrust District. My Chief is Barend Makapan. During the last battle between the Boers and the Makapan Ndebele, there was a German missionary living amongst the tribe whose name I do not know. This happened some years after the murder at Moorddrift in 1854, after the then village of Potgietersrust was burnt down by the natives, the Boers trekked back South, this German Missionary was told to leave the place as he was a white man the natives were afraid that the Boers may spy on them through him.[35]

In this account, Frans Nuku Kekana does not even mention the siege and refers instead to the murders preceding it. These murders are then linked with the sacking of Potgietersrus and the Boer flight southwards, an event that occurred in the early 1870s. In terms of this telescoping, the siege becomes a relatively minor setback, while the long-term aim of driving out the Boers is seen to prevail. It is, of course, difficult to gauge what status this testimony has and with what accuracy it was transcribed. However, since it was given in a situation where two chiefdoms were vying for the allegiance (and the cash levies) of a group living outside Pretoria, Frans Nuku Kekana's account must have been an official account.

In another official account, Molalakgori Kekana, the narrator whose version of the siege story we examined above, presented an account of Ndebele history to a meeting that had gathered in the Native Commissioner's office to decide on whether the incumbent chief, Piet Shiloane Kekana, should be unseated as many people were demanding. The minutes of the meeting, which took place in 1949, were unfortunately taken down in summary form. The opening of Kekana's speech in which he attempted to mount a genealogical case that would disqualify the incumbent, was recorded as follows:

> Greetings. I will speak about this matter according to Ndebele custom. Will start at beginning of chiefs. First one was Makuti. Paternal uncle of Makapane. Grew old and hunted for Mokopane. Freedom was bought by chief and tribe from farmers and tribe was agreeable. Mokopane ruled and died ...[36]

In this account, which focuses on the history of the chiefdom since it moved to Sefakaola, the siege disappears completely and instead we have a summarised reference to the interregnum episode of the young chief's indenture and ransom from the farmer. The only vague trace that remains of the confrontation with the Boers is a slight hiccup in the otherwise relentless sequence of the dynastic line. Obviously, as the 1949 squabble over the chieftaincy was played out in the language of genealogy and succession, this account is coloured by those concerns. Yet, despite this immediate contextual pressure, the speech does at least give us some idea of how the siege event is placed in a wider Ndebele historiography.

As we shall see in the following chapter, from at least the 1890s white historians latched on to the siege episode and by conflating nineteenth- and twentieth-century history, construed this event as signifying the end of Ndebele independence and the beginning of Boer power. By contrast, the two accounts produced above concatenate events very differently. The Boer victory shrinks away almost completely, making scarcely a dent on the smooth surface of chiefly control. The only mark that the siege leaves is that of a brief interregnum in which the chiefly line is momentarily threatened.

Such interregnum narratives, as I indicated at the beginning of the chapter, are plentiful and characterise many traditions that talk of the heightened divisions of the nineteenth century. As such, the concept of interregnum becomes a useful bracket that can fix the meaning of events as part of a wider tradition. By portraying a defeat or some other reversal as part of an interregnum, it can relatively easily be subordinated to and subsumed into a pattern of continuity and control.

The question that arises, of course, is how long such a sense of control can be sustained in narrative when, in the world to which it refers, authority has long been lost. For some royal men who were old enough to have had a thorough education in the *dikgoro*, the possibility of reproducing this world of control, if only in narrative, still exists. Their training in and knowledge of chiefly history is good, their commitment to chieftaincy is high, and even in the face of a hugely altered and contrary world they can still narrate chieftaincy coherently. For others, perhaps with less talent and also with less chiefly education, the possibility for historical narration exists, but in an attenuated form that has lost touch with some of the central meanings of chieftaincy.

One such example that we examined in the previous chapter concerned the transformation of the Boer woman. In Madimetša Kekana's account, the mutilation of the woman clearly betokens a sense of Ndebele prerogative and control. This episode is still in touch with a world in which chiefly aggression and initiative have some meaning, a world where a chief was hailed by the name *Sekete* meaning a thousand after the number of people he had killed, and where praise names included admiring references to 'holding the head by its chin' (that is, bringing home a severed head from war).[37] In the account of Fred Ledwaba, by contrast, this aggressive intent has entirely disappeared. In his version, the Boer woman is rubbed in red ochre to protect her from the sun and wind. From a distance, the Boers, seeing a red figure, presume she has been skinned alive and this belief, in turn, prompts their harsh reprisals. In terms of this account, all sense of chiefly initiative has evaporated, to be replaced by a view of the Ndebele as hapless victims.

There are a number of accounts that are akin to Ledwaba's version and all of them swivel on a reactive view of history whereby the hapless Ndebele simply respond to Boer aggression. While in form some of these accounts resemble chiefly history, their content has shifted and indirectly is more shaped by written views of the siege than by any sense of coherent chiefly design. Whereas written views portray the Ndebele as irrational aggressors, the 'corrupt' oral accounts simply invert this model so that the Boers become mindless tyrants, and it is against their violence that the Ndebele respond rather than out of any sense of chiefly initiative.

However, to see the interaction of oral and written as simply one of corruption is to simplify the matter considerably, and we turn now to examine the written versions before we return in the final chapter to discuss their impact on the shape of Ndebele historiography and interpretation.

PART FOUR

The Three Ms: Memory, Manuscript and Monuments

Testimony into Text
The Making of the Makapansgat Legend

On the base of the statue of Paul Kruger that stands in Church Square, Pretoria, are four reliefs, each representing an episode in the life of the President of the South African Republic. One of the reliefs portrays Kruger carrying the body of Piet Potgieter from Makapansgat (see Plate 28). The location of this relief on Kruger's statue says a great deal about the central place that the Makapansgat episode has come to occupy in the mythology of Afrikaner nationalism. Often seen as the Transvaal equivalent of Blood River, in which the Boers defeated the Zulu army in what is now Natal, the event has been immortalised on other monuments, as well as in a range of popular publications. The story of how this event came to be institutionalised is a long and complex one that meanders through both oral and literate worlds. In this process, folkloric perception which formed the basis of most accounts of the siege became transformed and elevated into the supposed respectability of monument and print. It is the intention of this chapter to trace out this process in some detail.

In taking such an approach, I hope to avoid the nationalist logjam into which the historiography of the siege event seems headed. Dominated by Afrikaner accounts, most renditions of this series of events have portrayed it as a homily on the righteousness of colonial conquest whereby unprovoked African barbarism is justly chastised and suppressed in order to make the country safe for further white settlement. More recently this interpretation has been challenged, but unfortunately these accounts have inverted the existing Afrikaner accounts so that instead of the Boers being victims of African aggression, the tables are turned so that Africans now become helpless objects of largely unexplained Boer violence.[1] In order to sidestep this impasse, what follows will examine the provenance of the evidence and the changing contexts in which it has been used.

I

Like many minor nineteenth-century conflicts in the Transvaal, the events surrounding the siege were poorly documented as far as written accounts go.

The only extant accounts are several military despatches left by Pretorius, and in the historiography of the events surrounding the siege these documents have come to be seen by a wide range of interpreters as reasonably reliable.[2] Central to his account are the details of how the Boers were murdered, and since these descriptions were to play a crucial symbolic role in subsequent accounts, it is worth pausing to examine Pretorius's reports in more depth. As regards the details of the murder, Pretorius wrote that the two parties of Boers murdered in the vicinity of Moorddrift were severely mutilated. Bodies were decapitated, hands had been cleaved open and baked in pots of human fat. Several male genitals were tied together and suspended in a tree, while the cooked limbs of children were found in corn baskets.[3]

Given the nature of Ndebele war practice, some mutilation of the Boers' bodies must undoubtedly have occurred. Furthermore, decapitation in war was considered laudable behaviour as the following praises suggest:

> Are you going to be as brave as your grandfather? The one from whom you got your name? Are you going to fell the Boer with an axe? Will you enter in the royal house as your grandfather used to enter, holding the head by its chin?[4]

In addition, parts of the bodies may well have been removed for medicinal purposes.

However, while there is some truth in Pretorius's report, there is reason to doubt what he says. First, it is not clear whether he saw the mutilated bodies. In one account he claimed to have seen them.[5] In another, he wrote that he did not see the bodies, but was told of their condition by Piet Potgieter.[6] Since the bodies were probably buried soon after the murder, as testimony collected subsequently made clear, it is unlikely that he did see the bodies.[7] Furthermore, he only arrived at the site of the murder a month after it had happened. The possibility of the bodies, or parts thereof, surviving the heat of a Northern Transvaal spring is remote.

The fact that Pretorius may have exaggerated is hardly surprising. The total Boer population in the Potgietersrust area probably numbered only a few hundred and the death of 28 people must have represented a considerable loss. Surrounded by angry rumour, it is to be expected that he would send back sensational accounts, tinged with folkloric intimations of cannibalism.

Be that as it may, the more interesting question is from what sources he obtained his information. One major informant, as Pretorius mentions in his despatches, was Piet Potgieter. Another source of information was less prominent – a servant of Hermanus Potgieter who witnessed his murder. While Pretorius does not elaborate on the details of what this servant says, another participant of the siege event, Willem Pretorius, does. In testimony that was collected from him in the 1890s, Willem Pretorius maintained that an *Oorlams meid* (Oorlams girl/servant) had described Hermanus Potgieter's end as follows: "They skinned Hermaans alive while he begged for God's help. When they broke him open (the breastbones from each other), his heart was still beating."[8]

This reliance on the testimony of servants or other Africans associated with Boer society occurs elsewhere: another siege participant attributes information to *mak kaffers* (tame kaffirs).[9] In a situation where there was often considerable distance, both actual and social, between Boer and African societies, this reliance on go-betweens and intermediaries is hardly noteworthy.

However, in assessing how the Makapansgat event came to be constructed, these oral roots are important. To begin with, they indicate that there is no absolute division between the oral and the written, and that much nineteenth-century documentation of the type left by Pretorius has its origins in the oral reports of a particular interstitial class. Often Christian converts, the members of this class may indeed have had their own agendas for creating particularly gory accounts of 'heathen' excesses. It is from this quarter, too, that one can perhaps 'diagnose' the often folkloristic veneer that covers the description of the murders. The example of Hermanus Potgieter's heart being ripped, beating, from his chest is a particularly clear example of this tendency.

Whatever the case may be, the descriptions of the mutilated Boers have, in subsequent written accounts, come to play the role of core clichés that summarise the essence of the story. Hence, while many people do not know the story in detail, they will often remember that Hermanus Potgieter was skinned alive and that this event in turn led to the siege in the caves.[10] While it is possible to argue that the source of this core image derives from Pretorius's military despatches, it is interesting to speculate that these may in turn unwittingly have their roots in the folkloristic traditions of indigenous storytelling.

While the slender evidence today limits one to circumspect speculation, it was precisely the same lack of evidence that allowed people from an early date to appropriate the siege as a parable on white conquest. In this vein Pretorius sent a letter of thanks to a Bloemfontein newspaper via one of the Free State residents who had assisted in the campaign. In his portrayal, the campaign became a successful exercise in punishing the 'guilty authors' of the atrocities.[11] In a slightly different vein, the *Graham's Town Journal* printed an account of the events that evinced admiration for the firm and decisive approach of the Boers. Like residents in the Cape Colony, the article noted, the Boers

> border upon the Kafirs, and are exposed accordingly to the self-same liabilities in the shape of frontier alarms, attacks, and depredations. That they do not, however, content themselves with our mild system of reprisals, or deal in our fashion with their savage enemy, will be only too evident from the story which we are about to relate.

The story began by explaining how the 'Kafirs had given the Transvaal Boers most dreadful offence'. It ended by explaining how the 'miserable savages had perished in their holes'.[12]

II

However, not all voices were so unequivocally admiring of the Boers. In a climate where allegations of Boer slavery were mounting, and where British imperial designs on the Transvaal were beginning to take shape, there were a number of observers keen to publicise incidents of Boer aggression.[13] Within this context, a number of missionaries made mention of the siege incident as one instance of broader Boer aggression and slaving. The first of these was Robert

Moffat who in November 1854 recorded the words of a resident of Sechele's chiefdom which had experienced Boer slave raids. Moffat's informant had heard of the Boer attack on Mankopane and he narrated events as follows:

> Martinus (Commandant Pretorius) is now gone with a commando to destroy the Bamapela tribe. Have they rejected the Gospel? What has Mangkopane, their chief, done? I will tell you and why. He has killed nine Boers; I shall tell you that too. The Boers have for a long time been robbing and oppressing him and his people. When the Boers returned from Moselekatse a long time since, when they went to try to take his cattle – did Moselekatse not tell you? – they returned by the Bamapela tribe, fired on them and took many waggon loads of their children on the day. Mangkopane, their chief, got a present from another chief of a few guns and horses. As soon as the Boers heard this, they took them from them, because a kaffir must not have a gun or a horse. Ask Mangkopane how many of his own children and theirs have been taken and made slaves, how many of his people have been murdered![14]

The piece continues in similar vein detailing the slaving practices of the Boers 'who have red teeth'.[15]

Another missionary to comment on the siege event was Theo Wangemann, director of the Berlin Mission Society, who visited the area in the late 1860s and filed a report.[16] Although critical of the Boers and their methods, his piece was much more muted than others, reflecting, no doubt, the more cautious and conciliatory stance which the Berlin Mission Society took toward the Transvaal government.[17]

Apart from missionaries, another group who commented on the siege comprised travellers who from the 1860s began to make their way through the area in increasing numbers. One of the first of these was Thomas Baines. Like most travellers, he outspanned at Moorddrift, and in the account of his travels he narrates the story associated with this place which was the site of "the treacherous massacre of a party of Boers under circumstances of atrocious cruelty; I believe by Makapan's father". He continues:

> I understand he had a blood feud with the Republic; but no particular provocation from the individual victims. It was in the war following this that the tribe fortified themselves in caves, and the Boers adopted the effective but cruel expedient of bringing several hundred wagon loads of wood to the brow of the mountain, hurling them down to the foot of the cliffs in which the caves were, and then throwing fire upon the mass. These caves are said to be of wonderful extent, and many unsuspected passages lead up from them to daylight. Mynheer Potgieter was sitting on the edge of a deep cleft, little thinking it led down so far, when a Kafir, who from the obscurity of the cave beneath saw his figure clearly defined against the sky, fired up and killed him.[18]

Like so many other travellers who came after him, Baines obtained his information from oral sources. In Baines's case, his informants were probably Boer, although the sources of his information are not made clear. In other instances, travellers drew on African oral sources as well. One such traveller was

Sarah Heckford who visited Mokopane's chiefdom to trade in the late 1870s. Her testimony, quoted in the previous chapter, does not mention the siege specifically but instead talks of how "Makapan", "after a fearful massacre of the Boers, was at last reduced to submission by them".[19]

Another person to make inquiries into African oral accounts was J.M. Orpen, a surveyor and member of parliament in the Orange Free State. While he never visited the caves, he was in the Free State at the time of the siege, heard reports of it and developed a life-long interest in the episode. While the siege was still in progress, Orpen heard accounts of Hermanus Potgieter's slaving activities and his use of the ramrod which was quoted in Chapter 5. In subsequent decades, written accounts like Kruger's memoirs and G.M. Theal's *History of South Africa since September 1795* attempted to exonerate Hermanus Potgieter.[20] On reading Theal's account which first appeared in 1889, Orpen started making his own inquiries. He wrote to a friend in the Northern Transvaal and asked him to speak to African survivors of the siege. The friend found one such person whose account was reported as follows:

> The native's story was that Field Cornet Hermanus Potgieter and others had for a long time been forcing them into service of various kinds, had repeatedly committed acts of great cruelty and shot down numbers of natives. The chief ... thereabouts was called 'Makapan' by the Boers, but more properly 'Mokopane' and to distinguish him from others of that name, 'Setsuamadi'. His youngest brother was out hunting one day and killed a buffalo calf. While he and others were standing over it, Field Cornet Hermanus Potgieter arrived on the scene, flew into a temper and said that only full grown animals, and then not a cow in calf, must be killed, and without more words he turned upon the chief's brother and shot him dead.[21]

While Orpen's did not appear until 1908, a steady trickle of accounts of the siege appeared throughout the last quarter of the nineteenth century. By this stage the caves, or Makapansgat, as they became known, had become a recognised spot that merited a mention in the growing number of books that focused on 'the Boer problem'. Jingoistic in tone, these examples of travel journalism were often extremely critical of the 'backward Boers'.[22]

One of the more ironic renditions in this genre came from Mark Twain who visited the Transvaal in the wake of the Jameson Raid of 1896. While he never visited the cave himself, he was told about a siege:

> Dr. X told me that in the Kafir wars, 1,500 kafirs took refuge in a great cave in the mountains about 90 miles [about 145 kilometres] north of Johannesburg, and the Boers blocked up the entrance and smoked them to death. Dr. X has been in there and seen the great many bleached skeletons – one a woman with the skeleton of a child hugged to her breast.[23]

In characteristically dry tones, he continues by contemplating methods of colonial genocide:

> We humanely reduce our overplus of dogs by swift chloroform; the Boer humanely reduces an overplus of blacks by swift suffocation; the nameless

but right-hearted Australian pioneer humanely reduced his overplus of aboriginal neighbours by a sweetened swift death concealed in a poisoned pudding.[24]

As the Transvaal moved towards war with Britain, the level of anti-Boer propaganda mounted steadily, and again certain writers saw fit to invoke the Makapansgat siege as an object lesson in Boer brutality. One anonymous account prefaced its description of the siege with the following paragraph:

> There is no race of men who have collectively been through such experiences, or sounded so many of the depths and shoals of the harder phases of human existence. Their whole career has been one long bitter struggle with their environments. Bloodshed has been their occupation from infancy. Nature red in tooth and claw never had a more emphatic exponent than the average middle-aged Boer. It may safely be said, altogether independent of the present war, that there is hardly a Boer of the older generation who had not at one time or other of his being been responsible for a human life; while very large numbers of younger men carry the same responsibility.[25]

However, not all accounts were in this jingoistic vein, and from the 1880s the Makapansgat siege began to feature in historical texts like Theal's *History of South Africa*. This influential book discussed the siege at some length and so assured the event a place in a wider historical chronicle of colonial conquest that Theal was central in forging.[26] The account also appeared in other historical texts, and by the 1920s an historian, J.A.I. Agar-Hamilton, could pass over the siege event by saying, "The story is too well-known to need more than mention."[27]

Through these various accounts, the caves started to become a well-known landmark to which picnickers and sightseers travelled.[28] Part of the attraction for going there was to collect the skulls and artifacts that remained on the cave floor. One of the more famous fossickers to visit the caves was a naturalist, W.L. Distant, who removed six skulls which he subsequently deposited in the Royal College of Surgeons' Museum in London. His account of his visit to the cave appeared in 1892 under the title of *A Naturalist in the Transvaal*.[29]

III

It was not only travellers and historians, however, who were responsible for popularising the Makapansgat siege. Much of this work was undertaken by Afrikaner cultural activists as part of a concerted campaign to construct a nationalist history. Tied up with the struggle for the recognition of Afrikaans as a language, this movement emerged in the heightened nationalist climate of the 1890s, and it was during this time that a number of Afrikaner historical texts emerged. While much of this activity was centred in the Western Cape, the Transvaal became an important focus for the production of nationalist history. Much of this historical work was popular and appeared in newspapers.[30] As the

Transvaal moved closer to war with Britain, one focus for this historical construction became life stories of the President, Paul Kruger; between 1899 and 1902, three biographies as well as his own reminiscences appeared.[31] Some of these were obviously intended for international consumption, but at least two Dutch biographies were directed at a local audience. Apart from creating a strong association between the life of the President and the life of the Transvaal Republic, the accounts also focused on Kruger's participation in the siege and as such established this as a key event in the unfolding of Transvaal history.[32]

This idea also had fertile ground on which to fall since Kruger's reminiscences had already appeared in newspaper form; one of these episodes focused on his part in the siege.[33] This reliance on personal testimony should not surprise us since, like many other nationalist-inspired histories, Afrikaner historiography relied heavily on oral history, and throughout the 1890s and early 1900s personal recollections were used with increasing frequency.[34]

As part of this movement, other recollections of the siege began to see the light of day. One of the earliest of these appeared in *De Volkstem* at the beginning of 1890. Under the heading "Een Oude Geschiedenis uit de Transvaal" (An Old Story/History from the Transvaal), the article began:

> It is a sad fact that the bravery shown and the severe hardships suffered by our forefathers and relations in South Africa in the past, particularly in the Transvaal, are not sufficiently realised by Afrikaners, and the patriotic spirit that is so necessary for cherishing and inspiring a national self-image are to a large extent retained only in the historical documents of past centuries.[35]

While other newspaper accounts of the siege continued to appear, it was from an unusual source that the Makapansgat legend gained an unexpected fillip.[36] This turn of events occurred in 1896 and had as their author the noted industrialist and entrepreneur, Sammy Marks, who offered £10 000 to the Transvaal state to erect a statue of Kruger. A promising young sculptor, Anton van Wouw, was given the commission, and it was decided to include four major events from Kruger's life as subjects for the four bas-reliefs that would decorate the statue's pedestal.[37] One of these events was the siege of Makapansgat in which Kruger had, via his reminiscences, staked out an heroic role for himself. His valiant conduct apparently took place in two episodes. In the first he had, so he said, black-faced himself, entered the cave and addressed the people 'in their own language' in an attempt to persuade them to leave the cave. This intervention was greeted by cries of '*Magoa*' (white person), and many people ran deeper into the cave. Kruger claims that he ran after them and mingled with them so as to mislead those Ndebele who were searching for the white man. After things had quietened down, Kruger, deep in the cave, again addressed the people 'in their own language', apparently so faultlessly that about 180 women and children followed his call to leave the cave.[38]

This improbable account which, for example, has Sindebele-speakers talking Sesotho, was not the only act of heroism that Kruger remembers himself performing. His second feat, and the one that became the more legendary, was his dash to save the body of Piet Potgieter. It was this action which was to be immortalised on one of the bas-reliefs, and again Kruger's description bears all the hallmarks of heroic overstatement:

In one of the fights, Commandant General Potgieter was hit by a shot fired from a crevice in the rocks. He was standing close to the edge of a rocky wall, giving directions to his Kaffir, when the fatal shot struck him. Potgieter fell down into the midst of a Kaffir trench. I saw this happen, and rushed down at once to try at least to save the body. The Kaffirs aimed a furious fire at me from the loop-holes of their entrenchments, but the burghers answered the fire no less heartily; and I was able to leap over the wall of the entrenchment, to lift the body over the wall, leap back, protected by the smoke of the powder, and bring the body back to safety back with me. Potgieter was a big, heavy man, and I had to exert all my strength to carry my dead friend back to his people.[39]

According to other accounts, the heroism did not belong only to Kruger. Pretorius records that after Potgieter was shot, he sent Kruger and a few other men to retrieve the body. The testimony that Orpen collected towards the end of last century maintains that Potgieter's body was actually saved by reluctant Kgatla auxiliaries ordered into the cave by their Boer commanders.[40] While one perspicacious South African writer, Herman Charles Bosman, was to use this latter interpretation as a basis for a short story "Makapan's Cave" which originally appeared in 1930,[41] it is, of course, Kruger's version that came to triumph, partly through the sensational events that dogged the making and erection of his statue.

By the time war broke out, Van Wouw, who was casting the statue in Italy, had completed Kruger's figure and the four Boer soldiers that were to be located at the corners of the entire edifice. These he duly crated up and sent off to Delagoa Bay. By the time they arrived, however, the war had broken out and they had to remain in customs from where the four Boer figures were to be redeemed by a most unlikely person – Lord Kitchener. He had learned about the existence of the figures from Sammy Marks whose farm he had used as the headquarters for his British military campaign in the final stages of the war. While he was on the farm Kitchener came across some photographs of a model of the statue which he liked a great deal. Marks, having decided that Kruger was about to lose the war, made the statue over to the Lieutenant-General of the British forces. However, it was not the whole statue that Kitchener wanted. It was only the four Boer soldiers, and these he arranged to be transported back to England. There, two of the figures finally ended up in front of the School of Military Engineering while the other two graced the gardens of Kitchener's estate.

After the British victory the base of the Kruger statue, which had been erected in the city centre on Church Square, was moved to the outskirts of the town, and it was here that the statue of Kruger, unadorned by the now-completed reliefs, was unveiled in 1913. Many nationalists had made concerted attempts to retrieve the four Boer soldiers from England but Kitchener steadfastly refused to give up his garden gnomes. After his death in 1916, negotiations continued at the highest levels, and eventually, in 1923 King George V authorised the release of the figures. Two years later, the entire statue with all its component parts was unveiled in front of the Pretoria railway station (see Plate 29).[42] In 1954 it was finally moved back to its original site in Church Square.

PLATE 28   Bas-relief at the base of the Kruger statue in Pretoria. The relief shows Paul Kruger rescuing the body of Piet Potgieter from the caves (T.A., T.A.D., 5078)

PLATE 29   The unveiling of the Kruger statue in front of the Pretoria Station in 1925 (T.A., T.A.D., 23020)

PLATE 30   A scene photographed at the caves. The photograph is undated and the circumstances being depicted are not clear. However, this plate and the one below were most probably taken in the 1890s for Van Wouw who requested photographs of the cave to help him in the making of his bas-relief (T.A., T.A.D., 3256)

PLATE 31   See the caption above (T.A., T.A.D., 3257)

All these developments were surrounded by intense publicity, much of which helped to reinforce the original conceptualisation of the statue as a symbol of the life of Kruger and the Transvaal Republic. In addition, books, novels and plays on Kruger continued to appear in substantial numbers.[43] Both as part of the Kruger statue, and as part of Kruger's life story, the Makapansgat siege was assured a place in the canon of Afrikaner history.

IV

Its place was further entrenched when in 1912 another monument, this time near Potgietersrus, was unveiled at Moorddrift to commemorate the murder that had occurred there. The unveiling was done in 1909 by the Minister of Land and Natives, J.F.B. Rissik, on 16 December, a date that had recently become institutionalised as a public holiday commemorating the Boer victory over the Zulu empire at Blood River in 1838.[44] Known as Dingaan's Day, after the Zulu chief who was defeated, the public holiday soon became a major focus for Afrikaner cultural organisations. In Potgietersrus it was the Dingaan's Day Festival Committee that had organised the campaign for the monument which was paid for by public subscription.[45]

As the unveiling took place with the union of the four provinces only a few months off, the speeches, hardly surprisingly, stressed national white unity and supremacy, in keeping, too, with the more minimalist Afrikaner nationalism favoured by Jan Smuts and Louis Botha, leaders of the ruling Afrikaner party *Het Volk*. But in the Northern Transvaal where white control had always been shallow and had, in any event, largely been shaken off during the South African War, this stress on racial supremacy carried an urgent, local meaning rather than a vague national symbolism.[46] And it was largely to these local desires that some of the speeches, from residents in the area, were directed. One such talk, delivered by the mayor of the town, gave 'A Short History' of the events that the monument commemorated. According to his view of things, these events included first the murder of 23 (rather than 28) people by 'Chief Makapaan', which in turn led to the siege. Significantly, the mayor chose to portray what were in fact three separate murders by two chiefs as one collective massacre by the local chief's grandfather since this portrayal, no doubt, played more strongly on local white feeling. But, as the mayor's parable went on to illustrate, this massacre did not go unpunished and 'the blood of the Voortrekkers [was] avenged'. The monument, then, assumed the function of commemorating and sustaining a summary of local history reduced to a mnemonic outline of unprovoked black aggression, white retribution and victory that supposedly spelled the end of Ndebele power. It was, interestingly enough, virtually the same interpretation that was used in 1940 to motivate the conversion of this monument into one that was nationally protected and recognised. Part of this proclamation read, "It was on this site that natives massacred a number of women and children in 1854 ... a massacre that led to the destruction of native power in the central Transvaal in the same year at Makapansgat...."[47]

In reality, the Makapansgat siege had been followed by at least another half-century of Ndebele independence that had often entailed significant Boer retreat but, in the process of imagining white power, this series of events was but one of the many to be repressed.

V

Like many other monuments, this one in Potgietersrus legitimated local legend and it was on this local tradition that Gustav Preller, perhaps the most influential interpreter of the siege, was to draw. One of the central architects of Afrikaner nationalist history, he more than anyone else transformed the legend of Makapansgat into a national canonical event. Like many other Afrikaner professionals, he was turned to nationalism by the devastation of the South African War, and on returning from India where he sat out the hostilities as a prisoner of war, Preller found his house commandeered and his job as a clerk in the Department of Mines gone. On the point of emigrating to Argentina, Preller was persuaded by a prominent young writer and journalist, Eugène Marais, to assume editorship of a newspaper, *Land en Volk*. This move into journalism inaugurated a truly extraordinary career as a popular historian. In newspapers, magazines, books, pamphlets, films and plays, Preller dedicated himself to collecting, preserving and constructing Transvaal and Natal Boer history. Much of his considerable energy went into accumulating historical documents, diaries, letters and the like. In addition, he gathered life histories and oral testimony relating to various historical episodes including the South African War and the movement of emigrant Boers to the interior that we now call the Great Trek, a term that owes much to Preller's popularising ventures. In this latter area he was quite breathtakingly successful, and it was both his visual and conceptual interpretation of the Great Trek (a white, pioneer-style saga) that came to be accepted as the dominant one and has for decades been disseminated in all South African schools.[48]

By the 1910s Preller had done much work on the Natal Trekkers, particularly Retief, Dingane and the battle of Blood River. His research into Transvaal Trekker history had not been as extensive, and from the early part of the decade he turned his attention to the Makapansgat story. Most probably alerted to it by Marais who spent time in the Potgietersrus area, as well as by various articles that had appeared on the topic, Preller collected oral testimony from local residents, and by combining this with archival and written sources, produced his account of the cave story that appeared in two illustrated parts in his popular Afrikaans magazine, *Die Brandwag*, in 1914/15.[49]

Entitled "Baanbrekers" (Pioneers), the story is a shrill, exculpatory piece that sets out to rebut British and missionary allegations of Boer cruelty and slaving. The central idea through which Preller mediates these concerns is that of hospitality. In terms of this code, the Boers in the story are consistently hospitable. Their winter migration to the lowveld, from which they are returning, is passed off as a friendly social holiday, rather than anything as crude as a health necessity that such trips mainly were. Even Hermanus

Potgieter whom the story owns as a difficult but rugged frontiersman, observes the codes of hospitality and fair exchange. When, at 'Makapan's' invitation, he visits the chief's homestead to hunt in the area, Potgieter takes a suit of clothing as a present for the ruler. Equally 'Makapan' keeps some of the Boer's cows for '*melkgebruik*',[50] another token of Potgieter's fair exchange. All the trade transactions in the stories embody this just dealing on the part of the Boers who trade wheat and mealies for game. In historical reality, the exchange must in fact have been the other way around. Given the shaky and uncertain position of Boer homesteads in the area, they were often unable to sow crops during the 1850s.[51] However, in portraying the Boers as agriculturalists, the story naturalises their right to the land which they earn by honest labour, unlike the Ndebele who supposedly only hunt and gather wild honey. Similarly the settlers mark the land as their own with those microcosms of civilisation – the hedged garden. Furthermore, they cut proprietorial swathes through the region with "highways sliced through the Waterberg and Soutpansberg on which the Voortrekker wagons travelled backwards and forwards".[52]

The Ndebele on the other hand transgress all conventions of hospitality. They invite Potgieter into their midst and then kill him. They offer deceitful exchanges: at one point an Ndebele man offers the Boers some wild honey with the object of waylaying them. Moreover their dealings are never open and fair, but rather dark, hidden, devious and disguised. For example, they set sunken, concealed traps in the river, and during the siege one man escapes dressed as a woman. Indeed they offend all known law and custom by becoming cannibals during the *Mfecane*.

In the story, this cannibalism 'accounts' for their apparently unprovoked killing of the 28 Boers, which in turn justifies the Boer siege, subsequent reprisals and Boer possession of the land, symbolised by the establishment of Pietpotgietersrust in the region. In the light of this Ndebele perfidy, Preller claims both moral and historical rights for the Boers by comparing the Makapansgat siege with other colonial atrocities, particularly of the cave blasting and smoking variety, reports of which he assiduously garnered over the years.[53] The climax of the argument is a shrill genocidal call. If the Ndebele will cling to the dark, deep cave of their heathendom, then wiping them out is justified.

> Against barbarians and cannibals, survival justifies any method of warfare in the case of a limited white population ... if forty years ago, Pretorius and Kruger in the north had eradicated the Ndebele and Venda and the English had done likewise to the Zulus and Basothos in the south – how much sorrow and suffering and adversity would they not have saved their own nation.[54]

In constructing his account, Preller drew heavily on his interpretation of Blood River, an event which in his hands came to signify the Boer victory over the Zulu empire. By the time he came to write the Makapansgat story, he had already done a lot of work on this episode which had appeared in his highly successful book, *Piet Retief*. He was also busy thinking about a film.

Like the Makapansgat story, his account of Blood River falls into two clear parts. To begin with we have an episode of betrayed hospitality and unprovoked violence in which the Zulu invite the Boers into their midst and then kill them. In the second episode, the Boers seek retribution which they find in the battle of Blood River at which the Zulu forces were routed. In "Baanbrekers" we have the same pattern, and Mankopane, for example, invites Hermanus Potgieter into his midst and then kills him. At Moorddrift much the same thing happens. Mokopane's warriors invite the Boers to trade sheep and then slaughter them in cold blood.

There are other similarities between Preller's accounts of the Makapansgat and Blood River stories. The atrocity scenes in both books, for example, are virtually identical, with their battered baby skulls, dead women and drifting feathers from the ripped and stabbed mattresses. What these similarities suggest is that Preller was trying to build up a Transvaal equivalent of the Blood River mythology. Having successfully constructed the latter event into a clear and accessible homily on black barbarism and Boer righteousness, he set out to do the same to the Transvaal story.

In doing so, Preller relied on a set of techniques and themes that were designed to be popular and accessible. These techniques include an appeal to customary notions of hospitality; the use of oral witness and experiential evidence; the conventions of popular colonial fiction with its marooned cluster of redoubtable white protagonists, even perhaps the haranguing tones of the sermon.

However, there is another strand of popular experience at which this story tugs. Like much of Preller's other texts, this one appeals to a popular and widespread memory of violence and bloodshed. Virtually all Preller's texts read as an inventory of atrocities which eventually calcify into a set of almost legendary codes. These shorthand images, in turn, acquire the status of implicit historical explanation and justification. For example, when a local journalist decided to do a story on Makapansgat in 1938, she went out interviewing people to see what they remembered. The memory of the siege, she discovered, was still strong. One woman for example held forth splenetically:

> Is it possible for you to grasp how we loathe the kaffirs when it was their very own fathers and grandfathers that committed those terrible atrocities at Moorddrift? My father who was together with General Potgieter, told me that the kaffirs tore small, helpless children from their mothers' arms and smashed their heads to bits against the wagon wheels.[55]

In this account, the woman is grasping the past through a cluster of Preller-type images which by 1938, the year of the Great Trek centenary, had reached quite frenzied heights. The mythical version through which she experiences both the past and the present is derived from that popular haze of images that Preller's work on Makapansgat had helped create and perpetuate.

Largely because Preller relied on popular forms of legend and expression, his article proved to be extremely popular and was subsequently printed in book form. In utilising popular forms of expression, Preller was able to bank a variety of associations in the story as well as locating the episode as part of the broader narrative of the Great Trek. This strongly affective history was extremely popular and the publication of 'Baanbrekers' was followed by the arrival of fan mail. Some of these letters came from Potgietersrus residents who had helped

Preller collect testimony; the writers were part of a growing fraternity in the town who were turning to local history as a powerful political resource.[56]

VI

Given the chronic lack of resources that most Northern Transvaal towns faced until they were 'saved' by separate development in the 1960s, the one area which such towns could seek to develop was history, and as early as the 1910s Potgietersrus promoted itself as a centre of historical interest.[57] From the turn of the century, the town had a range of Afrikaner cultural, youth and political organisations that all had a strong historical dimension. Some of their activities included historical re-enactments and tableaux (see Plates 32 and 33), and their committees took an active part in things like cleaning and maintaining monument sites.[58] This historical industry gained momentum during the 1930s when Afrikaner nationalist mobilisation took off. Central to this exercise was the massive Voortrekker centenary of 1938 (see Plate 32).[59] In Potgietersrus, a veritable Voortrekker mania took hold of the town, and when the convoy of wagons passed through the area their wheels were dragged through a wet concrete slab that had been placed directly behind the Moorddrift monument. In this act, the association between the national symbolism of the Great Trek and the local legend of the cave siege that Preller had so effectively established was, quite literally, cemented again.

PLATE 32   The procession of the 1938 Great Trek Centenary passes through Potgietersrus (Combrink, *Eeufees*, 182)

PLATE 33   Participants in the 1949 Rapportryers Fees (Dispatch Riders' Festival) approach to Potgietersrus. The flags being carried are those of the old South African Republic (T.A., T.A.D., 14920)

Throughout the 1930s a number of local historians began to employ this set of shorthand associations in lobbying for the declaration of the caves as a monument. In terms of the popular perception of the story, it had two clear parts, the massacre at Moorddrift and the retribution at the cave site. While the Moorddrift site had been monumentalised, the caves had not, and from the 1930s local voices began calling for the declaration of the caves as a national monument. The immediate factor sparking the request was excavation for travertine that a lime-works company was carrying out near the caves. Because of blasting operations, the caves were in danger of being destroyed. A report in *Ons Vaderland* ran as follows:

> The caves are not only interesting as a natural phenomenon, but they also have great historical meaning for the Afrikaner nation because at the entrance of one of these caves, Potgieter, the great Voortrekker leader, lost his life and this is also where Paul Kruger carried out his heroic act when, under fire from the kaffirs who were trapped in the cave, he entered the mouth of the cave to bring the body of Potgieter to safety. Will these caves which act as a reminder of the brave Voortrekkers who sacrificed so much for our land and nation, be allowed to be destroyed? We hope not.[60]

However, apart from the historical interest of the caves, the lime-works excavation had also uncovered significant palaeontological finds. These hastened the declaration, and by 1938 the caves had become a national monument for both historical and archaeological reasons.[61]

The caves continued to be a focus of white curiosity and tourism, particularly during the 1940s when it became apparent that the cave area contained australopithecine remains.[62] As a result of these finds and of growing public interest in the caves, the vicinity came to be more and more thoroughly fenced off, particularly when the area surrounding the caves became a research station under the aegis of the University of the Witwatersrand.[63] Access was barred to all but researchers and their guests. Madimetša Kekana remembers this time:

[T]he fence around that cave was put up by whites. Even these gates were established by whites, so that we should not go to that place. That place is frequented by them alone and these people [Africans] if they go there, they ask for permission from the government....[64]

In addition, a popular legend grew up that white 'doctors' from Johannesburg were coming to remove bones from the cave since these had potent medicinal and magical properties.[65]

This monument declaration continued as a strong theme in the Northern Transvaal, and by 1941 nine of the Transvaal's eighteen monuments were located in the north. If one includes Pretoria, which if not physically was always emotionally part of the Northern Transvaal, then the figure rises to fourteen, nearly the entire complement of the province's monuments.[66] Two of these monuments, Moorddrift and the caves, were in Potgietersrus, and by 1949 a third was added to the list when some *Acacia abbida* were declared national monuments. Known locally as *anabome* or *aapiesdoorn*, these trees were said to have great botanical value and it was on these grounds that the declaration was made, although the local legend that both Livingstone and the Voortrekkers had tarried under the shade of the trees to rest and play sport respectively, strengthened the motivation for declaration.[67]

The chief of Valtyn, Piet Shiloane Kekana, opposed the declaration since the one hectare that was to surround the monument, in fact, constituted somebody's field. The Native Commissioner airily suggested that the owner be compensated with land elsewhere and the proclamation went through.[68] Like many other monuments, these trees continued to be the subject of legend, and one of these emerged in 1964 when eight African women were charged with cutting down the trees and the surrounding fence. In the report on the case, the Potgietersrus newspaper stated authoritatively that the trees had been brought from Egypt by 'our great-grandparents' – whoever they might have been.[69] This report may in turn have some link to the widely told legend that the river that runs near Potgietersrus was named the Nyl (Afrikaans for Nile) by the Voortrekkers who believed they had reached Egypt.

VII

This tree declaration, however, was by no means the last attempt to monumentalise the town, and from the 1940s there was a growing interest in reinterments (see Plate 34). The major mover in this development was a local historian, Hans 'Purekrans' (lit. Pure Cliff) van Rooyen who had earlier inducted Eugène Marais into local Boer history. Marais subsequently wrote a short story entitled ''Die Laaste Mapela-Moord'' (The Last Mapela Murder) which dealt

PLATE 34   Reinterment in Potgietersrus. The gravestone reads: Died on the farm Pruizen No. 1538, Potgieter Region, Waterberg District, Transvaal in a fight on 1 October 1901 Christoffel du Toit Born on 22 January 1872 and Petrus Johannes Janse van Rensburg Born on 17 February 1881 Reburied at Potgietersrus on 18 December 1910 and Petrus Stefanus van Emmenes (T.A., T.A.D., 1498)

with the death of Hermanus Potgieter, and much of his information must have come from Van Rooyen.[70] Since Preller was in close contact with Marais, it is more than likely that Van Rooyen also provided background for "Baanbrekers".

In 1941 Van Rooyen approached the Native Commissioner's office for permission to unearth the remains of three men who had been killed by Mapela's followers during the South African War. The issue was very much alive in people's minds as witnesses to the murder were still living and the relatives of the dead men wanted to reinter the remains in white territory. Mapela, however, refused to reveal the location of the bodies and Van Rooyen had to give up his plan. His next scheme was to save the bones of a certain Wolmarans who had died during the same war. His remains were on a company farm that was occupied by black tenants who were ploughing in the vicinity of the grave. Van Rooyen wanted to dig up the bones and "put them in a proper coffin ... and reinter them in a Christian churchyard".[71]

This theme of reinterment with its stress on 'saving' white earthly remains from black 'contamination' had powerful associations with the Makapansgat story itself since it was a similar act of saving that Kruger supposedly performed in wrenching Potgieter's body back from beyond the black pale, the depths of which, as Preller put it, "no white [person] has yet plumbed".[72] What this type of symbolism did was to enforce a powerful segregationist view in which one meaning of history became the violent wrenching apart of those areas where black and white memory might intermingle.[73] In Van Rooyen's case, this struggle was a very physical one which gained its violent piquancy from a memory of black independence that was still uncomfortably recent.

This symbolism of reinterment, then, was profound, and it reached its apogee in 1964 when the remains of Piet Potgieter were relocated to the centre of Potgietersrus. At the ceremony the historical associations, needless to say, came thick and fast. According to newspaper reports, Potgieter's remains were said to be languishing unhappily in a 'non-white area' and needed to be buried in white respectability. A Voortrekker and military leader, the martyr of Makapansgat, the eponymous hero of the town – all these facets were incorporated into a ceremony that took place on 31 May, Republic Day, which commemorated the departure of South Africa from the Commonwealth in 1961. The audience of four thousand was addressed by J.J. Fouche, Minister of Defence, who lauded the South African Defence Force, promised it more resources and threatened the world in the confrontationist discourse of the time. Potgieter's remains were lowered to the singing of the hymn, "Straf tog nie in Ongenade" (Do not Punish without Mercy).[74]

This reinterment did much to remind spectators of the historical associations that linked the siege and the town through the person of Potgieter. In terms of this perception, the victory of the siege had became the precondition for the town's establishment and it was this view that the town's centenary, which occurred in 1954, propagated. One of the publications celebrating this event, which incidentally leaned heavily on Preller's "Baanbrekers", set out this popular periodisation that portrayed white settlement following closely on the heels of black humiliation. This temporal image also attains a spatial dimension so that white settlement is imagined as being established on top of black defeat.[75] By the end of the decade these views had wide purchase, and publicity material on the town routinely referred to them. Or, as one newspaper article put it, 'Here [at Makapansgat] the power of Makapan was smashed.'[76]

Taken together, the tradition of the Makapansgat legend, as with most popular history, is characterised by a high degree of inversion, repression, ellipsis and displacement. To begin with, any interpretation of Makapansgat that would see it as a white victory must necessarily repress a great deal of nineteenth-century history during which the Ndebele clearly controlled the area and on more than one occasion sacked the town of Potgietersrus. Furthermore, most popular written accounts bleach away the theme of slavery entirely from the story. As far as Preller's story is concerned, these brazen inversions are particularly marked: the slavers have become the apparently enslaved and the destroyers of hospitality, the hospitable.

As the popularity of the written accounts of the siege show, these formulations have held a wide appeal, and it is partly in their unconscious dimensions that their success must be sought. The symbolism, for example, of a black community literally being repressed and smashed into the dark holes of the earth is extremely suggestive in this regard and, given the predominance of the popular written traditions, it is as though any memory of that society beyond the narrow Boer-sanctioned view is suppressed and buried there too.

VIII

Given the Afrikaner nationalist orientation of the written tradition, there are obvious differences between the oral and textual accounts of the siege episode. However, there is also a fascinating undercurrent of similarity that is worth discussing briefly. Most obviously, as we have seen, the printed texts have had their roots in oral reports, and in this way much of the chiefly interpretation of the episode has made its way into written accounts. Preller, for example, introduces many motifs from the chiefly tradition into his stories. These include the scene of someone dressed up as a woman escaping from the cave which relates to the story of a substitute, often disguised, being sent out. Preller includes, too, the sheep-selling scene in which the Ndebele, on the pretext of trade, lure the Boers at Moorddrift to their deaths. This information is in turn derived from the testimony of Willem Pretorius which has an Ndebele man utter the phrase, 'Don't you want to buy a sheep?' Exactly the same phrase occurs in the account given to me by Madimetša Kekana. This sheep-selling incident also features in the testimony that Orpen collected late last century.[77] It is, of course, difficult to tell in which direction this motif moved, and it may well have been that chiefly traditions absorbed the account from Boer oral renditions. However, either way, the widespread presence of the motif attests to an interaction between oral and written accounts.[78]

Another similarity between these two traditions is their emphasis on the theme of 'bringing back the body', and it is around this motif that both stories turn. For the Afrikaner version, it is Piet Potgieter's body which must be retrieved. In the chiefly version, it is the kidnapped heir who must be saved. In both cases, there is fairly elaborate detail on how the body – alive or dead – is redeemed from behind enemy lines. Furthermore, since both these traditions come from dominant groups, much of their symbolism is tied up with political leadership in which the loss of a leader or his body is tantamount to the loss of an entire society. The retrieval of a body, then, represents the redemption and continuity of a social order, and it is around this political legend that both traditions cohere.

As the histories of two chiefly classes, the Boer and Ndebele traditions share further similarities. Both, for example, rely heavily on topography as a mnemonic device, and both bank their historical memory in geographical features of the landscape. While this tendency may be clearer in relation to chiefly accounts, local Afrikaner traditions cohere around the points of Moorddrift and the caves. Furthermore, the Afrikaner tradition does not simply rest in the printed page, and much of its meaning depends on monuments, ceremonies and reinterments that, like the oral tradition, have a strong performance dimension.

Finally, the two traditions also cohere in the muted emphasis that both give to the idea of interdependence between Boer and African society. Since the stories are so flagrantly about conflict, this theme of co-operation may sound strange. Yet lurking in most stories are details of an interaction that binds the two groups together. In Preller, for example, Hermanus Potgieter is linked to the chief Mankopane by his cows that reside in the latter's care. Similarly, Potgieter gives the chief a suit. Likewise, some of the oral accounts portray the abduction and seizure of the Boer woman as an act of protection, and the red ochre that is smeared on her is intended to shield her from the harsh sun and wind. Equally, Molalakgori Kekana's account of the way chiefship influences Boer society speaks of cultural interaction.

What these details suggest is that, despite their overt differences and unequal status, Boer and African societies do enter subtle forms of exchange that are not purely military and economic but are also cultural and intellectual. In the available historiography on rural Transvaal societies, it is often the differences and inequalities that have by and large been stressed. What these various accounts do is open an alternative perspective.

The story given here of how the Makapansgat legend came to be constructed has attempted to show how the interpretation of an historical event is subject to a series of changing contexts. Shaped by the political climate in which they are written, both oral and literate composers have drawn on a range of local historical resources and, like the tellers of *dinonwane*, they have combined these to meet the exigencies of a particular situation. While many of the written accounts attempted to elevate the event into one of national canonical importance, they continued to have a local meaning that could at crucial junctures reactivate the national interpretation. In this way, much of the event's meaning was forged in this local arena, and, as with all historical meaning, it was determined in the end by social struggle. Or, as Scott phrases it,

> The struggle between rich and poor ... is not merely a struggle over work, property rights, grain, and cash. It is also a struggle over the appropriation of symbols, a struggle over how the past and present shall be understood and labelled, a struggle to identify causes and assess blame, a contentious effort to give partisan meaning to local history.[79]

8

History as Farce?
Oral History as a Changing Phenomenon

As a number of commentators on oral tradition have noted, oral memory has a close mnemonic relationship with place and location, and in a variety of societies people often 'bank' information in the landscape. In analysing this process, scholars have examined the various ways in which landscape is used to record memory. Aspects of the landscape can, for example, serve to separate bodies of stories into coherent units; a series of topographical features may store a temporal sequence of events in a spatial order while the surrounding geography may have the effect of preserving the life of a story when it might otherwise have disappeared.[1] In addition, as Glassie has shown in relation to oral history in an Irish community, landscape plays a crucial mnemonic role by providing "the artifacts in which [the] past is entombed". Elsewhere he comments:

> In the noble native tradition, history in Ballymenone is part of the durable idea of place. Place is space rich enough to provide travel for the mind while the body sits still, space so full that it forces people to become responsible for its future. History is the essence of the idea of place.[2]

Yet one question that such research has never persistently pursued is what happens when people lose access to the topography that helps to uphold memory. The common-sense answer to this question would be that such recollection withers and dies. However, the situation is by no means so simple. Much thinking on the production of oral tradition maintains that it thrives on fragments, and that its producers are like bricoleurs who go to work with material originally intended for another purpose.[3] Given this method of working, a fragment of historical recollection unmoored from its geographical anchor could just as well be appropriated into some other story as disappear entirely.

The issues raised by the question of the relationship of oral tradition to a changing geography are, in many ways, paradigmatic of the broader question of oral tradition as a phenomenon that changes in time. While the common-sense view is that oral tradition inevitably wanes in the face of the literate, industrial world, there is much evidence to suggest that the situation is much more complex than these popular perceptions allow. As the second part of this book has indicated, oral forms not only exhibit an amazing tenacity, they can also transform the literate institutions they encounter. However, such transformations generally occur in a context where an oral society retains a large degree of coherence, independence and territorial integrity. What happens when that coherence and integrity fracture?

Part of the answer to this question is that some oral performance skills do indeed wane, particularly when the key institution for their reproduction – like, for example, the *kgoro* – disappears. However, since the basic techniques for oral historical narration are not dissimilar to those used in the telling of *dinonwane*, the possibility of acquiring a modicum of skill still exists. In regard to oral historical narration, this means that the skill can still continue despite the fact that its key institution of reproduction has been swept away by forced removals. Without a centre of gravity, the craft of chiefly historical recollection can only circulate in ever-decreasing and aimless circles. It is this process of corruption and transformation that this chapter will attempt to illustrate.

I

As we have seen in the previous chapter, the canon of chiefly history is plotted on the earth and stored in the landscape. In chiefly memory, an area is imagined as being criss-crossed with the paths of secession, migration and battles that make up the official history of the polity. Or as Tswana historians envisage it, a 'map' is constituted by an intricate pattern of 'ruins' or places where the chiefdom once resided, and together these points record the passage and migration of polities across an area.[4] Such organisation, however, presupposes the integrity of both a real and imaginative map on which the epic events of chieftainship unfold.

In the past, this imaginative map of chiefly coherence was a powerful reality, and even after the Location Commission of 1890 had dispossessed the chiefdom a narratively constructed topography of control remained intact. In 1906, for example, Frans Nuku Kekana, in giving evidence to another Location Commission, said, "In former days we used to own all the land round about here, down to and including the town of Pietpotgietersrust and the farms surrounding it, which of course no longer belong to us."[5] Some three decades later, in 1933, the incumbent chief, Barend Makapan, was claiming tribute from farmworkers as far south as Pienaars River – some 250 kilometres south of the chiefdom – on the basis that his jurisdiction properly stretched so far.[6] However doubtful these coercive claims might be, they do none the less illustrate some sense of a coherent political map.

It is a similar kind of map that one encounters in the testimony of Molalakgori Kekana. His narration unfolds against the background of a world of Ndebele control in which the polity lies at the centre of a set of radiating relationships that link it to other societies. These societies with whom the polity 'is acquainted', as he terms it, can be called upon to recognise the authority of the Kekana chief. Even if the political claims inherent in such a map were entirely without foundation, the notion of the 'map' is important in so far as it sustains a coherent sense of the past. As regards Madimetša Kekana's narration, much the same situation applies, and his story plays itself out against a topography of Ndebele initiative and control.

All the men mentioned above, with the exception of Frans Nuku Kekana, were born into a situation where the imaginative map of the chiefly world bore very little resemblance to the dramatically curtailed border of the chiefdom. Yet growing up as these men did in a world still centred on the *kgoro*, and being schooled in historical tradition, they could continue to keep the imaginative world of chiefly control in orbit long after its actual territorial base had been thoroughly shredded.

These men are (or were) able to do this largely because they are (or were) by no means ordinary citizens. All firmly within the aristocracy, they include some of the finest graduates of a chiefly education. Molalakgori Kekana, for example, is noted as a truly outstanding historian and narrator who acquired his knowledge from his father, Magube Ratanang, also a respected historical authority. From an early age, Molalakgori Kekana showed a strong talent and interest in historical tradition and was, as one of his contemporaries put it, "always among the old people".[7] Among this royal group, the commitment to a chiefly system is understandably high. Since the aristocracy were often the first to move when betterment resettlements were instituted, they could settle with kin and so keep alive some semblance of old social relationships and cultural practices.[8] Furthermore, as an ethnic minority in a Sotho-dominated homeland, the royal lineage has an added inducement to traditionalism.[9]

Yet this ethnic aristocracy is fighting against the tide. Many younger men, having experienced only formal schooling, are either entirely ignorant of chiefly history or see it as quaint in much the same way as many people today see *dinonwane* as suspiciously fantastic and non-realistic.[10] In addition, for those without a royal background, or for those who had to settle among strangers, the attrition rate of the skills of historical narrative have been much higher. Without any props to hold these skills approximately in place, the impact of formal schooling has been more corrosive.

Yet the demise of the *kgoro* is recent enough to ensure that there are still a number of people who are familiar with the basics of historical narration which they gained in these courtyard arenas. In addition, the skills of historical narration can be 'borrowed' from the *dinonwane* tradition, and since these are available from school and some households, albeit in an altered form, some tellers can supplement their lack of a proper historical education with techniques gleaned elsewhere. However, as the chance to practise these skills is limited and, for some, the foundation of their skill is, in any event, slightly shaky, the style and orientation of their telling show a number of differences from the 'orthodox' tradition as exemplified by narrators like Molalakgori Kekana and Madimetša Kekana.

The first of these differences is predictable and involves a radical attrition of memory brought on by lack of practice. The second set of differences is more unexpected and involves amplitude rather than diminution. Let us examine each of these transformed traditions in more detail.

II

As Scheub has argued, oral narrative is stored in a series of core clichés or images that the teller recalls and elaborates on in performance. These cores are the units in which the story resides and it is through constant practice and active performance that one gains the skill of expanding them into stories.[11] If such practice is lacking, it makes sense that the details surrounding the core will wither, leaving only the bare kernels from which the story has, in the past, been constructed.

This process is clear in the following testimony from Cecil Lesiba Kekana who, in attempting to narrate the siege of Gwaša episode, produced the following:

> They discovered there are people, things, beasts, kids [inaudible] people and beasts there. They've, uh, oh, all the 'Kaffirs are here inside'. [Laughter] Wood, wood, wood, wood, wood [some bystanders talk but inaudibly]. And then that to bloody burn, bloody, mouth of the cave, thinking that they are burning people. Suffocation here and because of sickness and the breath that was in the cave.[12]

What we see in this passage are two core images of the Gwaša story that were identified in Chapter 5. The first concerns the dumping of the wood in front of the cave and the resultant attempt to smoke out those inside. The second relates to the 'disease of the breath' that was said to assail those in the caverns. In the excerpt above, these episodes have been stripped down to their most basic cores. Deprived of their animating detail, the cores have became a stark list made incoherent through over-drastic summary.

There are admittedly a number of factors which account for this incoherence. The informant was slightly drunk and he was speaking, by his own choice, in English. Moreover, the printed word does not convey the gesture and action that rendered the passage slightly more sensible. Yet, these factors notwithstanding, the story is still garbled and incoherent, and unless one has some prior knowledge of the story the passage is incomprehensible. In recalling these core images, and in techniques like repetition and direct speech, the speaker indicates that he still has access to the basic skills of oral storytelling. Yet, overall, these skills have become so rusty that they can no longer produce coherence.

Let us examine another example from Mosoamadite Kekana.

MK: What I can say——
JM: Mm.
MK: ——is one thing.
JM: Mm.

MK: Yes———when the Ndebele were fighting against the Boers———

JM: Mm.

MK: ———the years when this happened, that I can't remember. It is long ago.

JM: Mm.

MK: Now, when they were fleeing away from the Boers, they took refuge in that cave of Gwaša.

JM: Yes.

MK: Yes, that of Gwaša———

JM: Mm.

MK: ———that's where many died, and now we go there to pray for rain, we go there———

JM: Yes.

MK: ———when we realise that there is no rain.

JM: Yes.

MK: Do you see?

JM: Mm.

MK: Going beyond this, no. Now I don't think I can proceed.[13]

The interviewee would not be drawn any further on the topic and instead steered the conversation towards a topic with which he was more familiar: his war experiences in Egypt. In this brief account it is only the barest outlines of the story that survive along with the knowledge that the chief's grave is a site for rain sacrifices. As with Cecil Lesiba Kekana, Mosoamadite Kekana was in his sixties and was regarded as someone with historical expertise. But as this expertise is seldom called upon these days it has largely atrophied.

But not everyone's skill has calcified in this way and there are any number of tellers who will talk in capacious detail. Familiar with the techniques of constructing oral historical narrative, they can generate extensive stories. The content of such tales, however, is often awry.

Let us examine some examples. The first concerns the skill of beginning a story. As Miller has pointed out, the technique of initiating an oral historical account generally revolves around a crisis, "a sudden and visible shifting of fortunes".[14] One informant, Mahula Kekana, clearly possessed such initiating techniques in his storytelling repertoire, and indicating that the story I wanted to hear had its roots far in the past, he began his account as follows:

The whole thing started like this, when out there in Bulawayo, near Stanger, the chief quarrelled with Shaka over a woman called Pampata. Chaos resulted and chief Khona and his people had to run away.[15]

In terms of technique, this opening episode is impeccable. Not only does it begin with the requisite crisis, it also anticipates the trajectories of genealogical disruption and migration along which the narrative will be funnelled. However, its content is less impressive, implying as it does that it was as a result of Shaka's activities that the group now known as the Transvaal Ndebele moved to the localities where they are presently settled. As we have already mentioned, the Transvaal Ndebele moved into their present-day areas in the sixteenth or seventeenth century.

A second example concerns the historical skill of etymological deduction, a principle on which both historical and imaginary narration depends. Many people still use this form as a structuring principle in their historical narrations, but its content is often dubious. One informant, Moletsi Mahlangu, in telling the story of the Gwaša siege, linked it to the Berlin Mission station, Makapanspoort (Makapan's Gateway), at which he was telling the story. Here he explained that the mission had got its name because Makapan's footprints or *spoor*, as Afrikaans terms it, passed through the site on which the station now stands. As a result of this *spoor* which betrayed the whereabouts of the chief to the Boers, the mission came to be called Makapanspoor or Makapanspoort.[16]

Another example of such form without content concerns the principle of using the landscape as a mnemonic reference and hence a crux of composition. Within the historical canon of the chiefdom, one such reference is a place referred to as Maroelaskop (Maroela Hill). According to one tradition collected at the turn of the century, Maroelaskop was the place to which the Kekana fled under the onslaught of the Pedi armies. Here they encountered the Kgatla.[17] This account of events is borne out by Kgatla tradition, also collected at the turn of the century, which maintains that it was at Maroelaskop that they were defeated by the Kekana.[18] In a tradition that I collected, Maroelaskop became the place to which the indentured child chief was sent.[19] For Madimetša Kekana, the Forest of Lions was also a place characterised by maroela trees.[20] Since the first two episodes bear each other out, it seems reasonable to assume that the actual Maroelaskop was, in fact, well beyond the chiefdom's boundaries to the south in Kgatla territory. In the latter two versions, however, this core of content has largely disappeared, until Maroelaskop becomes a purely symbolic reference. Any more precise meaning that the place had no longer exists.

One possible reason why this reference to Maroelaskop survives is that the maroela tree is extremely common in the Northern Transvaal. It is also large and conspicuous and references to it could be construed as forming part of the *nonwane* technique which relies on constructing an ordinary quotidian background against which a fantastic plot can unfold. Seen from this perspective, any reference to Maroelaskop involves using an everyday botanical feature to create a credible background for the more legendary events of chiefly history. In addition, the tree becomes a repository for a number of historical events, and as a result a profusion of episodes could ostensibly attach themselves to the tree.

What this *ad hoc* historical system of recollection means is that the real co-ordinates of the epic map of chieftaincy are lost. In the narratives of Molalakgori Kekana and Madimetša Kekana, these geographical points served to anchor the plot of chiefly history and keep the story segments that surround them in some sort of regular orbit. With a loss of both the places for transmitting historical education in the *kgoro*, and the almost total erasing of the territorial world of chiefly control, it would seem that this orbit of plot segments circles out of control. The plot segments still remain, the skills which underlie them are still obtainable, but the social universe that held them in place has shifted substantially.

The sense of a chiefly landscape that underwrites any historical narrative can still be detected in much narration, but it and the memory of events it supports has contracted radically. Hence for many informants the sense of an epic landscape has shrunk to the present-day borders of the chiefdom. Here only a handful of historical markers remain. These are set out in the song which we have previously encountered:

> We come from MmaChidi/We come from MmaChidi/And reached Ngwa-ditše quite well/We come from MmaChidi/We come from MmaChidi/And reached Ngwaditše quite well/Sefakaola has already arrived/Sekafaola has already arrived/Sefakaola has already arrived/At Mokopane's place/Sefakaola has already arrived/Sefakaola has already arrived/Sefakaola has already arrived/At Turfloop, at Ngwaditše.[21]

As we have seen, the song marks three major historical points. The first of these is the previous site of the chiefdom at Chidi, the second refers to the river at which the chief and his followers were said to have paused as they made their way to the third point, Sefakaola, the hilltop site of the relocated chief's capital. For skilled narrators like Molalakgori Kekana and Madimetša Kekana, these topographical references form part of a wider mnemonic web that stretches beyond the chiefdom's present boundaries. Yet for most narrators the shrunken sequence as set out in the song is all that remains of a wider chiefly map. This map still has some meaning because one of its points, Sefakaola, lies within the chiefdom's boundaries and can be seen for miles around. The river also used to be visible, but since it was diverted by the Potgietersrus municipality it has been completely dry, and unless one knew that a river once ran there one would be none the wiser. So, apart from the hilltop, the geographical references in the song have literally become faint or distant.

This sense of a fading mnemonic system crops up in other contexts as well. For example, in his testimony Cecil Lesiba Kekana tried to think his way into history via the landscape. "If only I knew that piece of history from Zebediela," he commented, "you know those names when we left here to camp there at gaMmaChidi, where we arrived and camped. [...] You pass there when you climb the steep slope."[22]

This disappearance of the landscape as a system of mnemonic ordering does not mean that all recollection has disappeared. There are, of course, new historical markers that carry information of the past. Among these are schools which often bear the names of chiefs and so act as reminders of recent genealogy. There is a certain irony in this situation since many of these schools began to appear at the time of betterment resettlements which coincided with the spread of the National Party government's version of mass schooling known as Bantu Education. A widely told popular rumour maintains that it was the promise of having a school named after him that finally pushed the chief into ratifying the implementation of the betterment proposals.[23]

Other historical markers that, as Chapter 3 has shown, came to summarise information about the past were things like beacons and fences. Not only did the implementation of these features require that the objects of historical recollection shift to include a memory for meetings, boundary decisions and fence adjudications, but fences and beacons themselves could come to act as mnemonic resources in which the story of the struggles and circumstances surrounding their genesis could be banked.

Like beacons which stood as fixed reminders in the earth, monuments, too, became a form in which historical memory was stored. As we have seen in the previous chapter, Potgietersrus supported a veritable culture of monuments and historical re-enactments. While the obvious intention of these monuments and ceremonies was aimed primarily at creating and sustaining the idea of Voortrekker history, this was not how everyone saw them. For Madimetša Kekana, for example, the Moorddrift monument acted as a reminder of Afrikaner racism. Or, as he explained it, "That [that is, the monument] is why we are not on good terms with the Boers. Every white child, if it misbehaves, is taken to the monument and then told, 'You can read there, look what the kaffirs did'" (the implication being that they will do the same to the child).²⁴ There is much insight in this comment. As we have seen in the previous chapter, the sense of an Afrikaner identity as put forward by someone like Preller was dependent for its definition on the idea of the threat of black violence and the ability to quell this menace. In discussing the monument, Madimetša Kekana clearly grasps the role that it plays in this process of cultural definition.

However, not everyone saw the monument, and the Voortrekker tradition it embodies, quite so critically and, as we shall see, many people have absorbed a Trekker model of history into their oral historical explanations. This 'osmosis' can perhaps best be described as a process of bricolage whereby tellers cobble together different techniques, ideas, themes and resources in their historical narration. Since the basis of historical narration can be gleaned from *dinonwane*, and there are furthermore alternative sources of historical information that can be garnered from formal schooling or historical pageants in Potgietersrus, anybody with the inclination or talent can theoretically start processing historical narrative.

III

One such person is Lucky Kekana whose stories provide an interesting example of the corruption that an historical imagination sundered from its proper contexts of transmission and performance can undergo. This corruption is not one of diminution, it is rather one of proliferation. An outstanding *nonwane* teller, Lucky Kekana uses her skills to generate seemingly endless amounts of oral historical narrative. Clearly influenced by a 'Voortrekker' view of history acquired both in school and through observing life in Potgietersrus, her stories, with quite exuberant avarice, swallow up motifs from Afrikaner history and weave them into a well-nigh Rabelaisian farce. In this pageant the traditional admixture of the fabulous and the quotidian, the extraordinary and the ordinary has been quite comically dislocated. In the narration of someone like Molalakgori Kekana, the fabulous energy of historical storytelling is kept in control by reference to a wider world of everyday detail, topographical references and geographical sequences that form part of a coherently imagined universe. In the tellings of Lucky Kekana there is little sense of a wider coherent chiefly world, and unfettered by these constraints her joyous penchant for the fabulous can run riot. Add to this an equally fecund but debased appropriation of a 'Voortrekker' discourse, and you have a style of storytelling that is quite anarchically humorous. Let us consider some examples.

The first concerns an episode of genealogical history in which the 'founder' of the Kekana lineage broke away from his brother Ndzundza. In the official chiefly canon, one explanation for this breakaway maintains that as a young girl in the group had begun to menstruate (*ukuthomba*), part of the group remained behind with her and in this way a new lineage emerged.[25] Another name for the 'founder' of the Kekana lineage is Mathombeni, and this name is said to derive from and commemorate this episode.

According to Lucky Kekana, however, things went slightly differently. Like all versions of chiefly history, her account begins with the movement of the Ndebele from Natal to the Transvaal. This movement, however, belongs to the period of the emperor Shaka and not, as it should, some three hundred years earlier. Be that as it may, in their wanderings in the area that we now call the Transvaal, the Ndebele encounter the unusual sight of a tree that grows only in Natal. The tree has a number of useful properties: it has tasty fruit, its roots have healing properties and in its shade lies a well. The Ndebele duly spend three months at this welcome oasis and, as a mark of their respect, they name themselves after the tree which they know by the name, Mthombo. The story continues:

LK: They called themselves after the tree, they said, 'We are no longer Zulu, we are Mthombeni.' That's right. Now they call themselves Mthombeni. They say, 'We are Ndebele, we are trained under Ndebele.'

JM: We are trained under the Ndebele.

LK: Yes, we are Ndebele. We are no more the Zulu. They call themselves after that tree Mthombo. They call themselves after this tree. Yes. They said, 'We are Mthombeni.' It means that this tree is father to them ... And their names are Ndebele names, they've been 'Ndebeled' by this tree.[26]

In this excerpt which purports to explain ethnic distinctiveness, the storyteller takes a fragment of genealogical history and combines this with a detail of the everyday world around her. In addition, she also draws on a well-known historical precedent relating to trees in the Potgietersrus area. The episode which we encountered in the previous chapter concerns a clump of rare trees that fell within the chiefdom's border. This cluster of *Acacia abbida* or *anabome/aapiesdoorn* as they are known in Afrikaans, had been declared a national monument in 1949.[27]

Since the chief had unsuccessfully opposed the declaration of the memorial on grounds that someone's field occupied the area that was to become the monument, the trees must have been well known within the chieftaincy.[28] In 1964 these trees again came into the news when eight African women were sentenced to 40 days' imprisonment or a fine of R20 for chopping off part of the trees and damaging the surrounding fence. The local newspaper reported that the trees were unique to the Northern Transvaal and implied that the trees had been brought from Egypt by the ancestors of the Boers.[29] The story has such striking parallels with that of the Mthombeni tree that one can only assume that this legend of the arboreal monument had seeped into the chiefdom and had in turn made its way into Lucky Kekana's narration.

In constructing her account of the Mthombeni tree, Lucky Kekana relies on an etymological principle which sets out to explain origins and derivations by using retrospectively deductive reasoning. This principle forms the basis of much *nonwane* telling but in Lucky Kekana's hands it becomes a relentless logic whereby any proper name forms the object of etymological speculation. For example, the main road in Potgietersrus, as with virtually all Northern Transvaal towns, is called Voortrekker Street. According to Lucky Kekana, this street was named after a man called Piet Voortrekker. By the same logic, a store called Waterberg and Gilbertson was run by Mr Gilbertson and Mr Waterberg. While Gilbertson is the name of a famous farmer in the district, the word 'Waterberg' in fact refers to a geographical district.[30]

Apart from this slightly crazy etymology, Lucky Kekana also uses Voortrekker history as one of the sources of her history. In setting out the background to the siege event, she told the following story.

LK: Potgieter came here from Cape Town. They were using wagons. You see where Mr Smerk [Mr Smith] lives there at the dairy?

JM: That road when a person comes from Naboomspruit?

LK: Yes, when you come from Naboomspruit, there at Dromaleya [Drummondlea, the farm next door to Moorddrift].

JM: Dromaleya?

LK: That's right, just there at Dromaleya, you see that place?

JM: Yes.

LK: Yes, there at Mogalakwena. That's where Potgieter parked his white nation. Now the white man came to grow up, here on our land. They parked there and started building tents, alongside those useless cars [wagons]. Do you understand?

JM: Yes.

LK: While they were parked there, they started cooking with those great pots. So great [she indicates size]. You see?

JM: Yes.

LK: But mind you, Dingane was still alive at that time. I still remember the fight between Dingane and Potgieter. It was on the 16th, that's why this day, December 16, they say it is in memory of Dingane, because Potgieter and Dingane fought on this day.

JM: Yes.

LK: Dingane's herdsmen were busy taking care of the cattle. Then they see the white people wearing big hats with big dresses [that is, standard female Voortrekker garb]. They were busy cooking pork, do you understand? You must listen to me very carefully.

JM: Yes.

LK: While they were busy cooking that pork, mind you there were no clothes in that time, they were wearing *stertriems* [cruppers]. I don't know if you know a *stertriem*?

JM: Usually I see them in pictures.

LK: But does the woman [I.H.] know them?

JM: *Do you know setsiba, stertriem?*

IH: *Yes.*

JM: Right.

LK: Now, tell her I'm going to talk about something that might hurt her.

JM: *Now she says she is starting with something that will make you very, very uneasy.*

IH: *No, no, let her talk and not be afraid.*

JM: She says talk and be free.

LK: Yes, now the man wearing the *stertriem*, the Ndebele one who was busy herding cattle smelt some meat, pork in fact. Then he went to ask. He had to enter a river and swim across. He says, '*Thobela*', he greets. They don't give him an answer. A white man says, 'What is this baboon?'

JM: Yes.

LK: And that young boy says, 'Sir, I ask for meat, there is nothing in my stomach.' But he doesn't know how to speak their language. You see?

JM: Yes.

LK: Then that white man says, 'Oh, he is asking for food.' Then another one says, 'No, we cannot give a baboon food.' They beat him with their hands. Then the poor herdsman ran away and fell into the water. Mind you, they were using those old guns, isn't it?

JM: Yes.

LK: They try to shoot him. He keeps on swimming until he arrives at an overhanging ledge. Then he tells the other ones, 'You must always know that the whites are here, wearing big hats, they cook meat that smells very nice. I was so hungry that I went to ask for some but they beat me and shot me with a thing that goes dudum-dudum-dudum.'[31]

In response to this aggression, the chief decides to attack the Boers. He summons up warriors and the fight again occurs on 16 December and this time Dingane kills Potgieter. Paul Kruger, identified by a praise name, 'the hero, I don't load a gun but I can shoot', arrives and 'the blacks run away to Makapansgat'.

In this account, one can feel the weight of a 'Voortrekker' interpretation pushing in on the story. As the previous chapter has indicated, Preller attempted to portray the event of Makapansgat as a Transvaal equivalent of the battle of Blood River of 1838. This clash, which occurred on 16 December, has for some time been commemorated as a public holiday formerly known as Dingaan's Day, but now referred to as the Day of the Covenant. In Lucky Kekana's account, the two events – the Makapansgat siege and the battle of Blood River – swirl together in a comic confusion that indiscriminately mixes up locations and names. So, for example, the Blood River scenario which occurred in Natal is relocated to the Transvaal. The major protagonists of the conflict, Dingane[32] and Andries Pretorius, are also shifted to a new locale, while Andries Pretorius's name changes to Potgieter. This confusion of Pretorius and Potgieter is, however, understandable since M.W. Pretorius and Piet Potgieter were the major Boer actors in the Makapansgat siege. To confound matters further, there is another Voortrekker leader, Andries Hendrik Potgieter. He, however, had nothing to do with either the siege event or the battle of Blood River. Given the similarity and duplication of these names, and given that Voortrekker history as taught at school is monotonously repetitive, this gallimaufry is to be expected.

In the burden of its explanation, Lucky Kekana's story with its emphasis on hospitality exemplifies another interesting parallel with Preller's story. Like his story, which was arranged around the idea of betrayed hospitality, her account portrays the cause of conflict as inhospitable behaviour, but this time on the Boers' part. I am not, of course, suggesting that her explanation is directly indebted to Preller's, since it is quite clearly drawn from everyday images of eating and hospitality. None the less, what her story does do is to invert the Preller model, and in this sense her account which responds to the 'Voortrekker' version is in some way shaped by it.

This reactive model is further discernible from the stress that her story places on misunderstanding. By her account, one factor precipitating conflict between Boer and Ndebele is their inability to understand each others' languages. As Chapter 5 has illustrated, this emphasis on misunderstanding is one that frequently occurs in other oral accounts. In one of these, the Ndebele take a Boer woman captive and cover her in red ochre to protect her from the sun. They then release her and as she makes her way back to the Boer camp, the Boers see her in the distance and from her appearance believe that she has been skinned alive. On the basis of this, they institute the punitive siege against the Ndebele.[33]

This episode, which resonates with the belief that Hermanus Potgieter was skinned alive, portrays the Ndebele as hapless victims of misunderstanding. The overall impression of such a portrayal is that the Ndebele were innocent victims of misplaced Boer aggression, and it is very much this form of explanation that Lucky Kekana's version embodies. This explanation, of course, simply inverts the Afrikaner interpretation which painted the Boers as hapless victims of Ndebele violence.

However, as we have seen in Chapter 6, not all versions rely on this idea of misunderstanding and hapless victimhood. Madimetša Kekana, for example, portrays the Ndebele as noble aggressors initiating an attack against illegitimate interlopers. This aggressive intent of the Ndebele is made quite explicit in the way in which they appropriate a Boer woman and refashion her into an Ndebele, thus making her a signifier of male chiefly authority. But, in a climate in which the Voortrekker version of history presses in on the chiefdom from school, monument and pageant, this militaristic emphasis has become 'tainted' largely because it appears to conform to the Afrikaner historiographical emphasis on unprovoked black aggression. So, instead of stressing Ndebele military initiative, someone like Lucky Kekana relies on a reactive model that simply inverts the major categories of Afrikaner historiography. Under such circumstances, the burden of explanation has shifted from one of initiative to one of reaction.

However, while much of its content may be drawn from the legends of Voortrekker historiography, the form of Lucky Kekana's story comes from the world of oral performance. Much of the story, for example, is told in accordance with the rule of two characters to a scene. Repetition and enacted speech also characterise her style, while the piece identifies Kruger by a praise name. In this narrative, the skill of oral narration is still intact. However, the content is so corrupted that overall the story seems properly to belong to that other genre of accidental humour, the howler.

IV

In dealing with the testimony of Lucky Kekana, it might, of course, be argued that it is largely her status as a woman that has ordained this incoherence. Relegated to the realm of female storytelling and excluded from the *dikgoro*, when these existed, she can hardly be expected to exhibit historical competence. Indeed, one might argue that her exuberant style of telling is, in fact, a buoyant form of resistance to her exclusion from the male world, and, contrasted against the world of silence to which women are generally relegated, the sheer volume and capaciousness of her narration represent no small achievement.

While these points do have some validity, her testimony can also be taken as a vivid illustration of the fate of oral historical narrative since it has become unmoored from the *dikgoro*. No longer so tightly controlled, it has in one sense become more democratic and can freely be exercised by a woman. Yet at the same time, because it no longer has an ideological centre of gravity, the meaning of such narration has become vapid, corrupted and at times incoherent.

The idea that such oral history is 'incoherent' or corrupted is, of course, controversial. Incoherent to whom? Corrupted by whose standards? Is this 'invention' of history not something that has been typical of all oral history which, after all, responds to contemporary circumstances and is forever up to date?[34] Also, is an informant like Lucky Kekana, indeed, not much more creative than I allow for? Is she not perhaps the subversive bricoleur, the one who "breaks down the images and symbolism of dominant and subordinate cultures in order to recombine them in a way that subverts cultural dominance"?[35] What of the idea that historical understanding is inseparable from narrative form? If the narrative form remains intact, then does it not, somehow, preserve a particular form of historical understanding?

To all these questions I would give a qualified no. To begin with the last question first, narrative form and historical understanding gain their meaning partly from a wider, institutional context which determines firstly their correct transmission and reception. The *kgoro* provided such a context. Its removal not only shattered the major forum of historical education, it also robbed people of their accustomed, everyday social spaces, one of the major sources we use for creating a context of meaning and continuity.[36]

In addition to creating an image of continuity, the *kgoro* also stood as a symbol of the chiefdom and an entire traditional order. By abolishing this daily, mnemonic, physical reminder of the proper social order of the chiefly universe, the resettlements marked a crucial threshold in the transformation of the chiefdom. They marked a decisive border beyond which the skills of an oral culture could certainly still be reproduced but with reference to a world that was entirely remade.

One crucial feature of oral historical narration is the implicit elaboration of a normative chiefly world and it is against this background that events become coherent. Since 1890, when the chiefdom lost most of its territory, the possibility of imagining that chiefly world has been in doubt. Yet, given the tenacity and effectiveness of oral education, it proved possible to reproduce an imaginative notion of an epic chiefly world. But, when simultaneously both the institution in which historical education occurred and the last physical reminder of the chiefdom disappeared, the skill of historical narration rapidly disintegrated.

All that remained were the features of the landscape itself, and these alone were not strong enough to keep control on the galaxy of plot segments that made up the corpus of the chiefdom's official history. These topographical features still help people to recall certain events of the chiefdom but it is as if the centre of gravity has gone so that the plot segments float around in jumbled limbo, combining and reproducing themselves by an apparently aimless fission. While such fission has always been at the heart of both historical and non-historical storytelling, it has now become so aimless that it can no longer be said to be similar to the invention of history in the past. The type of comic invention I have documented in this chapter surely represents a qualitative departure from the more elevated narration and understanding embodied in the testimony of someone like Molalakgori Kekana. Combining both the skills of narrative ability, historical insight and an outstanding memory, his stories come close to the qualities of a good oral historian that Alpheus Ledwaba outlined. He phrased the issue like this: "When we say someone is good, we mean a person who can memorise everything and know it, a person who would not forget when asked about old issues ... and also old things." Elsewhere he added, "When old people are with him [that is, a good oral historian], you find them endorsing his statements ... he should have a good memory and not rush over issues to conclusions. He should follow issues according to how they unfold themselves from the beginning to the end."[37]

One way in which Molalakgori Kekana obtained these skills was by spending a lot of time with old people in the *kgoro*.[38] However, the possibility for others to follow his example has been radically curtailed both by migrancy and the disappearance of the *kgoro*. Wrenched out of its context in this way, oral historical knowledge has been irrevocably dislocated. It has also been marginalised by the teaching of history in formal education. Schools dispensed a massively institutionalised history in novel genres and unusual forms. A rigid sense of chronology – requiring that one 'understand years' – became its defining characteristic.[39] In terms of its content, history at school legitimated colonial dominance. 'Traditional' history did feature in muted forms in certain reading books, but it never attained the same kind of prominence as *nonwane*. In addition, the 'message' of such historical stories could be Christianised.[40] Also, as with *dinonwane*, the transference of oral history to print erased its performance aspects. Like *dinonwane*, too, such traditional history as did appear was relegated to the lower standards and so acquired a 'junior', 'child-like' status.[41] And while formal education effectively ensconced a new style of history, it, along with missions, dented the prestige of the existing institutions of oral history, particularly initiation schools.

Against this background, chiefly history was rendered more marginal and less coherent. But what of Lucky Kekana? Is her 'cross-over' style that flagrantly draws on both formal school, public and oral historical sources, not more coherent? As a style that bridges a wide range of experience, could it not be said to be more accessible and meaningful than an 'orthodox' chiefly tradition? Furthermore, could her narrative not be said to be subverting the cultural dominance of chieftaincy? While her story may unintentionally do this, Kekana herself sees the story as being an authentic and orthodox account of chiefly history. She is not alone in this view, and I was referred to her more than once as an historical authority. Also, her stories are not without appeal, and on both occasions that I interviewed her she held an audience of four or five bystanders spellbound.

Her stories with their humour, action and dramatic enactment clearly have some popular appeal. However, they are stories with little intellectual content. As we have seen, the 'orthodox' proponents of a chiefly tradition, like Molalakgori Kekana and Madimetša Kekana, used their stories as intellectual explorations of chieftaincy and its wider meanings. In Lucky Kekana this intellectual foundation is entirely absent. One reason for this absence has to do with her gender which precluded her from the forum of the *kgoro*. Yet at the same time her work illustrates some of the more general tendencies of post-*kgoro* oral history. Deprived of a proper historical education in the *kgoro*, or alternatively having only partial or artificial access to a post-betterment, reconstituted substitute of the *kgoro*, many people have not mastered the intellectual rigours and traditions of chiefly history. Instead, such historical education as they have obtained in formal schooling has been a particularly debased and propagandistic version of the Afrikaner historiography which has for some time been taught in schools. Out of a combination of these two corrupted traditions, subject in turn to the oppressive climate of homeland politics, grows a kind of popular history which can best be described as comic. It is a case of history quite literally being repeated, the first time as tragedy, the second time as farce.

Conclusion

Any literary discussion of oral history is forced to shuttle between four major co-ordinates: the event/s referred to by the informants; the present-day context in which those narrations occur; the conventions and forms which enable narration; and an intervening period during which both the conditions and craft of telling, as well as the meaning and form of the story itself, have undergone considerable changes. While the details of the events narrated – in this instance the cave of Gwaša siege – and their changing ideological meaning have occupied part of this study, it is along the other three co-ordinates that its major horizons have been drawn.

The first horizon concerns the historical period through which a particular chiefdom as well as its texts and tellers have passed from the 1850s to the 1990s. Such a history has, of course, to be conceptualised so as to enable the major forces shaping the community to come into view while simultaneously bringing into focus those institutions in which oral literature is reproduced. In order to bring both the larger historical background as well as the literary foreground into focus, and in order to imply a relationship between them, this book has used the notion of orality and literacy as central organising concepts. In pursuing this style of analysis, it has maintained that much nineteenth- and early twentieth-century political struggle in the Transvaal countryside can be interpreted as a confrontation between the oral performance politics of chiefdoms and the control of literate institutions.

Anyone doubting this statement should examine the 1953 amendments to the Bantu Authorities Act of 1951. Apart from laying down the conditions for a cheap repressive homeland administration,[1] the Act attempted to enforce literate procedure on rural chiefdoms. These provisions for this literate imposition are set out in great detail and include the procedures for meetings and minute-taking as well as the methods of record and account-keeping. Such a 'tribal record book and minute book' was also to become a 'permanent record' of the community's history. Alongside copies of government notices, names of office bearers and vetoes exercised by the Native Commissioner, "there may be recorded in such record books particulars of historical events concerning such

175

tribe or community handed down by tradition and particulars concerning the genealogy of the chief or headmen". To destroy, damage or render any part of such a book illegible was to invite punishment.[2]

This theme of literacy imposed from above is not limited to the Bantu Authorities Act, which is one in a long line of legislative attempts to coerce chiefdoms into literate rule.[3] One way to interpret this theme in the legislation is to see it as a manifestation of a wider struggle between the political precepts of a predominantly oral world and those of an overwhelmingly literate social order.

It might, of course, be argued that putting forward such broad divisions of orality and literacy is questionable, particularly since so much recent scholarship has challenged the usefulness of positing gross psychological and cognitive distinctions made simply on the basis of the mediums that people use.[4] However, while this study has indeed made a distinction between orality and literacy, it has not been of the kind which maintains that the mediums of writing or speech as technologies of the intellect have cognitive implications and that, for example, in incorporating writing into their communicative repertoire individuals change the way they think as they supposedly move from a state of being 'oral' to one of being 'literate'. As the Introduction already made clear, these are not separable 'states' and there can only ever be a movement from a predominantly oral situation to one in which both orality and literacy combine in complex ways.

In order to illustrate the complex interweaving of orality and literacy, much of Part Two has been taken up with illustrating the porousness of spoken and written forms in the chiefdom itself as well as the complex way in which people combined the spoken and the written in their everyday communicative strategies.

Like most contemporary studies of literacy, these case studies have sought to show that there are no automatic consequences that follow from the introduction of literacy. So, for example, the qualities of standardisation, decontextualisation and permanence that some would see as inherent in writing were not discernible to members of the chiefdom. Instead, they appropriated writing and transformed it, particularly in their letter-writing which obliged the written word to be heavily context-dependent.[5] Similarly, the Native Commissioner's office could not behave as the depersonalised and distant institution that some would assume a bureaucracy – by virtue of its literacy – to be. Instead, because of the context in which this office operated, the commissioner frequently had to abandon impersonal rule and literate governing for face-to-face interaction and public audience. From these examples it is clear that the impact of literacy and the way it is appropriated cannot be predicted beforehand, and the precise nature of any interaction between orality and literacy must be sought in the details of each particular context.

Much of this book, then, has stressed the intermingling of the two mediums. At the same time, however, I have attempted to argue that at some levels, *the idea of* orality and that of literacy operated in opposition to one another. In this guise, these two modes of communication became important symbols that were mobilised in the political disputes between a particular chiefdom and the surrounding white world. Put another way, it can be said that the idea of writing or speech can be surrounded by symbols and images which in turn can be used to defend, rationalise or inform other areas of life. These technologies provide metaphorical 'banks' of images through which both historical life and political life are conceptualised.

At this symbolic level, the notion of literacy and orality often influenced political thinking and the action that people took on behalf of those ideas. In relation to Valtyn specifically, this process is perhaps most apparent in the successive attempts made by the Native Affairs Department to control rural communities. As Chapter 3 has shown, these schemes aimed to penetrate ever more deeply into the chiefdom by imposing a rigid, surveyed, mapped and documented order that would reach into the heart of every household. Informing much of this political thinking was a cluster of notions about order, control and documentation that were symbolically connected to notions of literacy. One side effect of these repressive initiatives was an attack on some of the central institutions that upheld the reproduction of oral literary forms.

So much for the first horizon shaping this book. What of the other two: the present-day context in which narration occurs and the conventions and craft enabling such narration? Here again, I have tried to accommodate a simultaneously broad and narrow approach that considers both the details of a particular craft and its wider context. Holding these two poles in view at the same time requires the consideration of a complex range of factors which Landeg White in speaking of oral poetry has set out as follows:

> Ideally, in interpreting oral performance, one would wish to pay the closest possible attention to the actual meaning of the poems, supported by oral testimony of their significance to the people who performed or listened to them, and supplemented by investigation into the social position of the performers, into the conventions of the forms they are using, into the context and contingencies of the performances, and into the place of such poetry in the oral literature and general culture of the region as a whole.[6]

Within the confines that a study of this kind imposes, I have attempted to address these issues. The most concentrated point of focus has been oral historical narrative, and in relation to this genre I have attempted to outline the meaning of particular texts both in terms of their internal conventions and in relation to the shifting historiography – both inside and outside the chiefdom – of the events they depict. In addition, the social position of these tellers as men of royal standing has been examined, while the way in which this genre of storytelling is viewed and evaluated has been analysed on the basis of comments made by those acquainted with historical storytelling.

As regards the placing of this one genre in a wider literary 'canon', this task has been attempted in two ways. First, the area of storytelling has been approached in terms of gender, a category that exercises a powerful ordering force in the definition, interpretation and reception of storytelling genres. Secondly, the business of male historical storytelling has been situated along a continuum of genres that were, at one stage, performed in the male courtyards of the chiefdom. However, since the genres associated with this locale are on the cusp of descending into a passive tradition, it has not been possible to probe the 'context and contingencies of the performances' in any detail. Similarly, the role of the 'oral literature and general culture of the region' have not been considered, largely because existing research on oral forms in the Northern Transvaal is limited. Hence any broader regional assessments are not possible at this stage.

This, then, in broad outline, is how the three major conceptual boundaries of this study have been explored. But to have a more complete picture one not only requires a description of the horizons, one also needs to know how they intersect, or, at least, what relation they bear to each other. With regard to the three horizons of this study, the question then arises as to how processes of historical change have registered themselves in the area of craft, convention and the present-day context of telling. Or, put another way, at what point do these three concerns intersect?

One such point of intersection arises from a major theme in this book, namely the political impact of literate institutions on rural societies. As much of this book has attempted to argue, it is not literacy *per se* that transforms oral forms. Indeed, with the exception of two of my informants, all were literate and had gained at least a primary-level education. The acquisition of literacy itself did not fundamentally affect a knowledge and commitment to certain oral performance styles. Instead, what affected those styles most drastically was the political intervention of literate institutions. Whether it be church, state or school, these institutions operated from a set of symbolic assumptions that surrounded the idea of literacy. The search to implement these ideas shaped the nature of both mission and colonial intervention in rural Transvaal societies.

It is this idea of the political 'embeddedness' of literacy that had been used to align the first horizon of this study with the second two, namely the present-day context in which narration occurs and the conventions and craft enabling such narration. With regard to the present-day context of performance, its changing fate has been traced out by following the ever-increasing state intervention in rural societies. As we have seen, this process culminated in the rearrangement of the internal geographies of Transvaal communities. As a result of this forcible reordering, the male courtyards and the historical storytelling they had hosted largely disappeared.

What, however, of convention and craft? How have these responded to changing political circumstances? These questions are infinitely more complex, and without recordings of stories over an extended stretch of time it is difficult to answer in any direct way. This book cannot pretend to have formulated any comprehensive answers. Instead, it has attempted to point to the complex range of forces and institutions that, in one place, have had a bearing on forms of oral storytelling. These institutions have been schooling, the enclosure and fencing of the chiefdom and direct state intervention. These forces often weighed heavily on the nodes at which the production of oral narrative occurred and often deformed existing styles of performance and convention of narration by tampering with the spaces of storytelling.

Nevertheless, the influence of schooling was not uniformly destructive and by introducing written texts, for example, formal education did promote new styles of storytelling. Similarly, the introduction of a literate religion could reinforce existing performance styles while encouraging the emergence of new ones. The overall impact, then, of these agencies of colonialism on oral performance was ambiguous.

At the same time, these changes also registered on a chiefdom with pre-existing divisions and tensions. Many of these stratifications, particularly those of age and gender, flared up under the impact of colonial penetration and these social tensions also influenced oral performance styles. In this regard, one minor theme of this study has been migrancy, initially a response of younger men to existing forms of generational control by going elsewhere to accumulate resources. Their movement in turn introduced new cultural resources and performance styles, while the social tensions generated around migrancy have 'imprinted' themselves on the historical record of the chiefdom, as the narrative of Madimetša Kekana shows.

This interaction of struggles – both within and without a society – and oral literature is vital to any assessment of how historical change affects oral forms. In the Transvaal countryside in particular, where conflict has been so marked, any consideration of oral performance genres needs to be located against this broader political background.

In using these various horizons as shaping frontiers, one is, of course, required to accommodate and integrate a dauntingly large number of considerations. However, if one wishes to do any scholarly justice to oral literature, then all these points have to be visited, a process that makes the analysis of oral forms unavoidably interdisciplinary. Or, as Karin Barber phrases the issue:

> There is an obvious and very good reason for taking an interdisciplinary approach to African oral texts, and that is that the text[s] themselves can combine 'literature', 'history', 'music', 'medicine', 'religion' and other things. The unity of these fields within oral texts suggest that the method of interpretation should also be unified. Rather than a collaboration between specialists from different disciplines, what is needed is the reintegration of an artificially divided field. A unified approach need not be seen, however, as a special measure for dealing with the special case of 'oral' or 'traditional' culture. There has been a strong move in the humanities in Europe and America to break down disciplinary barriers and to study culture and culture-production – of a given society at a given period – as a single complex phenomenon.[7]

Like much other work in the field of cultural studies, this book has tried to understand cultural production as a 'single complex phenomenon'. As such, this text has positioned itself in the marketplace of social history, the zone where the purveyors of various disciplines meet in an attempt to grasp the multi-dimensionality of cultural processes. In making one's way through this terrain, one has always to navigate between two poles: that of intellectual practice and that of political power. Feierman in his study *Peasant Intellectuals* phrases the issue as follows:

> It is profitable, in exploring the web of discourse and power, to ask about the social position and tacit knowledge of the intellectuals who create or transmit a particular form of discourse, and then to understand that discourse within the full context of their interests and their life situations. To view the social position of the intellectuals within the larger society and

in relation to production and power, to understand their discursive practice within this context, is a satisfying and potentially rigorous way of understanding power/knowledge.[8]

In trying to chart the intersections of intellectual production and political power, this book has generally listed toward the former. This proclivity can partly be explained by the lack of attention that intellectual issues have attracted in the field of Southern African studies. One reason for this situation has been the difficulty of coming to terms with intellectual production in precolonial society. Tracing the intellectual influence of church, school and formal political organisation is, of course, relatively straightforward because the sources are plentiful and accessible. Trying to grasp how these ideas mesh with pre-existing indigenous intellectual traditions has been much harder and here, less studied.

If this book has anything to contribute to the area of Southern African studies, then it lies in this area of examining intellectual traditions. The analysis presented here suggests that there are two major analytical points of entry into the topic. The first concerns the manifold institutions and forums in which intellectual activity occurs. The second relates to literary convention, most notably narrative, the form in which much pre-colonial intellectual dicourse is encoded. As regards the institutional determinants of intellectual activity, this book has tried to outline a number of factors – such as household, gender and place – that have played a part in defining the cultural and intellectual activity of men and women in a particular community. This analysis has in general striven to highlight the social relations that control texts and audiences.

As regards literary form, this book has sought to demonstrate that it is primarily through attention to questions of narrative structure that aspects of intellectual tradition can best be accessed. In addition, this book has tried to emphasise that literary form in general and narrative in particular have cognitive content and that it is only careful attention to the literary encoding of ideas that will reveal their substance. This point would, of course, be self-evident to anyone with even a passing interest in the philosophy of history, contemporary literary theory or any other scholarly tradition which demonstrates that the intellectual and analytical content of texts is inseparable from the literary form in which they are cast. However, this point is often lost on much Southern African studies which has generally bypassed debates on the constitutive nature of language and linguistic convention. Instead, most scholars working in Southern African studies have tended to favour a view of language and discourse as transparent. There are, of course, a number of exceptions to this, most notably the Comaroffs. Also, a growing number of South African literary critics have pointed to the blindspots of Southern African studies and the ways in which it could benefit from literary wisdom. However, few literary scholars have actually tried to take their own advice by looking at historical material with a literary eye.[9] Instead, their application of these ideas has been narrow and has largely focused on a canonical range of literary texts. For those interested in both questions of discourse and historical change, these literary critics have relatively little to offer.

Overall, then, one confronts a situation where questions of text and context cannot be satisfactorily aligned. On the one hand, one has a body of historical and sociological research which, in attempting to defuse the power of racially based or ethnic explanations of South African society, has with good reason sought more materially based interpretations of inequality and apartheid. One result of this approach is that the traces of economic determinism are always present. To have a detailed concern for words and their impact in the world in this climate is often difficult since one is seen to be speaking of issues which are far removed from, and so apparently irrelevant to, the major forces that shape people's lives. When one moves to those whose business it is to interpret texts and words, one encounters a tradition of literary studies that has kept its eyes closely focused on the written page.

One way out of this impasse is an involvement with oral literature whose qualities constantly force one to reassess both these positions. With regard to the fraternity of historians, even a slight acquaintance with oral literature in a field-work situation reminds one of the respect with which many rural communities view words as a form of eloquence and power. Such an encounter compels one to reconnect intellectually with the ordering force of language in society. Furthermore, as this study has tried to show, much popular understanding and analysis is embedded in narrative which encodes political ideas and historical thinking in particularly effective ways. Anyone wishing to come to terms with popular consciousness and the role it plays in political behaviour would do well to pay close attention to words and stories, granting them an independence that is not inevitably yoked to a material base.

With regard to the text-centred literary status quo in South Africa, any involvement with oral literature quite literally forces scholars to lift their eyes from the page. Such involvement also compels us to leave our libraries and make journeys to meet informants, to speak to them, to hear their stories and to try to understand something of the world in which they live. In so doing, one not only has to confront context as a very material reality, one also confronts anew the complex links that unite producer, text, audience and the world in which they exist. At a time when an astonishing and often seductive array of reborn literary formalisms continue to constrain us to bury our heads in the text, this insight remains fundamental.

APPENDICES

Appendix 1: Extracts from Reading Books

Part A: Dinonwane from Padišo B

The word *nonwane* has been rendered here as 'folktale' since it is clearly in this spirit that the missionaries intended these renditions.

Mpša le Phiri

Nonwane e re: Kgalekgale phiri le mpša di be di kwana di ratana gagolo. Mosegare le bošego di be di tsomišana diphoofolo; di di be di robala felo gotee. Fela, phiri ya thoma go ba le megaburu; ge e bolaile ya ja e nnoši, ya tima mpša. Mpša ya ba ya tenwa ke bojato bja phiri.

Bošego bjo bongwe ge di tsoma, tša tla bodibeng e le ngweding. Mpša ge e okamela, ya bona ngwedi a bonala mo meetseng; ya fora phiri ya re: "Monna! Makhura šia mo bodibeng."

Phiri, ka gobane ke selo sa tlala e kgolo, le gona ke setlatla, ya kgolwa se mpša e se bolelago; ya tabogela bodibeng, ya thinya, ya hwetša go le laraga fela. Mpša yona e be e šetše mo ntle e tšhologa letshego.

Ya ba gona phiri e lemogago bofora bja mpša. Mpša yona šilee! E lotobetše le mmoto, e a tšhaba. Go thoma fao phiri le mpša ga di sa kwana.

> Anthe kwano e senyega ka megabaro.
> Leratano ga le kwane le dikwero.
> Le rena batho re tsebe tšeo. (*Padišo B*, 33-4)

The Dog and the Wolf

The story says: Long, long ago the wolf and the dog were on good terms and loved each other very much. Day and night they hunted other animals together, and they slept

182

together at the same place. However, the wolf started to be avaricious; when it killed it ate alone, not sharing the food or leaving some for the dog. Eventually the dog could no longer tolerate the wolf's greed.

One night when they were hunting, they arrived at a pond and the moon was shining. Then the dog looked down in the pond, saw the reflection of the moon in the water; and then lied to the wolf: "Man! There is some fat in this pond."

The wolf, because it is an ever-hungry animal, and also because of its stupidity, believed what the dog said; it dived into the pond, plunged deep down only to find mud. In the mean time the dog was standing out there, dripping with laughter.

The wolf started to realise how shrewd the dog was. There goes the dog! It is going up the hill, running away. Thenceforth the wolf and the dog were on bad terms.

After all, good relationships are ruined by greed.
Love and sarcasm do not go together.
We people should also know that.

Kgomo le Segwegwe

Ka tšatši le lengwe ge kgomo e fula khwiting ya noka, ya bonwa ke segwegwe. Sona ge se bona bonyenyane bja sona, sa duma bogolo bja kgomo. Sa khupela moya ka teng, sa buduloga; sa botšiša kgomo sa re: "A ga ke lekane nago?" – Kgomo ya se lebelela ya re: "Lesa tšeo; o tla segwa ke batho."

Segwegwe sa boela gape sa buduloga sa tiiša; sa botšiša gape sa re: "Bjalo gomme ke yo mokakang?" – Kgomo ya se lebelela ya retologa ya tloga e re: "Segwegwe sela se se botsana bjalo se itshentše; bjalo se swana le kgorokgoro."

Bjalo segwegwe sa tlalwa ke pelo, sa buduloga ka matlamatla gore se tle se lekane ke kgomo; me sa re se sa budulogile sa palega, sa hwela gona fao.

Nonwane ye e re rutang? E re motho a se ke a ikgogomoša. Ge a ikgodiša o tla segwa ke ba bangwe. Wa go ikgantšha o senya bothakga bjo bo lego mo go yena.

Gomme moikgogomoši ga a ipone. Bogolo bjo a bo kganyogago a ka se ke a bo fihlela; o tla ba a hwa a nyatšegile. O a ikgodišago o tla kokobetšwa. (*Padišo B*, 34-6)

The Cow and the Frog

One day when the cow was grazing on the banks of the river, it was seen by a frog. When it realised how small it was by comparison, it envied the great size of the cow. It sucked more air into itself and expanded; it asked the cow: "Am I not as big as you are?" – The cow looked at it and said: "Just stop doing that, for people will laugh at you."

The frog repeated the same thing and expanded, and once again it asked: "Now how big am I?" – The cow gave it a glance, turned around and said as it left: "That beautiful frog has ruined itself; it looks monstrous."

The frog became fed up, it inhaled more air so as to expand and become as big as a cow; however, in the process of expanding, it exploded and died just there.

What does this folktale teach us? It says that a person should not be vain. When you exalt yourself, others will laugh at you. He who is boastful often ruins the beauty that is within him.

Moreover, a person with vanity is never aware of this himself. He will never reach the greatness that he yearns for; he will ultimately die with a bad reputation. He who exalts himself will be laid low.

Tšhweni le Nkwe

Ba re: Kgalekgale nkwe le tšhweni di be di sa hloyane ka mokgwa wo wa mehla yeno. Di be di gwerane di bile di etelana. Tšhweni ge e tla go nkwe ya e hwetša e patlame gabotse segoleng sa yona, go fsietšwe, go kgopilwe mo go fela. Tša dula lapeng la nkwe di thabile la ba la dikela; tšhweni ya tseba go boela gae.

Mohla nkwe e tlago go hlola tšhweni, tšhweni e akgofe e etšwe lapeng la yona ka bjako; gomme di gahlane ka ntle ga lewá, di thabišane gona. Kwa segoleng sa tšhweni nkwe e be e sa go tsebe.

Ka tšatši le lengwe la pula nkwe ya tšhabela lapeng la tšhweni. Tšhweni ka go tšhaba go koloba ya se ke ya tšwa ya e kgahlanetša. Nkwe ya tsena ka ngwakong wa tšhweni. Gomme mohla woo tšhweni e llwe ke dihlong, gobane lapa la yona ga le fsielwe; me go be go se na botsenyo bja nko ka baka la mefsia e mebe, go nkga go re šang. Le bana ba tšhweni ba be ba sa hlapišwe, ba tletše ditšhila tša matšatši a mantši. Mehlamo ya hlokega; nkwe ya selekwa me ya nyama ya re: "Anthe ke tšona ditšhila tše tšhweni e bego e di uta; lehono ke e lemogile."

Gomme ge nkwe e laela e tloga, tšhweni ya re: "Thaká; fela o se ke wa hlwa o nketela puleng; o tle ge go khudile." – Nkwe ya re: "Aowa! Ga ke sa boa; ke be ke sa tsebe ge o le wa ditšhila." Go tloga moo ya ba ntwa; le bjale ga di sa kwana.

Le go rena batho ba re nyakago kwano go bjalo. Ge o lemogile gore motho ke wa ditšhila, gona ga o sa tlo mo rata. (*Padišo B*, 38-9)

The Baboon and the Leopard

It is said: Long, long ago the leopard and the baboon did not hate each other as they do today. They were friends and often paid each other visits. When the baboon visited the leopard, he found him lying in his lair which was well swept and well painted. They stayed at the leopard's resting place until sunset; and then the baboon returned home.

When it was the leopard's turn to visit the baboon, the baboon would rush out of his cave immediately so that they could meet outside the cave, and entertain each other there. The leopard did not know the baboon's hiding place.

One rainy day the leopard took refuge at the baboon's place. Because the baboon was scared of getting wet, he did not rush out to meet the leopard. The leopard entered the baboon's hut. Well, that day the baboon was shy because his hut was never swept; and one's nose could not stand the unpleasant odours in that cave. Even the baboon's children were never bathed, and they remained dirty for many days. That day the two did not even chat; and the leopard was outraged as well as disappointed, and he said, "Is this really the filth that the baboon has been hiding all along? Only today I now realise this."

And when the leopard was just about to leave, the baboon said, "My friend, you should not visit me when it is raining; come when it has stopped." – The leopard said, "No! I'm not coming back any more; I did not know that you are the filthy type." From there onwards, it was war; even today they do not like each other.

Even to people who want co-operation and understanding, it is just like that. If you find out that people are filthy, you no longer like them.

Part B: Example of a Quasi-Historical Story from Padišo III

Masasara

Masasara ké monna yo ba xabô ba bexo ba mmeile mohlapetši; a ba mohlodi wa bôná wa xo dula thabaneng à hlapetša, ka xobane xo be xo na le manaba a bexo a e-tla a thopa dikxomo, a bolaya batho, a fiša metse.

Masasara a dula, à hlapetša à ituletše à nnoši thabeng. A re xe a bôna mebotong ya kua kxolê xò bônala se se mo rônaxo, a lebeleša. Xe a bôna marola è le a mehlape e yaxo mafulong le badiša, a tseba xe xo se molato; le seši a bôna xe e le sa naxa xe e e-fsa, le xe e le mokubêxô wa masolo, a tseba a ikhomolêla.

Mahlô a Masasara, ka xobane a be a bôna bo-ka a lenong, a tseba marole xe e le a mehlape ye e thopiwaxo; le meuši a tseba xe e e le ya manaba a a fišaxo metse ya batho è sa le kua kxole-kxolê.

Moo a kxanyêla xo ba xabô, a êma lefsikeng le le okametšexo motse, a xoêlêla a re: "Manaba! Thšabang!"

Batho ba napa ba thšabêla dithabeng; dikxomo ba di nametša dihlabeng. Manaba xe a fihla, a hwetša xò se motho le o tee, xò se kxomo ye e šetšexo mo xaê le xe le mebotong le mexwaneng.

Masasara e fêla a phediša ba xabô ka mokwa woo, mokxoši wa xaxwe bà fêla ba o kwa bà mo holofetše. Ba phela, xo se bolawe motho, xo se thopiwe kxomo. Xomme manaba ao a bonwexo ke Masasara, ba bantši ba se kê ba bá ba a bôna.

Ka mohla o mongwê xe ba boile dithabeng, le Masasara à boetše seokamong sa xaxwe, banna ba bangwê ba motse woo ba re: "Masasara ó a re fora. Manaba ao, rena xa se ra bá ra a bôna ka mahlô. Mohla a tl'o xo hlaba xapê mokxoši wa xaxwe, re tlo itulêla fá motseng. Re itapišetša'ng ka methšabô rè ipolaiša merotoxa?"

Ka la ka moswana ba bôna Masasara à eme lefsikeng, ba mo kwa xe a re: "Manaba! Thšabang!"

Ba bangwê ba thšaba. Ba bantši ba itulêla motseng. Ba thšoxa manaba à tsene, à ba bolaya, à tloxa le dikxomo. Mohla woo xe ba fêla, ba ithsôla ba re: "Anthe Masasara ó be a rerеša!"

Taba yé e a ruta.

Mohlapetši wa rena ké Lentšu la Modimo. Le re sêbêla manaba a a bolayaxo mmele le môya.

Ba ba le holofetšexo, ba a le kwa ba pholoxa.

A re se nyatše bahlapetši motseng ba re ba beilwexo.

Ba ba bolailwexo, ba senyêxa bà ituletše, bà nyatša mokxoši wa mohlapetši, ké ba bantši ba ba xobaditšexo, le ba ba bolailwexo, le ba thopetšwexo tše ba bexo ba na natšo'. (Padišo III, 24-6)

Masasara

Masasara was a man who had been appointed by his people as a watchman; the man who stayed at the mountain and guarded against invaders, because at the time there were enemies who looted cattle, killed people and burnt down their huts.

Masasara then stayed there alone at the mountain as a watchman. He would look very carefully when he saw anything suspicious far away. When he saw the dust caused by the cattle that were going to the pastures with the herders, he knew that there was no problem; he could also recognise if the fire was just a veld-fire or not, or if it was the dust caused by the local regiments, he would know and just keep quiet.

Because Masasara's eyes could see just like those of the eagle, he could distinguish between dust caused by the herds that were being confiscated and the smoke of fire caused by the enemies who were burning other people's huts far away.

Then he would make the people of his homestead aware by standing on top of the large rock above the homestead and he would scream: "Enemies! Run away!"

People would then take refuge in the mountains; and they would take their cattle along to the top of the mountain. When the enemies arrived, they would not find even a single person, nor a stray cow in the hills or in the veld.

Masasara continued to protect his people in this way while they, in return, took heed of his warning and took it seriously. They survived, and nobody was killed, and not even a cow was confiscated. And most of his people never even saw the enemies which Masasara had seen.

One day when the people had returned from the mountains, and Masasara had gone to his watchtower, some men from his homestead said: "Masasara is deceitful. We have never seen those enemies he is talking about. Next time he screams that we should run away, we are just going to stay in the homestead. Why should we bother running away and expend such great effort climbing the hills?"

The following day they saw Masasara standing on top of the rock, and they heard him say: "Enemies! Run away!"

Some fled. But the majority just stayed in the homestead. They panicked when the enemy invaded, killing them and leaving with the cattle. That day they were defeated and they repented, saying: "So Masasara was talking the truth indeed!"

This story teaches us a lesson.

Our watchman is the word of God. It whispers into our ears about the enemies who kill the body and the soul.

Those who believe in it listen to it and they are redeemed.

Let us not underestimate the watchman whom we have appointed.

Those who were killed perished because they stayed where they were, having disparaged the watchman's warnings. There were many who were wounded, and those who were killed, let alone those whose valuables were confiscated.

Appendix 2: Extract from Interview with Molalakgori Kekana

Like all the appendices that follow, this one has two parts. The first gives the full transcript of the section of the interview from which the narrative of Molalakgori Kekana, analysed in Chapter 6, was taken. The second part is a translation of this transcript. The interview with Molalakgori Kekana was originally conducted in Sesotho. The following two appendices are extracts from interviews in which Madimetša Kekana spoke predominantly in Sindebele but, as is customary in the area, Sesotho is used from time to time. The final extract in Appendix 5 is in Sesotho. In the case of the first three appendices these transcriptions and translations were done by Peter Lekgoathi. The last interview was transcribed and translated by Charles Makgoba. Since the Sindebele used in the two middle interviews is a dialect that has not been written down, there is no orthographical clarity on which conventions should prevail. As a result Peter Lekgoathi, a speaker of the dialect, has had to make his own choices.

The conventions used in these appendices are the same as those used in the body of the text. For details, the reader is referred to the Preface and Note on the Text.

In order to facilitate cross-referencing between the transcript of the original interviews and the translations, they are placed on facing pages.

Part A: Sesotho

MK = Molalakgori Kekana
FM = Felix Malunga
SM = Sidney Maaka
IH = Isabel Hofmeyr

Date: 10 August 1988

MK: *All right* Maburu a———a ba a a mo thopile Mok- wo Mokopane ba tsamaya
      ba ya le yena kwa.

FM: Mm.

MK: Ntwa yona ya no lwa e ntše e elwa bjale go fihlella e be e tle ba bolayane
      le boPotgieter e e lwa bjalo- a go ne taba.

FM: Mm.

MK: *Well* ge, ge ešetše ntwa e fedile———

FM: Mm.

MK: ———dintwa di fedile.

FM: Mm.

MK: Bjatše M– yena mokgalabje Setšwamadi, a hwile———

FM: Mm.

MK: ———a laetša ngwanagagwe, ngwanabo———

FM: Mokopane.

MK: Mokop– ngwan– ngwanabo Matsebe papago Mokopane.

FM: Ee.

MK: Wo a rilego go hwa Mokopane a ke re bjatše Maburu a mo tšere e sa le
      mošemanyana, wa bo———*eleven or twelve years.*

FM: Mm.

MK: Bjale a laetša rangwana, rangwane'a Mokopane set– ntogatse Makute.

FM: Makute?

MK: Wo ke———Setšwamadi a rile go hwa, a tšeya setulo.

FM: Ee.

MK: *Ja*, a tšeya setulo. Bjale a be mokgalabje a mmoditše a re, "Wa nkwa, ge o
      bona gore———a ke re Maburu a thopile ngwana wola eh? Ge o bona gore
      dithaka tša gagwe tše di leng mo gae di godile di fihlile bogo– eh
      bogolong boo re ka———ba ka———ba ka išwa komeng, ba yo wetšwa, ke go
      k- ngwanaka o nyakišiše o———ngwanagago———ngwana———yena
      Mokopane, o mo nyakišiše. Ge o ka mo humana a sa phela, o mo dire
      gore o be o tle o mo———o tlo o mo fe bogoši bjo, a buše."

Part B: English translation

MK = Molalakgori Kekana
FM = Felix Malunga
SM = Sidney Maaka
IH = Isabel Hofmeyr

Date: 10 August 1988

MK: All right, these Boers———have now kidnapped Mok— this Mokopane and took him away with them.

FM: Mm.

MK: The battle still continued in the same pattern until they killed the Potgieters like that— no problem.

FM: Mm.

MK: Well now after the battle was over———

FM: Mm.

MK: ———the battles were over.

FM: Mm.

MK: Now M— the old man Setšwamadi, after his death———

FM: Mm.

MK: ———he had told his younger brother about his son——— [that is, the younger brother's son]

FM: Mokopane.

MK: Mokop— his bro— his brother Matsebe, Mokopane's father.

FM: Yes.

MK: After his father had died and Mokopane had already been kidnapped by the Boers while still a boy of about———eleven or twelve years.

FM: Mm.

MK: Now he [Setšwamadi] had told his uncle, Mokopane's uncle———the so-called Makute.

FM: Makute?

MK: The one———who took the throne after Setšwamadi's death

FM: Yes.

MK: Yes, he took over the chieftainship. Now the old man had already told him that, "Listen, when you see———you know the Boers have kidnapped that boy, not so? When you see that his peers here at home are fully matured, they can———er——— they can be taken to circumcision school, to be initiated, my son, I ask you———you should look for your son———this Mokopane, you should look about for him. If you still find him alive, bring him back and———give him his chieftainship, so that he can rule."

Bjale mošeman– yena rangwanagagwe Makute a kwišiša lentšu la papagwe. Ka paale ge a– mola Mokopane a le mo le Maburu, aowa yena ntše le yena a tshwere bogoši mo papagwe a hwile a tshwere bogoši, kwa le yena Mokopane o a gola.

E rile ge a bona gore bjatše ba- bankane ba gagwe ba godile bjatše ba ka ya komeng, o biditše bakgomana a re, "Banna, nke, a le gopole ngwana yola ka gore gona bjatše bankane ba gagwe le a ba bona ba godile, ke ba––ke ba ba ka išwa komeng?"

Banna ba re, "Aowa ke nnete."

Ke ge napile ba bitšana ba re, "A go bitšwe dingaka."

FM: Ke gore tš– a ke le tsene ganong. Eh, ke gore eh, ke gore a ke re taba tše ke tša ka morago ga ntwa?

MK: *Ja.*

FM: Le ka morago ga lehu la Setšwamadi?

MK: *Ja.*

FM: Eh bjale a nkere go be go rena khutšo bjale a nkere?

MK: *Ja.*

FM: Go be go se sa lwewa *nie.*

MK: Ee.

FM: Eh.

MK: Gape–––gape o tsebe gore taba ye ya ntwa ye–––

FM: Ee–––

MK: –––e be e ema, go re tuu!

FM: *Ja. Oh–––no.*

MK: Ka sebaka e thome!

FM: *Right.* E reng ke mo hlalosetše go fihla mo re fihlileng gona.

MK: *Ja.*

FM: Nka tla ka lebala tše dingwe. *He says after the war–––no, which time and again erupted or–––*

IH: Uhu.

FM: *Eh, he says after the death of, eh–––*

SM: Setšwamadi.

FM: *Setšwamadi, eh, the old man had given word to his other son known as Makute.*

SM: Makute.

FM: Makute.

MK: Ke gore sekolo se sa– sa Sekgakgapeng se theeletšwe yena kgoši yeo.

FM: *Oh, Makute, his other son, said that, "After my death, eh, you will take over for the time being. But never forget that you must search for my son and bring him back so that he should take over the chieftainship."*

SM: Morena.

Now the boy's uncle, Makute, understood his father's [that is, the chief's] *word. Indeed, when Mokopane was there with the Boers, he* [Makute] *continued as a regent while Mokopane was growing up.*

When he saw that Mokopane's peers are fully matured and they could be initiated, he called the gentlemen and said, "Gentlemen, now that you see that the peers of that boy are matured and they can be circumcised don't you remember that boy?"

The gentlemen said,"Well, it's true."

Then they called each other and said, "Let the traditional doctors be called for."

FM: *In fact, eh, let me just interrupt you. Eh, basically all this happened after the battle?*

MK: Yes.

FM: *And also after Setšwamadi's death?*

MK: Yes.

FM: *Eh now peace was reigning now, isn't it?*

MK: Yes.

FM: *There were no longer clashes.*

MK: *Yes.*

FM: Eh.

MK: *By the way———you should know that this issue of battle———*

FM: *Yes———*

MK: *———would stop, and it would be quiet!*

FM: Yes. Oh———no.

MK: *Suddenly it would start!*

FM: Right. *Let me explain to her up to where we have reached.*

MK: Yes.

FK: *Otherwise I may forget things.* He says after the war———no, which time and again erupted or———

IH: Uhu.

FM: Eh, he says after the death of, eh———

SM: Setšwamadi.

FM: Setšwamadi, eh, the old man had given word to his other son known as Makute.

SM: Makute.

FM: Makute.

MK: *In fact this school in Sekgakgapeng is named after that chief.*

FM: Oh, Makute, his other son, said that, "After my death, eh, you will take over for the time being. But never forget that you must search for my son and bring him back so that he should take over the chieftainship."

SM: *Yes sir.* [With this phrase of agreement, speaker encourages informant.]

FM: *Now he says this, eh, son of Setšwamadi remained faithful to the word and promise he had given to his father. That as the young ones, eh, who were of the same age as Mokopane, as they were growing up into, eh, young, fit fellows, and they were ready to be taken to the initiation school——*

IH: Uhu.

FM: *——he called his elder- elders and said, "By the way, before his death the chief indicated that when the time comes, you must go out and look for Mokopane and bring him back so that he joins his contemporaries at the initiation school. And thereafter he should come back and take his rightful place with the people."*

MK: Bjale ba dumela banna ba bitša mangaka. Ba re nke le re bontšheng mangaka gore ge——ge go le bjale ka serena, ma- ditsela re di bontšhwa ke lena mangaka. E rile ge ba re mangaka ba re ka marapo ba re, "Aowa, o gona o a phela o ka mo thoko ye. Le gona, ge re lebeletša, lentšu le tla tle——le tla hlakana le lona le ka se sobele, lentšu le tla hlakana le lona. Mokgoši o tla lla gona mo. Le tla o kwa mokgoši, mara ka thoko ye."

      Ke ge a ntšha banna ba bararo kgoši a eya gona kwa. A ke re wa bona?

FM: Mm.

MK: Bjale ge ba fihla kwa——

FM: Kana o be a le mo kae?

MK: Eše?

FM: O be a le mo kae? Ke gona kwa Mi- Middelfon-

MK: Mo, ja.

FM: Eh.

MK: Ja, ke ge go feta beke ba re ke kogo——gona mouwe ke ge ba re *somewhere* bo Pienaarsrivier kwa.

FM: Oho.

MK: Yena Mokopane ba re o be a le thokonyana tša bo Pienaarsrivier tšela.

FM: Mm.

MK: Bjale, ge ba fihla gona mouwe, ba fihla go kgoši——ke ra ba fihla mo tulong ye nngwe ya Ma- ya Bakgatla gona mola, ba re ke gaMakau.

FM: Ja——ke a go bona.

MK: Ja. Bjale ba gaMakau ba be ba tsebana le ba bagešo ba.

FM: Mm.

MK: A ke re wa bona?

FM: Mm.

MK: Ja. Bjale ge ba fihla go bona, ba re——ba lotšha.

      Aowa ba ba iša kgotleng ba dira——ba dumela ba re, "Re lotšha bjatše re a nyaka. Bjatše re re re nyakišeng." Ngwana' rena e sale a thopiwa ke Maburu ka dintwa." Ba re, "Dulang fase. Ja! Re šetše re di jela man!"

FM: E re ke——

FM: Now he says this, eh, son of Setšwamadi remained faithful to the word and promise he had given to his father. That as the young ones, eh, who were of the same age as Mokopane, as they were growing up into, eh, young, fit fellows, and they were ready to be taken to the initiation school———

IH: Uhu.

FM: ———he called his elder– elders and said, "By the way, before his death the chief indicated that when the time comes, you must go out and look for Mokopane and bring him back so that he joins his contemporaries at the initiation school. And thereafter he should come back and take his rightful place with the people."

MK: *Now the elders agreed and the doctors were summoned. They ask them to show them the way, because under such circumstances ways are indicated by doctors. When the doctors threw their bones down, they said, "No he is still alive and well, he is in this direction. And also, the word will———meet you on the way, you won't penetrate very deep in before the word meets you, but in this direction."*

The chief then appointed three men and they went there. You see?

FM: Mm.

MK: *Now when they arrive there———*

FM: *By the way where was he?*

MK: *I beg your pardon?*

FM: *Where was he? Was he there at Mi– Middelfon–*

MK: *There, yes.*

FM: Eh.

MK: Yes, *a week passed on their way there———*somewhere *at Pienaarsrivier.*

FM: Oho.

MK: *They say Mokopane was somewhere at Pienaarsrivier there.*

FM: Mm.

MK: *Now, when they arrived there, they went to the chief———I mean they arrived at the area of the Ma– the Bagkatla people there, called Makau.*

FM: Yes———*I see the place.*

MK: Yes. *Now the Makau people were acquainted with our people.*

FM: Mm.

MK: *You see now?*

FM: Mm.

MK: Yes. *Now when they arrived, they said———they greeted each other.*

Well, they were taken to the council———and they said, "We greet you and at the same time we are searching. Now we–we–we are asking you to help us search. Our child was last kidnapped by the Boers during the time of wars." They said, "Sit down. Yes! We understand you already."

FM: *Let me———*

MK: *Ja.*

FM: ———ke ke mo fe tšona.

SM: Ee.

FM: Ke ra ka———le tla tla le laodiša tše dingwe.

MK: Ee.

FM: *Right, he says eh the, the, the, the caretaker chief, together with his elders, they then called the bone-throwers, to help them as the eyes of the tribe, to try and find out whether the young Mokopane was still alive or not.*

IH: Mm.

FM: *And when they threw down their things, their bones, they said, "No, he is alive and well. And in fact it would be easy for you to find him."*

     And therefore the caretaker chief sent out three people. And, eh, they, the doctors had given them the, the direction. And these people then took the direction of Pienaarsrivier where he was more or less around there, where he was being kept. But then in that area, we have the Bakgatla people, eh, who were staying at the place called Makau———Makau, that's right.

     So these three people who were sent by the caretaker chief arrived at this place and, eh, they said, "We've been sent by the Ndebele people, we're looking for the son of the chief."

     And those said, "In fact we've all along been wondering."

     And incidentally, the two tribes were friendly.

MK: Ja. Bjale ba re———"Re re tla———re tla robala e tla re ka bošego, ka nako ya ge di———" ka gore o be a diša dinku tša———tša Leburu leo———"e tla re ge dinku tšela di tšwele ka gore di ja mo mof- ka mo mohlakeng ka mo, re tla di lebelela. Ge e šetše di———di boetše ka mo a di dišitše kwa, re tla le botša ra tsamaya le lena le yo mmona."

     Bjale ka paale ka boše- ba letše ba robetše ka bošego bona ba *guard*, e re ka paale ka dinako ge a tšwela le dinku tšeo di eya ka mo moeding ka mo, ge di eya kwa, napa ba re, "Ja di wetše, kga re yeng." Ba, ba theoga ba ya. Ka paale ba fihla ba mo humana.

SM: Ba mo tseba.

MK: Ba mo tseba. Le yena e bile a bongwanabo o mongwe e ba tlile le yena o ba re———ba re———ba re nto ba re Lehlabapelo———ba a———ba mo tseba, bjale ge ba mo———fihla mo ba mo tseba, a ke re yena ga ba sa———ga a sa ba tseba? O, o tšerwe e sa le mošemanyana.

     Bjale ke a bona ge re ekwa polelo ye ba re o mongwe a re, "Banna, a re motshwareng."

     O mong, ba bangwe ba re, " Hei! O ka tshwara motho a le kaaka monna? O nyaka———o nyaka go tlo re bakela kotsi monna eye? A a a a! Gona ga o bone gore ke sena———ke———ke tau motho wo?"

MK: Yes.

FM: ———*transfer the words to her.*

SM: *Yes.*

FM: *I mean———you will explain other issues afterwards.*

MK: *Yes.*

FM: Right, he says eh the, the, the, the caretaker chief, together with his elders, they then called the bone-throwers, to help them as the eyes of the tribe, to try and find out whether the young Mokopane was still alive or not.

IH: Mm.

FM: And when they threw down their things, their bones, they said, "No, he is alive and well. And in fact it would be easy for you to find him."

And therefore the caretaker chief sent out three people. And, eh, they, the doctors had given them the, the direction. And these people then took the direction of Pienaarsrivier where he was more or less around there, where he was being kept. But then in that area, we have the Bakgatla people, eh, who were staying at the place called Makau———Makau, that's right.

So these three people who were sent by the caretaker chief arrived at this place and, eh, they said, "We've been sent by the Ndebele people, we're looking for the son of the chief."

And those said, "In fact we've all along been wondering."

And incidentally, the two tribes were friendly.

MK: Yes. *Now those ones said———"We will———we will sleep and in the morning, when it is time"———because he looked after———after the sheep of———of that Boer———"when the sheep appear because they graze here in these r– reeds here, we will look for them. When they———they have gone this side and he is looking after them, we will tell you and will go together with you to see him."*

Then indeed, tomorrow- actually they slept there that night and the following morning those ones went to guard, *and the sheep appeared at their regular time, going towards the valley, this side, on their way there, and then they said, "Yes, they have come down." They came down and went there. Indeed they found the boy.*

SM: *They recognised him*

MK: *They recognised him. One of the three men was his brother called——— Lehlabapele———they———hey knew him, now when they———arrived, they knew him, but he could not recognise them. He had been kidnapped while still a small boy.*

Now I think we understand through hearsay that one of the men said, "Chaps, let's catch him."

The other one, the others said, "Hey! How can you capture such a big man? You want———you want to cause us trouble ay? Ha, ha! After all can't you see that this guy is stro———he is———a lion this person?"

Ke ge ba re go yena a ke re Mokopane lebitšo la gagwe e be ba re ke Mantšhimodi?

Ge ba re go yena ba re, "Mantšhimodi! Mantšhimodi!", ga a sa le tseba ka gore o tlogile s– [laughs].

Ba bona gore––––nape ba re, "Kgareyeng banna re yo––––re ye go lekgowa re yo––––reo––––re yo––––re yo bontšhana le lona."

A re, "Aikhona, le ka se ke. Mm. Le yo bontšhana ke––––le––––le Maburu? Aikhona."

FM: Mm.

MK: O mongwe a re, "Ai nna ke a ya *man*."

MK: Nape a tloge a ye, ba le ba šale ba tšhaba.

FM: E re ke mo hlalošetšeng.

MK: *All right.*

FM: *Right. He says, eh, when the three people, eh, arrived at Makau–the Makau people, eh, the Makau people said, "Well, we know him. He's taking care of the sheep of a neighbouring white Boer. Eh, and eh, we always see him taking care of those sheep. So, wait, sleep, early in the morning we'll show you."*

So the following day indeed the young man came down herding sheep. And then they went to him. And then they identified him and they––––among the three there was the younger brother––––the younger brother to, eh, the young Mokopane. Eh––––

MK: A bone––––bona wo o– wo– a ko re––––kahle. Wa bona wo ke mmolelang wo ke re––––o––––o ntogatse, eh––––Lehlabapele.

FM: Lehlabapelo? Ee.

MK: E be e be e se ngwanabo Mokopane.

FM: Ee.

MK: E be e le papagwe, eh, ke ngwanabo papago Mokopane. Wa bona?

SM: *The uncle.*

FM: *Oh, I see, oh, he was the uncle, not, not the brother, eh, Lehlabapelo.*

SM: Lehlabapele.

FM: *Lehlabapele. Lehlabapele. Lehlabapele. He was the uncle to Mokopane. So he easily identified the young Mokopane. Then an argument ensued among the people who've been sent to come and collect Mokopane.*

Some said, "Let's grab him and take him over."

Others said, "No man. Can't you see this man is strongly built? You won't manage. Eh, the best is let's go and explain to the Boer that this person is actually the chief of the Ndebele people."

IH: Uhu.

FM: *Release him.*

MK: Bjale ba gana go ya eye?

O tee a tsamaya a re, "Nna ke a ya le ge a ka mpolaya go lokile."

Then they said to Mokopane–––isn't it his other name was Mantšhimodi?

When they said to him, "Mantšhimodi! Mantšhimodi!", he could not even recognise the name because he left while– [laughs].

They realised that–––they then said, "Let's go fellows–––let's go to the white man--and negotiate with him."

One said, "Impossible, you can't do that. Mm. You are going to–––to––– negotiate with a Boer. Impossible!"

FM: Mm.

MK: *One said, "I'm going then, guys."*

MK: *Then he left and went, and the others were left scared.*

FM: *Let me translate.*

MK: All right.

FM: Right. He says, eh, when the three people, eh, arrived at Makau–––the Makau people, eh, the Makau people said, "No, we know him. He's taking care of the sheep of a neighbouring white Boer. Eh, and eh, we always see him taking care of those sheep. So, wait, sleep, early in the morning we'll show you."

So the following day indeed the young man came down herding sheep. And then they went to him. And then they identified him and they––– among the three there was the younger brother–––the younger brother to, eh, the young Mokopane. Eh–––

MK: *You see–––see there–––Just wait. You see this one I'm talking about the–––so-called–––Lehlabapele.*

FM: Lehalabapelo? *Yes.*

MK: *He was not, he was not Mokopane's younger brother.*

FM: *Yes.*

MK: *He was his father, eh, he was Mokopane's father's younger brother.*

SM: The uncle.

FM: Oh, I see, oh, he was the uncle, not, not the brother, eh, Lehlabapelo.

SM: *Lehlabapele.*

FM: Lehlabapele. Lehlabapele. Lehlabapele. He was the uncle to Mokopane. So he easily identified the young Mokopane. Then an argument ensued amongst the people who've been sent to come and collect Mokopane.

Some said, "Let's grab him and take him over."

Others said, "No man. Can't you see this man is strongly built? You won't manage. Eh, the best is let's go and explain to the Boer that this person is actually the chief of the Ndebele people."

IH: Uhu.

FM: Release him.

MK: *Now they refused to go, you see?*

Only one went alone and said, "I shall go and even if he [the Boer] kills me it's fine."

A fihla a humana batho ba re———ba re go ne lephusmanyana ke le, a nape a ya go lona a re, a dumediša a fihla a re, "Banna, ke a nyaka. Ke nyaka———"

"O nyakang?"

"Ke nyaka motho e sa le a———a timela kgale ka dintwa a thopiwa ke makgowa. Bjale ke a nyaka ke re na e kaba o kae? Mara ke b– ke nyaka ke bile ke mmoni o ka mo fase ka mo, o dišitše dinku."

"Eya!"

"And motho wo ke kgoši. Ke yena a swanetšeng go ba kgoši kwa gae kwa."

"Eya!"

"Ee."

O botša lephusman le———eh lephusman le eya Leburung, le ya go tšeya———le mo iša Leburung. Go fihla ba tšeye ba ye go bontšha Leburu le mosadi a lona. Leburu le re go yena, "O tšwa kae?"

Eh le re, "Bjatše motho wo rena ga re mo tsebe wo. Wena kgane o mo tsebago o mmone kae gona mo?"

O re, "No, ke mo humane ka mo o dišitše dinku. Ke yena o a dišitšeng dinku ka mo———ka mo mohlakeng."

Wola o re, "O ra Klaas."

"Eya!"

"Ee."

O re, "O tšwela kae wena? O mo nyaka bjale o tšwela kae?"

O re, "Ke tšwela gaM– gaMakapan.

Ah! Leburu nape le tsena ka ntlong. La re tšeya sethunya. E rile ge le etšwa ka sona le tšeya koloi le re, mof– mosadi a re, "Hei, pa! Nee, nee, nee, nee. Nee, nee, nee, nee. Nee, nee, nee, nee. Nee, nee, nee, nee. U nga iyete leyo. O se ke wa ba wa e dira nto yeo. Monna, tlogela makhwela a banna ba geno, man. O ska, wa bona, wa kwa mo– mogatšaka. Tlogela makhwela a banna ba geno. Wena, o a a———a ke re o a bolela gore motho wo ke kgoši?"

A re, "Bjale? Wena o———o thibela lehumo le le swanetšeng go tsena ka ngwakong wa gago? Nyaka lehumo e tle lehumo le tsene ka mo man, ka gore ke kgoši!" Ka paale, monna a bowa a tšeya sethunya a se beya.

Ke ge a re, "Bjatše, o noši ge o le bjale?"

A re, "Aowa, ga ke noši."

"Ba bangwe ba kae?"

Wola a re, "Ba ka kwa fase go———go yena wola ka mo———ka———ka mo ka mo moeding ka kwa, mo dinkung."

"Ba reng bona ba sa tle?"

He arrived and found the people saying—–they say here is a certain little coloured man, and he went to him, greeted him and said, "Chaps, I'm searching. I'm searching—–"

"What are you looking for?"

"I'm looking for a person who—–was last lost a long time ago during the time of the wars with the whites. Now I'm looking and asking where can he be? But as– I look I've already seen him down there, he's herding the sheep."

"Really?"

"And this person is a chief. He is supposed to be the chief at home there."

"Really?"

"Yes."

He told this coloured man and he went to the Boer, and he took him—–to the Boer. They arrived at the Boer and his wife. The Boer asked him, "Where do you come from?"

And he added, "Now, this person you are talking about we do not know him. Where have you seen him?"

He said, "No, I've found him herding the sheep. He is the one who is looking after the sheep down there—–in the reeds."

That one said, "He is referring to Klaas."

"Really?"

"Yes."

He said, "Where do you come from? Looking for him now, where do you come from?"

He said, "I come from M- Makapan."

Suddenly, the Boer entered the house. He took the gun. When he rushed to the wagon with the gun, the lad—–the woman said, "Hey father! No, no, no, no. No, no, no, no. No, no, no, no. No, no, no, no! Don't do that! You must never do that! My husband, forget the jealousy of your own folk, man. Don't. You see, you hear, my husband? Despise the jealousy of you own folk. You—– [that is, the Ndebele man], *isn't it that you are saying that this person is a chief?"*

She said, "Now! You—–you [that is, the Boer] *prevent wealth from entering into this house? Demand wealth so that it can enter into this house, man! Because he is a chief!" Indeed the man returned and put down his gun.*

Then he said, "Now, are you alone like this?"

He said, "No, I'm not alone."

"Where are the others?"

That one said, "They are down there with—–with that one—–in the valley with the sheep."

"Why didn't they come?"

A re, "Ba a tšhaba."

A re, "*Magtig!* Wena ke wena a sa tšhabeng ga o tšhabe Leburu wena? Ge bona ba tšhaba? Tsamayang le yo ba bitša."

A roma lephusman le——le yo ba bitša, ke ge ba ba bitša ba tla mo.

FM: Ba etla le yena?

MK: Ja. "Hei lena go reng motho a re a etla mo lena le šale——le kwa keng?" Ba hloma dihlogo fase ba sega ba re, "Re be re tšhaba."

"Le tšhaba! Le be le tšhaba? Bjale woo! Ke mmolaile wo? E le gona le tlang bjale?"

Ga ke sa tseba taba tša bona, a re, "*All right.*"

A boya Leburu la re, "Le ya nkwa? Ka gore le re motho wo ke kgoši, *all right.* Nna ke re go lena, pele ke tla mo lokolla, tsamayang le yo ntšeyela dinku ka mo le ke kgonang ka gona. *Then* ke tle ke——ke ke lo——le nna e tle ke mo lokolle ka gore, le a mmona gore o kaakang? Ke mo o tlile, ke senyagaletšwe, ke mo godišitše, a ke re wa——le a kwa? Bjale le nna nhlatsweng diatla."

FM: Ja.

MK: Ke re——

FM: Gona mouwe.

MK: Ja.

FM: Gona mouwe. Eh, a ke re, go na le lentšu le lengwe, ke sa le kwang. Eh, ba rile ba mmotšiša, motho wo, gore "Na wena o tšwa o le kae?" A re, "Ke tšwa ke le Makapan?"

MK: Ja. Bjale——

FM: ——poort *or* o no re Makapan?

MK: O no re Makapane.

SM: ——stad.

MK: A ke re——

FM: Makapanstad?

MK: Ah, eh Makapan.

FM: *Okay.*

MK: Eh ka re a ke re bjale go tle a bone Leburu le le dira bjatše le——le nyaka go mo thunya ka sethunya——

FM: O gopola taba tšela?

MK: Ke ka taba ya bona.

FM: *Right. Now he says, eh, one man out of the three and the others, volunteered that, eh, since, eh, the possibility of grabbing this man——*

IH: Uhu.

FM: *——abducting him actually was, eh, far-fetched and out, he then volunteered that he would go and face this Boer——*

IH: Uhu.

He said, "They are scared."

He said, "Good Heavens! And you are not scared, you are not scared of a Boer! If they are scared? Just go and call them."

He sent a coloured man———to call them in and indeed they came.

FM: *They came with him?*

MK: Yes. *"Hey you, what's wrong with you? Why did you remain behind while one man came to me?"*

They hid their faces and laughed and said, "We were scared."

"Scared? You were scared? Now this one, did I kill him? Now that you have come?"

I don't know what he said further, he said, "All right."

The Boer came back and said, "Are you listening? Because you are saying this person is a chief, all right. *What I'm saying is that before I release him, go back and bring me as many sheep as you can. Then I———I———I will release him. Do you see how big he is? I fed him, I spent a lot for him, and I brought him up——— you hear? Now you should also wash my hands."*

FM: Yes.

MK: *I say———*

FM: *Just there.*

MK: Yes.

FM: *Just there. Eh, there is a certain word I did not hear very well. Eh, when they asked this man where he came from, and he said, "I come from Makapan?"*

MK: Yes. *Now———*

FM: *———poort or you said Makapan.*

MK: *You said Makapane.*

SM: *———stad.*

MK: *Isn't it———*

FM: Makapanstad?

MK: *No. Makapan.*

FM: Okay.

MK: *Eh, isn't it by doing this the Boer wanted to shoot him———*

FM: *He remembers those incidents?*

MK: *It is because of them.*

FM: Right. Now he says, eh, one man out of the three and the others, volunteered that, eh, since, eh, the possibility of grabbing this man———

IH: Uhu.

FM: ———abducting him actually was, eh, far-fetched and out, he then volunteered that he would go and face this Boer———

IH: Uhu.

FM: ———*and ask him to release, eh, the future chief. So he went. When he arrived on the farm, he, he met a coloured man and he explained to the coloured man his mission. And the coloured man said, "No, I will take you to the owner of the farm."*

He took the gentleman to the Boer and then he started explaining his story, that, eh, they'd actually come to ask the Boer to release he Ma—eh Mokopane who was the ch—the future chief of the Ndebele.

And he was asked, "Where do you come from?" He said, "I come from Makapan."

Just that word triggered a negative reaction. The Afrikaner or the Boer went into his house and came out with a muzzle, loading it.

IH: Uhu.

FM: *When he was busy loading it, his wife came out and said, "Stop it, because you're s—going to spoil the whole thing. Eh, don't react in that manner."*

Eh, the husband was pacified. Then he started asking questions.

"Now if you are alone, eh———where are the others? Did you come alone here in search of this future chief?"

He said, "No I am not alone I'm with the others who at this point in time are with the man I'm talking about."

So the coloured was sent to go and call the others. So when they came, eh, this Boer said to them, "I understand your story, but you must remember that I have been taking care of this young man. And today he's a strong young man. So if you want him———"

MK: O kho kahle.

FM: ———*you must ref*———

MK: O kho kahle. Nko eme gona mo———gona mo re tlang go e kwa eye?

FM: Ee.

MK: Ka gore mola o hlalošitšeng, go fihla gona mo o di———mo o se tšho o———mo o setšho o bolele.

FM: Ee.

MK: A ke re ba tlile bale ba kgobokane?

FM: Mm.

MK: Bjale a botšišane le bona gore na le be le tšhaba eng lena? Bjale ba--ba ba fetole ka mo ba boneng gore eh wa re go———eh———a re go bona, "All right dulang mola." Ba dula. Tša———dinku mantšibowa tša tsena. A ke re bona ba hlwele mo lehono bjale?

FM: Ja.

MK: Ja———bjatše ge a goroša dinku mantšibowa di tsena ka šakeng, lekgowa Le———Leburu le la dira maano, le nyaka go bona batho ba gore na nnete ba ya mo tseba na. Bjale ge e se no go tsena, a tšeya mathopiwa a ke re be ba tsa———be be tsamaya ba thopa———ba ba thopa batho gohlegohle mo Maburu a?

FM: Mm.

FM: ———and ask him to release, eh, the future chief. So he went. When he arrived on the farm, he, he met a coloured man and he explained to the coloured man his mission. And the coloured man said, "No, I will take you to the owner of the farm."

He took the gentleman to the Boer and then he started explaining his story, that, eh, they'd actually come to ask the Boer to release he Ma– eh Mokopane who was the ch– the future chief of the Ndebele.

And he was asked, "Where do you come from?" He said, "I come from Makapan."

Just that word triggered a negative reaction. The Afrikaner or the Boer went into his house and came out with a muzzle, loading it.

IH: Uhu.

FM: When he was busy loading it, his wife came out and said, "Stop it, because you're s– going to spoil the whole thing. Eh, don't react in that manner."

Eh, the husband was pacified. Then he started asking questions.

"Now if you are alone, eh———where are the others? Did you come alone here in search of this future chief?"

He said, "No I am not alone I'm with the others who at this point in time are with the man I'm talking about."

So the coloured was sent to go and call the others. So when they came, eh, this Boer said to them, "I understand your story, but you must remember that I have been taking care of this young man. And today he's a strong young man. So if you want him———"

MK: *Just wait.*

FM: *———you must ref———*

MK: *Just wait. Just wait there where I stop you, so that we———we can hear it, okay?*

FM: *Yes.*

MK: *Because up to where you have explained, up to where we are———where you have not yet explained.*

FM: Yes.

MK: *Isn't it those people have come and gathered together?*

FM: Mm.

MK: *Now he asked them what they were scared of. Now those———those men answered in the way that fitted them best———and he said to them, "All right, sit down there." They sat. The———sheep arrived in the evening. Isn't it they have spent the whole day there now?*

FM: Yes.

MK: *Yes ———now when the boy herded the sheep into the kraal, the white———B– Boer made a plan in order to test if these men really knew the boy. Now he took all the other slaves———like I said they went about kidnapping———these Boers went all over kidnapping.*

FM: Mm.

MK: Ba tšeya mathopiwa a, ba a beya bjale.

SM: A a be a le mo polaseng?

FM: Mm.

MK: *Ja*, a a be a le mo polaseng yeo, ba ba beya bjale. Ba ya go banna ba le, Mokopane ba mo lesa, ba mo lesa ka ntle ka kwa. Ba mo fihlile. Ba---ba ya go---go---go bona ba tšeya o tee ba re, Leburu la re go yena la re, "O a kwa? Ge o fihla go batho bale, o sehlo o nyaka o re---o re o---o nyaka go---ge e le gore o a mo tseba, ge o---go---ge a bona o mo tseba o mo tshware o re, 'Ke yo!'"

"Ja."

Bjale ge, nnete e rile ge o motee a tšwela, ba re, "*All right*, ba šumo šupe." Ge a re, a re, "*No!* Ga a go mo."

A re, "O reng, o re ga a go?"

"Ee."

A re, "Na o a mo tseba?"

A re, "Morena ke re ga a go."

"Ao---o reng a se gona monna? Kanthe ke---ke bona batho ba?"

A re, "*No* morena a---ke še– ke šiya go bolela maaka, ga a go."

A mo tšeya a ya---a mmušetša ka kwa, a yo tšeya o mongwe.

A re, "O a nkwa? Ge o fihla mola, o se ke wa hlo o dira bjalo o---o no fihla o re. ke wo, ge e le gore o a mo tseba."

Bjale, le yena a fihla a re, "*No* morena ga a go."

"Ga a go?"

"Ee."

"Ga o mo tsebe monna aowa."

Napa a re, "*No* ga a go mola."

Ke ge a mo tšeya, a yo mo fihla ka kwa, a yo tšeya wa mafelelo bjale.

SM: *Last event.*

MK: "Bjale ke re le wena monna o ska hlo o re---ge o fihla o mo tshware o re, 'Ke wo'."

Well o fihlile le yena, ge a re, a re, "*No* morena ga a go."

A re, "Bjang?"

Motho wola a re, "He! Bjale ke tla bolelang ka gore morena ga a go?"

"Gona ga a mo tsebe."

A mo tšeya a yo mo fihla ka kwa. Bjale a yo tšeya---ba yo tšeya Mokopane a ke re o ba---o ba phatlaladitše batho bale, o mong o mo fihlile ko, o mongwe a mo fihlile kwa, ba yo tšeya Mokopane bjale. A fihla ba mo re ka gare---mo garegare a fihla a mo re---a mmeya.

A yo tšeya wola wa mathomo a re, "Monna, o a mo tseba wena?"

A re, "Ah eh papa ke a mo tseba."

A re, "O---o---e tla o re bontšhe yena monna. Nkane o paletšwe bjale?"

MK: *They took these slaves and put them like this.*

SM: *Those who were on the farm?*

FM: **Mm.**

MK: Yes, *the ones who were on this farm, they put them like this. They went to the men while Mokopane was left, was left outside. They had concealed him. They——they——went to one of them and picked one and the Boer said, "D'you hear? When you arrive at those people* [slaves], *you should not hesitate, when you recognise him——just touch him——and say, 'Here he is'."*

"Yes."

*Now, indeed when one appeared, they said, "*All right, *point at him." He said, "No, he is not here."*

He said, "What? You say he is not among these?"

"Yes."

He said, "Do you really know him?"

He said, "Sir, I say he is not here."

"So——why is he not here man? Aren't——these the only people?"

He said, "No, sir——I'm scared of lying, he is not here."

He took him back——and brought another one.

He said, "Do you hear? When you arrive there, you should not hesitate——if you know him. Just point at him."

Now he also arrived and said, "No, master, he's not here."

"Not here?"

"Yes."

"You do not know the man?"

They said, "No, he is not here."

Then he took him back, concealed him so that he cannot give others a signal of his findings and went for the last one.

SM: Last event.

MK: *"Now you should also not hesitate——when you arrive there just grasp him and say, 'Here'."*

Well, *he also arrived and when he saw them he said, "No, my lord, he is not present."*

He said, "How come?"

That man said, "What else can I say because he is not present here?"

"Then you do not know him."

He took him to be hidden on the other side. Now he went——they went for Mokopane——isn't it he had scattered them [that is, the three slaves already exhibited], *he has hidden one here, one there, and now he went for Mokopane. He arrived and put him right in the middle of the other slaves, and left him there.*

He went for the first man, "Man, do you know him?"

He said, "Well, father, I know him."

He said, "Well——come and show us. Why now have you failed?"

Ge a re——ge a eya, o no fihla a re, "Ke wo mo!"

Nape a tšeya, a yo mo fihla——a——a——a——ke ra a mo tšeya a yo mmeya mola bjatše ga a sa mo tšhabiša.

A yo tšeya wo mongwe gapegape a re, a fihla a re, "Monna o ko——o re——o re ga a go monna? Nko re bontšhe mo."

Ge a fihla o no re, "Ke wo!" Ba mo tšeya ba mmuišetša mola, ba tšeya wa mafello. Wa boraro le yena a re, "Ke wo!"

A bona gore *ja* ba a mo tseba ka paale. Ke ge a re go bona a tlo ba ntšh– a ba laetša.

"Agaa! Bjale ke re go lena pele ke tla mo lokolla ka gore le a bone o gotše ke mo otlile, ke senyagaletšwe, tsamayang le yo ntšeela dinku ka mokgwa wo le ka kgonago ka gona."

FM: *Okay——right, eh, eh, he says eh, the——the Boer decided that eh, there had to be some identification. He decided that the three had to take part in this——[slightly inaudible because of hammering outside] Eh, he called all the workers, the slaves at his farm and brought them together, but with the exception of Mokopane. Mokopane was not among them. And those people had come in search of Mokopane were put one side, and one by one they were called and they were instructed, "Among these people, identify Mokopane just by touching him."*

So the first one came, looked and said, "No he's not here."

And then the Boer said, "All right, you'll go and stay at such and such a place, so that there shouldn't be any communication with the others."

He called the second one. He came and said, "No! He's not here." Then he passed.

Then the Boer said, "Most probably these people know the person they are looking for." He then called in Mokopane to join the others. And then those people who had already confirmed that Mokopane was not among the initial group, they were called back once more one by one, to come and identify whether Mokopane was among the people or not, and indeed the first just said, "This is the person we're looking for."

They said, "One side."

Then the second came and said, "This is Mokopane."

The third one, "This is Mokopane."

And it was only thereafter that he said, "All right, you have identified your man. But now, eh, all my expenses of bringing up this man, I must be refunded. And I must be refunded by sheep. I need sheep as a refund for the expenses I have incurred in bringing up this lad."

MK: *Ja.* Bjale ge—— [Pause, because of hammering outside.]

MK: Bjale ke ge ka paale a laelana le bona bjatše——bjatše le bona ba——ba——ba——ba lotšha ke tsela, ba thoma ba boela kwa le ba gaMakau, ba fihla ba laelana le bona, ba wela tsela ba etla keno.

FM: Ba mo tlogetše?

When——he arrived, he just said, "Here he is!"

Then he took him and hid him and——and——and I mean he took him and put him there, now he does not conceal him.

He went for the other one and he said on arrival, "Man, you——you said he is not present here. Show us."

When he arrived, he just said, "Here!" They took him and put him aside. The third one also said, "Here!"

He [the Boer] realised that yes, indeed they recognise him. It is then that he too——he instructed them.

"Fine! Now I say to you before I can release him, you can see that he is grown up and I've maintained him, I spent a lot, so, go back and bring me as many sheep as you can."

FM: Okay——right, eh, eh, he says eh, the——the Boer decided that eh, there had to be some identification. He decided that the three had to take part in this——[slightly inaudible because of hammering outside] Eh, he called all the workers, the slaves at his farm and brought them together, but with the exception of Mokopane. Mokopane was not among them. And those people had come in search of Mokopane were put one side, and one by one they were called and they were instructed, "Among these people, identify Mokopane just by touching him."

So the first one came, looked and said, "No he's not here."

And then the Boer said, "All right, you'll go and stay at such and such a place, so that there shouldn't be any communication with the others."

He called the second one. He came and said, "No! He's not here." Then he passed.

Then the Boer said, "Most probably these people know the person they are looking for." He then called in Mokopane to join the others. And then those people who had already confirmed that Mokopane was not among the initial group, they were called back once more one by one, to come and identify whether Mokopane was among the people or not, and indeed the first just said, "This is the person we're looking for."

They said, "One side."

Then the second came and said, "This is Mokopane."

The third one, "This is Mokopane."

And it was only thereafter that he said, "All right, you have identified your man. But now, eh, all my expenses of bringing up this man, I must be refunded. And I must be refunded by sheep. I need sheep as a refund for the expenses I have incurred in bringing up this lad."

MK: Yes. *Well now——* [Pause, because of hammering outside.]

MK: *Now indeed they agreed with each other and——and left, going firstly to the Makau people to say goodbye, and then came back here.*

FM: *They left him?*

MK: *Ja* ba mo tlogetše. Ba fihle ba bega kgošing, go rangwane'agwe Makute. Ba re, "Re mo humane kgoši, ngwanagago, 'mme re mo humaneng, Leburu tša lona šetši o re, 'Ka gore ke mo otlile, tsamayang le yo ntšeyela dinku ka mokgwa wo le ka kgonang.'"

SM: Ga se a ba botše palo?

MK: Ga se a re botše palo. A nkere wa bona? Makute ke ge a thoma a bitša banna ba——ba——ba——ba motse wa gagwe, ba boledišana a re, "Taba še."

      "Eya papa."

      "Etse go nyak– Leburu le re le nyaka dinku ka mokgwa wo go ka kgonegago ka gona."

      Ba dumelelana gomme ba bitša pitšo ya setšhaba gore e tle ba e rere. Gwa tsena mašaka ka mašaka, ka dintona ka dintona go tšwa dinku. Bjale dinku tše di ileng kua ga re di tsebe gore na ke tše kae. Go ba ke masome goba ke makgolo ga re tsebe re no kwa ba re go tšwele dinku mašaka ka mašaka tša išwa kua. Bona bale ba go rongwa ka bararo ba di tšeya ba di iša kwa. Bjale a yo begela Langa yena Mokopane a nke re o a bona? Ka taba ye——eh le ka——ngwana wa——yena Mokopane ge ba mo humane, 'me Leburu le nyaka dinku ka mokgwa wo go ka kgonagalang ka gona. Bjale Langa, ke ge a tla ntšha meno a ditlou—— *four.*

FM: Langa kae? Bakenburg?

MK: Ah eh. Gape Bakenburg ye ke——ke Mapela leina ke ntho e tee——

FM: Ma——

MK: Ba no kgaola gona bjatše ke nto e tee ke——ke ge mmušo e sa le o tee e setšho ba lwe o kgaogane.

FM: Oho.

MK: *Ja.* Ke ge a ntšha meno a ditlou ka mane a makaaka.

FM: *Ja.*

MK: A re, "Ngwana' monkane wa ka wo ke thaba kudu nke a ka bowa, ke thabile kudu ge ba mo humane e bile a tlo tla. Ke re ge eba ba yo ntšha dinku bjale ka ge Leburu le realo, le nna ke re mpho ya ka še ke re ke ntšha ma– meno a ditlou šea."

      A fa, a a tliša ga——Mokopane ba——kgoši a leboga. Ba——ba romiwa ge ba iša dinku kua ba——ba rwe——ke gore ba ne dinku a bile ba rwele le ma——le meno a le a ditlou a le ka mane. Ba ile kua.

FM: *Right. Okay. Right, eh, the——the——the emissaries who were sent over, eh, by the chief, the caretaker chief, then came back to report that we have discovered his whereabouts. He remained behind. And they indicated that the Boer, however, would like compensation. So, eh, the caretaker chief called his tribe and informed them. So from each kraal a number of sheep were collected. A number of sheep rather were collected. But he says he doesn't have a definite number as to how many they were eventually taken over. But otherwise each kraal, eh, they did bring in something. Apart from that, the caretaker chief then sent word to——*

FM: Mapela

MK: Yes, *they left him. They arrived and reported to the chief, his uncle, Makute. They said, "We found him, chief, and having found him, here is what the Boer says, 'Because I brought him up, go back and bring me as many sheep as you can.'"*

SM: *He did not specify the number.*

MK: *He did not specify the numbers to us. You see now? Then Makute summoned the men of——of——of——he homestead to discuss the matter and he said, "Here is the issue."*

"Yes, master."

"By the way we want– the Boer says he wants as many sheep as possible."

They agreed with one another and an assembly of the nation was called to iron this issue out. Kraals and kraals of sheep entered from different headman. Now we do not know how many sheep were sent there. Whether it was tens or hundreds we do not know, we only know that kraals and kraals of sheep were sent there. Those three men who were intitially sent were sent again to deliver those sheep. Now Mokopane [speaker probably means Makute] *himself reported to Langa, you see now? About this issue——and——and about this child Mokopane who was found, and that the Boer wanted as many sheep as they could afford. Now Langa offered the teeth of the elephants——four.*

FM: *Langa where? Bakenburg?*

MK: *No. By the way this Bakenburg, its——its name is Mapela. It is one and the same thing——*

FM: Ma——

MK: *They were just separated recently, it is just one thing——it was at a time when it was one nation, not yet divided.*

FM: Oho.

MK: *Yes. It is then that he offered four elephant tusks this size.*

FM: Yes.

MK: *He said, "I'm very glad that my brother's son– I wish he could come back. I'm very glad that he has been found and he is going to come back. When they take the sheep to the Boer, here is my present. I offer four tusks, here they are."*

They were brought to——Mokopane's place——and the chief was thankful. Th—— the messengers drove the sheep there while they also——that is while they carried those four tusks as well. They went there.

FM: Right. Okay. Right, eh, the——the——the emissaries who were sent over, eh, by the chief, the caretaker chief, then came back to report that we have discovered his whereabouts. He remained behind. And they indicated that the Boer, however, would like compensation. So, eh, the caretaker chief called his tribe and informed them. So from each kraal a number of sheep were collected. A number of sheep rather were collected. But he says he doesn't have a definite number as to how many were eventually taken over. But otherwise each kraal, eh, did bring in something. Apart from that, the caretaker chief then sent word to——

FM: Mapela

FM: ———*to say, "The lost chief whom we did not know where he was, we've discovered where he is. But, however, for his return, there is this condition."*

IH: Uhu.

FM: *Now the Mapela people were so overjoyed that they said, "All right, instead, we're now going to help you by also sending in four tusks of the elephant———"*

SM: *Ivory.*

FM: ———*of, of, of, of, of elephant.*

IH: Oh.

FM: *Ivory, you know the———*

IH: Mm.

FM: *That's right. They gave them four. So, together with the sheep, those were sent over to the Boer in order to release chief Mokopane.*

SM: *Right.*

MK: Bjale ba di tšere ba tsamaya ba fihla ka tšona kwa.

FM: *Yes.*

MK: E rile ge ba fihla, Leburu la mong'a polase le mosadi ba bone gore hei ka paale motho yo ke kgoši. E be e le mohlape wa dinku le ge re sa tsebe gore na e be e le tše kae. Bjale e rile ge ba tlo ntšha meno a———

SM: Meno a le a ditlou———

MK: Leburu la re, "Hei, mang! Tše dilo tše, bjale ge le be le tshwere dilo tše dinku tše le be le sa di iša kae?"

Ba re, "Aowa rena gape re kwele gola o re ke nyaka dinku."

A re, "Ja, mara ge nka be le ile la ba le tsebo ge le be le———ge be le nkwele, nka be le di lesitše ka gore le a tseba gore na dilo tše ka segagaborena ke eng."

Ba re, "Aowa."

"Le mphile lehumo le le sa feleng *man* ka dilo tše. Ke kgoši ka ntle le lehumo le *klaar.*"

Ba re, "Aowa."

A re, "*No* le gone go lokile."

Ke ge a bowa Leburu bjatše le ba———be le ba beya fase le laetša Mokopane le re, "O a kwa? Ka bošego o se ke wa lala o———o ntšhitše mo dinkung go diša. O nape o bolele le banna ba."

Le ntšhitše nku ya lona ya———la e hlaba, gore ba je———ba je e be———e be sešebo le gona a ba thibela gore, "Nke le fetše matšatšinyana a mabedi a mararo nke le fodiše dinao tše."

FM: ———to say, "The lost chief whom we did not know where he was, we've discovered where he is. But, however, for his return, there is this condition."

IH: Uhu.

FM: Now the Mapela people were so overjoyed that they said, "All right, instead, we're now going to help you by also sending in four tusks of the elephant———"

SM: Ivory.

FM: ———of, of, of, of, of elephant.

IH: Oh.

FM: Ivory, you know the———

IH: Mm.

FM: That's right. They gave them four. So, together with the sheep, those were sent over to the Boer in order to release chief Mokopane.

SM: Right.

MK: *Now they drove them* [the sheep] *and arrived with them there.*

FM: Yes.

MK: *When they arrived the Boer, the owner of the farm and his wife realised that indeed this person is a chief. It was a flock of sheep altough we do not know how many there were. Now when they offered those teeth———*

SM: *Teeth of the elephants———*

MK: *The Boer said, "Hey! Who! These things these, now if you have brought these, then where were you taking those sheep?"*

They said, "No, in fact, we heard you saying you want sheep."

He said, "Yes, but if you had the knowledge, if you'd listened to me you would have left the sheep because you know what these things [the tusks] *mean in our culture?"*

They said, "No."

"You have offered me the eternal wealth with these things, man! I am already a chief [with this ivory] *even if you exclude this wealth* [that is, the sheep]*."*

They said, "Well."

He said, "No, it's still fine."

Then the Boer came back———and let them get seated, and told Mokopane saying, "Do you hear? Tomorrow do not———take the sheep out to the pastures. You should talk with these men."

He offered his own sheep———slaughtered it so that———they———hey should eat and stopped them from leaving and said, "Just relax a bit here, while you rest for two or three days."

Ka paale go die– go diregile bjalo. Pele, ge ba tlo go tsamaya ka bošego, ke ge e šetše ba––––ba khutšitše, a botša mosadi a tšeya nku gapegape ya gagwe, a e hlaba, a botša mosadi a re, "Eeeee gadike ka mo setofong." Ba e––––a ba gadikela gore e be mphago. Gomme ka paale mosadi a dira bjatše. Ka bošego ge ba tlo tsamaya ke ge ba rwalelela mphago wola ba boela keno bjale, ba ne le yena Mokopane, o a bona?

FM: *Right. When they arrived the Boer became convinced that indeed this man is the real chief.*

IH: Uhu.

FM: *He was impressed by the number of sheep the people had brought––––*

IH: Uhu.

FM: *––––in order to secure the release of the young chief. So when they presented this––––these sheep to him and ultimately also took now the ivory––––*

SM: *Four.*

FM: *––––the four ivory, he said the––––the chie– the Boer said, "Man! Had you known, you should have forgotten about the sheep, because this is what really counts. This is real wealth."*

IH: Uhu.

FM: *For these people. And then he told them that they should remain, cool down their feet for a few days, and then thereafter they could return back to their chief. And, eh, on the day they left he also slaughtered another sheep as the provision on their way back to the Ndebele people.*

IH: *I see.*

MK: Bjale a ba botša a bitša lephusmane lela la go ba––––la la gagwe le le––––e e le be ba tsene ka lona, a re, "Botša batho ba. Ge ba tloga mo, ba se ke ba tsamaya bošego––––ke ra mosegare. Ba tsamaye bošego. Mosegare gore go esa letšatši le––––le hlaba kwa ba––ba tsene ka dikgweng ba––––ba dule ba nyake mo ba tla––––ba dule."

E rile ge letšatši le sobela monyama o tshwara nape ba wele tsela ba ye ba––––ba––––ba ye magaeng a bona, ba tshware tsela ya go boela gae.

"Ka gore ge Maburu a ka ba bona, e re ge ba ba bone, ba be ba tle ba tseba gore ke ba––––ba tšwa gaMakapane, ba fedile *klaar*, ba tla ba fetša Maburu *klaar*. Bjale wena ba botše ba kwišiše taba ye, *and, eh,* ke go fa pere še, o tsamaye le bona, o tsamaye o be o yo fihla mola ga Moketekete."

A mo laetša. A re, "Moketekete a ke re o a mo tseba?"

A re, "Ee."

"O ye go fihla moo o ba gomele o boele keno. O tla be o ba––––o tla be o ba tsamaišitše o ba ntšhitše ka gare ga––––ga––––ga––––ga––––"

FM: Ga polase.

Indeed it so– it happened as he said. Prior to, when they were about to depart the next morning, they had already rested, and he told his wife, he took another sheep and slaughtered it, and he said to his wife, "You should put this on the stove to fry." They———she roasted it for them as a provision on their way home. Indeed this is what the woman did. The next day they then carried their provisions and came back home, together with Mokopane, you see?

FM: Right. When they arrived the Boer became convinced that indeed this man is the real chief.

IH: Uhu.

FM: He was impressed by the number of sheep the people had brought———

IH: Uhu.

FM: ————in order to secure the release of the young chief. So when they presented this———these sheep to him and ultimately also took now the ivory———

SM: Four.

FM: ———the four ivory, he said the———the chie– the Boer said, "Man! Had you known, you should have forgotten about the sheep, because this is what really counts. This is real wealth."

IH: Uhu.

FM: For these people. And then he told them that they should remain, cool down their feet for a few days, and then thereafter they could return back to their chief. And, eh, on the day they left he also slaughtered another sheep as the provision on their way back to the Ndebele people.

IH: I see.

MK: *Now he told them and called his coloured man———the one through whom they went to him [the Boer] and said, "Tell these people. When they leave here, they should not walk at night———I mean during the day. They should walk at night. During the day when the sun rises there, they———they should enter the forests and———and get seated and look for——for a place to sit."*

When the sun set and darkness took over, they———they left via the way that led them home.

"Because if other Boers can just see them and know that they come from Makapane, they———they are finished completely, the Boers would finish them. So now, tell them to understand this issue, and I give you this horse, you should accompany them up to such-and-such a place."

He instructed him and said, "Such-and-such a person, isn't it you know him?"

He said, "Yes."

"You should reach that place and then come back. You would then have——— accompanied them far enough out of———o———o———"

FM: *Out of the farm.*

MK: ———ga boima bjo bo———bo le kgauswi bjo. Ke ge ka paale lephusman le ba tšeya bjalo, le le be le fihla mola le re, "Le a kwa, ke a boya mo. Ke mo a reng ke boye gona. Ke le bontšhitše tsela bjatše."

Ke ge a boya, bona le bona ba šala le Mokopane, ke ge ba tshwara tsela bjalo. Ke a bona e rile, kapa ba rile ba sobelelwa mo tseleng, ke a bona ba tsena dikgwa ba robala, ke ra--e--e mosegare ba robala ge ba hlabetšwe ke letšatši, goba e rile ba no tsamaya ke mo ke sa tsebeng ke a bona. Mara ba rile ba tla ba fihla mo.

SM: Mara ba ba boditše gore ba se ke ba tsamaya masegare?

MK: Masegare.

SM: Letšatši ge———le tš– le sobela———e le hlaba ba tsena ka sekgweng ba khuta.

MK: Mm.

FM: *Fine. Eh, now when he released the chief Mokopane this Boer gave these people an advice. He said, "On your way back you must only move in the evening. During the course of the night you hide yourself and be resting because should———"*

SM: *Just a minute———move in the night.*

FM: *Ja, move in the night, rest———*

SM: *———during the day.*

FM: *Rest———*

SM: *———you rest.*

FM: *Ja, the reason being if the other Boers discovered that you are from Makapan———*

IH: Uhu.

FM: *———they'll finish you off. Now to sort of create a double surety for their lives, he instructed a coloured man who was working on his farm. He said, "You accompany these people."*

IH: Uhu.

FM: *He was on horseback. "You accompany these people until they are out of the danger zone and then you come back and after that they will continue."*

IH: Uhu.

FM: *And he says that happened until these people actually arrived back home with the future chief.*

MK: Mm.

IH: *I see.*

MK: Bjale ge ba fihla mo gae mo, e rile ge ba etla mola leporogong la setimela a ke re o a le bona?

FM: Mm.

MK: Ba dula moriting ba sa khutša.

SM: Moorddrift?

MK: ---out of this difficulty---that is very close. Indeed the coloured man did accompany them in this manner until he reached that place and said, "You hear, I return here. That's where he said I should return. I showed you the way."

He then returned, and they were also left with Mokopane and took their journey. I think they, whether they slept on their journey, or entered the forests---during the day when the sun rose, or whether they just walked, that's what I do not know. But they ultimately arrived here.

SM: But they were told never to walk during the day?

MK: During the day.

SM: When the su- when the sun set---when it rose they entered the forests to hide.

MK: Mm.

FM: Fine. Eh, now when he released the chief Mokopane this Boer gave these people an advice. He said, "On your way back you must only move in the evening. During the course of the night you hide yourself and be resting because should---"

SM: Just a minute---move in the night.

FM: Yes, move in the night, rest---

SM: ---during the day.

FM: Rest---

SM: ---you rest.

FM: Yes, the reason being if the other Boers discovered that you are from Makapan---

IH: Uhu.

FM: ---they'll finish you off. Now to sort of create a double surety for their lives, he instructed a coloured man who was working on his farm. He said, "You accompany these people."

IH: Uhu.

FM: He was on horseback. "You accompany these people until they are out of the danger zone and then you come back and after that they will continue."

IH: Uhu.

FM: And he says that happened until these people actually arrived back home with the future chief.

MK: Mm.

IH: I see.

MK: Now when they arrived here at home, when they were on that train bridge [that is, Moorddrift], can you see it?

FM: Mm.

MK: They sat under the shadow of the tree to rest.

SM: Moorddrift?

MK: *Ja* bjale ke ge ba roma motho——o——o mong——o mong wa bona ba re, "Tsamaya o yo——tsamaya o yo re begela gore etse le a welwa setšhaba sa gaMokopane setšhaba le a welwa. O etla ngwana' lena re mo humane."

FM: Mm.

MK: Bjale wola ge ntše ba khutša yena o a tsamaya. Ba bona gore bjale gona bjatše o tsamaile, le rena re tla be re mo šala morago. Ge ba ema ba tseba gore bjatše le rena ge re——ge re tlo tloga mo ge re yo fihla nhleng yela o tla be a šetše a tsena mola. A ke re ke ge re le mo Ple– mo Pruissen mo?

FM: Mm.

MK: Ka paale o ile bjale. Bona ge ba etla bjalo ntše ba etla yena le yena o a tsena ko gae.

Ge a fihla gae a fihla a re, "Agaa! Kgoši, re mo humane e bile o etla, le a welwa."

FM: Mm.

MK: Ah! Ge ba re, mokgoši wa re, ba re, "Sebatakgomo!"

Gwa tsogwa gohlegohlegohle gwa——ya be ba ba a tšwela. Ge ba tšwela, ge ba tšwela ge a f– a fihla a humana setšhaba šetše se thabile go iwa ka mo le ka mo [inaudible] go sa loke selo. Aowa, ba mo amogela.

Ke ge ba re, "Aowa, o tsene ka gae. *It's all right.*"

Ke ge e bile ba——ba mo agela lešakana la gagwe gore a se ke a tsena ka motseng. Ba aga mo yena e tla ba yena a nnoši e——ke setšha e le ntlo ya gagwe, mara ba sa——ba e dirile ka mašaba bjale. Bjale ge——ka gore ke——–Sesotho o a se tseba nape, ba be——ba bereka ka dipheko gore ba mo dikeletše moo, go lokile *is klaar.*

Bjale *one, two, three,* kgwedi——digkwedi e se tše kae ke ra kgwedi ge e ile go fela ba re, "O gotše motho wo ke——o swanetše a ye komeng ka gore ke monna le a mmona."

Ke ge a tla——go tla ntšhiwa koma napa a ya komeng a ya go wela. Ge ba boya kwa——ke ge ba tla re mphato a bona ba re ke Magasa.

FM: Magasa?

MK: Magasa.

FM: Magasa?

SM: Magasa.

MK: *Ja.*

FM: Magasa.

MK: *Ja.*

MK: Yes, *now they sent one––––of their men and said, "Go to––––go to inform the nation that something unexpected is happening. Your child is coming, we've found him."*

FM: Mm.

MK: *Now that one, when they rest, he continued to walk. They saw that now he has left, and they also followed him. When they stood up, they knew that when they––––arrive at that side, he would have already entered there. Isn't it we were still at Pl– Pruissen?*

FM: Mm.

MK: *Indeed he went like that. When they came like that he was also entering at home. When he arrived at home he said, "Well! Chief, we found him and he is on the way coming. Be ready."*

FM: Mm.

MK: *Suddenly when they––––the ululating started, "The beast is among the cattle!"* [A war cry]

People woke up––––all over the place. When they appeared, when they appeared, they found the nation very happy, people going this way and that way [inaudible]*––––nothing was going okay. No, they received him.*

Then they said, "Well, he has arrived at home. It's all right."

A kraal was then built––––for him so that he should not enter the home. They built it where he could live alone––––it's as if it were his house, it was built from leaves and branches––––like this. Well now––––in fact––––you know according to Sotho tradition, they––––they used muti [medicinal herbs] *to strengthen him, and it is* completely *fine.*

Now after one, two––––three months––––after several months, I mean towards the end of the month, they said, "This person is matured––––and he should be taken to the initiation school, you can see he is a man."

Then he––––they formed it and he was sent to be initiated. When he came back they called his age group the Magasa.

FM: Magasa?

MK: Magasa.

FM: Magasa?

SM: Magasa.

MK: Yes.

FM: Magasa.

MK: Yes.

FM: *Right, eh, he says eh, they are——they were approaching, Pruissen is where they were settled. As they were approaching Pruissen, they sent word by one of them to forewarn the people at home that the chief——the future chief is on his way back home. So, when they arrived there they——this person who was sent, he gave where the——the chief is waiting. And there was general excitement all over that eh, the north star is now coming back home. And so they went out to meet him. And, eh, eventually a kraal——a home for him was built away from the other people and in due course it was decided that now that he was back, he had to be ta– taken to the intiation school, together with his old compatriots. And when he came back with his group, that group was known as Maga–*

SM: Magasa.

FM: Magasa.

IH: Magasa.

FM: Magasa. *That's right.*

MK: Bjale, ka morago ga moo ke ge mokgalabje rangwane'a gwe Makute a tla—– a mo fa setulo, a se tšeye.

FM: *Thereafter, after initiation, when the boy was back, the caretaker chief——*

SM: *Regent. Regent a ke re ntate?*

FM: *Yes, yes, regent. He handed over——*

IH: *Is it?*

FM: *——the reins of, eh——*

SM: *Chieftainship.*

FM: *——of chieftainship over to the young Makap– Mokopa– ne.*

IH: *I see.*

FM: *And that's how he took over.*

MK: Bjale Mokopane wo o bušitše *all right.* Ke ge a tla tšeya basadi, mme go basadi ba a belega ngwana wa mošimane wo o kwang ba re ke Valtyn.

FM: Right, eh, he says eh, they are———they were approaching, Pruissen is where they were settled. As they were approaching Pruissen, they sent word by one of them to forewarn the people at home that the chief——— the future chief is on his way back home. So, when they arrived there they———this person who was sent, he gave where the———the chief is waiting. And there was general excitement all over that eh, the north star is now coming back home. And so they went out to meet him. And, eh, eventually a kraal———a home for him was built away from the other people and in due course it was decided that now that he was back, he had to be ta– taken to the intiation school, together with his old compatriots. And when he came back with his group, that group was known as Maga–

SM: Magasa.

FM: Magasa.

IH: Magasa.

FM: Magasa. *That's right.*

MK: *Now thereafter the old man, his uncle, Makute———came and abdicated the chieftainship so that he should take over.*

FM: Thereafter, after initiation, when the boy was back, the caretaker chief———

SM: Regent. Regent *isn't it father?*

FM: *Yes, yes,* regent. He handed over———

IH: Is it?

FM: ———the reins of, eh———

SM: Chieftainship.

FM: ———of chieftainship over to the young Makap– Mokopa-ne.

IH: I see.

FM: And that's how he took over.

MK: *Now this Mokopane ruled* all right. *He then married women and from these women he gave birth to a boy, the one you hear them call Valtyn.*

Appendix 3: Extract from Interview with Madimetša Kekana, 1/10/88

Part A: Sindebele

MK = Madimetša Kekana
CM = Caroline Mashao
AB = Anonymous Bystander

Date: 1 October 1988

Note: The tape recorder was switched on a few minutes after Mr Kekana had started.

MK: Mbili mphumela embili, a ka yo teka tikomikana lapho, selani mangati.
CM: Mm.
MK: *Then* ba teka tikomiki, *then* ba ti teka ba ti teka ba re, "Neh re lebogile."
       Ba re, "*Ja*, le rena go leboga rena, bašimane bagešo."
       Ba re, "Mh! Dinku tše tša lekgowa la geno, lekgowa la gona le mo kae?"
CM: Mm.
MK: Ba re, "Lekgowa la gona le gona ka mo sekgwaneng ka mo."
       Namile ba——o——ba a ti hlalela, ko re nga munye nkhathi kabo o re, "Banna na bahlangana laba le ba bona njani?"
       Ba re, "He! O ra njani?"
       A re, "Ao kambe ku ne mundwana wo monye wa kqosi llo a thunjwe makgowa lla, o nga bonakaleko."
CM: Mm.
MK: "O mot– m– m– mohlangana llo nga u fana naye llo——o montima lowa."
CM: Mm.
MK: Mm ngu lokhwa khona lapha, laba ba——re——
CM: *They are listening* [Laughter]
MK: "A si nga khambi! Si nga khambi, le sale le te se mmone kahle."
       Laba bona ba re, "Aowa, thina yena Mukombani——"
       A re——lowa a re, "Nna mmonganami, e be nhlala naye. A nga sikhe a mpalele *nie*."
CM: Mm.
MK: A re, "Na ke a mpalelako e ngaba kore mara bandu bona ba ya fana, a ba fani, tikqomo."
       Eyano, kusasa nakho ba hlwa ba hlwele. E re tinango tona leti ta ta timbuti ta wela, ti to sela.

Part B: English translation

MK=Madimetša Kekana
CM=Caroline Mashao
AB=Anonymous Bystander

Date: 1 October 1988

Note: The tape recorder was switched on a few minutes after Mr Kekana had started.

MK: *Before you proceed with your journey, let him take cups so that you should first drink.*

CM: Mm.

MK: Then *they took the cups*, then *they took them, they took them and said, "Thanks, okay."*
They said, "Yes we also thank you my boys."
They said, "Mh! These sheep of your white employer———where is he?"

CM: Mm.

MK: *They said, "Our white man is right in this bush this side."*
Then they———they got seated. One person amongst them said, "Gentlemen, do you see anything familiar in any one of these boys here?"
They said, "What do you mean?"
He said, "In fact there is a certain son of the chief who was kidnapped by these whites and he has since vanished."

CM: Mm.

MK: *"This ch– this chap over here looks like him, this———dark one."*

CM: Mm.

MK: *Yes. Thereafter some of them———said———*

CM: They are listening. [Laughter]

MK: *"Let us not go away. We should not go away until we have scrutinised him more closely to see if it is him." Others said, "No, we, Mokopane himself———"*
He said———that one said, "He is my friend and I stayed with him. I can't be mistaken in recognising him."

CM: Mm.

MK: He said, "If I could be mistaken, then all people would look all the same, but they are not the same, like cattle."
Now they spent the following day there. Then the time for the goats to come and drink came.

CM: Mm.

MK: Ke ti selako ba vela bahlangana ba re, "Re sa ntše re kgopela meetse."
Ba ba pha tikomikana ba sela, ba sela, ba sela, ba re, "He! Le tseba go
diša dinku tša--tša *baas* wa gago, na ga geno ke mo kae?"
A re, "Ah gagešo ke gona mo lekgoweng mo."

CM: Mm. Ba se timbolasini.

MK: "Bjatše ga re tsebe re ne gagešo. Gagešo ke gona mo lekgoweng le."
Le bona ba re, "Ah eh. Kulungile. *No* unga mo tlatlawetši."
Ba re, "*All right* ba leseni le nga ba hlalephisi."

CM: Mm.

MK: Name laba ba nyuka ne timvu ba ya lle, name ba thwala methwalwana,
nabaya ba a khamba.

CM: Ba khamba?

MK: Ba khamba ba ta neno ekhaya.

CM: Ba boya?

MK: Ee, ba eta ekhaya, ba jama ba thobala, ete ba ngene lapha ngendabeni la.
E re ku be ba ngene endabeni la ba thobele. Nge masa ke ba vuka a re,
"Kha re yeni si yo lotšhisa nkqosi, Makute."

CM: E be engu Makute nkqosi nnango leyo?

MK: *Ja* e be engu Makute.

CM: Mm.

MK: Name khona lapho———name ba a ya ba———dl– mangaa madoda,
mahlano. Name ba ya e kqosini ba fika ba re———[inaudible as someone is
making a noise in the background].
"Eše Morena! Morena!"
A re, "*All right.*"
Name ba hlala khona lapho.
"Le lele le ngene le makarapa?"
Ba re, "Ee kqosi, si te ndambama."
Ba re, "Mokgomana———nkhe le si lotšheleni e mošate."
Nge mokgomana a be a hleti nenkqosi, a ba dlulisa e kqosini, kqosi e re,
"Aowa, ba bonwi."
Ba———o monye a khupha tiponto nga tihlano, a re nkqosi o ta thenga
motsongo, njalo.
E banye ba khupha tiponto ngatihlano, o re, "Nkqosi e ta thenga tek-
tikqabolana."
E banye ba khupha tiponto ngatihlano ku fikella ba bile ba———ba phelella
ngabahlano babo.
A re lokhwa ba phelele, name lowa Makute o re ku lowa mokgomana o
re, "Monna, teka bandu laba o ba ise ngale, segodlweni lesa si ngale."

CM: Mm.

MK: *While they were still drinking the boys came and said, "We are once again asking for water."*

They gave them cups and they drank, they drank, they drank and said, "Hey! You can look after the sheep of your master *very carefully———where is your home?"*

He said, "Ah, my home is in the white man's area."

CM: Mm. *They are staying on the farms.*

MK: *"Now we don't know if we have our real home somewhere. Our only home is on this white man's farm."*

Those men said, "Well, it's fine. No, don't intimidate him."

*They said, "*All right*, leave them alone, don't make them aware"* [of what the mission is]

CM: Mm.

MK: *Then they ascended with the sheep and went that way and they carried their bags, there they went away.*

CM: *They went away?*

MK: *They went away, they are coming back home.*

CM: *Coming back?*

MK: *Yes, they are coming back home, spending nights on the way, until they arrived at this mountain. After arriving at that mountain they slept there. At dawn, when they woke up, one said, "Let's go to greet our chief Makute."*

CM: *Was the chief Makute at that time?*

MK: *Yes it was Makute.*

CM: Mm.

MK: *Then just there———they they———they were five, these men. Then they went to the chief and when they arrived they said———*[inaudible as someone is making a noise in the background].

"Greetings, our lord! Our lord!"

*He said, "*All right*."*

Then they sat down there.

"Are you the migrants that arrived last night?"

They said, "Yes chief, we arrived in the evening."

They said to one elder, "Sir, please pass our greetings to the royal family."

It is then that the elder who was with the chief, introduced them and the chief said, "Well, they've been seen."

They———one took out five pounds and said that the chief should buy tobacco.

Four took out five pounds each and one said, "The chief should buy some shoes."

Others issued out five pounds until the five had been———covered.

After completing this process then Makute said to the elder, "Gentlemen, take these people to the other side to the house yonder."

Name lowa a re, "A re yeni!"

O ba isa ngale, o fika o ba beka lapho a ba a hleti khona. Ke a ba be kako, name o----o a hlala, name banna ba re, "Na eyano o----si hlala khona lapha?"

"Ee."

Ba re, "Ah eh, wena khamba si ta te si to ku bita."

A boyela lle e nkqosini, a fike a teka mfati o monye lapha a teka boyalwa, boyalwa lobo a bo ise ngale nga kibo ngale. Nga mbale ba thwala mojeka ba fika ba o lahla kibo lle. Ke ba fikako ba re, "Mm."

A o hongola a o hongola, a ba thelela ba sela ba re ku sela, ke ba khokha metsongo nje, ba----ba goga ba goga.

Name ba re, "Mokgomana."

A re, "Ee."

Ba re, "Eyano o nga si bitela nkqosi na si be si fune ku bonana naye?"

A re, "Ao, le nga bonani naye njani na? Mfanelo."

Name a ya kuye. A fika a khunama phase a re, "Kqosi, ba----bandu laba ba re ba funa ku ku bona, ba ne mosomaelo nawe."

Name nkqosi ya jama a re, "Uyente kahle mokgomana."

Namile ya khona lle, a kuka setulo a fika a si beka khona lapha kudute nabo nama ba re nkqosi e hlale esitulweni ba re ba a mo lebuka. Aowa, a hlala. Ba re tu.

Ba re, "He, Mokgomana, nkqosi lle e bitwa ngithi. Nkho re nkhaya lapha, a ku na mundwana o munye o timeleko khona nkhaya?"

CM: E le kore ba velaphi madoda lla?

MK: Ba vela endamane.

CM: Ngu kuphi lapho?

MK: E makgoweni lle ba phuma ku berenga.

CM: Oho.

MK: E ba ye ku berenga.

CM: Mm.

MK: Name ba re, "Ah eh. Ngubani llo a timeleko?"

A re, "Ee, mundwana we mogolo wami. O timele, na eyano nje a singa tšhebe si mmone, a si mo veleli, na lapho a khona a si mmati kore o a phila koba ka a phili."

CM: Mm.

MK: "A ku wati mundu."

Name ba re, "Mokgomana, si ya kaya ena, ku kaela nna."

Eyano ku be ku somaela lowa.

A re, "Nna ndi ya kaya, ndi bone mohlangana o munye nge o fana naye. Lokhwa ba re bandu ba ya fana, mara llo yena ndi kholwa e nga ngu ye."

"Ee."

Then he said, "Let's go."

He took them yonder and got them seated there. After getting seated he———also seated himself and they said, "What now———Do we just sit here?"

"Yes."

They said, "Well, you go and we'll call you."

He went back to the chief and took one woman with him to carry beer, this beer he took to the men yonder. Indeed, they carried the calabash and placed it among them. When they arrived they said, "Yes."

She removed the foam, removed the foam and served them and they drank, after drinking, they smoked tobacco like that, they———smoked and smoked.

Then they said, "Elder."

He said, "Here I am."

They said, "Now could you call the chief for us please, we would like to see him?"

He said, "Of course, why not? It is right."

Then he went to him. He sat on his knees and said, "Chief the———those people would like to see you, they would like to have some words with you."

Then the chief stood up and said, "That's nice of you, elder."

Then he went yonder, took his chair and put it down there next to them and they said that the chief should sit on the chair, and they thanked him. Well, he sat down. They were quiet.

They said, "Well, elder, this chief was called by us. At home there, is there no child who has been lost?"

CM: *Where did these men come from?*

MK: *They came from the diamond fields* [Kimberley].

CM: *Where is that?*

MK: *From the white man's area where they had been working.*

CM: Oho.

MK: *They were working.*

CM: Mm.

MK: *Then they said, "Well, who got lost?"*

He said, "Of course my elder brother's child, he got lost and even today we have never seen him again, nor heard about him. Moreover, wherever he is, we are not even sure whether he is alive or dead."

CM: Mm.

MK: *"Nobody knows."*

Then they said, "Elder, we are just guessing, in fact, I speculate."

Now it is that other one who is talking.

He said, "I guess I saw a certain chap who looks like him. Even if certain people look alike I suspect that it's him."

"Yes."

"O khona o motima nje o ne bahlangana ba nga, nga bathathu."

"Ja.".

Ba re, "Ee. Ngiye we bothathu llo."

Name khona lapho, name lowa a re, "Makute, bita sehlabamokhose."

O hlaba mokhose, namile ke a hlaba mokhose name madoda kusasa ba re putuku! Ba hlala lapho.

Ke ba hlala lapha, name ba re, "Agaa! Madoda! Makarapa nakqa a vela e makgoweni. Eyano ke ba jama ba thobala ne matamo lla ba ta neno, ba re si bone lapha ko ne timvu e tinyeti e tinyetinyeti, ti loswe bahlangana nga banga. Eyano nkhathi ka bahlangana laba, si yaka nge o munye llo o motima llo nga ngu ye nkqosi ye khethu, modwana' nkqosi ye khethu. Eyano llo a wati Mukombani ngu bani?"

Madoda name ba bita lla ba wati Mukombani, ba re, "Thina si ya mo wati, kqosi, thina si ya mo wati. Si ya mo wati, na ke si nga mmona si nga mmati."

Ba re, "Agaa! Ke le ta mmati ke, tekani timbuphu, le tekeni timbuphu, le te le khambeni ne madoda lla ngamahlano lla, le be sihlophanyana se madoda le ye khona lle. Ke le fikako mohlamunyi le ta fika le ba fumane."

Nga mbale, aowa ba jama ba thobala ba hleti ba ya khona lle. Ba jama ba thobala ba hlete ba ya, ba fika khona lapho llanga le lapha, e be le ta suka le ya ku sobela. Name ba fika ba hlala khona lapho e letanyeni, ba thokga tikqonyana ba pheka-pheka, ba phemba mellwana, ba pheka-pheka, ge ba kqetša ku pheka lapha ba hlala ba thobala. Kusasa e re lokhwa mahube a re la, name ba vuka ba hlamba, ba hlamba ne tihloko, ba hlamba kohle lapha, ba hlala. Ba phala tipotwana tabo, ba phala tipotwana tabo, ba pheka. E re kube ba pheke aowa ba dla ba dla——ba dla ba šeba ngetinyamana leto tabo, a ba na ndaba ba hleti. Ba re, "Na—— -lokhwa nnango e yo betha madine li ta ba bona ba ta vela."

Name ba re, "Aowa li ta ba bona, Makgale o ta bekela." Ba re ba hl- ba sa hlete——nn- nnango lle ba fanele ngabe ba te, ba bona lethwidlana le vela nkhathi ke mithi ba re, "Le ya le bona lethwidlana leli, ntimvu ti yeta. O ta ti bona ti ta be ti kgamoke khona lapha." Nga mbala ba sa re si hleti name ta vela timvu ti kijimela ku yo sela. Ti fike ti kqongwa nge madolo ti ya sela, ti ya sela, ti ya sela, ti ya sela ta be ta hunyelela tokqe ti ya sela, muvha name ku vela bahlanganyana.

Ba re, "Haa, eyano ke lapho bona ba yeta eyano. Si ta te si le ve kore le to rene." Ba re e re ke ba fika lapha e letanyeni, ke ba podeni ngalapha ngemma——nge ba ba botisa matinyo we bombili——

CM: Mm.

MK: Kore ba ve kore na ngi bo koba a se ngibo——nama aowa lapha ba kgopela meetse, gobe ba ba re, "Tekane tikomikana nate."

Ba sela bokqe ba re——sele ba mo thele mmahlo bokqe aba. Ba sela, ba sela, ba sela.

"There is a darker one like this and he is among the three boys."

"Yes."

They said, "Yes, he is the third one."

Just there that man said, "Makute, call the person who is responsible for sounding a horn to get people together."

He did this and the following morning men arrived. They sat down.

When they've settled, then they said, "Well, gentlemen! Here are some migrants who come from the white man's land. Now, on their way from work, when they spent some nights next to the dams on their way home, they say they saw a place with many sheep, many, many and they were looked after by many boys. Now amongst them we suspect the other one, the darker one, is our chief, the son of our chief. Now, who knows Mokopane?"

Then the men called those who knew Mokopane and they said, "We know him, chief, we know him. If we could see him we would recognise him."

They said, "Well! If you could recognise him, take mealie meal, you should take mealie meal so that you should go back with these five men and form a larger group of men to go there. When you arrive perhaps you would find it is him."

Well, indeed, they left and spent some nights on their way there. They slept on their way until they reached the place while the sun was about there, just before sunset. Then they camped next to the dam, they chopped down some wood and prepared food, lit a fire, they cooked and afterwards they slept. The next day, just after dawn, they woke up and washed themselves, washed themselves and washed their heads, washed their pots and cooked. After cooking, they ate———and ate, they ate and supplemented their food with meat, no problem, they are relaxed. They said, "When———it is just about time for dinner, you will see they will appear."

Then they said, "Well, you will see, Makgale, [one of the party] will guard." When they———when they were still relaxed———a– and according to the time they should have arrived, they saw dust hovering over the bush and said, "Do you see that dust? It's sheep coming. You will see them, they will soon appear here." Indeed, while they were still relaxed like that, the sheep appeared running to drink water. They crouched on their knees and drank, drank, drank, drank until they were satisfied and retreated. After a while the boys appeared.

They said, "Well, now here they come. We'll hear what you are going to say." It is said that when they arrived at the dam they started———asking them their second names———

CM: Mm.

MK: *So that they should know whether it is them or not———well then, they asked for water and afterwards they said, "Take these cups."*

They drank and———these men were looking at him. They drank and drank and drank.

Kibe ba re ndoda ennye ya re, "Bomolekane, lena mabit o a lena, ke lena bo mang?"

Lowa o munye a re, "Ndi ngo Kleinbooi."

O munye o re, "Ndi ngo Swartbooi."

Lowa a re——lowa a re, "Nna ndi ngo Klaas."

CM: Mm.

MK: Ba nama ba re——ba——ba——ba hlala kahle ba re, "Ai, ai, ai, ai!"

Ba re, "O ngo Klaas bani?"

A re, "Ah eh. Ndi no ba ngo Klaas ka phela."

Ba re, "A se wena Klaas Mokopane?"

Wa vuma a re, "Ee, yena."

Ba re, "Ngu ye llo."

CM: Mm.

MK: Ba nama ba re, "Ah eh, ku lungile bobaba khambani."

Ba nyuka ne timvu leta ba khamba ba ya lle. Ba fika lle ba hlwa ba lusile te be ta buya ndambama ti yo ngena, ta thobala, ta re ku thobala, kusasa *vroeg*, lokhwa llangana li sa re lapha le re, ba nama ba——ba phatha methwalo ngetandla. Ba ya ku hlangana nge ndlu ye lekgowa. Ba va nja e re, "Hou hou!"

Nama lekgowa le re, "*Jy*," le jame nge tinyawo e tut ke——i-ngemmundwana. Name ke ba fika lapha name o fumana madoda ba re, "Morena, morena, morena!"

Nama ba fika ba hlala phase, ndoda nga nnye ya jama ya re, "Morena! Eti siya funa. Si tinyelelwe."

"Mm."

"Si tinyelelwe mundwana, mundwan'ethu e se ke a timela kade. Eyano a si wati kore na ukuphi kuba ukuphi."

A fike a re, "Aowa, lapha a ku na, a kuna mundu o mo njalo lapha. Laba ba lapha mbami ka phela la."

Nama o a ba bita o re matinyo abo o ba bita nge matinyo a bo, kube ba fike lapha ba fika ba jama nge bathathu kabo ba fika ba re——a nama a re, "Le ya ba bona laba embami? Naba bona."

Ba re, "Morena, eba ngilo engu wethu nakqo. Lo e ba ngilo si mo funako, o montima llo, ngu ye wethu——"

CM: Mm.

MK: "Nkqosi yethu ke a lapha."

"Eye?"

"Mm."

"Aowa," lekgowa la re, "Eyano ke ngiba enkqosi yenu le ta mmona njani, nami ndi mo phiwe nna, ndi mo phiwe mmundu."

CM: Mm.

Afterwards one man said, "Guys, what are your names?"

That one said, "I'm Kleinbooi."

The other one said, "I'm Swartbooi."

The next——said, "I'm Klaas."

CM: **Mm.**

MK: *Then they said——they——they relaxed and said, "Well, well, well!"*

They said, "You are Klaas who?"

He said, "Nothing. I'm just Klaas."

They said, "Are you not Klaas Mokopane?"

He agreed and said, "Yes, him!"

They said, "That's him!"

CM: **Mm.**

MK: *Then they said, "Well, it's fine boys, you may go."*

They went up with the sheep and went there. They spent the day in the pastures and brought the sheep back in the evening, led them to the kraal to sleep. The following morning, early, they——carried their bags. They went to the white man at his own house. They heard a dog barking, "Hou! Hou!"

While standing on the veranda of his house, the white man said, "Hey you!" He went to those men and they said, "Master, master, master!"

Then they sat down and one man stood up and said, "Master, we are searching. Somebody is missing."

"Mm."

"Our child is missing, our child has been missing since a long time ago. Now we don't even know where he is."

Then he said, "Well, no, here we don't, there is no such person here. All these who are here are mine."

Then he called them, he called out their names, yelled out their names and they came, the three of them and stood in front of them and he said, "Do you see these which are mine? Here they are."

They said, "Master, ours is this one. The one we are searching for, this one is ours——"

CM: **Mm.**

MK: *"He is our chief if you see him here."*

"Really?"

"Mm."

"Well", the white man said, "Now if he is your chief, what can you give me for him because I was given him by someone else——"

CM: **Mm.**

MK: "—a—ebile mundwana wami."

Eyano ti fike ti ba tlabe khona lapho. "Eyano lena banati ba khona, lokhwa le mmatiko, le ya mmati."

Name e re lokhwaeya lekgowa le re—lekgowa le re, "Ja, ma kuba le ya mo funa, e ba mundwana wenu nga mbalambala—"

Nge kuba naye o a mmutisa o re, "Madoda lla o ya wa wati?"

"No, a ku na llo ndi mo watiko kibo nge moka."

Name lapha name ba a hlala. Name o re, "Lena, a ndere le ya mva? Le fike le bote ise makube o ya mfuna, ndi funa masome ngamathathu e timvu."

CM: Mm.

MK: "Ne matinyo we tindlovu. Ma kuba le mo funa phaya le nga mo funiko—"

CM: Ne matinyo we tindlovu?

MK: Ee, matinyo we tindlovu. Ngore o a bona lle—

CM: Mm.

MK: —kubo *Olifant* lle—

CM: Mm.

MK: —e name ba re, "Morena, ah eh, si vile."

Name ke ba suka lapho name mokhosi o a lla. Ba re, "Hai, wuye, hai! Wuye! Wuye! Wuye! Wuye!"

Aowa e name ke ba fika lapha ba no welawela timbahla tabo, nama ba wela ndlela ba ta ekhaya. E jama ba thobala, ba thobala, ba thobala, e re lokhwa ba to ta lapha ekhaya—lapha emuganwini o mmovu, esikgweni sengwenyama ngale, nkqolo ya lla. Ba ya va laba e banye endabeni.

Nama ba hlala e tulu ke maye ba re, "Ba yeta."

CM: Be ba hlala kuphi nge nnango leyo? E be le hlala kuphi?

MK: Nga lapha, ngungalapha—

CM: Ngala?

MK: Ngemathupini a le—

CM: Emathupini?

MK: Miti yokqe lle e phuma ngalapha—ngalapha nge mathupini ngale.

CM: Eya!

MK: Lapha e tiswe nguneMukombani ngesibanga se ku palelwa ku khwela ndaba lle.

CM: Oho.

AB: Eyano pa—

MK: Mh?

AB: Sekgwa lesi be e hleti si khona?

MK: Ini? Sekgwa e be si hleti—sekgwa si sabisako.

MK: *"———uh———he is even my child."*

Now they contradicted one another there. "Now you, his people, if you know him, you know him."

After a while the white man said———he said, "Yes, if you really need him, if he is indeed your child———"

In fact, he asked the boy, he said, "Do you know these men?"

"No, there is none that I recognise."

Then they relaxed. Then he said, "You, do you hear me? Go and tell his father that if he needs his son, I want thirty sheep."

CM: Mm.

MK: *"And the elephant's tusks. If you need him you will, if you don't———"*

CM: *And also the tusk of the elephant?*

MK: *Yes, ivory. In fact you know where there are elephants in the vicinity———*

CM: Mm.

MK: *———in the vicinity of the Olifants River———*

CM: Mm.

MK: *———then they said, "Well sir we've heard."*

When they left, the horn was sounded. They ululated in jubilation. "Huye! Huye! Huye! Huye! That's him! That's him! That's him!"

Well they went back and grabbed their bags and came back. They slept nights on their way until they arrived here and when they were at the red maroela tree, in the Forest of Lions, the horn was sounded.

All the other people in the mountains heard and they stood on top of the rocks and said, "They are coming."

CM: *Where were they staying by that time? Where were you staying?*

MK: *This side, it is on this side.*

CM: *This side?*

MK: *At the ruins there————*

CM: *At the ruins?*

MK: *All these homes came from there——from these ruins on the other side.*

CM: *Really!*

MK: *They come here because Mokopane's mother could not climb this mountain any longer.*

CM: Oho.

AB: *Now sir———*

MK: Mh?

AB: *This bush, was it there?*

MK: *What? This bush was still——frightening.*

AB: Eyano hlalosa ke.

MK: A o ve ke ba re ngu setikgweni, ngu seti——ku ne sifate se ngwenyama. Ke ba ta ngeSikgakgapeni ngalapha, nkqolo e a lla, ya re, "Pše! Pše! Pše! Pše!"

O ta va ba re, "Tladi e a lla, ngu Monhla wa bo——"

E ta re ke ba fika ku boNgwaditše lapha, a re a kgamoka ku bo Mantwane lapha, a re ku thamba a ya lle, a boye a thambe a ya lle.

A re, "Ja ba mmonne o yeta."

Name ba vhele lapho ba re, "Ho, ho, ho, ho, ho, ho, ho!"

Name ba ta betha mmate we Ngwaditše, ba khwela ngenkqane. Namile ba a khwela, ke ba khwelako, ke ba fika ngale, nnena name o——o—— ongomela madoda lawa wohle ngale nge mmahlweni, o a ba beka o fumana e ngore mmadoda ka phela a ku ne mundwana, llo ngabe o nga- ngabo labo.

CM: Mm.

MK: Name nnina o boela nkhaya. Ke a boela nkhaya——

CM: [Talking to someone else] Ungakhambise mm– m– koko o to khamba mohlomunye ba to mo khambisa.

MK: Ba hlala phase. Name nkqosi o re, "A si veneni, madira, kore le khambe njani." O munye o re, "Ao kgoši, sa mo fumana."

"Ee, eyano bothata bo velaphi?"

CM: [Still talking to someone else] A ba to khambisa lokhwa ba phambana——

MK: "Eyano bothata?"

"Bothata ntimvu."

CM: [Another comment directed outside the interview] Bokoko——ba fanele ku khambisa bokoko.

MK: "Eyano ke——lekgowa lela le re le funa masome a mathathu e timvu ne matinyo we tindlovu."

"Jo, jo, jo, jo!"

CM: Masome mathathu?

MK: Ja, masome a mathathu e timvu.

CM: Mm.

AB: Ke lekgowa?

MK: Aowa, ee ke lekgowa.

AB: Le——le——le—— funa timvu leti——

CM: ——khona lapho ba mo fumene khona.

AB: Ee, le ti funa ku bani? Kore mundu lowa a longollwe?

MK: Ja. Ti to longolla Mukombani.

AB: Ti to longolla Mukombani?

MK: Ee. [Several people speak at once]

AB: *Then you should explain.*

MK: *That's why it is said that is is the bush of——there is a tree of the lion. When they came via Sekgakgapeng, the horn was sounded, "Pše! Pše! Pše! Pše!"*

They said, "Thunder is sounding, it is the sharp one of Monhla——" [probably the horn-blower]

And when they came to Ngwaditše over here, they started ululating and dancing this way and that.

They said, "Yes, they have found him, he is coming."

Then they appeared there singing, "Yo! Yo! Yo! Yo! Yo! Yo! Yo!"

They then crossed the waters of Ngwaditše by force. They then ascended and after ascending, they arrived on the other side and——his mother is looking at all the men's faces, looking at them only to find that they are all men and no boys.

CM: Mm.

MK: *His mother then went back home. When she went back home——*

CM: [Talking to someone else] *Don't b–be in a hurry. Grandmother is going, perhaps they would take her there.*

MK: *They settled down and the chief said, "Let's hear, soldiers, how you journeyed."*

One said, "Well, chief, we found him."

"Yes, now what is the problem?"

CM: [Still talking to someone else] *They won't hurry up when they meet——*

MK: *"Now what's the problem?"*

"The problem is the sheep."

CM: [Another comment directed outside the inverview] *Grandmother——they should take grandma with them.*

MK: *"Well, now——that white man says he wants thirty sheep and ivory tusks."*

"Yo, yo, yo, yo!"

CM: *Thirty?*

MK: *Yes, thirty sheep.*

CM: Mm.

AB: *Is that the white man?*

MK: *No, it is the white man.*

AB: *He——he——he——wants these sheep——*

CM: *——just where he found them.*

AB: *Yes, but from whom does he want them? So that that boy should be released?*

MK: *Yes. They are going to release Mokopane.*

AB: *They are going to release Mokopane?*

MK: Yes. [Several people speak at once]

MK: Lowa Makute o re , "Matinyo we tindlovu eyano a to si khathata." Name ba re——ba khupha madoda nga mahlanu ba re, "Eyanani kaLanga le——le yo khombela matinyo we tindlovu."

Ngu lokhwa ba sukako ba ya kaLanga ba fike ku Masebe.

"Masebe si thunywe nkqosi. E si thume kore si to funa matinyo we tindlovu, mundwana we kqosi lowa a be a timeleko si mmonne. Eyano lekgowa la khona o re o funa matinyo we tindlovu."

"Eya!"

"Ee."

Wa fika wa re tlabe!

Wa re, "All right, hlalani phase."

Wa bita madoda kambe nga mahlanu akhe.

Wa re, "Na le a mva?"

Ba re, "Si ku vile kqosi."

A re, "Tsama– khambani le ye kaMolengwa——"

AB: KaMolengwa ngu phi?

MK: Ka Molengwa ngale ke moše eMogalakwena, phase.

AB: Lle kubo Mashegoana lle?

MK: M– khona phase lle. Name ba kqwala, ba khamba, ba khamba ba fika ba re lle gaMogalakwena. Kube ba re Mogalakwena name ba khwela tindabana leti. Ke ba fika khona, aowa, ba fumana nduna ya khona, ba fika ba lot ha, ya fika ba re———aowa khona lapho name ba re, "Ah eh, wena nduna, si thunywe nkqosi———ngore———eh———si to khombela matinyo we tindlovu."

AB: Matinyo we tindlovu eyano ba———ba a khombela e———e lengwe———

MK: Ee, nlingoni, nlingwena ma o lija———o lija lesinga. O leja nsimbi madoda ke a vela lapha, ba fika ba hlabela lapha madoda, ba kgobokane name ke ba kgobokanako name a re, "Ba kaMolengwa."

Name ba re, "Morena!"

A re, "Le a nkwa? Kgoši o romile batho ba gagwe šeba bona, ba re ba tlile go nyaka meno a ditlou."

"Eya?"

"Ee."

Hono———kwa jama ndoda nga nnye, e nnye nayo nama a re, a re———o munye na o munye a jama a khombola nga kakhe, o munye a re———o munye a ta a phuma nga kakhe o pha———o ta a phethe nga mathathu, o munye a phethe nga mambili, o munye a phethe nga mathathu o munye a phethe ngamang- agi, njalo a———

AB: E Maburu lla a to khombela matinyo we tindlovu lawo?

MK: *That Makute said, "Ivory is going to give us problems." Then they said——they appointed five men and said, "Go to Langa's place and——ask for ivory."*
They went to Langa's place and found Masebe.
"Masebe, the chief, has sent us here. He sent us to come and look for ivory. The son of the chief who has been missing has been seen. Now the white man under whom we found him wants ivory."
"Is that so?"
"Yes."
He [Masebe] was puzzled.
He said, "All right, be seated."
He called his five men.
He said, "You hear?"
They said, "We have heard you chief."
He said, "Go– go to Molekoa's place——"

AB: *Where is Molekoa's place?*

MK: *Molekoa's area is across the Mogalakwena river, down there.*

AB: *There at Mashegoana there?*

MK: *Ye– down there. Then they started, they walked, they walked until they reached Mogalakwena. After crossing Mogalakwena they climbed these mountains. When they arrived, well, they found the headman of the area, they greeted and then said——well just there they said, "Well, you headman, we have been sent here by the chief. In fact we——we are asking for elephant's tusks."*

AB: *The tusks now--when they asked for them were they——*

MK: *Yes, the chief ordered one of his men to ring——the iron bell so that men should gather together. He summoned the men, they came, those men, and after gathering together, he said, "The Molekoa people."*
They said, "Chief!"
He said, "D'you hear me? The chief has sent his men here to come and look for ivory."
"Really?"
"Yes."
Now——one by one the men——one by one the men went to their huts and each came back with three or two tusks and some came with many, like that——

AB: *Was it the Boers who came to ask for ivory?*

MK: Leburu lela lapha ku na Mukombani.

Name khona lapha, name khona lapha———matinyo we tindlovu———name Molengwa o re, "Le ya mva lena ba kaMolengwa? Ku to phuma madoda nga mahlanu a ta———le– khamba ne bandu laba eye? E be le yo fika lapha bandu laba ba ya khona. E be le fike le bone mundu lowe ba re ba re oa———a———ba mmonne. Ke le te naye le fike le te le mbote kore na nge mmahlo le re si mmonne."

Name khona lapho ba thwala matinyo we tindlovu, name ba yeta.

Ba fika ba a thula kaMasebe, ba fika ba re, "Masebe, matinyo———matinyo we tindlovu nakqa."

AB: E re ndi——— [inaudible because of noise]

MK: Ee———ee e be ti khona.

CM: Wa bona ndaba lle e sele ba e funa kqulu e iyini? N– tindaba ta se ligolweni la kaGwaša lle.

MK: Ee ngi lokhwa khona lapho, name laba ba fika lapha ba ta nabo ba———ba thunywa ngu Langa lapha ba ta ba fika nge ndabeni ba fika ba re, "Matinyo we tindlovu nakqa wona kqosi." Nama a khupha bandu nga bathathu, ba ya kaMakhujisa.

Ba re, "Makhujisa, nkqosi e re ku funeka masome e mathathu e timvu. E ngasi leti ti na tivanana, e ngasi leti ti dušako. E ti fresh ka phela."

CM: Mm.

MK: Nga mbala ba ti kgetholla, ba ti kgetholla, ba ti kgetholla ne sibaya lesa, nga mbale kambe e be e sa ngemošate. Ba ti kgetholla, ba ti kgetholla ta ba ta re masome a mathathu ba re, "Nati tona ti lengene masome a mathathu."

A re, "A ti khambe."

CM: Ta ya khona lle ku longolla Mukombani?

MK: Ta ya lle, ta ta khona lapha name ti ngene nga lapha. Kube ti ngene nga lapha, aowa name ke ba fikako ba re, "Aga, namhlanje khona——— khona———a le se se mašiwana."

Name madoda wokqe ba re, "A ku ne llo———a si sale. Nathi si funa ku yo suka naye lapha a suka———a yo suka khona."

CM: Mm.

MK: Wa bone name ba kgatla mekhokhwana nkqosi o———e wisa nkqomo phase ku tekwa tinyama ba ngenisa ngemi———ngemikotlaneni ba ngenisa ngemikotlaneni. *Then* kusasa ba wela lle ne timbutšhana ta bo ne tipotwana. Ba jama ba———a banye ba sembili ke———timvu, ba banye ba se mahlanguthini, ba banye ba ngasamuva, timvu ti nkhathi kabo ti ngemuka. Emini nje ati khambi *nie*. Ti———ti hlwa ti lusiwe ti dla, ti dla, ti———lokhwa llanga li subelako ba ne ku tiparapara. Name ba re———timvu ndlela tidla emini———ti ngabe ta hlwa ti si tshwenya lapha.

CM: Mm.

MK: *It is that Boer on whose farm they found Mokopane.*

Just there then, then the ivory——then Molekoa said, "Do you hear me you Molekoa people? Five men will be appointed among you to go with these men, okay, until you reach your destination with them. Till you reach the place where they say——they say they saw the person. After arriving with him you should come and tell me you saw him with your naked eyes."

Then they carried that ivory and came here.

They delivered them to Masebe and said, "Masebe, ivory, here is the ivory."

AB: *Let me——*[inaudible because of noise]

MK: *Yes——yes, they were here.*

CM: *You know, do you know the main story they want to know? I— it is the story of the cave of Gwaša.*

MK: *Yes, it is then that they arrived here, sent by Langa here and arrived in the mountains and said, "Here is ivory, chief." Then he appointed three more people to go to Makhujisa.*

They said, "Makhujisa, the chief says that thirty sheep are wanted. Not the ones with lambs or those that have conceived. He needs only the fresh ones."

CM: Mm.

MK: *Indeed they selected them, selected them, selected them in the kraal as a whole and indeed it was still the royal kraal. They selected them, selected them until they reached thirty and they said, "Here they are and they are thirty."*

He said, "Let them go."

CM: *They went there to secure Mokopane?*

MK: *They went there, they came here and entered in here. After entering in here, well, when they arrived he said, "Well, well, today——you don't leave anybody behind."*

Then all the men said, "There's none——you won't leave us behind. We also want to leave with him [Mokopane] wherever he is going to leave."

CM: Mm.

MK: *You see, they then prepared themselves and the chief——slaughtered a cow for them. The meat was taken and put into their——bags, and put into their bags. Then the following day they started their journey with their mealie meal and small pots. They were——some were in front of the sheep——some on the sides and some at the back while all the sheep were in the middle. During the day they did not move. T——they leave the sheep to feed and when the sun sets they—— surrounded them. Then they——start to walk while during the day——the sheep feed, so that they don't trouble them.*

CM: Mm.

MK: Mm. Name nga mbala ba khamba ba khamba, e be ba ye ku fika khona lapho esikhisini leso, ke ba fika khona lapho ba lale ba lare khona lapho ba thobele, aowa ka ku ne ndaba. Kusasa ke ku sako, a ndere ku ya emadineni [inaudible], ba thwele ne matinyo we tindlovu lawa. Ke ba fika esikgwaneni lapha, mvu name ya lla yakhe ya re, "Hoo!" Name te madoda ta re, "Hoo! Hoo!"

Name ta pheletšwa nja ya re, "Hou! Hou!" [Laughter]

Lowa ke a phumako lekgowa o jama emmondwaneni o bone, o bone ku vela ku vela lešaba le bandu. Ke ba fika lapha name ba re,"Eše morena, eše morena."

Ba re, "*Ja.*"

Ba re, "*Maak oop die hek pa.*"

La vula ngeite ta ngena, ta ngena timvu, ta ngena, ta ngena, o a ti bala. A ti bala ta be ta fumana masome a mathathu.

A re, "*Ja*, ti lungile."

A teka matinyo we tindlovu la ba wa kgobela esitupwini lapho. Wa wa kuka wa wa isa nge ndlini ku misis. Ngu lokhwa khona lapho name———

AB: Phumela embili, o be o sele———o———tšwela pele.

MK: Ee———name khona lapha aowa, name ba ti ba teka ndokati leya ngi laba be nte———oho.

AB: Phumela embili le ta no bušeletša e nnye nayo e khona.

MK: Oho———ya re lokhwaeya lapho name kwa———ngabe ne mathata name ba mmita.

"Mukombani! Bekhenu naba nemhlanje ba to ku teka."

A re, "O a ti bona timvu leta ti ngena lapha, ti to lungulla wena. Ne matinyo we tindlovu lla a to lungulla wena. Eyano ndi ya ku bopholla namhlanje kore bekhenu ba ku teke."

AB: Thobela.

MK: "*Ja*, o kha———ba khambe nawe."

AB: Ee.

MK: A re, "Morena."

"*Ja*".

Ba re, "Khamba, teka tinguyana takho ngale."

Name o ya ngale o yo teka tinguyana takhe nape o———madoda ba mo tekela tona, name ti tekwa mmadoda ti phathwa mmadoda.

AB: E rene pa *before* le phumela embili mbutise kore Mukombani lo yona nnango le be ba mo tekile, o hleti nnango e kangani ne Maburu lawo?

MK: Ba mo teke a se se kangana ngale ba mo fumana e se se lešoboro le ku kgeila.

AB: *Is it?*

MK: Mm. Ba mo teke a se se kangana.

MK: *Yes. Indeed they walked and walked until they reached that valley. When they arrived, they spent the night there, well, no problem. The following day when it was nearly dinner time,* [inaudible] *they carried the ivory to a little bush. When they arrived in the bush, the Boer's sheep bleated and the ones led by the men also bleated.*

Finally the dog barked, "Hou! Hou!" [Laughter]

That white man came out of his house and stood on the veranda and saw many people coming. When they arrived there they said, "Greetings, master, greetings."

They [probably should be *he*] *said, "Yes."*

They said, "Open the gate, master."

He opened the gate and they entered, the sheep entered, they entered, entered while he was counting them. He counted them until they reached thirty.

He said, "Yes, they are fine."

He took the ivory while those men were putting it on the veranda. He took them into the house to the madam. Just there then——

AB: *Go ahead, you were just about——to proceed.*

MK: *Yes, well then——they took what we call this——all right.*

AB: *Go ahead, you'll just repeat it because there is still something else.*

MK: *All right——afterwards then——without problems they called him.*

"Mokopane! Here are your people, they have come to fetch you."

He said, "Do you see these sheep that are entering here, they have come to release you. These ivory tusks here also come to secure you. Now today I release you so that your people should take you."

AB: *Indeed.*

MK: *"Yes——you g–they go with you."*

AB: *Yes.*

MK: *He said, "Yes, sir."*

"Yes."

They said, "Go, take your clothing in there."

Then he went to take his clothes and——and the men carried them for him, and they were taken by the men and carried by the men.

AB: *Excuse me, sir,* before *you proceed, the time Mokopane was taken, how long did he live with the Boers?*

MK: *They took him while he was still young, not yet initiated.*

AB: *Is it?*

MK: *Mm. They took him while he was still young.*

CM: Eyano lokhwa a boya o be a kangani?

MK: E se uwo————

AB: Ema pele ke felletše.

MK: E se se ngu wo mongane llo, e nge lokhwa e se se mohlanganyana, a yo hlalepha, a lo————a lusa tikqo————ti timvu. Mm. Eyano khona lapho aowa *no* name lekgowa la bopholla Mukombani, madoda name a te– ai! Mokhosi wa lla, mabatata kwa lla mabatata, ko šwahlwa methe lle ba šwahla kohle lapha, a banye esele ba mo paraparile.

AB: Eyano e sa hlola e iyini methe? Lethabo? Ngekore o bo————

MK: Ee lethabo————ee ba thakgele.

     "He buya, he."

     Lekgowa le mangele lapha le re na bandu ba yenta ini?

AB: *And eh————*

MK: Mm.

AB: ————e le kore ngayo menyaka ya bo Mukombani le be le batha marokgo *or* e be e se se ntivunno?

MK: Aowa, boMukombani e ba batha tivunno. Mm.

AB: O ka nna wa tšwela pele.

MK: *Ja.* Eyano khona lapho aowa, ba suka na Mukombani. Ba ta naye. Ke ba ta lapha, ba fika lapha, ba re aowa, ba te ba khamba naye nnangu lle yokqe, ba re ke ba ta nga lapha nge sekgweni se ngwenyama————

AB: Mm.

MK: ————Nkqolo ya lla.

AB: Khona nge Sikgakgapeni nga la?

MK: *Ja* eSikgakgapeni. Ba thobala ngale ngemuva nga————ka ka lla.

AB: Ndaba ya khona e tulu la?

MK: Nga le nge Sihlabeni ngale.

AB: Ee ee.

MK: Ai. Ba va ne mabatata a lla name ba re, "Ah! Nemuhla khona ba ta naye."

     Nga mbale ba to vela lapha, ba to kgamoga eNgwaditše lapha emasimini lapha, ba bona bandu ba re ku iwa lle ne mahlanga, ku iwa lla, laba e banye ba mo ngenise nkhathi ke mašaba, o nge mašabeni. A ka bonakali ku no re, "O ho, bo, bo, bo!" Ba ta naye ba be ba nyuka Ngwaditše.

     Name ba nyoka naye ba nyuka Ngwaditše, ke ba to khwela lapha esiphandeni lapha, name nnina o hleti, o hleti lapha emmundwini endakaneni.

MK: Mm.

MK: Name ke ba dlula lapha ya be o mo teka nge mkhono, ya be o mo teka o mo isa nkhaya. E ba nama ba ya enkundleni, ba teka tikqomo, tikqomo, tikqomo nga tine, "Thu! Thu! Thu! Thu-thu! Thu! Thu!"

     Name tikqomo leta ti pitikama phase.

CM: *Now how old was he when he came back?*

MK: *He was still———*

AB: *Let me finish first.*

MK: *He was still very young, still a boy, starting to be conscious and looking after the catt– the sheep. Yes. Now, well, no, the white man set Mokopane free and the men came close and started celebrating and sounding the horns, jumping over the trees and surrounding him.*

AB: *Now why were they jumping over the trees? Was it happiness? Because he was———*

MK: *Yes, happiness———yes, they were happy.*

"Hey, come back, hey!"

The white man was stunned and was asking what they were doing.

AB: *And eh———*

MK: *Mm.*

AB: *———during the time of Mokopane were people wearing trousers or was it still the leather loincloths?*

MK: *No, those of Mokopane were wearing leather loincloths. Yes.*

AB: *You may proceed.*

MK: *Yes. Now, just there, well, they went away with Mokopane. They are coming with him. When they arrive here, arrive here, they say well, they've been with him all the way and they are now in the Forest of Lions———*

AB: *Mm.*

MK: *———the horn was sounded.*

AB: *Just here in the vicinity of Sekgakgapeng?*

MK: *Yes at Sekgakgapeng. They slept on that side, behind———this one.*

AB: *That mountain up there?*

MK: *That side of Masehlaneng there.*

AB: *Yes, yes.*

MK: *Suddenly, they heard the sound of the horns and said, "Well! Today they are with him."*

Indeed they are coming with him and they moved across the Ngwaditše just there next to the fields, and saw people going to that side with canes, going there, while some put him in the midst of some branches, surrounding and concealing him with the branches. He is invisible and it is just a buzzing noise. They came with him until they crossed Ngwaditše.

Then they crossed with him and went up from Ngwaditše, and when they were moving between two, two mountains, then his mother is seated, seated here on the veranda of the house.

MK: *Mm.*

MK: *When they passed by her she took him by the hand, took him to the house. The others then went to the council place, they brought the cattle, cattle, cattle and started shooting them, "Thu! Thu! Thu! Thu-thu! Thu! Thu!"*

Those cattle were skinned.

AB: Ta thuntšhwa?

MK: *Ja* ta thuntšhwa.

AB: Ku ba Mukombani a buye?

MK: *Ja*. Eyano ta kqwalwa ngi laba ba sekhaya, ba ti sindla lapha kwa———
        lapha ku sa thanjwa lapha———

AB: Ti thuntšhwa Maburu *or*———

MK: Aikhona! Bona, bona bekhethu.

AB: Nge lethabo?

MK: *Ja* nge lethabo labo. Mm. Name khona lapho a ndiri ngi lokhwa tithunya,
        tithunya ti se se khona. E tithunya ti———ti———e ntabo, engasi te mundu.
        Ba no teka lesi ba se bonako.

AB: Tithunya e se se ntabo bani?

MK: Nta bona bekhethu laba.

AB: Ekhe ya ba ntabo thina tithunya?

MK: Ee a ndiri ba ti teke ki laba———[he is interrupted]

        Ja, a ndiri, lokhwa ba berenga lle———[another interruption]

AB: Be ba ba golisa tithunya?

MK: ———e be ba ti nabo ba ti, eh———ba ti thenga. Kube ba fike lapha nabo ba
        kaLanga nabo ke ba berengako, ba thenga tithunya ba ya nato ekhabo
        bona. Eyano ba re lokhwa ba lwako, ba lwa na ba kaLanga laba
        bekhethu, ba re ku bulala ba kaLanga e phele ba ba muka tithunya ti
        boela nga kibo. Ba bulala ba kaLanga ba———ba ba muka tithunya ba yo ti
        bekela nga kibo.

        Kuba ti thuntšhwe ti ya sindlwa tikqomo name ti phele ku sindlwa name
        kwa jama yena Makute o swele, "Le ya theeleja lena Mandebele ndi ya le
        lebuka nge mokgwa llo le berenge ngakho. Kqulu ndi lebuka Ma- n-
        Langa. Langa, ndiri o a mva? Nkqomo yakho ngile. Wena lle ngi ya———
        ngi ya bandu bakho. Lle, o a e bona lle, ngi ya Molengwa lle. Eyano ngi
        ye mošate lle, lle e lapha lle."

        Ku sele ku———ku sele ku———ku khotšhwa ti———tindokati, ma———
        maphaphu lla, ku a dliwa, ku a dliwa anga tšhabi a, a nga tšhabi a iswe
        na sendoka tini———

CM: O a wa dla a njalo?

MK: Eye?

CM: Ba wa dla a e ye matala?

MK: Ee. Ne si———ne sibindi lesi, si hleti si vuta tingati ba si dla, mm. Name
        khona lapho ba re, "Aowa, si kodukile kqosi."

        Aowa, nkqosi ya re, "Aowa nami ndi ya lebuku lokhwa mundwana we
        mogolwami a phile kuhle. Name nhlitiyo yami nemhlanje e hlaba ngi ye
        hlophe." Ao name ku hlalwe khona lapho.

AB: *They shot them?*

MK: Yes, *they were shot.*

AB: *After Mokopane came back?*

MK: Yes. *Now those who were left at home started to skin them while others were still dancing for joy———*

AB: *They were shot by the Boers or———*

MK: *No ways! These, these our people.*

AB: *As a result of joy?*

MK: Yes, *because of their happiness. Yes. Now, just there, didn't this happen while our people still had guns? These guns were still available. These guns were——— were still theirs, not belonging to other people. They just used the kinds they wanted.*

AB: *Whose guns were they?*

MK: *They were belonging to our people, these.*

AB: *Did they ever own guns?*

MK: Yes. *Isn't it they took them from these———*[he is interrupted] Yes, *isn't it by the time they worked there———* [another interruption]

AB: *Did they pay them in guns?*

MK: *———they bought them. When they arrived here, these people of Langa, after working, they bought guns and carried them home. Now while they were fighting, our people, fighting against the people of Langa, they killed the people of Langa———and confiscated their guns. They killed the people of Langa, confiscated their guns and stored them here.*

After being shot, they were skinned and after the skinning, the arrogant Makute stood up and said, "Listen, you the Ndebele. I thank you for the way in which you performed this work. More important I also thank you the———Langa people. Langa, are you listening? Here is your cow. You, this is the cow for--for your people. This one, you see this one? It's for Molekoa. Now this one is for the royal family, this one over here."

Then they started taking out the what-we-call, the———lungs and they started eating them, without, without cooking them or frying them———

CM: *They were just eating them like they are?*

MK: *Yes.*

CM: *Were they just eating them uncooked?*

MK: Yes, *also———this liver as well, when blood was still dripping, they ate it, yes. Then they said, "Well, we've come back, chief."*

Well, the chief said, "I am also thankful that my brother's son is well. Also, my heart that has always been dark is bright today." They then settled down.

Appendix 4: Extract from Interview with Madimetša Kekana, 28/11/87

Part A: Sindebele

MK = Madimetša Kekana
PK = Peter Kekana
IH = Isabel Hofmeyr

Date: 28 November 1987

MK: *Ja*, be ba thunjwa makgowa———*Ja*, eyano ngu lokhwa llo Makute a busako lapha, a busako naye, a busa la a hlete a busa a busa, ya re bandu be ku ya emakgoweni lle e hleti ba ya emakgoweni lle ba boya———ba boya ba ya lle ba boya, kwa ta ba banye emuva, ba lala ba tako ba se lle endleleni khona lle ematanyeni lla be a khona lapha be ba khutša khona, ngu se titišini tabo, be ba hlala khona, ba bona ba to wela timvu te lekgowa te tinyetinyeti, ti luswe bahlangana nga banga———nga bathathu. Name khona lapho ke ba ti welako ba fika ba re, "Bopapa, re kgopela meetse——— nto ya go nwa meetse."

Name ba ba pha tikomikana ba sela, ba sela, ba re, "*Ja*, ke lena badiša ba dinku na bopapa?"

Ba re, "Ee."

Llo o munye wa ba bekelela, wa re, "Ha! Mundu llo, mundwana we nkqosi llo, hleng e khe mundwana we nkqosi o munye? Eh lena———lowo ndokati———a le mo wati Mukombani?"

La ba ba re, "Ah eh. Thina yena si nga se———a si mo wati."

A re, "Nna yena be e mmongani wami, ndi ya mo wati, mara ndi mo fanisa ne mohlangana o munye nga ngu ye lowa."

"Eya?"

"Mm."

Ba re, "Aowa, ndaba lle eyano, a re ye o ta e somaela ekhaya."

PK: *Ja*.

MK: Nga mbala, ba lala ba thobele, na bahlangana laba ba khamba ba ya lle. Eyano a o bone ke———be ba phethe ndlela, be ba thobala endleleni. Kusasa ke ba vukako, ba to kqwala ba ngene ekhaya. Ba ngena llangana le sele le sobela nje. Ba ngena, aowa lapha, nambe ba fika ba thobala.

Kusasa ke ba vukako name ba re, "A re ye se yo lotšhisa emošate."

Name ba ta ba lotšhisa emošate, ku Setšwamadi ngale nge mathupini ngale, e ngasi lapha. Lapha ku dio ta bo nne Mukombani, e ngase se ngale nge ndabeni ngale etulu. Name khona lapho, name ba phuma ba bitana makarapa ba ya khona, e mmadoda nga mahlanu.

Part B: English translation

MK = Madimetša Kekana
PK = Peter Kekana
IH = Isabel Hofmeyr

Date: 28 November 1987

MK: *Yes, they were often kidnapped by the whites. Yes, now, when Makute was in authority, when he was in charge, ruling as he was, there used to be migrants who walked long distances to white areas and back after some time. They would walk and rest on the way, especially next to the dams which became their stations. One day as they were resting, they saw an extraordinarily large flock of sheep belonging to a particular white man being taken care of by three boys. Then when they saw them they said to the boys, "Young men we are asking for water, something to use to drink water."*

They gave them containers and they drank and drank, after which they said, "Well, are you shepherds of these sheep, young men?"

They said, "Yes."

One of them looked at them and said, "Aha, this person is the son of the chief. How could he look so identical to one of the chief's sons? Uh, you over there don't you know Mokopane?"

The other men said, "No. We would not——in fact we don't know him."

He said, "As for me, he was my peer, so I know him, but I suspect that that boy over there is him."

"Really?"

"Yes."

They said, "Well, this issue, you will have to relate when we arrive home."

PK: *Yes.*

MK: *Indeed, they walked back home all night, and those boys also went back there. Then you see, as they were on their way, these migrants often slept several times on the way. The following day when they woke up, they would walk again until the reached home. They arrived here at sunset. They arrived, very well, then they slept.*

The following day when they woke up, they said to one another, "Let's go to the capital and pay our repects."

Then they came to the capital, to Setšwamadi at the old place, not here. The capital moved here later as a result of Mokopane's mother. During that period it was still yonder, on top of the mountain. Then the migrants called one another, and went there. Those men were five in number.

Ke ba fika lle ba fika ba re, "Eše morena, eše morena."

Ba mo funana Makute, aowa, a hleti———a hleti ne bakgomana ba khe. Ba name ba re, "Si lotšheleni emošate."

Aowa, ba ba lotšhela, nkqosi ya ba vumela ya re, "Aowa, ku lungile."

Name e munye o setšha nge mokodleni, o khupha *five* ponto, o re, "Nge ndo lle nami ndi be ndi re nami ndi lotšhisa nkqosi, nkqosi e ta thenga motsungu."

PK: *Ja.*

MK: Lowa naye a munye naye a setšha nge mbodleni, a khupha *five* ponto o re, "Ndi re nkqosi e ta funa lesi e si funako."

Lowa naye———bokqe laba ba phelela ba khupha *five* ponto, *five* ponto bokqe laba, nga bahlano kwabo. Kube ba phelele ba re, "Aowa."

Eyano khona eyano nje khona ba phelele ba re, "*All right.*"

Name, yena Setšwamadi lowo———Makute o re ku munye mokgomana o re, "Wena Mokgomana, teka bandu laba o ba ise ngale esigodlweni lesa se ngale."

Lowa o a ba teka o ba isa ngale. Kube a ba ise ngale, ba fika ba hlala lapho, ke a ba isako. Ke a buyako lowa o fika o re ku ye, "Khamba o yo teka mofati o munye a thwale boyalwa nga lapha, le yo ba pha ba sele."

Nga mbale lowa o fika o teka mofati, ba thwala mojeka lowa, ba fika ba o lahla nga le. Ma ba o lahla nga le aowa lowa name a hlata tiphungwana, o a ba hlatela, o a ba hlatela, wa ti kqetša, wa ba khelela, ba sela, ba sela.

Ba re ku be ba kqetše ku sela lapha name ba re, "Mokgomana, na e be si nga e bona nkqosi na?"

Name a re, "Ao! Le nga si e bone le na ini? Nta ya ndi yo mmita le te le somaetisane naye."

Name ba re, "Aowa, si bitele yena nkhe si te si somaeti..sane naye."

Nga mbale lowa wa suka, wa fika wa bita nkqosi, a kqonge nkqosi a re, "Kqosi, makarapa lawa ba re 'be se funa nkhe si ku bone, si somaetisane nawe, si ne tindaba nawe.'"

Name lowa o re, "Teka setulo lesi o si thwale kê."

Lowa o thwala setulo o ya ngale e bandwini laba. Ke a fika ngale o a fika, ba hlala, o beka nkqosi lapha, aowa a ku ne ndaba. Namile ke ba hleti ba sela, ba sela, name ba re, "*All right*, ndi re wena mokgomana, nkho se butisele nkqosini lapha kore nkhaya lapha a ku na mundwana o munye llo a timeleko na?"

Name mokgomana a re, "Kqosi, ba re makarapa lla ba re si ya butisa ko re na nkhaya lapha a ku na mundwana llo a timeleko we nkqosi na?"

Lowa a re, "Ee, o khona o timele."

Ja, lowa a name a re, "Ee, si bone mundwana o munye, si mo fanisile, kodwa a si kqinise nga ngu ye. Mara si re o fana naye, a ndi wati na e nga ba ngu ye na."

Nkqosi e re, "Ngu kuphi?"

When they arrived there they said, "Greetings, our lord, greetings our lord."

They found Makute, well, he was with his advisors. And then they [migrants] said to them, "Pass our greetings to the capital."

Well, they passed their greetings, and the chief accepted them and said, "Well, it's okay."

Then one of them searched his bag, took out five pounds and said, "With this thing I am also greeting the chief, the chief will buy tobacco."

PK: *Yes.*

MK: *The other one also searched his pocket, took out five pounds and said, "With this I say that the chief will look for whatever he needs."*

The next one also–––all of them each took out five pounds, all five of them. After they had all done that they said, "Well."

Once they had all done that they said, "All right."

Then, Setšwamadi himself–––I mean Makute said to one of his advisors, "You, elder, take these people to the house on the other side."

That one did likewise and took the men to the other side. After doing just that, they got seated there and came back only to be told on his arrival, "Go, take one of the women to carry beer from here, to give to those men to drink."

Indeed, that one did as he was told, took one woman to carry a calabash and to drop it on the other side. Then the woman also washed the drinking utensils after putting down the calabash, and then started serving them while they drank and drank.

After drinking, they said to the elder, "Can we possibly have a word with the chief?"

He said, "Of course? How could you not see him? I shall go and call him so that you can have a discussion with him."

Then they said, "Well, call him for us so that we can have a word with him."

Indeed he left and called the chief, he knelt before the chief and said, "Chief, those migrants said that they would like to have a word or two with you."

Then he said, "Take this chair and carry it over there."

He carried the chair to those people on the other side. When he arrived there, he put the chief over there, and well, there is no problem. They then continued to drink their beer again, and then they said, "All right, I address you, elder, to ask the chief here if there is no particular child from this family who had disappeared."

Then the advisor said, "Chief, these migrants would like to know if there is no particular child of the chief from this family who has disappeared."

Then he said, "Yes, there is one who has disappeared."

Yes, that one then said, "Yes, we saw one child who looked similar to the chief's son but we are not very certain that it is him. However, we are saying that he looks just like him, we don't know if it is actually him."

The chief said, "Where?"

Ba re, "E letanyeni lle, lapha——lokhwa ke e ngore le funa ku ya khona, si nga no le teka se le ise, si yo bona ko re na ana ngu ye koba se buye na."

Nga mbala nkqosi nama ya bita madoda, kusasa ba ta e likqundleni ba tala.

Ke ba tala lapha name o re kubo o re, "Madoda!"

Ba re, "Morena."

A re, "Mundwana we mogolo wami lowa a te a thunjwa makgowa le ya mo wati bokqe lapha? Laba ba mo watiko nkhe ba jamise tandla."

Ba bona bandu ba jamisa tandla nge bonyeti ba re, "Si ya mo wati."

Ba banye ba re, "Nathi si ya mo wati."

Name a re, "*Oh*, lena laba le mo watiko, ku lungile."

Eyano ke madoda lapho bona ba re bona ba a mo wati, lokhwa ba nga mmona ba fumana e ngu ye, ku ta te ku somaeleke nnete. Name o bone lapho nga mbala, name ba teke timbutšhana, ba teka ini, nkqosi name e hlaba nkqomo. Bandu laba ba teka tinyama, ba ba pha titho, tinyama te ko re ba jame ba šeba lokhwa ba ya lle. Aowa, nga mbala name ku phuma madoda e sihlolero nje ba ya khamba ba ya ku wela khona ngale. Ba ya ku fika khona lle a ba lahlekele laphaya. Name ba fika ba re khona lapha e letanyeni lapha ba lala khona, name ba hlala, ba pheka, ba pheka, ba pheke lapha, aowa ba ti hlalele, ba ndlala tingubo ta bo, ba thobala.

PK: E re ke go tsene ka ganong ke mo hlalošetše gannyane.

MK: *Ja.*

PK: *You see now what happens here, they are tracing that boy now who was taken by the Boers. In other words it happened when these people were already starting to work in industrial areas in the south. You see, they used to leave here on foot, to work and come back after some months. So, as they were coming back in a group of five, they came to a farm. They saw some——a herd boy and a flock of sheep. Then they went to him to ask for water. As they were there drinking, they started to recognise this boy. Then they tried to ask him but he couldn't tell them the truth. When they came home, they came to the chief to report that they have seen a boy who they thought had been shot by the Boers.*

Now the chief called the other people and said, "Any of those people who know this boy should raise their hand."

Then quite a number said they could recognise him. Then he sent them to that place. So now we are just at that point where now we are on the way to the farm.

IH: *Okay.*

MK: *Ja,* eyano khona lapho ngu lokhwa madoda lawo a sukako ba boela lle. Ke ba boela lle, ba fika ba hlala khona lapho ba be ba hleti ba thobala, eletanyeni la khona.

Ke ba thobalako kusasa ke ku sako, name ba hlala kuhle, name ba re, "Aowa, ba ta te ba fike, lena le no hlala."

Nga mbala ba hlala lapha ya be ya betha *ten o'clock.* E re ke e re *eleven o'clock,* lethwili la bonakala nkhathi ke sekgwa. Ba re, "*Ja,* ti yeta eyano timvu."

They said, "At a certain dam there——if you want to go there, we can actually take you there so as to verify if it is really him or else we should come back."

Undoubtedly, the chief called the men to the kgotla and they filled it.

When they had gathered together he said to them, "Gentlemen!"

They said, "Our lord!"

He said, "My elder brother's son who has been kidnapped by the whites, do you all know him here? Those who know him, please raise your hands."

They saw many people raising their hands saying, "We know him."

Others also said, "We also know him."

Then he said, "Oh, those of you who know him, it's okay."

Then those men who said that they know him, and that they could recognise him if they could see him, prepared themselves for the long journey. In point of fact they took some mealie meal along as provision, they took other things, and the chief slaughtered a cow. Those people took some meat along, they took along different portions, meat as provisions on the way to that place. Well, indeed a group of men came forward and went to the place. They are going to that place where he was last seen. They arrived at that dam and camped, then they stayed, they cooked and cooked, and after cooking, well, they stayed and prepared blankets and then slept.

PK: Let me interrupt you and interpret a bit.

MK: Yes.

PK: You see now what happens here, they are tracing that boy now who was taken by the Boers. In other words it happened when these people were already starting to work in industrial areas in the south. You see, they used to leave here on foot, to work and come back after some months. So, as they were coming back in a group of five, they came to a farm. They saw some———a herd boy and a flock of sheep. Then they went to him to ask for water. As they were there drinking, they started to recognise this boy. Then they tried to ask him but he couldn't tell them the truth. When they came home, they came to the chief to report that they have seen a boy who they thought had been shot by the Boers.

Now the chief called the other people and said, "Any of those people who know this boy should raise their hand."

Then quite a number said they could recognise him. Then he sent them to that place. So now we are just at that point where now we are on the way to the farm.

IH: Okay.

MK: *Yes, now at that time it was when those men departed and left for that place. When they returned there, they arrived at that place and camped where they had rested before at the dam there.*

They slept and the following morning at dawn, they woke up, relaxed and said, "Well, they will arrive later, you must just sit and rest."

Veritably they sat there until it struck ten o'clock. When it was eleven o'clock, some dust became visible from within the bush. They said "Yes, now the sheep are coming."

No, ba hleti khona lapho eletanyeni lapho ba hleti kahle ba bekane na lapha ti vela khona. Name timvu ta kgamoka ti ta ti kijima ti kijimela mmati. Ke ti kijimela mmati, name ke ti fika lapha——ke ti fika lapha, name ti a sela, ti a sela, name ta jama. Lokhwa ti jamako, ba vela bahlangana nge bathathu, ba re, "Haa, nakho ke ba yeta."

O munye na o munye a re, "Mmutla ga o ake."

O munye naye a re, "Mmutla ga o ake."

Ba re, "Yena llo a montima llo, ngu ye."

Name ba yeta, ba fike ba re, "Barena!"

La– ba ba re, "Ja, dumelang masogana."

Name ba re, "Aowa, re be re kgopela dilo tša go nwa meetse."

Ba ba pha tikomikana ba sela, ba sela, ba sela, name ba re, "He! Lena le diša dinku tša lekgowa?"

Ba re, "Ee."

Ba re, "Lena le le bomang?"

O munye a re, "Ke Swartbooi."

O munye a re, "Ke Kleinbooi."

O munye a re, "Ndi ngu Klaas."

Ba nama ba kqwala ku ba bekelela, Klaas——

PK: E re gannyane ke ba hlalošetše gona fao. *So now when these boys who are looking after sheep are quite a number of them. So these old men sat at a dam where the sheep usually come to drink. So, when they sat there, they came——the boys came with their flock, and they asked for something to use for drinking water. And then they started asking their names.*

Then one said, "I am Swartbooi."

Another one said, "I am Kleinbooi."

And another one said, "I am Klaas."

IH: [Laughter.]

MK: Name khona lapho, name laba ba re, "Ndi ngu Kleinbooi."

O munye a re, "Ndi ngu Swartbooi."

O munye a re, "Ndi ngu Klaas."

Lowa o munye name o re——mokgalabe——mokgalabe o munye llo a mo watiko, o re, "O ngu Klaas bani?"

Lowa a re, "Aowa, ke Klaas fela."

A ndi re o somaela Sesotho?

PK: *Ja.*

MK: Nkade a khambile kambe, menyaka.

Name khona lapho name o a boya o re, "He, ga se wena Klaas Mokopane?"

O re, "Ee."

Well, they sat there next to the dam facing the direction from which the sheep are coming. Then the sheep appeared, running towards the water to drink. When they ran towards the water, they arrived and started drinking and drinking and then they stood there. When they stood there, the three boys arrived and they said, "Aha! Now here they come."

Each one of them said, "A hare never lies."

Another one said, "A hare never lies."

They all said, "This dark one this is him."

Meantime, they are still coming, and when they eventually arrived, they said, "Our lord!"

These ones said, "Yes, greetings to you, young men."

Then they said, "Well, we are asking for things to drink water."

They gave them cups, they drank, drank and drank, and then they said, "Hey, are you looking after the sheep of a white person?"

They said, "Yes."

They asked them, "Who are you?"

One said, "I'm Swartbooi."

Another one said, "I'm Kleinbooi."

And one said, "I'm Klaas."

Then they started scrutinising them closely and Klaas———

PK: Wait a minute, let me interpret just there. So now when these boys who are looking after sheep are quite a number of them. So these old men sat at a dam where the sheep usually come to drink. So, when they sat there, they came———the boys came with their flock, and they asked for something to use for drinking water. And then they started asking their names.

Then one said, "I am Swartbooi."

Another one said, "I am Kleinbooi."

And another one said, "I am Klaas."

IH: [Laughter.]

MK: *Just there, then those boys said, "I'm Kleinbooi."*

Another one said, "I'm Swartbooi."

And the other one said, "I'm Klaas."

Then one said———an old man———an old man who knows him said, "You are Klaas who?"

He said, "No, just Klaas."

Isn't it he was speaking in Sotho?

PK: Yes.

MK: *As a matter of fact, he had been away from home for a long time, for many years.*

Then he responded by asking him, "Hey, aren't you Klaas Mokopane?"

He said, "Yes."

O re, "Bjale ke——*hoekom* o nga somaele letinyo la kho *man*?"

A re, "Aowa, thina kambe si bandwana be lekgowa leli."

Ba nama ba re, "Eyano lekgowa leno le kuphi?"

Bona ba re, "Aowa, khona esekgwaneni lapha lekgowa lethu le khona."

Ba nama ba re, "Aowa——"

PK: *Sorry——the other one, the one they——they know as Mokopane was the one called Klaas. So then they asked him, "What is your surname?"*

Then he said, "Ah, well——I'm just Klaas."

You see, they said, "Are you not Klaas Mokopane?"

And he said, "Yes, I am."

"But now why do you tell us you are just Klaas?"

"No, it's because we belong to that Boer."

MK: Aowa, eyano ngu lokhwa khona lapho ba re, "Aowa, khambani masokana."

Name lokhwa ba khambako ba ya lle, ba phuma ba nyuka ne timvu, laba ba sala ba hleti lapha ba sala ba re, "Ha! Ngu ye, ngu ye!"

Name llanga e bile le ya sobela, ba thobala. E re kusasa *net* lokhwa llanga le ta le sele le to phuma, be ngena nge sekgweni. Ke ba ngena nge sekgweni, name nje e re, "Hou! hou! hou!"

Name ba re, "Ja, ngu kho khona lapha."

Lekgowa name le a phuma le va nja e kqokqotha. Lekgowa name le jama nge molentana we ndlo, le jama e situpini, name o bona madoda a vela.

Ba re, "Morena, morena, *morê baas, morê baas.*"

A re, "*Ja, morê boys.*"

Ba re, "Morena, si tinyelelwe, si ya funa."

"He, le funa ini?"

Ba re, "Si tinyelelwe mundwana, mundwana o se le wa khamba kade, wa thunjwa makgowa. Eyano si mo funa ne nnaga lle a si mo wati na lapha a khona."

"Eya?"

"Mm."

A re, "Aowa, laba mbami laba, lapha ku bo lapha a ka kho."

Ba re, "Eya?"

"Mm."

Name a ba bita a re, "Swartbooi! Kleinbooi! Klaas!"

Ba re, "Morena!"

Name ba ta ba jama lapha nga ba thathu kabo, ba jama *so.*

A nama a re, "A le ba boni."

A name a re, "Bami na ba bona, laba mbami laba, le a ba bona?"

Then he said, "But now why didn't you tell us your real name from the outset, man?"

He said, "No, by the way we are the children of the white man."

Then they asked, "Now where is this white man of yours?"

They said, "Well, just over here in the bush our white man stays."

Then they said, "Well———"

PK: Sorry———the other one, the one they———they know as Mokopane was the one called Klaas. So then they asked him, "What is your surname?"

Then he said, "Ah, well———I'm just Klaas."

You see, they said, "Are you not Klaas Mokopane?"

And he said, "Yes, I am."

"But now why do you tell us you are just Klaas?"

"No, it's because we belong to that Boer."

MK: *Well, now they said to them, "Well, young man, you may go."*

Then as they were leaving, they drove the sheep away, and these ones stayed behind saying, "Ha! That's him, that's him!"

Meanwhile, the sun was setting, and they slept. The following morning, just as the sun was rising, they entered the bush. As they had just entered the bush, then the dog barked.

Then they said, "Yes, that is the place."

Then the white man came out as he heard the dog barking. The white man leaned against the pillar of his house and stood on the veranda to see the men coming.

They said, "Lord, lord, morning boss, morning boss."

He said, "Yes, morning boys."

They said, "Our lord, we lost someone and we are looking for him."

"Hey, what are you looking for?"

They said, "A child, a child is lost since he disappeared long ago after being kidnapped by whites. Meanwhile we have been looking all over for him but we don't know where to find him."

"Really?"

"Yes."

He said, "No, these ones are mine, he is not amongst them."

They said, "Is that so?"

"Yes."

Then he called them by their names, "Swartbooi! Kleinbooi! Klaas!"

They said, "Our lord!"

Then the three of them came and stood there like this.

He then said, "Do you see them?"

He then said, "These are mine, these are mine, do you see them?"

Ba nama ba re, "Morena, o ta si va?"

A re, "Ee."

Ba re, "Yena llo montima llo, mundu llo nkqosi yethu, yena llo. Ngu ye llo si mo funako. Si funa yena llo ke o va si re si funa mundu, e sa le a thunjwa makgowa, ngu yena llo, nakqo?"

Lowa a re, "Eya? Ngu ye yena llo?"

Name ba re, "Ee."

A re, "Oho, eyano, ke e nguba le ya mo funa, le fanele le mo———mo——— [inaudible].

PK: *So at dusk they went to the farm and the Boer came out. Then they greeted him.*

They said, "We are———we are looking for a boy who was taken away by the Boers some time ago. We are looking all over for him."

Then this Boer said, "Well, I don't have him. I've got only these ones."

Then he called them by their names. They came and stood there in front of him.

He said, "These are mine!"

Then they said, "You see that dark one———Klaas———is our chief."

So he was just going to tell us what happened next.

MK: Name khona lapho a o bone lekgowa le re, "Eya! Ngu ye llo?"

Ba re, "Yena llo ngu yena nkqosi yethu llo."

Lekgowa la re, "*Ja*, na ke le mo fumanako mara a si ngulo nga li pha yena nie."

"Eya?"

"Ee."

"Eyano?"

A re, "Ke e nguba o na boise e khaya, khambani le yo bota boise kore mfuna masome-a-mathathu we timvu ne matinyo we tindlovu nga le pha mundu llo."

Ja.

PK: *They said, "We want him."*

He said, "No, this one you can't have. If you want him, go back and tell your chief that I want thirty sheep and some uh———what you call them, uh———ivory———elephant tusks."

MK: *Ja*, name o bone khona lapho, ba re, "Ah eh, ku lungile morena lokhwa ku njalo *so lank* thina si mmonile."

Name tikqôlô ta lla, ba thamba, lekgowa le dio bona bandu ba no wela mithi lle ba ya lle na lle, ba boya, ke ba fika lapha e letanyeni lapha khange ba sa hlala o munye a re, "Mpha sami."

O munye naye a re, "Mpha sami."

They said, "Lord, will you listen to us?"

He said, "Yes."

They said, "This very dark one, this person is our chief, this one. This is the one we are looking for. We are looking for this person as we have already told you that we are looking for someone. He was kidnapped by white people, that's him, here he is."

That one said, "Is that so? Is that him?"

Then they said, "Oh yes."

He said, "Oh well, now if you want him you can't just get him so easily———" [inaudible]

PK: So at dusk they went to the farm and the Boer came out. Then they greeted him.

They said, "We are———we are looking for a boy who was taken away by the Boers some time ago. We are looking all over for him."

Then this Boer said, "Well, I don't have him. I've got only these ones."

Then he called them by their names. They came and stood there in front of him.

He said, "These are mine!"

Then they said, "You see that dark one———Klaas———is our chief."

So he was just going to tell us what happened next.

MK: *Just there then the white man said, "Really! Is this him?"*

They said, "This one is indeed our chief."

The white man said, "Yes, even though you desperately want him, he is not the kind of person I can easily give away."

"Really?"

"Yes."

"And so?"

He said to them, "If he still has parents back at home, go back and tell his father that I want thirty sheep and ivory as compensation, then I will release him."

Yes.

PK: They said, "We want him."

He said, "No, this one you can't have. If you want him, go back and tell your chief that I want thirty sheep and some uh———what you call them, uh———ivory———elephant tusks."

MK: *Yes, then they said, "Well, that is just fine, lord, that is the deal so long as we have identified him."*

Then they started blowing their whistles, dancing, the white man just wondered as people hit against the trees, going this way and that way, on their way back home. When they reached the dam, they did not hesitate and one said, "Give me my things."

Another one said, "Give me mine."

Name ba teka tipotwana ta bo ba phathakga, name ba boela neno. Aowa ba ta ba lungele lapho ba thobala endleleni. Kusasa ke ba vukako, ba wela ndlela. Ke ba to ngena lapha ke ba ta nge Sekgakgapeni lapha, nkqôlô ya be ya lla. Ba re, "Ba yeta, ba mo fumene."

Ba name ba phuma, ba jama emayeni khona lapha etulu lapha endabeni. E re ke ba kgamoka lapha, ba bona bandu ba teka ne mahlanga ba——ku thanjwa, ku thanjwa, ku yentwa njani.

Ba re, "Hao, ba mo fumene."

Aowa name ba yeta ba ta ba khwela siphande lesa, ba khwela so ba khwelela nge ndabeni, ba fika ngale ba re, "Haa! Kqosi, mmutla ga e ake. Si mo fumene. Si mo fumeneko, lekgowa la khona kqosi, o re o funa masome-a-mathathu we timvu, ne matinyo we tindlovu."

Nkqosi ya re tuu ya re, "Ai, ndo lle e to si tshwenya matinyo we tindlovu. Timvu tona a si lle ngato."

Name a re——a khumbule nga mbila a re, "Hey, madoda nga mahlanu nkhele khambeni le ye ka Langa lle le yo khombela Langa le mmote ko re kha– ke e be o ne matinyo we tindlovu lapho nkhe ba si thuše. Matinyo we tindlvou lawo si ne mmerengo kqulu si haastig nawo."

Aowa, nga mbala ba khamba ba wela lle ka Langa ku Masebe. Ke ba fika khona ba fika ba lotša aowa nkqosi ya ba vumela.

Ba re, "Aowa, si lotšhwe——si thunywe ngu Kekana la. Kekana o re si te ku we si khombele matinyo we tindlovu. Matinyo we tindlovu lla si wa ndokatako la– si wa funako la, mundwana we mogolo'akhe o be a timele, eyano ba mmone lle etimbolasini te makgowa. Eyano lekgowa la khona le re le funa matinyo we tindlovu."

Lowa a re, "He?"

Ba re, "Ee."

Name a re, "All right, hlalani phase."

A bita be khabo, nga bahlanu, a re, "Khambani le ye ka Molengwa, le nyuke e Mogalakwena le khwelele tindabeni leta ta ka Molengwa leta."

Nga mbala name ba suka, kwa suka masokana nga mahlanu. Ba khamba, ba wela lle, ba o nyuka Mogalakwena, ba khwela tindabana leta, ba fika enduneni name ba lotšhe enduneni. Aowa, nduna e ba vumele, ba re, "Aowa, wena nduna, si te kuwe, si thunywe nkqosi. Ja, nkho si bitele bandu bakho laba, llo e ngaba o ne matinyo we tindlovu a te a te a thuše nge matinyo we tindlovu. A ya funeka Masebe o a a funa."

Name a betha nsimbi, nduna. Madoda a vela nga lapha na aga lapha, kwa ta la kwa re kgatla! kgatla!

Ba re, "Morena!"

A re, "Kgoši šo yena Masebe a rometše barena ba gagwe šeba. Ba re thušang ka meno a ditlou o a nago le wona, le tle le ba feng."

Then they took their pots and carried them on their way back home. Well, they came straight back home sleeping on their journey back home. The following morning when they woke up, they would hit the road. When they arrived here, as they were still around Sekgakgapeng, a horn was blown. The people said, "They are coming, and they have found him."

They then went out and stood on top of the rocks just here on the mountain. When they emerged here, they just saw people carrying reeds and dancing and doing many different things.

They said, "Aha! They have found him."

Well, they were still coming and ascending the mountain to the capital and when they arrived, they said, "Aha! Chief, a hare does not lie. We have found him and with our finding him the white man with whom he stays says he wants thirty sheep and elephant tusks."

The chief was dumbfounded for a while and then said, "Well, we are going to have some difficulties finding elephant tusks. Sheep are no problem."

Then he quickly remembered and said, "Hey, you five men, go to Langa and ask for elephant tusks. Tell him that if he has them he should come to our rescue. We have a very serious mission with those elephant tusks."

Well, indeed they left to Langa's place to Masebe. When they arrived there, they greeted the chief and he accepted their greetings.

They said, "Well, we have been sent here by Kekana. Kekana sent us here to come and ask for elephant tusks. These tusks are going to be used to get back the son of the chief's elder brother who disappeared long ao. He is presently at a white man's farm there. Now, that white person says he wants elephant tusks."

That one said, "What?"

They said, "Yes."

Then he said, "All right, get seated."

He called five of his men and said to them, "Go to Molekoa across the Mogalakwena river and those mountains."

In truth they left, five young men left. They walked across Mogalakwena, up these mountains, and then arrived at the induna's place and then greeted the induna. Well, the induna accepted their greetings and they said, "Well, induna we have come to you. We have been sent by the chief. Yes, please call your people here and inform them that those who have some elephant tusks should come to our rescue. They are desperately wanted, Masebe wants them."

Then the induna rang the bell. The men appeared from all directions and they filled the whole kgotla.

They said, "Our lord!"

He said, "Here is the chief, Masebe sent his lords here. They are saying please us with elephant tusks those of you who have them."

Aowa, o bone madoda ba dio jama, ba jama ba ya nkhaya. Ke ba jama ba ngena nge tindlini, o munye o ta a phethe nga mambili, o munye a phethe nga mathathu, o munye a ta a phethe nga mangaki, o munye a phethe nga mangaki. Ba velela ba banye ba hleti ba a kgwerenya———ba a kgwerenya, ba a phethe matinyo we tindlovu.

Ba re, "Ha! Aowa, ke a fikileko, eyano le a mva ba ka Molengwa? Matinyo we tindlovu lla ke ba a funa nje, na ni le ya nawo. Mfuna madoda nga mahlanu, a khambe ne bandu laba ba ka Langa laba. Ba khambe ne matinyo lla we tindlovu ba ye ku a bona lapha a ya khona, *ja* ba te ba le bote nnete lokhwa ba phuma ku boya."

PK: *So now when these people came back, they came back to report that they found the boy, it's him. Now the problem is the Boer wants thirty sheep and elephant tusks. So now———*[Tape ends] *He sent his men to Mapela to chief Langa to go and ask for elephant tusks. Then they explained to him that these tusks are going to be used to buy back the chief's son who is with the Boer there. So then chief Langa didn't have elephant tusks but he referred them to somebody else, Molekoa who is attached to the same tribe as Langa. So they went there and found the tusks. And this Molekoa chose five of his men to come together with the people who came from his place so that they could see that these tusks are going to be used for the purpose they are asked for.*

"We must see if they are actually going to release the chief's son."

So they are coming back now this way with the elephant tusks.

IH: *Oh, I see.*

MK: *Ja,* eyano a o bone khona lapho ba ta nabo ba ka Molengwa, ba fika ba a thula ka Masebe, ba re, "Masebe, nakqa wona matinyo we tindlovu."

Name a re, "Aga, mohlamunye mundu wa ka Kekana lowo o ta khe a thušeke."

Ba lle ba ka Langa, eyano ku phuma bandu nga bahlanu kambekambe lapho, le tatisela laba ba ka Molengwa laba, le be lesome le bandu, na laba ba ka Mukombani le be ngu *fifteen* lokhwa le hlanganako.

"Eyano le thwala matinyo lla we tindlovu le khamba nawo, na laba be khethu le khamba nabo le fike le ye khona lapha mundu llo a khona, le ye ku fika le mmone nge mmahlo lokhwa le mo patelelako. *Ja.* Kore ndi te nkholwe ndaba lle le e kqejileko."

Ngu lokhwa khona lapho aowa ba name ba re, "Aowa kqosi ku lungile."

Ba thwala matinyo lawo we tindlovu, ba ta nawo la. Ba ta ba wa thula lapha e kqosini ba re, "Kqosi, matinyo nakqa wona we tindlovu, si a fumene."

PK: *So there are five men from Molekoa's tribe who accompanied those who took the tusks to chief Langa and chief Langa also sent out five. So they were ten coming this way. He said all of them should go there which means five would also come out of Kekana. So in all they would be fifteen, going to release the boy. So that each group should go and report back to their chief.*

Well, the men just stood up and went home. They entered their huts and emerged with those tusks, one carrying two, others carried three while others carried this many and so on. Some came back blowing them, carrying these tusks.

They said, "Ha! Well, now that they have arrived, now listen to me you the people of Molekoa. You must also accompany these tusks with these people of Langa. You must go alone to see where these tusks are going, yes, so that you could know the truth when they have returned."

PK: So now when these people came back, they came back to report that they found the boy, it's him. Now the problem is the Boer wants thirty sheep and elephant tusks. So now———[Tape ends] He sent his men to Mapela to chief Langa to go and ask for elephant tusks. Then they explained to him that these tusks are going to be used to buy back the chief's son who is with the Boer there. So then chief Langa didn't have elephant tusks but he referred them to somebody else, Molekoa who is attached to the same tribe as Langa. So they went there and found the tusks. And this Molekoa chose five of his men to come together with the people who came from his place so that they could see that these tusks are going to be used for the purpose they are asked for.

"We must see if they are actually going to release the chief's son."

So they are coming back now this way with the elephant tusks.

IH: Oh, I see.

MK: *Now they are coming along with the people of Molekoa and dropped the tusks at Masebe's place and said, "Masebe, here are the tusks of elephants."*

He then said, "Well done, perhaps the poor child of Kekana will be rescued."

An additional five men were selected from the Langa people to supplement those of Molekoa to bring the number to ten, and when this is added to five of Mokopane's people, all in all it's fifteen.

"Now you carry these tusks and go along, you all go together to the place where this person is kept, you go there and see him with your own eyes as you pay for him. Yes, so that I can believe once this issue has been resolved."

Just there then they said, "Well chief, it's all right."

They carried the tusks and brought them here. They dropped them here at the chief's place and said, "Chief, here are the tusks of the elephants, we have found them."

PK: So there are five men from Molekoa's tribe who accompanied those who took the tusks to chief Langa and chief Langa also sent out five. So they were ten coming this way. He said all of them should go there which means five would also come out of Kekana. So in all they would be fifteen, going to release the boy. So that each group should go and report back to their chief.

MK: *Ja,* eyano wa bona khona lapho kube ba thule matinyo we tindlovu, name nkqosi e ba thuma ba ya e moše e Magofaneni ka Mabhogo. Ba fika ba re ku Mabhogo ba re, "Mabhogo, nkqosi e re le si phe masome-a-mathathu timvu, leti ti nga dušeko, e ngasi leti ti ne timvanana."

PK: Mabhogo ke mang bjale?

MK: Mabhogo o be a khona e moše e Magofaneni lapha.

PK: Ke ntona?

MK: Ngu we nkqosi, lapha nkqosi e be e sikisa——timvu ta khe ti hlala khona. Name lokhwa nga mbala name ba suka lapha ba boela ka Mabhogo.

Ba fumana Mabhogo, aowa ba teka ndaba lle ba a mmonisa, Mabhogo name o re, "Ah eh, ngenani nge sibayeni lapha le dio khetha leti le ti bona ti *fresh* tokqetokqe leti."

Nga mbala bati khetha, ba ti khetha ba ti phumisa nga nnye nga nnye nga nnyee, ta ba ta fika masome-a-mathathu a re, "*Ja,* ti fikile e mbalweni yato na."

Ba re, "*Ja.*"

"Si funa leti ti ta re lokhwa ti khambako, ti nga hlwe e nnye ba re e tele, e nnye e a duša, e nnye e yenta njani, e nnye e ne mvanana. Ti khambe ti nje tokqe leti."

Nga mbala, ba re, "Aowa, wena Mabhogo, si a ti kqora."

Ba ti tswitswitla, ti to khwela nga lapha endabeni, ti fika la.

Ba re, "Agaa, nati kqosi."

Name a re, "Haa!" Mokhosi wa lla eyano emošate.

Wa re, "Madoda bohle, hunye hunye hunye bokqe."

Madoda ba name ba hunyelela bokqe, ba hunyelela bokqe, ke ba fika lapha a re, "Aga! Eyano timvu nati tona ti tile, eyano bokqe laba madoda, e nnye na ye nnye ndoda lle e ti vako, e fanele e ngene nkhathi ke madoda lla, le khambe le yo teka mundwana we kqosi lowo."

Ha! Ba name ba re, "Kqosi."

O munye a ngena nkhaya a re, "Mekqondo yami iphi yona?"

O munye a re, "*Hey,* lebatata lami liphi?"

"*Hey,* nkqolo yami iphi yona?"

"Siyala sami siphi sona?"

Name nkqosi ya wisa nkqomo phase, ba ba abela tinyama leto, ba ba abela, ba ti ngenisa nkhathi ke megodla.

Ba re, "A re yeni kê. Le ta ti parapara timvu leti, lapha e ngu se sikgweni le ta re lokhwa le thobalako, le phembe mello nga kohle lapha kore timbungu ti nga ti bulale, ti nga bambe e nnye."

MK: *Yes, now after they had put down those tusks, you see the chief now sending them yonder to Magofaneng, to Mabhogo. They arrived and informed Mabhogo, "Mabhogo, the chief said that you should give us thirty sheep, those that are neither pregnant nor have small ones."*

PK: *Now who is Mabhogo?*

MK: *Mabhogo was staying across the river at Magofaneng.*

PK: *Was he an induna?*

MK: *He belonged to the chief, he was a client of the chief, the chief's sheep were kept there. Then indeed they left and went to Mabhogo.*

They found Mabhogo, and well, they related their story, and Mabhogo said, "Well, just enter the kraal and choose those that look fresh to you."

They did likewise, they selected and selected and took them out of the kraal one by one until they reached thirty, and he said, "Yes, have they reached the required number?"

They said, "Yes."

"We want only those that won't give problems on the long journey so that we would not have to wait because one had just given birth, or one was heavily pregnant, and so on. They must just be like this."

Indeed, they said, "Well, Mabhogo we are now driving them away."

They drove them away, ascended this mountain until they reached here.

Then they said, "Aha, here they are chief."

Then there was ululation at the capital.

He said, "All men must come together there."

The men came in large numbers in fact all of them, and he said to them, "Well! Now here the sheep have arrived, and now to all of you I say, any man who feels fit is free to join these men here to go and fetch that poor child of the chief."

Well, they all said, "Our lord."

One man went to his hut and said, "Where are my spears?"

Another one went to his own and said, "Hey, where is my horn?"

"Hey, where is my whistle?"

"Where is my head gear?"

Then the chief slaughtered a cow and divided portions of it among them, and they put them in their bags.

Then they said, "Let's go. You shall surround these sheep, and when you go to sleep in the bush, you must light fire all around them so that the jackals should not catch them or even kill one of them."

Ja, nga mbala name ba suka ba te ba wele nato lle. Ke ba fika endleleni, lokhwa ba bona llanga le subelako, name ba kqwala ku phemba mello, timvu ti thobale nkhathi kabo. Kambe ku be ku phume na bandu ba lle, kambe ku be ku phume na ba ka Lekalakala laba bokqe laba, ba phumile ku iwe khona lle. Timvu ti se khathi kabo, bona ba nga semahlanguthini lapha. Aowa, ngu ti khambela kuhlenyana kwa thoyalwa, ke ku sako lapha ba re, "A re yeni."

Name ba ti tswitswitla, ba ti tswitswitla, ba lija ne matinyo we tindlovu, 'nkwenkweri-kwenkweri'. Ke ba fika khona lapha eletanyeni la khona ba fika ba re kgatlakgatla! Wa le bona llanga nalo le a subela.

Name ba re, "Hai, eyano khona eyano nje khona, ku lungile."

Nato ti re ku sela mmati ti name ta hlala khona lapho. Bona ba ti dikanejile nga kokqe lapha kore mbungu e nga be ya ngena nga kito lapha.

Nga mbala ba thobala, kusasa e re ke ku sako, e re ku sa re nge mahube ke ku sako, ba re, "A re yeni, a se mo ngeneni."

Ba ti kqora ba ti paraparile, ke ti ngena nge sikgweni name mvu e re, "Mmê!"

E nnye ya lla nge sibayeni nayo.

Nja ya re, "Hou, hou, hou!"

Lekgowa la phuma la jama esitupini.

O bona timvu ti velela, name o re ku bahlangana o re, "*Hey, maak oop die hek daar voor!*"

Name laba ba vula n'gate, ti ngena ngale, laba be matinyo we tindlovu nabo ba ta nawo ba fika ba re esitupini khona lapha ku jame lekgowa ba fika ba re "Aowa, mokgobo nakqo wona morwa lekgowa, nakqo *hey*."

Name ba katuka ba hlala lapha. A nama a re, "*Ja*, bandu laba nhlitiyo yabo e ya futha nga mbala."

Ba thwala ndokati leya, matinyo we tindlovu lao, ba wo a nika *misis* nge ndlini.

Ba fika ba bonisa *misis* nge ndlini, a phuma lapho a re, "*Ja*, eyano, khona eyano nje le rene?"

Ba re, "A si se ne monagano wo muhle lekgowa, se re wena-wena lokhwa o dio si lungulla, wena o dio si lungulla."

Name nga mbala o re, "Klaas!"

O re, "Baas!"

O re, "Tana."

O re ku ye o re, "Klaas."

O re, "Baas."

O re, "Madoda lla o a ba wati?"

Lowa a re, "Ah eh. A ku na llo ndimo watiko."

Yes, indeed they left together with those sheep. On the way, as the sun was setting, they lit fires around them and let the sheep sleep in the middle. By the way, even people from as far as Lekalakala's place were all there. The sheep were right in the middle and they [the men] *were surrounding them. Well, they moved on fairly well, and they slept. When it was dawn, they said, "Let's get going."*

Then they drove them on and on, blowing the tusks of elephants on the way. When they arrived at the dam, they settled. You see the sun was also setting.

Then they said, "No, well, well, well."

The sheep after drinking water also slept there. They themselves were still surrounding them so that a single jackal could not get them.

Veritably, they slept and the following morning at dawn they said, "Let's get going, let's invade."

They drove them along still surrounding them and when they entered the bush, one sheep bleated, "Mmê!"

Another one bleated from the kraal.

A dog was barking, "Hou, hou, hou!"

The white man came out and stood on the veranda.

He saw the sheep coming and ordered his boys, "Hey, open the gate there at the front!"

Then they opened the gate and the sheep entered while those [men] carrying elephant tusks came to the veranda and put them down saying, "Well, here is a heap for you, you son of a white man!"

Then they took a couple of steps backwards and he said, "Yes, those people are really desperate [to get the boy]*."*

They carried these tusks into the house to show to the white lady.

They showed her inside the house and she came out and said, "Yes, now what are you saying?"

They said, "There is nothing pleasant on our minds. You must just allow us to leave [with the boy]*."*

Then indeed he called out, "Klaas!"

He said, "Baas!"

He said, "Come here."

He said to him, "Klaas."

He said, "Baas."

He said, "Do you recognise these men?"

He said, "No! I don't recognise any of them."

"*Ja*, bandu laba ba lande wena. Timvu leta o ti bona ti ngena lapha leta ti thenga wena. Matinyo we tindlovu lla o a bona ndi wa ngenisa nge ndlini lla a thenga wena, ngore wena ndi ku bopholle ba ku teke o khambe nabo o ye ekhenu, o ye ku busa bandu lle o ye ku busa setšhaba lesa se lle. Ee, o ya va?"

A re, "Morena!"

A re, "*Ja*, o hlale nje nga lokhwa o hleti, nhleti nawe lapha ndi ku bona nge mogkwa llo o be o lunge ngakho. Eyano nemuhlanje o ndi lahlile, ndi nga se hlwe ndi sa ba ne modiša llo ndi nga mo thembako. Laba ba lapha laba ba salako laba a si laba ndi ba kholophela nje ngawe."

A name a duduka, a hloma nhloko phase, name a re, "*Ja*, teka tinguyana takho kê."

Name o teka tinguyana takhe o teka tinguyana takhe, name ke a fika laphaya madoda ba re, "Tisa."

Ba mo phathela tona.

Ba re, "A o phathi ndo wena, si ya ku phathela. A o sa phathi ndo."

Name lapha ba re, "Ku phelile?"

Baas a re, "Ku phelile."

Ba re, "Hey!"

Kwa sa ka mbili eyano. Kwa re, "Ki ki, ki ki!"

Mokhosi a re, "Iwuu!"

Ba fika ba re lapha e letanyeni ba fika ba re khona ba re kgatla kgatla!

Ba re, "Ah eh! A si hlaleni phase, si phekeni, si dleneni, si kgona si wela ndlela. A si sa kqore ndo nemhlanje nge koba si mbandu ka phela."

Nga mbala kwa phekwa.

PK: *Ja*, e re ndi mo fanisele. So now they have arrived there, the Boer came out. Then he saw a flock of sheep and opened the gate for them and then they came to him and put the elephant tusks down.

They said, "Okay. We have now come for our chief, can you release him?"

Then he called the boy and asked him, "Do you know any of these men?"

The boy said, "No, I don't know any of them."

Then he said, "But these people have come for you. They need you, for you are their chief. So all these sheep and elephant tusks are to buy you. So go there and stay with them, be as honest as you were here with me."

Then they took him away.

IH: Uhu.

MK: Ku be ba fike lapho, name ba phalokota tidutu, name ba ya mo phalokotela sidutu sakhe, ba mo nika, ba mo nika ne tinyama o a dla, nabo ba a dla.

Kube ba kqetše ku dla lapha name ba re, "Eyano kê, si to khamba ebusuku na se mini. A si sa to thobala endleleni."

"Well, these people have come for you. These tusks that you see me putting in the house are meant to buy your freedom, so that they can take you back home where you are going to preside over your community. Yes, are you listening?"

He said, *"My lord!"*

He said, *"Yes, you must remain what you were when you were still with me. I have stayed with you long enough to know you. Now, today you are forsaking me. I will never have another shepherd I can trust. Those that are remaining are not really the kind that I could trust like you."*

Then he kept quiet and stooped down, then he said, *"Yes, now take all your belongings."*

Then he took all of his clothes, took all his clothes, then when he reached there close to the men, they said, *"Bring them here."*

They carried them for him.

They said, *"You are not going to carry them, we will. You shall never carry anything again."*

Then they asked, *"Is that all?"*

The baas said, *"That's all."*

They said, *"Hey!"*

They started singing and dancing, playing with their spears, *"Ki ki, ki ki!"*

They ululated, *"Iwuu!"*

They arrived at that dam and they all rested.

They said, *"Well, let's stop here, cook and eat before we hit the road. We are no longer driving any livestock, it's only us men."*

Indeed, they cooked.

PK: Yes, let me translate. So now they have arrived there, the Boer came out. Then he saw a flock of sheep and opened the gate for them and then they came to him and put the elephant tusks down.

They said, "Okay. We have now come for our chief, can you release him?"

Then he called the boy and asked him, "Do you know any of these men?"

The boy said, "No, I don't know any of them."

Then he said, "But these people have come for you. They need you, for you are their chief. So all these sheep and elephant tusks are to buy you. So go there and stay with them, be as honest as you were here with me."

Then they took him away.

IH: Uhu.

MK: *Thereafter they dished out their cooked mealie meal and gave him* [Mokopane] *some as well as some meat and he ate and they all ate.*

After eating they said, "Now, we are going to walk day and night. We are no longer going to sleep on the way."

Aowa lapha name ba ba mogobo, ba mo ngenise nkhathi kwabo ba re, "Woo woo!" [denotes singing]

Mpata lle ba jama ba re, "Woo woo woo woo!"

PK: Singing?

MK: *Ja*, ba ta neno ekhaya, llanga la be la ba subelela endleleni, na se busuku nakho e dio kgatlana busuku bokqe kwa be kwa re lokhwa ko re hwibi lapha, ba re, "Haa, e ne mala eyano khona nje si ya fika ekhethu."

Nga mbale ba ngena ba ta nga lapha nga se Sekgakgapeni lapha, lepatata le a lla, nkqolo e a lla. Ai, ba hlašeka nge ndabeni ba re, "Ba eta, ba eta."

Nga mbala ba va mogobo e sele e ngu wo monyeti, ba banye ba jama emayeni, naye nne Mukombani a hlala emmundwini, etikweni, a re, "Ei, mundwanami, ko kunye ngabe ba ta naye."

Aowa, lapho ba velela ba vela emasimini lapha eNgwaditse lapha ba nyuka Ngwaditse llo, ba dla phase nge tikqatha *man*, ko re hla! hla! hla! hla!

Aowa name ba to nyukela lapha ekhaya lapha, o nkhathi ke bandu lapha a ba mmoni a ndi re ba yente nje na nge mašaba, ba mo sithe na nge mašaba.

Ba re ke ba to khwela la esiphandeni lapha name ba khwela kuhle ba re, "Ha, o khona, nakqowa! O mongatanyana kibo laba ngu ye llo."

Lla mmadoda *mos* bokqe laba? Name aowa ba ta ba khwelela lle, name nnina a mo re nge mokhono a mo re *ubu*! A mo isa nkhaya. Ke a mo ise nkhaya, name madoda ba re enkqundleni kwa re kgatla kgatla! Ba buisa tikqomo ba re tikqomo nga ti nga, ba ti wisa phase.

Songwana'khe Makute, *ja*, a ti wisa phase name ke ku sindlwa lapho kwa phenjwa mollo o mokqulu, ku dio beswa tinyama ba re, "Beša nama ka mollo, nama ya pitša modiego."

Ba beša tinyama leta, ba re ku dla tinyama lete ba sêlê mmati tiso ti name tô be kanga.

Ba hlala khona lapha ba name ba re, "Aga! Eyano aowa khona nje khona ke phelile, si le lebukile bandu ba ka Langa na ba ka Molengwa si ya le lebuka nge mokgwa llo le si pepule ngakho."

Ba re, "Aowa, ku lebuka thina kqosi, si lebuka lokhwa mundwana we kqosi a bonakeleko a be a ta a fika nkhaya, nathi sa ba sa mmona. Si re si yo bota tikqosi tethu lle ebani si mmone na nge mmahlo."

Ha, nga mbala lapho name ndambama ba laela ba ka Langa na ba ka Molengwa. Aowa lapha ba re, "Aowa, mundu nga munye a ka laela name a si laelele bokqe laba."

Name na ba ka Lekalakala laba name ba khamba ba re, "Aowa, nathi name si ya gašeka, o ta sala na ba se Mošate ka phela."

Aowa, name ba ti khambela lapha aowa, kwa sala ku hletwi, aowa nnina wa mo singa singa ne mekgwa e menyeti a re, "Mundwanami, ke mundwanami."

Well, then they started singing, keeping him right in the middle, saying, "Woo, woo!" [denotes singing]

They sang all the way home.

PK: *Singing?*

MK: *Yes, they were on their way home and the sun set, but they continued to sing as they walked all night long until the sun rose and they said, "Well, this road is lying, we are almost home."*

Indeed they arrived by the road of Sekgakgapeng and the horn and the whistle were blown. Well, those on the mountain heard them and they said, "They are coming, they are coming."

Veritably, they heard the singing clearly, and others stood on top of the rocks. Even Mokopane's mother sat on the 'veranda' next to the fire place and wept, "My child, I wish that they are bringing him along."

Well, just then they appeared from this direction of the fields, just here at Ngwaditše, they crossed this river, and all the time they were singing and dancing. It was just, "Hla! Hla! Hla!"

Well, they were now ascending to this place and he was right in the middle where people could not have a clear view of him and they were hiding him with branches from trees.

Then they steadily climbed the mountain and people said, "Ha! He is with them. There he is! The smallest of them all is him."

By the way, all the others were men, you see? Well then they climbed the mountain and his mother got hold of his hand and led him home. As she did those men proceeded to the kgotla and they filled it. Cattle were brought in and so many cattle were slaughtered.

His uncle, Makute, yes, he brought them [the cattle] *down and the men started skinning them while others prepared a huge fire so that they could just roast the meat. They said, "Just roast the meat, cooking is a waste of time."*

They roasted the meat, ate it and then drank water and their bellies were this big.

They sat there and said, "Well! Now it's over. We thank the people of Langa and those of Molekoa we thank you as well for the way you carried us on your backs."

They said, "Well, we should be the ones to thank you, chief, we are grateful that the chief's son has been found and he has safely arrived at home and we are privileged to see him with our own eyes. We are now in a good position to relate the story properly to our own chief."

Indeed, in the evening the Langa and Molekoa reported that they were going back home. Others said, "Well, if one person can just make an indication that he is departing, he has done that for the rest of us."

Then the people of Lekalakala left and said, "Well, we are also dispersing, you will remain with these of Mošate."

Well, most left while others remained there, while the mother was busy with him asking him this and that, saying, "Oh, my boy, my child."

O fumana ku sele ku belethwe bopapa eyano. Bopapa eyano o funana bopapa e sele ba hlolekile, papa na Ntata, *ja*, no no' Kgare llo wa se Teberius, nnina. Papa—Mukombani llo e be e ngu wo bone, bandwana be mfati nne'Mukombani llo.

Name khona lapho ba ti hlalela khona lapho, name Makute o re, "Hm, Mundu llo mara ndoda *man*, a nga fanele ku hlala nje."

Ba ka Langa, name nge moso ku be ba fike ekhaya lle, ba yeta nge tipere, nabo ba funa ku to mmona. Nga mbala ke ba fika lapha ba lotšha ku Makute, Makute a ba vumela.

Ba re, "Aowa, si phalalele mokhosi we mundwana we nkqosi lokhwa a tileko."

Ba re, "Aowa."

Name ba mmita nkhaya, wa ta name ba ka Langa ba re, "Hao, *ja*, ke monna *man*. Ee, *hey*, naga yela ke kgale makgowa a sepetše."

Ee, aowa, a ti boelela nkhaya, name Makute o re ku laba ba ka Langa o re, "Lena ba ga Laka, motho yo ke nyaka gore a se a šo a hlalefe bjatše, ke mo hlalefetše a ye go wela."

Namile nga mbala ko re laba ba ka Langa ba re, "Aowa, ke monna, ga a botšwe. Le rena re tla tliša ba rena re tla ba šiya gona kua ba tle ba mo tlaleletše."

A re, "Aowa, nka leboga."

Nga mbala ngoma name ya phuma, kwa ya ku welwa e Majakaneni khona e moše wa Mogalakwena lapha.

Aowa, kwa sôkwa, ba soka, ba goduka, kube ba goduke lapha a name a re, "Aga, eyano khona nje khona o ndoda wena Mukombani."

Aowa, name o re, "Ah eh, songwana, wena jana o phethe wena."

A re, "Wena, o funa ku bota bangani bakho lokhwa a ne madoda e manye lokhwa o sele o hleti nabo ba phele ba re, 'Songwana llo o a ku dleleta, o dla ne tindo leti e ngi takho.' Eyano si be si te si kqwale si lwe. A ndi funi ku lwa name."

Ah, name nga mbala a re, "Ah eh, setulo se ihlo nase!"

A bita madoda lapho o bita ne tinduna leti, o re, "Banna, nemhlanje nje ndi ya si theoka setulo lesi ndi be ndi si hleti. Monatiso makqo yena o tile."

*When he [Mokopane] came back my [that is narrator's] father and others were
already born. He found that my father and others were already in existence, my
father and Ntata yes, also this Kgare from Teberius, his mother. My father———
this Mokopane was the fourth of the children of his mother.*

*Then they just relaxed and Makute said, "Mm, this person is a man, he cannot
just sit around here like this."*

*The following day the people of Langa arrived on horseback after their messengers
had arrived. They came to see him. Indeed they arrived and greeted Makute and
he accepted their greetings.*

*Then they said, "Well, we are responding to the message of the lost and found
child."*

They said, "Well."

*Then they called him from his home and when he arrived, the people of Langa
were surprised, "Yes, he is a man, man! Yes, hey, it's a long time since the whites
departed."*

*Yes, well, he returned home and Makute said to the people of Langa, "You people
of Langa, I intend to be shrewd and send him to initiation school."*

*Then the people of Langa concurred, "Well, he is a man, he must be informed. We
shall also bring our own [young men] and we shall leave them there to
supplement him."*

He said, "Well, I will be grateful."

*Veritably, the initiation school was then established, and they were sent for
initiation here in the Christian section, just across Mogalakwena.*

*Well, they were initiated into manhood, they were initiated and initiated and
then they came back, and thereafter he [Makute] said, "Well, now you are a
man, Mokopane."*

Then he [Mokopane] said, "No, Uncle, just continue as regent."

*He responded, "You, you want to start talking with your peers when you are
discussing with other men, and they will start influencing you by saying, 'This
uncle of yours is cheating you, he eats even the things which are rightfully
yours.' Ultimately some animosity between us will develop and we will fight. I
don't want to fight you."*

Then indeed he said, "Well, here is your father's throne!"

*He called the men to the kgotla as well as these indunas and said, "Gentlemen,
today I am stepping down from the position I have been holding. The heir is back,
here he is."*

Appendix 5: Extract from Interview with Mahula Kekana

Part A: Sesotho

PK = Peter Kekana
MK = Mahula Kekana

Date: 12 December 1987

MK: Mokopane, o rile ge a rekišitšwe polaseng, gwa tla lebaka la gore banna be ba etšwa taemane ba mo humane a dišitše dinku.

PK: Gona kua Makapanstad?

MK: *Yes.* Ge ba mo humana a dišitše dinku ba re, "Mošimane, a ke o re fe meetse."

So ba mmotšiša gore ke mang.

Monna yo a re, "Nna ke Mokopane."

Bjale o be a sa tsebe Sesotho goba Setebele, o be a bolela yona Afrikaans ka go felela. Bjale lebitšo la gagwe e sa hlwa e le Mokopane, e le Makapan.

PK: *So he says when they were coming, eh, men were now working in Kimberley where there were diamond mines. So as they were coming back from the mines, they came to this farm, they were travelling on foot, and they found the boy who was looking after sheep. They asked for water. Now as they were drinking, they asked him his name.*

He said, "My name is Makapan."

The thing is he couldn't speak Sesotho or Sindebele, he could only speak Afrikaans. So you can understand now that the word, the name, Mokopane, was changed to Makapan.

MK: Bjale gona moo ge a sena go hlalosa ba mo swantšha. Ba re re tla re ge re fihla ka mošate re fihla re botše kgoši, re bitše Mošupye, gore ge e ba ke yena, re e dire leano la go mo tšeya.

PK: Mošupye e be e le yena kgoši.

MK: Ka nako yeo go be go buša yena.

PK: *So these men came here and said, "All right." After talking to this boy, they could recognise his face. They said when we get home we will talk to the chief who was Mošupye and strategise on how to get him back.*

MK: Aowa ka nnete ke ge Mošupye a re, "Ge e le gore le bone yena, tsamayang le ye le boledišane le monna woo, a le fe yena le boye le yena."

PK: *So when they arrived here, indeed they told Mošupye about that boy and he sent them back to the farm to go and talk to the Boer, to release the boy.*

Part B: English translation

PK = Peter Kekana
MK = Mahula Kekana

Date: 12 December 1987

MK: *After Mokopane was sold to the Boer, there came a time when the men were coming from the diamond mines and found him herding sheep.*

PK: *Right there at Makapanstad?*

MK: *Yes. When they found him herding sheep, they said, "Young man, can you give us some water?"*

Then they asked him who he was.

The man said, "Me, I am Makapan."

He knew neither Sesotho nor Sindebele. He could speak only Afrikaans. His name was no longer Mokopane but Makapan [the Afrikanerised version of Mokopane].

PK: So he says when they were coming, eh, men were now working in Kimberley where there were diamond mines. So as they were coming back from the mines, they came to this farm, they were travelling on foot, and they found the boy who was looking after sheep. They asked for water. Now as they were drinking, they asked him his name.

He said, "My name is Makapan."

The thing is he couldn't speak Sesotho or Sindebele, he could only speak Afrikaans. So you can understand now that the word, the name, Mokopane, was changed to Makapan.

MK: *He looked familiar to them. They said, "Let us go to the chief's capital. When we get there, we will report to the chief, we will report to Mošupye. If it is him, then we will come and fetch him."*

PK: *Mošupye was a chief?*

MK: *At the time he was ruling.*

PK: So these men came here and said, "All right." After talking to this boy, they could recognise his face. They said when we get home we will talk to the chief who was Mošupye and strategise on how to get him back.

MK: *Well, indeed, then Mošupye said, "If it is really him then go and negotiate with this man and get the boy released."*

PK: So when they arrived here, indeed they told Mošupye about that boy and he sent them back to the farm to go and talk to the Boer, to release the boy.

MK: Bjale lekgowa leo la re le nyaka lekgolo la dinku.

PK: *Then the Boers said, "I want a hundred sheep."*

MK: Ka nnete setšhaba se ile sa dira bjalo, sa ntšha lekgolo la dinku ba ya go mo lokolla.

PK: *So, a hundred sheep were sent over to the Boer to release the boy.*

MK: Ka nnete o bile a lokollwa, a tla gae. E rile ge a fetša ngwaga o tee, a bušа.

PK: *So when they got there, there was no problem. They gave the Boer his sheep, they got the boy back. Then he stayed for a year, and after a year he was then made chief.*

MK: Go tloga moo a buša le yena a tenwa a yo hlasela gona ko a tšwang gona, gore a buše dinku tšela gae.

PK: A ya go hlasela ko Leburung le la?

MK: Ee. Go na koo. Gona kua Leburung le motse wa tikologo.

PK: *When he was now the chief, then he went back to that place, that farm, and areas surrounding it and attacked that place so that he could get back the sheep.*

MK: Bjale ke ka moo motse wola wa ga Mosehla a bitšwang Makapanstad.

PK: *That is why today that place is called Makapanstad.*

MK: E theeletšwe ka kgoši Mokopane.

PK: *It's named after chief Mokopane.*

MK: Ee, di sepetše ka wona mokgwa woo.

MK: *The white man said he wanted a hundred sheep.*

PK: Then the Boer said, ''I want a hundred sheep.''

MK: *Truly, the tribe did what was asked of it, they took a hundred sheep and he released him.*

PK: So, a hundred sheep were sent over to the Boer, to release the boy.

MK: *Truly he was released and went home. He stayed there for one year and then he ruled.*

PK: So when they got there, there was no problem. They gave the Boer his sheep, they got the boy back. Then he stayed for a year, and after a year he was then made chief.

MK: *While he was ruling he went back and attacked the place where he came from to recover the sheep.*

PK: *He went to attack the Boer?*

MK: *Yes. And the surrounding areas.*

PK: When he was now the chief, then he went back to that place, that farm, and areas surrounding it and attacked that place so that he could get back the sheep.

MK: *Now that is why that place that was called Mosetlha is called Makapanstad.*

PK: That is why today that place is called Makapanstad.

MK: *It's named after chief Mokopane.*

PK: It's named after chief Mokopane.

MK: *Yes, that is the whole issue unfolded.*

NOTES

Preface

1 R. Bauman, *Story, Performance, and Event: Contextual Studies of Oral Narrative* (Cambridge: Cambridge University Press, 1986), ix.

2 See, for example, D. Tedlock, *The Spoken Word and the Work of Interpretation* (Philadelphia: University of Pennsylvania Press, 1983). I cite Tedlock here since his work *in general* has focused attention on the problems of presenting oral literature in written form. The particulars of his sophisticated and intricate system for presenting translated performance in writing have not been followed here, because as I explain below, the historical narratives examined in this book belong to a predominantly passive tradition and hence were not collected in performance conditions.

3 Bauman, *Story*, ix.

Introduction

1 See L. White, "Power and Praise Poetry", *Journal of Southern African Studies*, 9, 1, 1982; and K. Barber and P.F. de Moraes Farias (eds), *Discourse and its Disguises: The Interpretation of African Oral Texts* (Birmingham: University of Birmingham, Centre of West African Studies, 1989).

2 K. Barber, "Introduction", in Barber and De Moraes Farias, *Discourse and its Disguises*, 1.

3 See, for example, H.A. Veeser (ed.), *The New Historicism* (New York: Routledge, 1989) and L. Hunt (ed.), *The New Cultural History* (Berkeley: University of California Press, 1989).

4 K. Barber, *I Could Speak Until Tomorrow: Oriki, Women and the Past in a Yoruba Town* (Washington: Smithsonian Institution Press, 1991), and L. Vail and L. White, *Power and the Praise Poem: Southern African Voices in History* (Charlottesville: University Press of Virginia, 1991). Their earlier work that has shaped debate would include L. White, "Review Article: Literature and History in Africa" *Journal of African History*, 21, 1980 and his "Power and Praise Poetry". As regards Barber's earlier work see her "Yoruba *Oríkì* and Deconstructive Criticism", *Research in African Literatures*, 15, 4, 1984; "Popular Arts in Africa", *African Studies Review*, 3, 30, 1987; "Introduction"; and "Interpreting *Oríkì* as History and as Literature", both in Barber and De Moraes

Farias, *Discourse and its Disguises*. See also the work of Elizabeth Tonkin which attempts to break down the disciplinary barriers between oral literature and oral history. I have relied on "The Boundaries of History in Oral Performance", *History in Africa*, 9, 1982; "Steps to the Redefinition of 'Oral History': Examples from Africa", *Social History*, 7, 2, 1982; "Investigating Oral Tradition", *Journal of African History*, 27, 1986; and "Historical Discourses: The Achievement of Sieh Jeto", *History in Africa*, 15, 1988.

5 E. Fox-Genovese, "Literary Criticism and the Politics of the New Historicism", in Veeser, *The New Historicism*, 215.

6 Barber, "Introduction", 1.

7 With regard to the term 'oral history', there is some confusion. For some, the term refers to scholarly work undertaken by academics involving the recording of testimony from informants. At the same time, it can refer to the historical endeavours undertaken by those living in oral or paraliterate societies. In this book, I have followed Elizabeth Tonkin in using the term in both senses. See Tonkin, "Investigating Oral Tradition".

8 As the various books in each category and the way in which I have used them will become apparent later on in this chapter and elsewhere in the book, I have not, at this point, burdened the reader with a mammoth footnote.

9 For a useful comment on the interdisciplinary nature of studying oral forms, see R. Grele, " A Surmisable Variety: Interdisciplinarity and Oral Testimony", an essay in his volume *Envelopes of Sound: The Art of Oral History* (Chicago: Precedent, 1985).

10 Finnegan's critiques are contained in *Oral Literature in Africa* (1970; Nairobi: Oxford University Press, 1976), 367-73; "A Note on Oral Tradition and Historiographical Evidence", *History and Theory*, 9, 2, 1971; and *Literacy and Orality: Studies in the Technology of Communication* (Oxford: Basil Blackwell, 1988), 169-70. The quotations in the paragraph are from *Oral Literature*, 373; and " A Note", 198 respectively.

11 D. Cohen, *Womunafu's Bunafu: A Study of Authority in a Nineteenth-Century African Community* (Princeton: Princeton University Press, 1977), 8.

12 See, for example, M.J. Herskovits and F.S. Herskovits, *Dahomean Narrative: A Cross-Cultural Analysis* (Evanston: Northwestern University Press, 1958), 17; and R. Finnegan (trans. and ed.), *Limba Stories and Storytelling* (London: Oxford University Press, 1967), 40. More generally, see A.M. Jones and H. Carter, "The Style of Tonga Historical Narrative", *African Language Studies*, 8, 1967.

13 This view is implicit in research like that of R. Rosaldo, "Doing Oral History", *Social Analysis*, 4, 1980 as well as in his book *Ilongot Headhunting: 1883-1974: A Study in Society and History* (Stanford: Stanford University Press, 1980), 54-60; J. Comaroff, *Body of Power Spirit of Resistance: The Culture of a South African People* (Chicago: University of Chicago Press, 1985), 66, 80, 119, 125, 141-3; and J. Rappoport, "Mythic Images, Historical Thought, and Printed Texts: The Páez and the Written Word", *Journal of Anthropological Research*, 43, 1987. My thanks to Anne-Marie Grindrod for the latter reference.

14 R. Dorson, "Africa and the Folklorist", in R. Dorson (ed.), *African Folklore* (Bloomington: Indiana University Press, 1972), 51-2; and D. Cosentino, *Defiant Maids and Stubborn Farmers: Tradition and Invention in Mende Story Performance* (Cambridge: Cambridge University Press, 1982), 2.

15 Barber, "Yoruba *Oríkì*"; "Popular Arts"; "Introduction" and "Interpreting *Oríkì* as History and as Literature", both in Barber and De Moraes Farias, *Discourse and its Disguises*; and *I Could Speak*.

16 See also D. Attwell, "The British Legacy in Anglophone African Literary Criticism", *English in Africa*, 11, 1, 1984.

17 With regard to the insistence on generic fluidity see Finnegan, *Limba*, 28-31; and her

Oral Literature, Chs 1-3. While someone like D. Ben-Amos, "Folklore in African Society", *Research in African Literatures*, 6, 2, 1975, makes much the same points, he does so through a fairly rigid taxonomy that would, in some respects, support the kind of critique that Barber mounts. See also D. Ben-Amos, "Analytical Categories and Ethnic Genres", *Genre*, 2, 1969. For another instance of a relatively rigid taxonomy see G.M. Shreve and O. Arewa, "Form and Genre in African Folklore Classification: A Semiotic Perspective", *Research in African Literatures*, 11, 3, 1980.

18   Quote from I. Okpewho, *The Epic in Africa: Towards a Poetics of the Oral Performance* (New York: Columbia University Press, 1979), 160. See also 181 and 191.

19   Harold Scheub's work *The Xhosa Ntsomi* (Oxford: Oxford University Press, 1975) is an apposite example.

20   Phrase from Barber, "Popular Arts", 5.

21   T. Beidelman, "Approaches to the Study of African Oral Literature", *Africa*, 42, 1972.

22   Barber, "Interpreting *Oríkì*", in Barber and De Moraes Farias, *Discourse and its Disguises*. Quotation from page 20. See also her "Power and Subversion in Yoruba Praise Poetry", paper presented to the conference entitled "Power, Marginality and Oral Literature", School of Oriental and African Studies, University of London, 17-19/2/91.

23   As regards the formal characteristics of oral historical narration, I have relied mainly on D.P. Henige, *The Chronology of Oral Tradition* (Oxford: Clarendon Press, 1974); and J.C. Miller, "Introduction: Listening for the African Past", in J.C. Miller (ed.), *The African Past Speaks: Essays on Oral Tradition and History* (Folkestone: Dawson/Archon, 1980). While the standard works on African oral history do not often explicitly address the question of oral tradition's formal characteristics, the topic does emerge in passing. See, for example, S. Feierman, *The Shambaa Kingdom: A History* (Madison: University of Wisconsin Press, 1974), 6, 11, 14, 64-9. I also found G. Prins, *The Hidden Hippopotamus: Reappraisal in African History: The Early Colonial Experience in Western Zambia* (Cambridge: Cambridge University Press, 1980) useful for the way in which he examines the symbolic and conceptual presuppositions of Lozi historical discourse. See, for example, 132-8. P. Irwin, *Liptako Speaks: History from Oral Tradition in Africa* (Princeton: Princeton University Press, 1981) was also useful in its sensitivity to the formal properties of oral tradition as well as the mode of its performance and transmission. The work of Elizabeth Tonkin has been illuminating. I have relied on the following of her articles: "The Boundaries of History"; "Steps to the Redefinition"; "Investigating"; and "Historical Discourses".

24   See work listed in note 13 above as well as V.W. Turner, *The Forest of Symbols: Aspects of Ndembu Ritual* (New York: Cornell University Press, 1967), Chs 4 and 6.

25   D.E. Faris, "Narrative Form and Oral History: Some Problems and Possibilities", *International Journal of Oral History*, 1, 3, 1980; L. Passerini, "Italian Working Class Culture between the Wars: Consensus to Fascism and Work Ideology", *International Journal of Oral History*, 1, 1, 1980; D. Bertaux (ed.), *Biography and Society* (London: Sage, 1981); A. Portelli, "The Peculiarities of Oral History", *History Workshop Journal*, 12, 1981, and his "'The Time of My Life': Functions of Time in Oral History", *International Journal of Oral History*, 2, 3, 1981; Popular Memory Group, "Popular Memory: Theory, Politics, Method", in R. Johnson (ed.), *Making Histories: Studies in History-Writing and Politics* (London: Hutchinson, 1982); B.J. Ancelet, "'And This is No Damn Lie': Oral History in Story Form", *International Journal of Oral History*, 4, 2, 1983; and Grele, *Envelopes of Sound*.

26   W. Labov, *Language in the Inner City: Studies in Black English Vernacular* (Oxford: Basil Blackwell, 1977), 354-96; L. Polanyi, "Literary Complexity in Everyday Storytelling", in D. Tannen (ed.), *Spoken and Written Language: Exploring Orality and Literacy* (Norwood: Ablex, 1982); C. Linde, "Private Stories in Public Discourse"; and W-D. Stempel, "Everyday Narrative as Prototype", both in *Poetics*, 15, 1986. Some of these

ideas from the work listed in this note and the one above were applied in I. Hofmeyr, "Introduction: Exploring Experiential Testimony – A Selection of History Workshop Papers", *Social Dynamics*, 14, 2, 1988.

27 This topic is terrifying in its immensity. I have found useful W.B. Gallie, *Philosophy and the Historical Understanding* (London: Chatto & Windus, 1964); L.O. Mink, "Philosophical Analysis and Historical Understanding", *Review of Metaphysics*, 21, 4, 1968; A.R. Louch, "History as Narrative", *History and Theory*, 8, 1, 1969; W.H. Dray, "On the Nature and Role of Narrative in Historiography", *History and Theory*, 10, 2, 1971; L.O. Mink, "History and Fiction as Modes of Comprehension", in R. Cohen (ed.), *New Directions in Literary History* (London: Routledge & Kegan Paul, 1974); L.O. Mink, "Narrative Form as a Cognitive Instrument", in R.H. Canary and H. Kozicki (eds), *The Writing of History: Literary Form and Historical Understanding* (Wisconsin: Wisconsin University Press, 1978); H. White, *Tropics of Discourse: Essays in Cultural Criticism* (Baltimore: Johns Hopkins University Press, 1978); and his "The Question of Narrative in Contemporary Historical Theory", *History and Theory*, 23, 1, 1984. An application of these ideas appeared in I. Hofmeyr, "Narrative and Oral History", paper presented to the African Studies Institute Seminar, University of the Witwatersrand, 16/5/1988. My thanks to Debra Nails for her patient attempts to guide one so philosophically untutored as I through the field.

28 C. Lévi-Strauss, *The Savage Mind* (London: Weidenfeld & Nicolson, 1966), 16-22.

29 A.B. Lord, *The Singer of Tales* (Cambridge, Mass.: Harvard University Press, 1964), 5, 12, 14-15.

30 R. Finnegan, "Literacy and Literature", in B. Lloyd and J. Gay (eds), *Universals in Human Thought: Some African Evidence* (Cambridge: Cambridge University Press, 1981), 247-8; and Finnegan, *Literacy and Orality*, 92.

31 These would include D. Ben-Amos, *Sweet Words: Storytelling Events in Benin* (Philadelphia: Institute for the Study of Human Issues, 1975), 42-3; and White, "Power and Praise Poetry".

32 L. Dégh, *Folktales and Society: Storytelling in a Hungarian Peasant Community* (Bloomington: Indiana University Press, 1969), *passim*. As regards active and passive traditions, or more properly active and passive bearers, I have relied on C.W. von Sydow, "Folktale Studies and Philology: Some Points of View", in A. Dundes (ed.), *The Study of Folklore* (Englewood Cliffs: Prentice Hall, 1965), particularly 231-4. See also K.S. Goldstein, "On the Application of the Concepts of Active and Inactive Traditions to the Study of Repertory", *Journal of American Folklore*, 84, 1971.

33 See Chapter 1 for a fuller discussion of this point.

34 For a Southern African example see C. Hamilton, "Ideology, Oral Tradition and the Struggle for Power in the Early Zulu Kingdom", M.A. Dissertation, University of the Witwatersrand, 1985.

35 For a more detailed exposition of these points see I. Hofmeyr, "Review Article: Feminist Literary Criticism in South Africa", *English in Africa*, 19, 1, 1992.

36 See, for example, G.M. Pitje, "Traditional Systems of Male Education among Pedi and Cognate Tribes: Part II", *African Studies*, 9, 3, 1950 which includes comments on changing patterns of storytelling and oral performance. See also A. Mafeje, "The Role of the Bard in a Contemporary African Community", *Journal of African Languages*, 6, 3, 1967; White, "Power and Praise Poetry"; L. Vail and L. White, "The Art of Being Ruled: Ndebele Praise Poetry", in T. Couzens and L. White (eds), *Literature and Society in South Africa* (Cape Town: Maskew Miller Longman, 1984); J. Hodgson, "The Genius of Ntsikana: Traditional Images and the Process of Change in Early Xhosa Literature", in Couzens and White, *Literature*; D. Coplan, *In Township Tonight! South Africa's Black City Music and Theatre* (Johannesburg: Ravan, 1985); E. Gunner, "A Dying Tradition? African Oral Literature in a Contemporary Context", *Social Dynamics*, 12, 2, 1986; J. Hodgson, "Fluid Assets and Fixed Investments: 160 Years of

the Ntsikana Tradition", in R. Whitaker and E. Sienaert (eds), *Oral Tradition and Literacy: Changing Visions of the World* (Durban: Natal University Oral Documentation and Research Centre, 1986); and D. Coplan, "Eloquent Knowledge: Lesotho Migrants' Songs and the Anthropology of Experience", *American Ethnologist*, 14, 3, 1987. My thanks to Deborah James for the latter reference. While these articles deal with various literary genres, very few of them look at storytelling *per se*.

37 This necessarily cursory assessment of the historico-geographical school is based on S. Thompson, *The Folktale* (1946; New York: The Dryden Press, 1951), 428-48; and Finnegan, *Oral Literature*, 326-30. As the reference to Von Sydow in note 32 indicates, the potential for historical analysis certainly did exist within historico-geographic thought. However, as a recent article by Dan Ben-Amos shows, the application of motif analysis by someone like Dorson could not be otherwise than ahistorical. See D. Ben-Amos, "The Historical Folklore of Richard M. Dorson", *Journal of Folklore Research*, 26, 1, 1989. As regards South African examples, see S.M. Mofokeng, "A Study of Folk Tales in Sotho", M.A. Dissertation, University of the Witwatersrand, 1951; and his D. Phil Thesis, at the same university, "The Development of Leading Figures in Animal Tales in Africa", 1954.

38 As this material is extensively discussed in Chapter 1, I have not catalogued it here.

39 For an overview of this historiography see B. Bozzoli and P. Delius, "Radical History and South African Society", *Radical History Review*, 46-7, 1990.

40 Much of this work has been associated with the History Workshop. See particularly some of the volumes produced from its conferences, notably *Town and Countryside in the Transvaal: Capitalist Penetration and Popular Response* (Johannesburg: Ravan, 1983); and *Class, Community and Conflict: South African Perspectives* (Johannesburg: Ravan, 1987), both edited by B. Bozzoli.

41 J. Cronin, "'Even Under the Rine of Terror': Insurgent South African Poetry", *Research in African Literatures*, 19, 1, 1988; and A. Sitas, "The Voice and Gesture in South Africa's Revolution: A Study of Worker Gatherings and Performance-Genres in Natal", paper presented to the History Workshop Conference, University of the Witwatersrand, Johannesburg, 6-10/2/90.

42 For a discussion of various trends in oral history in South Africa, see P. La Hausse, "Oral History and South African Historians", *Radical History Review*, 46-7, 1990.

43 The name Potgietersrus has undergone various changes and spelling alterations. Initially established in 1852, it was named Vredenburg. By 1854 the name had changed to Pietpotgietersrust. In 1902 this was shortened to Potgietersrust and in 1954 the 't' was dropped to become Potgietersrus. I have used the modern spelling throughout.

44 As is explained below, the community where research was done comprises a mixture of Sindebele and Sesotho speakers. In using words from these languages, the Sesotho is followed by the Sindebele. Thereafter just the Sesotho is used.

45 As with much segregationist terminology in South Africa, the word 'location' has several meanings. Most commonly, it refers to a smallish black residential area in the vicinity of a rural white town. If the black residential area is larger and/or is in a metropolitan area, it is referred to as a township. However, in the nineteenth century, the term location was also used to refer to chiefdoms whose substantially curtailed territory received official state recognition. Such locations most frequently took the name of the chief, and the chiefdom under discussion here was variously known as Makapan's Location or Valtyn Makapan's Location.

46 For an overview on betterment policy see W. Beinart, "Introduction: The Politics of Colonial Conservation", *Journal of Southern African Studies*, 15, 2, 1989.

47 For a detailed discussion of this period see D. Posel, "Influx Control and the Construction of Apartheid, 1948-1961", D. Phil. Thesis, Oxford University, 1987.

48 See, for example, B. Stock, *The Implications of Literacy: Written Language and Models of*

Interpretation in the Eleventh and Twelfth Centuries (Princeton: Princeton University Press, 1983), 5-6.

49 Stock, *The Implications*, 9.

50 .The Afrikaans word *gat* can mean cave, hole or anus. While the meaning of the word *Gwaša* is not entirely clear, some maintain that it derives from the verb *go gwaša*, to make a rustling sound. According to one informant, prior to the siege, the caves were said to emit a pleasant, rustling sound. However, after the siege, this sound ceased. Moses Ledwaba and Matthews Hlanga, interviewed by Amos Ledwaba, Madimetša Ledwaba and Isabel Hofmeyr (hereafter I.H.), GaLedwaba, 8/9/88. Molalakgori Kekana, interviewed by Felix Malunga, Sidney Maaka and I.H., Mahwelereng, 10/8/88.

51 Lévi-Strauss, *The Savage Mind*, 16-22.

52 For an interesting Northern Transvaal example of this process see R.T.K. Scully, "Phalaborwa Oral Tradition", Ph. D. Thesis, State University of New York at Binghamton, 1978, 118-19, who mentions the use of radio serials in historical tradition.

53 E.M. Letsoalo, "The Settlement System", in A. de Villiers (comp.), *A Rural Development Strategy for Lebowa* (Mankweng: University of the North, 1984), 100-1.

54 Lucky Mokgaetši Mokekolwane Kekana and Mantutule Joyce Mmushi, interviewed by Jacob Mthembu and I.H., Makapanspoort Mission, Potgietersrus district, 3/4/90. The phrase is a mixture of Sesotho and Sindebele.

55 Phrase from F.C. de Beer, "Groepsgebondenheid in die Familie-, Opvolgings- en Erfsreg van die Noord-Ndebele", D. Phil. Thesis, University of Pretoria, 1986, 229.

56 Development Bank of Southern Africa and the Lebowa Government, *Lebowa Development Information: Section 4: Population and Settlement* (Development Bank of Southern Africa: Sandton, n.d.), 7.

57 Occupational profile from Development Bank of Southern Africa and the Lebowa Government, *Lebowa Development Information: Section 5: Labour and Employment* (Development Bank of Southern Africa: Sandton, n.d.), 3. The exact figures are as follows: Production: 25,8 %; Agriculture: 24,4 %; Service Sector: 11,4 %; Sales Work: .6,8 %; Professional: 9,2 %; Clerical: 3,7 %; Managerial: 0,3 %; Not classifiable: 18,4 %. This occupational profile fits closely with Lebowa's educational statistics. According to 1980 figures, 55,8 % of the population had no formal education; 34,8 % had been to primary school while 9,1 % had some secondary or tertiary education. Only 0,3 % of the population had post-matric qualifications. Figures from A. de Villiers, "The Lebowa Economy", in De Villiers, *A Rural Development Strategy*, 28.

58 Development Bank of Southern Africa and the Lebowa Government, *Lebowa Development Information: Section 5*, 3.

59 Development Bank of Southern Africa and the Lebowa Government, *Lebowa Development Information: Section 4*, 13.

60 The villages and their housing totals are as follows: Blinkwater, 209; Madiba, 806; Magongwa, 386; Mosesetjane, 592; Sandsloot, 1 339; Sekgakgapeng, 83; Tsamahansi, 1 164; Tweefontein, 260. Figures from Development Bank of Southern Africa and Lebowa Government, *Lebowa Development Information: Section 4*, 20-2.

61 South African Institute of Race Relations (S.A.I.R.R.), *Establishment of the Bantu Authorities: First and Second Interim Report* (Johannesburg: S.A.I.R.R., 1959), 3.

62 Lucky Kekana interview, 3/4/90.

63 De Beer, "Groepsgebondenheid", 53, 89, 150.

64 De Beer, "Groepsgebondenheid", 43-5, 50, 53.

65 For a fuller discussion of this point see Chapter 4.

66 See, for example, N.J. van Warmelo, "The Classification of Cultural Groups", in W.D. Hammond-Tooke (ed.), *The Bantu-speaking Peoples of Southern Africa* (London: Routledge & Kegan Paul, 1959), 60 and 67.

67   The literature on the Northern Transvaal Ndebele is relatively sparse. While a few
     nineteenth-century travellers like Livingstone and Baines passed through the area,
     their observations on the region were limited to a few pages. See, for example,
     I. Schapera (ed.), *David Livingstone: Family Letters 1841-1856:* Vol. I (London: Chatto
     & Windus, 1959), 187-8, 200-2; I. Schapera (ed.), *Livingstone's Missionary
     Correspondence: 1841-1856* (London: Chatto & Windus, 1961), 97-8; and T. Baines, *The
     Gold Regions of South East Africa* (1877; Bulawayo: Books of Rhodesia, 1968), 67-8.
     Similarly, see W.L. Distant, *A Naturalist in the Transvaal* (London: Porter, 1892), 81-4;
     and C.L. Norris-Newman, *With the Boers in the Transvaal and Orange Free State in
     1880-1* (1882; Johannesburg: Africana Book Society, 1976), 58-60. The most extensive
     traveller's account comes from S. Heckford, *A Lady Trader in the Transvaal* (London:
     Sampson Low, 1882), 286-310.
        The ethnographic literature was until recently extremely limited and comprised
     only A.O. Jackson, *The Ndebele of Langa*, Republic of South Africa, Department of Co-
     operation and Development, Ethnological Publication No. 54 (Pretoria: Government
     Printer, n.d.); N.J. van Warmelo, *Transvaal Ndebele Texts*, Union of South Africa,
     Department of Native Affairs, Ethnological Publication No. 1 (Pretoria: Government
     Printer, 1930) which contains limited reference to Northern Transvaal Ndebele
     groupings; and A.O. Jackson, "The Langa Ndebele Calendar and Annual Agricultural
     Ceremonies", in The Ethnological Section (ed.), *Ethnological and Linguistic Studies in
     Honour of N.J. van Warmelo*, Republic of South Africa, Department of Bantu
     Administration and Development, Ethnological Publication No. 52 (Pretoria:
     Government Printer, 1969). Towards the end of the 1970s, the Committee for
     Development Research of the Department of Community Development declared the
     Northern Transvaal Ndebele a research priority; out of this state initiative came two
     theses, C.J. Coetzee, "Die Strewe tot Etniese Konsolidasie en Nasionale
     Selfverwesenliking by die Ndebele in die Transvaal", Ph. D. Thesis, University of
     Potchefstroom, 1980; and De Beer, "Groepsgebondenheid". There is also linguistic
     research in D. Ziervogel, *A Grammar of Northern Transvaal Ndebele* (Pretoria: Van
     Schaik, 1959).
        In terms of archaeological evidence, see J.P. Johnson, "Note on some Stone-Walled
     Kraals in South Africa", *Man*, 36, 1912; and J.H.N Loubser, "Ndebele Archaeology of
     the Pietersburg Area", M.A. Dissertation, University of the Witwatersrand, 1981.
        In terms of historical information the literature is richer. The Berlin missionaries
     who began arriving in the area from the 1860s have left extensive published records
     in *Berliner Missionsberichte* (hereafter *B.M.B.*). Using N.J. van Warmelo (comp.),
     Anthropology of Southern Africa in Periodicals to 1950: An Analysis and Index
     (Johannesburg: Witwatersrand University Press, 1977), I was able to locate the reports
     that dealt with the mission station in the chiefdom. These amounted to some two
     hundred pages which were translated by Syrith Hofmeyr. In addition, I have also
     used the edited diary of Daniel Heese who ran the Berlin Mission in the chiefdom
     from 1890 to 1901. The text is P. Gurr, *Daniel Heese: Ein Lebensbild aus der Mission in
     Makapanspoort in Nord-Transvaal* (Berlin: Berliner Evangelische Missionsgesellschaft,
     n.d.) which was also kindly translated by Syrith Hofmeyr.
        There are also rich local archival sources pertaining to the chiefdom. These are the
     Native Commissioner's archive for Potgietersrus (KPT) as well as the Native
     Commissioner's archive for the Northern Area (HKN). In addition, there are smaller
     and less fruitful archives, namely the Magistrate's papers for Potgietersrus (LPT) as
     well as the Municipal archive (MPT). These are all housed in Pretoria in the Transvaal
     Archives (hereafter T.A.), in one of its subsections, the Transvaal Archives Depot
     (T.A.D.).

68   Coetzee, "Die Strewe", 215. The figures given in this source only add up to 99 %.

69 Ziervogel, *A Grammar*, 6 and 9.
70 Job Patja Kekana, interviewed by I.H., Johannesburg, 7/6/90; Christina Raisitja Kekana and Mogotlane Kekana, interviewed by Alfred Lesiba Kekana and I.H., Sekgakgapeng, 6/4/90.
71 De Beer, "Groepsgebondenheid", 462. This point was also often made to me in conversation.
72 The two traditions are respectively recorded in Gurr, *Daniel Heese*, 5-6; and T.A., T.A.D., GOV 1088, PS 50/8/1907, History: Valtyn Makapaan (Mokopane), 3. For details of the Ndebele invasion see J.R.D. Cobbing, "The Ndebele under the Khumalos: 1820-1896", D. Phil. Thesis, University of Lancaster, 1976, 15-20, 40-1.
73 Coetzee, "Die Strewe", 385-418, 473-4.
74 Union of South Africa, Mines Department, *Geological Survey: The Geology of the Country Around Potgietersrust* (Pretoria: Government Printer, 1911), 16-17; J.H. Wellington, *Southern Africa: A Geographical Survey: Physical Geography:* Vol. I (Cambridge: Cambridge University Press, 1955), 80-2, 85-8; M.M. Cole, *South Africa* (London: Methuen, 1961), 646-7; and J.S. Marais, "Die Landbou-Potensiaal van Potgietersrust", in A.J. Combrink (comp.), *Eeufees Potgietersrust Centenary 1854-1954* (Potgietersrust: The Central Centenary Committee, n.d.), 127-8.
75 Quoted in B. Chatwin, *The Songlines* (London: Jonathan Cape, 1987), 237. A popular version of Dart's theory appears in R. Dart, *Adventures with the Missing Link* (London: Hamish Hamilton, 1959). See, for example, 109-19.
76 Chatwin, *The Songlines*, 235.
77 Chatwin, *The Songlines*, 240-1.
78 Finnegan, "Literacy", 169.

Chapter 1
"Stories go Hand in Glove with Building a Man and a Woman"

1 S.J. Neethling, "Die Xhosa Iintsomi: 'n Strukturele Benadering", D. Phil. Thesis, University of Stellenbosch, 1979, 245-6. The translation of the quotation is mine.
2 Examples include T. Cope, "Towards an Appreciation of Zulu Folktales as Literary Art", in J. Argyle and E. Preston-Whyte (eds), *Social System and Tradition in Southern Africa: Essays in Honour of Eileen Krige* (Cape Town: Oxford University Press, 1978), 195; M. Oosthuizen, "A Study of the Structure of the Zulu Folktale with Special Reference to the Stuart Collection", M.A. Dissertation, University of Natal, Durban, 1977, 38-9, 44; and P.M. Makgamatha, "Characteristics of the Northern Sotho Folktales: Their Form and Structure", M.A. Dissertation, University of South Africa, 1987, 19-20.
3 At the turn of the century James Stuart, a collector of Zulu oral traditions, noted that most tellers of imaginary oral narrative were women. Quoted in Oosthuizen, "A Study", 39.
4 J. Guy, "Gender Oppression in Southern Africa's Precapitalist Societies", in C. Walker (ed.), *Women and Gender in Southern Africa to 1945* (Cape Town: David Philip, 1990), 40. See also the introduction to this volume by C. Walker. Other studies include B. Bozzoli, "Marxism, Feminism and South African Studies", *Journal of Southern African Studies*, 9, 2, 1983; and M. Kinsman, "'Beasts of Burden': The Subordination of Southern Tswana Women, ca. 1800-1840", *Journal of Southern African Studies*, 10, 1, 1983. The nature of gender relations also forms an important theme in Comaroff, *Body of Power*.
5 Quoted in Kinsman, "Beasts", 49.
6 Comaroff, *Body of Power*, 71, 80-1, 98.
7 See, for example, M.Z. Rosaldo and L. Lamphere, "Introduction", in M.Z. Rosaldo

and L. Lamphere (eds), *Woman, Culture, and Society* (Stanford: Stanford University Press, 1974), 9-12.

8   On household space in Transvaal societies see Pitje, "Traditional Systems: Part I"; A. Kuper, "Symbolic Dimensions of the Southern Bantu Homestead", *Africa*, 50, 1, 1980, 16-17; C. Jansen van Vuuren, "Die Vestigingspatroon van die Suid-Ndebele", M.A. Dissertation, University of Pretoria, 1983, 41, 45-6; and Comaroff, *Body of Power*, 54.

9   Paragraph based on A. Kuper, "The Social Structure of the Sotho-speaking Peoples of Southern Africa: Parts I and II", *Africa*, 45, 1, 1975, 67-81, and 45, 2, 1975, 139-49; and Kuper, "Symbolic Dimensions". See also Jackson, *The Ndebele*, 119-22.

10   On terminology see M.J. Herskovits, "The Study of African Oral Art", *Journal of American Folklore*, 74, 1961.

11   Sarah Teffo, interviewed by Rose Lephondo and I.H., Mahwelereng, 6/3/90.

12   Paragraph drawn from discussions of Transvaal storytelling. H.A. Junod, *The Life of a South African Tribe: Mental Life*, Vol. II (London: Macmillan, 1927), 214; P.-D. Cole-Beuchat, "Notes on Some Folklore Forms in Tsonga and Ronga", *African Studies*, 17, 4, 1958, 187; C.D.T. Marivate, "Tsonga Folktales: Form, Content and Delivery", Vol. I, M.A. Dissertation, University of South Africa, 1973, 19-20, 28, 33; M.C. Bill, "The Structure and Function of the Song in the Tsonga Folktale", *African Studies*, 42, 1, 1983, 1; and Makgamatha, "Characteristics", 19-20. For comparative Southern African examples, I have relied on I.M. Moephuli, "Structure and Character in Cyclic Folktales in Southern Sotho", M.A. Dissertation, University of South Africa, 1979, 10; and Neethling, "Die Xhosa Iintsomi", 251, 259. Also Madumelana Shiloti, interviewed by Ruth Khaas and I.H., Mahwelereng, 28/2/90; Morongoa Kgosana, interviewed by Helen Maime and I.H., Mahwelereng, 1/3/90; Mosiwa Martha Lekalakala, interviewed by Jacobeth Ramupudu and I.H., Makapanspoort Mission, Potgietersrus district, 13/3/90; Moletsi Daniel Mahlangu interviewed by Jacobeth Ramupudu and I.H., Makapanspoort Mission, Potgietersrus district, 13/3/90; and Lucky Kekana interview, 9/4/90.

13   D. James, "Kinship and Land in an Inter-Ethnic Community", M.A. Dissertation, University of the Witwatersrand, 1987, 103.

14   H.O. Mönnig, *The Pedi* (1967; Pretoria: Van Schaik, 1988) maintains that in Pedi society, only circumcised men were permitted into the *kgoro*. However, all my informants said that this was not the case. Pitje, "Traditional Systems", supports this view. What may in fact be the case is that while this division operated at one stage, with migrancy it fell into disuse.

15   John Maselela Maleka, interviewed by Johanna Moima and I.H., Mahwelereng, 19/3/88; Sophie Lekgoathi and Emily Mashishi, interviewed by Helen Maime and I.H., Mahwelereng, 7/3/90; Grace Karolo Kekana, interviewed by Jacobeth Ramupudu and I.H., Mošate, Valtyn, 23/3/90 and 20/4/90; Lekalakala interview; Mahlangu interview; and Job Kekana interview, 7/6/90. See, also, Pitje, "Traditional Systems: Part I", 61; and G.P. Lestrade, "Domestic and Communal Life", in I. Schapera (ed.), *The Bantu-Speaking Tribes of South Africa: An Ethnographical Survey* (1937; Cape Town: Maskew Miller, 1966), 127.

16   Alfred Lesiba Kekana, interviewed by I.H., Sekgakgapeng, 29/3/90. Interview originally in English.

17   Alfred Lesiba Kekana, interviewed by I.H., Sekgakgapeng, 22/6/90; and Helen Maime, interviewed by I.H., Mahwelereng, 23/6/90. See also Ramasela Fransina Ramasela Sema, interviewed by Rose Lephondo, Sarah Teffo and I.H., 15/3/90. For comparative material on this point see Herskovits, *Dahomean Narrative*, 17; Finnegan, *Limba Stories*, 40; D. Ben-Amos, "Folklore", 180; and Cosentino, *Defiant Maids*, 6-7.

18   Lestrade, "Domestic and Communal Life", 123; and, comparatively, F.M. Deng, *Dinka Folktales: African Stories from the Sudan* (London: Africana, 1974), 14.

19 Lucky Kekana interview, 9/4/90.
20 Shiloti interview.
21 Ben Amos, "Folklore", 189. Other points in paragraph from Marivate, "Tsonga Folktales", 20; and Lestrade "Domestic and Communal Life", 127. H. Scheub, "Introduction", in A.C. Jordan (tr.), *Tales from Southern Africa* (Berkeley: University of California Press, 1973), 2.
22 Lucky Kekana interview, 9/4/90.
23 Sarah Teffo interview; Lucky Kekana interview, 9/4/90; and Dikgopana Rampula, interviewed by I.H., Mahwelereng, 30/4/90. See also Pitje, "Traditional Systems".
24 Pitje, "Traditional Systems: Part I", 68-9.
25 See Kinsman, "Beasts", 49-50.
26 C. Doke, "The Basis of Bantu Literature", *Africa*, 18, 4, 1948, 287. See also Cosentino, *Defiant Maids*, 2; and M. Jackson, *Allegories of the Wilderness: Ethics and Ambiguity in Kuranko Narratives* (Bloomington: Indiana University Press, 1982), 51.
27 Rampula interview. Interview originally in English.
28 This point is extrapolated from field work observations. Competent tellers like Alfred Lesiba Kekana and Lucky Kekana both had wide repertoires that drew from both historical and fictional traditions. Most other tellers stuck to one or other tradition. See also Scheub, "Introduction", 2.
29 Lucky Kekana interview, 9/4/90.
30 Kgosana interview, 1/3/90. See also Naomi Teffo, interviewed by I.H., Mahwelereng, 9/4/90 who made similar points.
31 Lekalakala interview; and Mahlangu interview.
32 Lekalakala interview; and Mahlangu interview.
33 Shiloti interview; Lekalakala interview; and Mahlangu interview.
34 Scheub,*The Xhosa Ntsomi*, 12.
35 For a fascinating comparative discussion of a similar oral educational system, in this instance that of ancient Greece, see E.A. Havelock, *The Literate Revolution in Greece and its Cultural Consequences* (Princeton: Princeton University Press, 1982), 122-49. My thanks to Debra Nails for this reference.
36 N.N. Canonici, "Educational Aspects of Trickster Folktales", in E. Sienaert and N. Bell (eds), *Catching Winged Words: Oral Tradition and Education* (Durban: Natal University Oral Documentation and Research Centre, 1988), 111. See also J.S. Mbiti (ed.), *Akamba Stories* (London: Oxford University Press, 1966), 7, for a useful, comparative statement. Local commentary includes Neethling, "Die Xhosa Iintsomi", 252; and Makgamatha, "Characteristics", 15, 19.
37 David Livingstone to Charles Livingstone, 16/3/1847 in Schapera, *David Livingstone*, 192-3.
38 G.P. Lestrade, "Traditional Literature", in Schapera, *The Bantu Tribes*, 296-7.
39 Mbiti, *Akamba Stories*, 3.
40 On praising see Lestrade, "Traditional Literature", 296; A.C. Jordan, *Towards an African Literature: The Emergence of Literary Form in Xhosa* (Berkeley: University of California Press, 1973), 21; and J. Opland, *Xhosa Oral Poetry: Aspects of a Black South African Tradition* (Johannesburg: Ravan, 1983), 42-3. For comparative examples on the universality of storytelling see E.E. Evans-Pritchard (ed.), *The Zande Trickster* (London: Oxford University Press, 1967), 19; and Cosentino, *Defiant Maids*, 8. For local storytelling as popular art see Marivate, "Tsonga Folktales", 21; and Bill, "The Structure", 1.
41 Naomi Teffo interview; and Lucky Kekana interview, 9/4/90.
42 N.N. Canonici, *The Inganekwane Tradition* (Durban: Department of Zulu Language and Literature, University of Natal, 1987), 3.
43 Again this is a feature noted throughout Africa. See, for example, Herskovits, *Dahomean Narrative*, 70; Mbiti, *Akamba Stories*, 26; Scheub, *The Xhosa Ntsomi*, 16; and

Deng, *Dinka Folktales*, 14. For local examples see Bill, "The Structure", 1. More generally, see B. Bettelheim, *The Uses of Enchantment: The Meaning and Importance of Fairy Tales* (Harmondsworth: Penguin, 1976), 18-19.

44 Bill, "The Structure", 5.

45 Scheub, *The Xhosa Ntsomi*, 13 and 15. Cope makes a similar point, "Towards an Appreciation", 203.

46 Lekgoathi and Mashishi interview.

47 For a range of comments on the complex issues of evaluation see S.A. Babalola, *The Content and Form of Yoruba Ijala* (London: Oxford University Press, 1966), 48; Mbiti, *Akamba Stories*, 24-6; Finnegan, *Limba Stories*, 69-70; Ben-Amos, *Sweet Words*, 52-3; D. LaPin, "Narrative as Precedent in Yoruba Oral Tradition", in J.M. Foley (ed.), *Oral Traditional Literature: A Festschrift for Albert Bates Lord* (Columbus: Slavica, 1981), 349.

48 Kgosana interview, 1/3/90, in which the informant favoured fluency, logical arrangement and unusual plots; Lekalakala interview and Mahlangu interview in which both participants praised humour and interest; and Naomi Teffo interview in which loudness of delivery and clarity of message were singled out.

49 A. Dundes, "Metafolklore and Oral Literary Criticism", *The Monist*, 50, 1966.

50 Finnegan, *Limba Stories*, 25-6; and Scheub, *The Xhosa Ntsomi*, 18-19.

51 Scheub, *The Xhosa Ntsomi*, 17-43; and Moephuli, "Structure and Character", 11-12.

52 J. Berry, *Spoken Art in West Africa* (London: University of London, 1961), 18; Finnegan, *Limba Stories*, 75-85; Marivate, "Tsonga Folktales", 17; and Neethling, "Die Xhosa lintsomi", 17.

53 Lord, *The Singer*, 42.

54 This pattern of reinforcing 'lines' or basic structural units is apparent in a wide range of oral forms. P. McAllister, for example, in "Conservatism as Ideology of Resistance among Xhosa-speakers: The Implications for Oral Tradition and Literacy", in Whitaker and Sienaert, *Oral Tradition and Literacy*, 296-7, notes that in the oratory of ritual events, the call-and-response patterns often demarcate short clipped sentences similar to praising. Marivate in "Tsonga Folktales", 17, notes that stories are delivered in units reminiscent of praises. See also LaPin, "Narrative as Precedent", 373, fn. 17. See also Rampula interview.

55 For 'subversive' readings of African oral narrative see Jackson, *Allegories*; and T.O. Beidelman, *Moral Imagination in Kaguru Modes of Thought* (Bloomington: Indiana University Press, 1986), 169-77. The generalised statements on *dinonwane*, made in this paragraph, are based on a reading of various collections, notably Mofokeng, "A Study"; Scheub, *The Xhosa Ntsomi*; and Makgamatha, "Characteristics". I have also relied on the stories collected during field work. The relevant interviews are Kgosana interview, 1/3/90; Shiloti interview; Lekgoathi interview; Makgabo Ramasela Langa, interviewed by Morongoa Kgosana and I.H., Mahwelereng, 7/3/90; Sema interview; Lekalakala interview; Mahlangu interview; Grace Karolo Kekana interview, 23/3/90; Ramasela Serosina Kekana, interviewed by Alfred Lesiba Kekana and I.H., Sekgakgapeng, 30/3/90; Christina Raisitja Kekana, interviewed by Alfred Lesiba Kekana and I.H., Sekgakgapeng, 3/4/90; Christina Raisitja Kekana and Mogotlane Kekana, interviewed by Alfred Lesiba Kekana and I.H., Sekgakgapeng, 6/4/90; Lucky Kekana interview, 9/4/90; Naomi Teffo interview; Dinah Raisibe Thabeta interviewed by Anna Kiki Kutumela, Obed Kutumela and I.H., Sekgakgapeng, 20/4/90; Priscilla Ramokone Rampula, interviewed by Anna Kiki Kutumela, Obed Kutumela and I.H., Sekgakgapeng, 20/4/90; and Rampula interview.

56 On this point see Scheub, *The Xhosa Ntsomi*, 56; and Cosentino, *Defiant Maids*, 8.

57 W. Ong, *Orality and Literacy: The Technologizing of the Word* (London: Methuen, 1982), 70.

58 D. Bynum, *The Daemon in the Wood: A Study of Oral Narrative Pattern* (Cambridge, Mass.: The Center for the Study of Oral Literature, Harvard University, 1978), 29 and 41.

59 Cole-Beuchat, "Notes", 187; and Marivate, "Tsonga Folktales", 52-3.

60 A. Kuper, *South Africa and the Anthropologist* (London: Routledge & Kegan Paul, 1987), 195 and 196-7.

61 R. Darnton, *The Great Cat Massacre and Other Episodes in French Cultural History* (New York: Basic Books, 1984), 30. Thanks to Molly Bill for this reference. Deng, *Dinka Folktales*, 193, notes a similar tendency in the Sudan.

Chapter 2
Jonah and the Swallowing Monster

1 For a fuller discussion of these issues see H.J. Graff, *The Literacy Myth: Literacy and Social Structure in the Nineteenth Century* (New York: Academic Press, 1979), 2-19; H.J. Graff, "Introduction", in H.J. Graff (ed.), *Literacy and Social Development in the West: A Reader* (Cambridge: Cambridge University Press, 1981); B.V. Street, *Literacy in Theory and Practice* (Cambridge: Cambridge University Press, 1984), Chs 1 and 2; Finnegan, *Literacy and Orality*, 1-14; and B.V. Street, "Introduction", in B.V. Street (ed.), *Cross-Cultural Approaches to Literacy* (forthcoming). My thanks to Professor Street for kindly making a copy of the latter article available to me.

2 Street, *Literacy in Theory*, and "Introduction".

3 For studies on colonialism and literacy in South Africa see A.T. Cope, "Literacy and the Oral Tradition: The Zulu Evidence"; E. Gunner, "The Word, the Book and the Zulu Church of Nazareth"; J. Opland, "The Transition from Oral to Written Literature in Xhosa, 1823-1909", all in Whitaker and Sienaert, *Oral Tradition and Literacy*. See also D.P. Kunene, *Thomas Mofolo and the Emergence of Written Sesotho Prose* (Johannesburg: Ravan, 1989), Ch. 1. For a comparative perspective see D.F. McKenzie, "The Sociology of a Text: Oral Culture, Literacy and Print in Early New Zealand", in P. Burke and R. Porter (eds), *The Social History of Language* (Cambridge: Cambridge University Press, 1987), 189.

4 This stress on the resistant power of oral cultures is a common theme in the scholarship. See, for example, J. Goody, "Restricted Literacy in Northern Ghana", in J. Goody (ed.), *Literacy in Traditional Societies* (London: Cambridge University Press, 1968); M.T. Clanchy, *From Memory to Written Record: England 1066-1307* (London: Edward Arnold, 1979), 198-216; J. Goody, *The Logic of Writing and the Organization of Society* (Cambridge: Cambridge University Press, 1986); and N.Z. Davis, "Printing and the People: Early Modern France", in Graff, *Literacy and Social Development*.

5 Fred Ledwaba, interviewed by Madimetša Ledwaba and I.H., Lebowakgomo, 7/10/88. See also D. James, "A Question of Ethnicity: Ndzundza Ndebele in a Lebowa Village", *Journal of Southern African Studies*, 16, 1, 1990.

6 D. Nel, "Die Drama van Makapansgrot: Soos deur die Naturelle Vertel" ("The Drama of Makapan's Cave: As Told by the Natives"), *Die Huisgenoot*, 24/3/33.

7 Paragraph based on J.J. de Waal, "Die Verhouding Tussen die Blankes en die Hoofmanne Mokopane en Mankopane in die Omgewing van Potgietersrus, 1836-1869", M.A. Dissertation, University of South Africa, 1978, 21-33; R. Wagner, "The Zoutpansberg: The Dynamics of a Hunting Frontier, 1848-1867", in S. Marks and S. Trapido (eds), *Economy and Society in Pre-Industrial South Africa* (London: Longman, 1980); and J. du Plooy, "Die Ontstaan- en Vestigingsgeskiedenis van Potgietersrust 1852-1904", M.A. Dissertation, University of Potchefstroom, 1989, Ch. 2.

8 Gurr, *Daniel Heese*, 30. Translated.

9 *Berliner Missionsberichte* (hereafter *B.M.B.*), 7, 1865, 103. Translated.

10   Gurr, *Daniel Heese*, 10; and D.W. van der Merwe, "Die Geskiedenis van die Berlynse Sendinggenootskap in die Transvaal 1860-1900", M.A. Dissertation, University of South Africa, 1975, 86-7.

11   *B.M.B.*, 5, 1869, 72-3. For discussion of similar issues in neighbouring societies see *B.M.B.*, 5, 1865, 84-92; and P. Delius, *The Land Belongs to Us: The Pedi Polity, the Boers and the British in the Nineteenth-century Transvaal* (Johannesburg: Ravan, 1983), Ch. 5.

12   *B.M.B.*, 5, 1869, 74; 6, 1869, 82-3; 7, 1870, 100-7; and Gurr, *Daniel Heese*, 10-17. For a comparative perspective see Delius, *The Land*, Ch. 5.

13   Paragraph based on *B.M.B.*, 5, 1869, 71-7; 6, 1869, 83; 7, 1870, 99; 7-8, 1875, 151; T.A., T.A.D., KPT 32, 2/9/2, Undated affidavit by Frans Noko Kekana giving the history of the chiefdom; S.P. Engelbrecht (ed.), *Paul Kruger's Amptelike Briewe 1851-1877* (Pretoria: Volkstem, 1925), 131-43; Van der Merwe, "Die Geskiedenis", 123-5; and Du Plooy, "Die Ontstaan", Ch. 2.

14   Quotation from Van der Merwe, "Die Geskiedenis", 125. Remainder of paragraph drawn from Heckford, *Lady Trader*, 288; and Gurr, *Daniel Heese*, 25-6.

15   T.A., T.A.D., KG 59, CR 1884/93; and SP 79, SPR 8717/95.

16   T.A., T.A.D., GOV 1085, PS 50/8/1907/9, Location Commission History of Native Tribes, Valtijn Makapan; and Du Plooy, "Die Ontstaan", Chs 2 and 5.

17   T.A., T.A.D., SP 79, SPR 8717/95. Translated. My thanks to Haldane Hofmeyr for this and all subsequent translations from the Dutch.

18   Gurr, *Daniel Heese*, 87; and Van der Merwe, "Die Geskiedenis", 207.

19   Gurr, *Daniel Heese*, 120-7; M. Wright, *German Missions in Tanganyika 1891-1941* (Oxford: Clarendon Press, 1971), 13-18; Delius, *The Land*, 160-7; and J. Krikler, "Agrarian Class Struggle and the South African War", *Social History*, 14, 2, 1989, 163-73.

20   T.A., T.A.D., KPT 15, 2/3/2, J. Neitz to Resident Magistrate (hereafter R.M.), 21/6/28; and Du Plooy, "Die Ontstaan", Chs 9 and 10.

21   *B.M.B.*, 19-20, 1877, 406; 19-20, 1889, 504; 23-24, 1892, 601-2; and Gurr, *Daniel Heese*, 32, 77. See also D. Gaitskell, "Devout Domesticity? A Century of African Women's Christianity in South Africa", in Walker, *Women*, 252-6.

22   *B.M.B.*, 13-14, 1886, 214; T.A., Central Archives Depot (hereafter C.A.D.), NTS 314, 12/55; and De Beer, "Groepsgebondenheid", 43-4. For a good description of the various interest groups in the chiefdom *B.M.B.*, 21-22, 1892, 573.

23   T.A., T.A.D., KPT 15, 2/3/2, J. Neitz to R. M., 21/6/28. On composition of mission see Calvin Mogahlahla Puka, interviewed by I.H., Makapanspoort Mission, Potgietersrus district, 8/4/90.

24   Church figures from T.A., T.A.D., KPT 14, 2/3/2. Remainder of paragraph from *B.M.B.*, 19-20, 1892, 506; 23-24, 1892, 596, 599, 601-2; and Gurr, *Daniel Heese*, 27, 34-8, 42-4, 57, 88, 96-7.

25   *B.M.B.*, 19-20, 1884, 418; 23-24, 1892, 599-601; and Gurr, *Daniel Heese*, 28, 32, 49.

26   On this point see S.B. Heath, "The Function and Uses of Literacy", *Journal of Communication*, 30, 1980.

27   *B.M.B.*, 19-20, 1884, 419; 23-24, 1892, 601; and Gurr, *Daniel Heese*, 28-9, 32, 49, 96-7. See also Obed Kutumela, interviewed by Anna Kiki Kutumela and I.H., Sekgakgapeng, 20/4/90.

28   Gurr, *Daniel Heese*, 31-2, 49, 96-7. See also Obed Kutumela and Piet Lesiba Kekana, interviewed by Anna Kiti Kutumela and I.H., Sekgakgapeng, 26/4/90; and Puka interview. The first informant attended the Makapanspoort mission school in the first decade of this century, the second during the 1930s.

29   Wright, *German Missions*, 15.

30   On this point see D. Cressy, *Literacy and the Social Order: Reading and Writing in Tudor and Stuart England* (Cambridge: Cambridge University Press, 1980), 1-6.

31 E. Eisenstein, "The Advent of Printing and the Problem of the Renaissance", *Past and Present*, 45, 1969, 56-77; R. Chartier, "General Introduction: Print Culture", in R. Chartier (ed.), L.G. Cochrane (tr.), *The Culture of Print: Power and the Uses of Print in Early Modern Europe* (Cambridge: Polity Press, 1989); and R. Chartier, "The Practical Impact of Writing", in G. Duby, P. Veyne and M. Perrot (eds), A. Goldhammer (tr.), *A History of Private Life: Passions of the Renaissance* (Cambridge, Mass.: Belknap, 1989). My thanks to Ulrike Kistner for the last reference.

32 Paragraph drawn from *B.M.B.*, 19-20, 1889, 486-7; and Gurr, *Daniel Heese*, 35, 44-5, 51, 73-4, 89, 110. Phrases translated. See also Wright, *German Missions*, 13-18; and Delius, *The Land*, 160-7.

33 Gurr, *Daniel Heese*, 32, 37-8.

34 Stock, *The Implications*, 241, 244, 254-9.

35 Gurr, *Daniel Heese*, 91.

36 ˙Gurr, *Daniel Heese*, 36, 96, 47. See also T.A., T.A.D., KPT 2, Secretary for Native Affairs (hereafter S.N.A.) to Native Commissioner (hereafter N.C.), 15/6/29.

37 *B.M.B.*, 19-20, 1884, 419; Gurr, *Daniel Heese*, 50; and De Beer, "Groepsgebondenheid", 397.

38 *B.M.B.*, 23-24, 1892, 602; and Gurr, *Daniel Heese*, 37-8, 42, 88, 97, 99. For a brief but insightful comment on Prussian popular culture see A. White, "Hysteria and the End of Carnival: Festivity and Bourgeois Neurosis", in N. Armstrong and L. Tennenhouse (eds), *Violence and Representation: Literature and the History of Violence* (London: Routledge, 1989), 160.

39 *B.M.B.*, 19-20, 1889, 433; and Gurr, *Daniel Heese*, 96.

40 Gurr, *Daniel Heese*, 107.

41 On this point see M. Bakhtin, H. Iswolsky (tr.), *Rabelais and his World* (Cambridge: M.I.T. Press, 1968), 2-29; W. Godzich and J. Kittay, *The Emergence of Prose* (Minneapolis: University of Minnesota Press, 1987), 8; and White, "Hysteria".

42 Chartier, "General Introduction".

43 *B.M.B.*, 19-20, 1884, 419. On this point of writing as an object see Goody, "Restricted Literacy", 201-2, 206, 230; and Rappoport, "Mythic Images".

44 M.F. Thwaite, *From Primer to Pleasure: An Introduction to the History of Children's Books in England from the Invention of Printing to 1914 with an Outline of Some Developments in Other Countries* (1963; London: The Library Association, 1972), 257-63; Wright, *German Missions*, 86; C.J. Esterhuyse, "Die Ontwikkeling van die Noord-Sothoskryftaal", M.A. Dissertation, University of Pretoria, 1974, 7-8; J.R. Maibelo, "The Structure, Content, Educational and Literary Value of the Padišo Series by Dr. P.E. Schwellnus", B.A. Hons Dissertation, University of the North, 1982; Canonici, *The Inganekwane Tradition*, 63; and C. Velay-Vallantin, "Tales as a Mirror: Perrault in the Bibliothèque Bleue", in Chartier, *The Culture of Print*, 126.

45 ˙School information drawn from T.A., T.A.D., HKN 10, 2/3/2; HKN 13, 2/3/2 36; HKN 60 78/0/3; KPT 54, 12/3/3; KPT 55, 12/3/3; and *Die Noord Transvaler*, 16/10/64. On informal schools see Job Kekana interview, 7/6/90.

46 For a comparative view on these issues in a central Transvaal Ndebele community see M. Groenewald, "Educating Attitudes: An Account of a Performance of Ndebele Iibongo", in Sienaert and Bell, *Catching Winged Words*, 70.

47 Marivate, "Tsonga Folktales", 19; M. Oosthuizen, "A Study", 40; and Canonici, *The Inganekwane Tradition*, 60.

48 Job Kekana interview, 7/6/90.

49 Obed Kutumela interview, 20/4/90; Job Kekana interview, 7/6/90; and Helen Maime interview.

50 Job Kekana interview, 7/6/90; Puka interview; and Obed Kutumela interview, 20/4/90. On this point see B.W. Andrzejewski and G. Innes, "Reflections on African Oral

Literature", *African Languages*, 1, 1975, 30.

51   Canonici, *The Inganekwane Tradition*, 63.

52   On this point see Herskovits, *Dahomean Narrative*, 71-2; Berry, *Spoken Art*, 14; Mbiti, *Akamba Stories*, 30; and Neethling, "Die Xhosa Iintsomi", 286-7.

53   For a fuller discussion of this process see D.R. Olson, "On the Language and Authority of Textbooks", *Journal of Communication*, 30, 1980.

54   For a comparative example see Velay-Vallantin, "Tales".

55   This point is widely noted in studies of oral narrative. See, *inter alia*, Beuchat-Cole, "Notes", 186; Finnegan, *Limba Stories*, 64-5; Deng, *Dinka Folktales*, 159-65; and Beidelman, *Moral Imagination*, 169-77. See also Lekalakala interview.

56   Thwaite, *From Primer*, 257-63; Opland, "The Transition", 136; and Velay-Vallantin, "Tales".

57   Deng, *Dinka Folktales*, 203.

58   Kgosana interview, 1/3/90. See also Maime interview.

59   Canonici, *The Inganekwane Tradition*, 60. Similar points were made by Mosoamadite Kekana, interviewed by Johanna Moima and I.H., Mošate, Valtyn, 19/3/88. See also Maleka interview.

60   Kgosana interview, 1/3/90.

61   Shiloti interview.

62   Shiloti interview. See also Lucky Kekana interview, 9/4/90; and Kgosana interview, 1/3/90.

63   Shiloti interview; Kgosana interview, 1/3/90; and Lekalakala interview.

64   Shiloti interview.

65   Lekalakala interview.

66   Lucky Kekana interview, 9/4/90.

67   Lekalakala interview.

68   Maime interview; Kgosana interview, 1/3/90; and see also Naomi Teffo interview.

69   Makgamatha, "Characteristics", 19-20.

70   The terms are widely used and cropped up in most interviews.

71   Lekalakala interview; and Kutumela interview, 20/4/90.

72   Ramasela interview.

73   Mahlangu interview, 20/3/90.

74   E.R. Maponya, "The Use of Communication by the Northern Sotho Speaking Blacks in the Pietersburg Region", M.A. Dissertation, University of South Africa, 1984, 148, 208, 232.

75   Mahlangu interviews, 13/3/90 and 20/3/90; Lekalakala interview; Dinah Raisibe Thabeta interview; and Priscilla Ramokone Rampula interview. See also Marivate, "Tsonga Folktales", 146; and Canonici, *The Inganekwane Tradition*, 60.

76   Two such studies would be J. Goody and I. Watt, "The Consequences of Literacy", *Comparative Studies in Society and History*, 5, 1962-3; and Ong, *Orality*, although, as with all work that makes brave generalisations, they remain useful pieces of scholarship.

Chapter 3
The Spoken Word and the Barbed Wire

1   T.A., T.A.D., KPT 2, 1/1/3, N.C. to Chief Alfred Masibi, 12/12/23. Unless otherwise specified, all officials are attached to the Potgietersrus office.

2   T.A., T.A.D., KPT 2, 1/1/2, N.C. to S.N.A., 27/5/29.

3   See correspondence in T.A., T.A.D., KPT 2, 1/1/2.

4   For a discussion of this point see R. Grillo, "Anthropology, Language, Politics", in R. Grillo (ed.), *Social Anthropology and the Politics of Language* (London: Routledge, 1989), 14-17.

5 ˙J. Fabian, *Language and Colonial Power: The Appropriation of Swahili in the Former Belgian Congo 1880-1938* (Cambridge: Cambridge University Press, 1986), 3. See also J. Opland, "The Bible in Front, the Musket Behind: Images of White Oppression in Xhosa Oral Poetry", paper presented to the Fourth National Technological Literacy Conference, Washington, 3-5/2/89 for a fascinating discussion of how in Xhosa oral poetry, literacy is perceived as part of colonial oppression. My thanks to Jeff Opland for making this reference available to me.

6 On this point see H. Scheub, "A Review of African Oral Traditions and Literature", *African Studies Review*, 28, 2-3, 1985, which discusses a range of points on such 'spoken writing'.

7 On this point of how images of writing can be transferred to other areas of life see J. Derrida, G.C. Spivak (tr.), *Of Grammatology* (Baltimore: The Johns Hopkins University Press, 1976), 9; and Fabian, *Language*, 78-84.

8 S. Dubow, "Holding 'A Just Balance between White and Black': The Native Affairs Department in South Africa c. 1920-33", *Journal of Southern African Studies*, 12, 2, 1986. The issues discussed here are more fully treated in his book, *Racial Segregation and the Origins of Apartheid in South Africa, 1919-36* (Basingstoke: Macmillan, 1989), 77-127.

9 On this point see Goody, *The Logic*, 89-90, 105, 110, 114, 124.

10 For details of the powers of the Native Affairs Department and Native Commissioners see M. Lacey, *Working for Boroko: The Origins of a Coercive Labour System in South Africa* (Johannesburg: Ravan, 1980), 84-115.

11 B. Sansom, "Leadership and Authority in a Pedi Chiefdom", D. Phil. Thesis, University of Manchester, 1970, 12-53.

12 For details of complaints see T.A., T.A.D., KPT 12, 1/15/4, Pitsu [Meeting – the spelling should be *Pitso*] of Native Chiefs and Headmen held at the Native Commissioner's Office, 16/2/34.

13 For examples see T.A., T.A.D., KPT 3, 2/3/2, Anon. to Assistant Native Commissioner (hereafter A.N.C.), Zebediela, 1/12/30; Special Justice of the Peace (hereafter S.J.P.), Zebediela to F. Madisha, 24/12/30; S.J.P., Zebediela to Abel Kekana, 17/3/31; and S.J.P., Zebediela to N.C., 5/12/32. For a comparative perspective see Clanchy, *From Memory*, 184.

14 Clanchy, *From Memory*, 257.

15 T.A., T.A.D., KPT 16, 2/3/3/4, P.R. Seboa to Sub-Native Commissioner (hereafter S.N.C.), 18/6/37; and KPT 16, 2/3/3/4, J. Madisha to R.M., 26/2/34.

16 T.A., T.A.D., KPT 29, 2/4/3/48, J. Lebelo to N.C., 24/11/38; and KPT 18, 2/4/3, A.H.P. Mako to N.C., 16/5/48.

17 T.A., T.A.D., KPT 16, 2/3/3/4, P.M. Kekana to N.C., Zebediela, 31/3/34; KPT 16, 2/3/3/8, D. Malepe to an unspecified recipient, n.d.; and KPT 26, 2/4/3, Chief A. Kekana to S.J.P., Zebediela, 20/4/32. See also KPT 16, 2/3/3/4, P. Kekana to S.J.P., Zebediela, 10/5/34.

18 T.A., T.A.D., KPT 16, 2/4/2, J. Ngwepe to N.C., 13/11/50; and Anon. to N.C., 7/1/51; and Headman F. Maeteletša to N.C., 15/10/47. 'Mill mill' is mealie meal.

19 Phrase from T.A., T.A.D., KPT 32, 2/9/2, 'Chief' to N.C., 19/4/26.

20 T.A., T.A.D., KPT 54, 10/1/2, J. Mashishi to N.C., 22/6/48. The letter which is in a Sindebele-tinged Sesotho with Afrikaans echoes reads as follows: *Kaboikokobetso Morena Amen Kere Lekhutla le kamola gaberate eseng kakgonthe garerate kgarebeso la Councerl. Ruri garerate lekgotla. Kamoka far Dorrondrae gabaerate eseng legaele garajani. Otsebe gore garerate Councerl. Reapatana Reapatana garerate Councerl. Otsebe gore garerate. I Rimain Johannes Mashishi.* My thanks to Kgomotso Masemola for help with translation.

21 T.A., T.A.D., KPT 2, 1/1/2, C. Leolo to W.S. Kekana, 19/11/28; KPT 16, 2/3/3/7, Chief P. Seloane to S.J.P., Zebediela, 2/6/40; and KPT 15, 2/3/2, W.D. Seshoka to

N.C., 5/9/35.

22 T.A., T.A.D., KPT 18, 2/4/3, Chief P. Makapan to N.C., 1/10/48; and KPT 29, 2/4/3/48, D. Lamola to N.C., 24/11/38.

23 T.A., T.A.D., KPT 2, 1/1/2, W.S. Kekana to N.C., Zebediela, 23/11/28; KPT 54, 10/1/2, T. Monene to N.C., 22/6/18; KPT 16, 2/4/2, C. Makhubele to N.C., 11/9/49; and KPT 15, 2/3/2, J.P. Kekana to S.N.C., 2/10/28.

24 Phrase from T.A., T.A.D., KPT 31, 2/8/2, S.J.P., Zebediela to N.C., 6/5/31.

25 T.A., T.A.D., KPT 45, 4/3/3, N.C. to S.N.A., 18/10/32.

26 Clanchy, *From Memory*, 233.

27 T.A., T.A.D., KPT 44, 4/3/3, 'Lekgotla' to 'Magerstreet', 12/12/34.

28 Clanchy, *From Memory*, 209.

29 Gurr, *Daniel Heese*, 89; and T.A., T.A.D., KPT 45, 4/3/3, Undated, unsigned document headed "The Present State of Affairs in Valtyn Location".

30 T.A., T.A.D., KPT 44, 4/3/3, Minutes of a Tribal Meeting of the Langa Tribe under Chief Mankopane Masibi, Bakenberg Location, 28/6/37.

31 For insistence on oral promise see T.A., T.A.D., HKN 46, 47/15/38, N.C., Nylstroom to Chief Native Commissioner (hereafter C.N.C.), 25/6/37. For allegations of invented claims see T.A., T.A.D., KPT 14, 2/54/3/21, A. Gilbertson to N.C., 30/9/50; and KPT 15, 2/3/2, H.S. Robinson to N.C., 23/5/35.

32 T.A., T.A.D., KPT 32, 2/8/2, Additional Native Commissioner (hereafter Ad. N.C.) to N.C., 21/10/29.

33 T.A., T.A.D., KPT 32, 2/9/2, S.N.C. to S.N.A., 19/3/20.

34 T.A., T.A.D., KPT 41, 2/11/6, A.N.C. to C.N.C., 8/9/39.

35 Phrase from C. Geertz, *Negara: The Theatre State in Nineteenth-century Bali* (Princeton: Princeton University Press, 1980).

36 Paragraph based on T.A., T.A.D., KPT 31, 2/8/2, S.J.P., Zebediela to N.C., 6/5/31; KPT 12, 1/15/4, Pitsu [sic] of Native Chiefs and Headmen held at the N.C.'s Office, 16/2/34; and KPT 32, 2/8/2, Moses Kgobe to N.C., 6/12/29.

37 B. Parry, "Problems in Current Theories of Colonial Discourse", *Oxford Literary Review*, 9, 1-2, 1987, 42.

38 This section is drawn from I. Hofmeyr, "'Nterata'/'The Wire': Fences, Boundaries and Cultural Resistance in the Potgietersrus District", *International Annual of Oral History, 1990* (New York: Greenwood Press, 1992).

39 As with all locations, the names vary enormously. At times officials used the name of the incumbent chief to identify the location. So, for example, Valtyn was also known as Makapan's/Macapaan's/Makapaan's location. Mapela for a long time was called Hans Masibi's location. Bakenberg often appeared as Bakeberg or Backeberg. Figures extrapolated from T.A, T.A.D., KPT 12, 1/15/6, Report on Native Affairs for the Year 1938; KPT 31, 2/8/2, *Verslag: Naturelle Sake: Potgietersrus*, n.d.; SN 2, Report on Native Tribes in the Transvaal, 24/11/1879; and C.A.D., NTS 7748, 6/35, Extracts from the Minutes of the Late Location Commission, 26/5/1890.

40 T.A., T.A.D., KPT 13, 2/28/7/4, Minutes of Tribal Meeting at Mapela Location, 30/8/39. Figures from KPT 41, 2/11/6, Undated document headed "Valtyn's Location: Potgietersrust, Location Reclamation Survey".

41 Union of South Africa, *Report of the Native Affairs Department for the Years 1945-1947*, UG14-1948, 1.

42 Hosea Bowale, interviewed by Peter Lekgoathi, Tamaties, Zebediela district, 5/5/89; and T.A., T.A.D., KPT 51, 8/18/31/1, Minutes of meeting held at Zebediela location, 9/6/31, statement by Induna Charlie Kekana.

43 T.A., T.A.D., KPT 14, 2/54/3/17, Chief Makapan to N.C., 15/9/38; and 2/54/3/12, Frans Seaneko to N.C., 23/7/49.

44 T.A., C.A.D., NTS 7748, 6/35, S.N.C. to N.C., Waterberg, 7/6/22.

45 Marais, "Die Landbou-Potensiaal", in Combrink, *Eeufees*, 157.
46 T.A., C.A.D., NTS 3544, 498/30, S.N.A. to P.J.D. Pieterse, n.d.
47 For reports on the condition of the town in the 1930s see T.A., T.A.D., MPT 131, 44/19; and MPT 137, 44/30.
48 T.A., T.A.D., LPT 1, 4/7/49, J. McIntosh to R.M., 21/9/25, 4/7/45; L.A. de Jongh to ·R.M., 19/5/25; and 4/7/4/1, C. Stewart Coppen to R.M., 23/4/26.
49 T.A., T.A.D., GOV 1085, PS 50/8/1907/9, Document headed "Native Location Commission", 2/11/06, evidence of Frans Nuku.
50 Union of South Africa, Minutes of Evidence of the Eastern Transvaal Native Land Commission, evidence of Lester Goldsworthy [Native Commissioner for Potgietersrus], UG32-'18, 198.
51 T.A., C.A.D., NTS 3626, 1149/308, R.M. to T.G.W. Reinecke, 10/10/35 and NTS 10211, 6/423/2, Director of Native Agriculture to Controller of Native Settlements, 5/2/36. The population and stock figures for the whole district were as follows: 11,2 people km² and 6 ha per cattle unit. (T.A., T.A.D., HKN 28, 35/0/17, Undated table headed "Statistics".) By the 1950s the population figure had risen to 20,7 people per km². (HKN 28, 35/0/17, Annual Agricultural Report for Year Ending 30th June 1952.)
52 The main file in this connection is T.A., C.A.D., NTS 10211, 6/423/2.
53 T.A., C.A.D., NTS 10211, 6/423/2, C.N.C. to S.N.A., 16/2/39.
54 T.A., T.A.D., HKN 33, 42/0, Evidence to the Witwatersrand Mine Native Wages Commission.
55 T.A., C.A.D., NTS 9531, 138/400(69), Assistant Erosion Officer to N.C., n.d.
56 Job Patja Kekana, interviewed by I.H., Westdene, Johannesburg, 5/3/89.
57 Jackson, *The Ndebele*, 237; Van Warmelo, *Transvaal Ndebele Texts*, 17 fn. 1; and Scully, "Phalaborwa", 145.
58 Job Kekana interview, 5/3/89.
59 C.L. Harries, *The Law and Custom of the Bapedi and Cognate Tribes* (Johannesburg: Hortors, 1929), 110; and Mönnig, *The Pedi*, 69.
60 Bowale interview.
61 T.A., T.A.D., HKN 33, 42/0, Undated document headed "Discussion on Land Regulations of Trust Land Acquired since 1936".
62 See, for example, T. Ranger, "The Invention of Tradition in Colonial Africa", in E. Hobsbawm and T. Ranger (eds), *The Invention of Tradition* (Cambridge: Cambridge University Press, 1983). For a Northern Transvaal case study see I. Hofmeyr, "Turning Region into Narrative: English Storytelling in the Waterberg", in P. Bonner *et al.* (eds), *Holding Their Ground: Class, Locality and Culture in 19th and 20th Century South Africa* (Johannesburg: Ravan/Witwatersrand University Press, 1989).
63 Quotations from Union of South Africa, *Report of the Department of Native Affairs for the Years 1944-1945*, UG44-1946, 9, 12, 68.
64 T.A., T.A.D., HKN 33, 42/0, Undated document headed "Discussion on Land Regulations of Trust Land Acquired since 1936". This discourse of documentary control characterises most Native Affairs Department policy statements. For further examples see Union of South Africa, *Review of the Activities of the Department of Native Affairs for the Years 1944-45*, UG44-1946, 32-3.
65 T.A., T.A.D., KPT 14, 2/28/7(38), P.J. du Preez to N.C., 18/10/45. Translated.
66 I. Schapera, *A Handbook of Tswana Law and Custom* (London: Frank Cass, 1970), 200-1; and J.L. Comaroff and S. Roberts, *Rules and Processes: The Cultural Logic of Dispute* (Chicago: University of Chicago Press, 1981).
67 T.A., T.A.D., KPT 78, Minute Book, Minutes of Special (44th) Meeting of the Bakenberg Local Council, 2/9/35.
68 T.A., C.A.D., NTS 7748, 6/35, Correspondence from 24/11/21 to 20/9/22; and T.A.D., KPT 31, 2/8/2, N.C. to S.N.A., 14/10/31.

69 T.A., C.A.D., NTS 7748, 6/35, S.N.A. to S.N.C., 29/10/20, 14/2/22; and S.N.C. to S.N.A., 2/9/20.
70 Union of South Africa, *Report of the Geodetic Work of the the Trigonometrical Survey, 1933-1938* and *Report of the Geodetic Work of the Trigonometric Survey, 1939-1953,* maps.
71 See file on beacon destruction, T.A., C.A.D., LDE 609, 7946; and LDE 273, 3023, A.Wayland to District Commissioner for Lands, 27/1/03.
72 T.A., T.A.D., KPT 13, 2/28/7, AD. N.C. to C.N.C., 22/11/38.
73 All quotations in this paragraph from T.A. T.A.D., KPT 13, 2/28/7/4, Minutes of meeting held at Mapela's Location, 30/8/39.
74 T.A., C.A.D., NTS 7748, 6/35, S.N.C. to S.N.A., 21/9/20.
75 T.A., C.A.D., NTS 7748,6/35, S.N.C. Graskop to S.N.A., 1/7/22.
76 For an example of this process see T.A., T.A.D., KPT 15, 2/3/2, J. Neitz to R.M., 21/7/28.
77 T.A., C.A.D., NTS 7748, 6/35, Correspondence from 24/11/21 to 20/9/22.
78 T.A., C.A.D., NTS 7748, 6/35, N.C. to S.N.A., 7/12/26; and S.N.A. to N.C., 13/12/26.
79 T.A., T.A.D., KPT 13, 2/28/7, A.N.C. to C.N.C., 22/11/38; and KPT 14, 2/54/3/12, Frans Seaneko to N.C., 23/7/49.
80 T.A., C.A.D., NTS 7748, 6/35, N.C. to S.N.A., 28/11/28.
81 T.A., C.A.D., NTS 7748, 6/35, S.N.C., Graskop to S.N.A., 1/7/22.
82 T.A., T.A.D., KPT 14, 2/54/3/9, Handwritten note from Agricultural Officer, 2/6/50.
83 T.A., T.A.D., KPT 14, 2/54/3/9, Meeting at N.C.'s office, 20/9/49.
84 T.A., T.A.D., KPT 14, 2/54/3/21, A.N.C. to A. Gilbertson, 4/4/46.
85 T.A., T.A.D., KPT 14, 2/54/3/17, Chief Piet Makapan to N.C., 15/9/39.
86 T.A., C.A.D., NTS 9531, 138/400(69), C.N.C. to S.N.A., 5/11/37.
87 T.A., T.A.D., KPT 14, 2/28/7/38, P.J. du Preez to N.C., 18/10/45 and 23/4/48.
88 T.A., T.A.D., KPT 14, 2/54/3/9, N.C. to Chief Piet Makapan, 25/7/50; and KPT 13, 2/28/7/2, J. Henkel to A.N.C., ?/3/40.
89 T.A., T.A.D., KPT 14, 2/54/3/17, Tribal Meeting at Valtyn's Location, n.d.
90 T.A., T.A.D., KPT 41, 2/11/6, Assistant Soil Erosion Officer to Agricultural Superintendent, 17/2/38.
91 T.A., T.A.D., KPT 78, Minute Book, Minutes of Meeting of Bakenberg Local Council, 2/10/32, 3/7/31, 4/1/35 and 5/7/35.
92 T:A., C.A.D., NTS 7475, 556/327, A.N.C. to C.N.C., 14/8/39.
93 T.A., T.A.D., KPT 14, 2/54/3/21, A. Gilbertson to N.C., 23/3/46; and C.A.D., NTS 1631, 32/238, Munnik Farmers' Association to S.N.A., 29/10/38.
94 T.A., C.A.D., NTS 1631, 32/238, S.N.A. to Deputy Chairman, Native Affairs Commission, 14/5/47, and Conservator of Forests to Director of Forestry, 18/9/47. T.A., C.A.D., NTS 10211, 6/423/2, Town Clerk to S.W. Naude [the M.P. for the area], 10/3/37.
95 Job Kekana interview, 5/3/89; Leka Thinta Mokhonoane and Mosoamadite Kekana, interviewed by Jane Letsebe-Matlou and I.H., Mošate, Valtyn, 10/11/89; and Revd Asaph Tsebe, interviewed by Jane Letsebe-Matlou and I.H., Mahwelereng, 10/11/89.
96 See, for example, the retaliation meted out against the rebellious Mabusela ward in Bakenberg. Accounts in T.A., C.A.D., NTS 3757, 2268/308; and NTS 7727, 201/333.

Chapter 4
"Digkoro tša Kgale" / The Courtyards of Long Ago

1   *Government Gazette*, 10, 662, Notice 1881, 6/12/63.
2   *Government Gazette*, 11, 751, Notice 437, 26/3/64; and *Die Noord Transvaler*, 9/10/64.
3   See, for example, Beinart, "Introduction"; F.T. Hendricks, "Loose Planning and Rapid

Resettlement: The Politics of Conservation and Control in Transkei, South Africa, 1950-1970", *Journal of Southern African Studies*, 15, 2, 1989; and P. Delius, "Sebatakgomo: Migrant Organization and the Sekhukhuneland Revolt", *Journal of Southern African Studies*, 15, 4, 1989, and his *"Dikgomo di ile* (The Cattle have gone): The Changing Context of Resistance in Sekhukhuneland 1950-1986", paper presented to the History Workshop Conference, University of the Witwatersrand, Johannesburg, 6-10/2/90.

4   Paragraph drawn from D. Posel, "The State and Policy-Making in Apartheid's Second Phase", paper presented to the History Workshop Conference, University of the Witwatersrand, Johannesburg, 6-10/2/90.

5   S.A.I.R.R., *Establishment*; and Posel, "The State". See also Posel, "Influx Control", Ch. 9.

6   On removals see G. Mare, *African Population Relocation in South Africa* (Johannesburg: S.A.I.R.R., 1980), 25-8; D. James, *The Road to Doornkop: A Case Study of Removal and Resistance* (Johannesburg: S.A.I.R.R., 1983), 42-3; and Surplus People Project, *Forced Removal in South Africa: The Transvaal*, Vol. V (Cape Town: Surplus People Project, 1983), 156-7.

7   Delius, "Sebatakgomo", 603.

8   L. Bank,"The Janus-Face of Rural Class Formation: An Economic and Political History of Traders in Qwaqwa 1960-1986", and E. Ritchken, "Chiefs, Migrants, the State and Ethnicity: The Leihlo le Naga Migrant Workers Organisation 1978-1986", both papers presented to the History Workshop Conference, University of the Witwatersrand, Johannesburg, 6-10/2/90.

9   M. Chaskalson, "Rural Resistance in the 1940s and 50s", *Africa Perspective: New Series*, 1, 5-6, 1987.

10   ·This literature includes Mare, *African Population*; J. Yawitch, *Betterment: The Myth of Homeland Agriculture* (Johannesburg: S.A.I.R.R., 1982); James, *The Road*; Surplus People Project, *Forced Removals*; and *Journal of Southern African Studies*, 15, 2, 1989, a special issue on betterment policy and its impact. Quote from P.A. McAllister, "Resistance to 'Betterment' in the Transkei: A Case Study from Willowvale District", *Journal of Southern African Studies*, 15, 2, 1989, 368.

11   Beinart, "Introduction".

12   This language is widespread in any documentation on this issue emanating from the Native Affairs Department. As examples, see their annual reports: Union of South Africa, *Report of the Native Affairs Department for the Years 1936-37*, UG41-37, 57-62; *1944-45*, UG44-46, 9-12; *1945-47*, UG14-48, 1; and *1949-50*, UG61-51, 8. For documentation specific to Valtyn see T.A., C.A.D., NTS 10211, 6/423/2. On virtually any page of this file the vocabulary outlined above can be found. Quotations in this paragraph from the latter file, Director of Native Agriculture to Controller of Native Settlements, 5/12/36.

13   For a comparative statement see C. de Wet, "Betterment Planning in a Rural Village in Keiskammahoek, Ciskei", *Journal of Southern African Studies*, 15, 2, 1989, 338-40. See also T.A., T.A.D., KPT 41, 2/11/6, Agricultural Supervisor to A.N.C., n.d.

14   Yawitch, *Betterment*, 48-9; James, *The Road*, 38-9; and Mokhonoane and Kekana interview.

15   For details of these plans see T.A., C.A.D., NTS 10211, 6/423/2.

16   For resistance in Valtyn see Union of South Africa, *Report of the Native Affairs Department for the Years 1935-36*, UG41-1937, 58; T.A., T.A.D., KPT 41, 2/11/6, Assistant Soil Erosion Official to Agricultural Supervisor, 17/2/38; C.A.D., NTS 9518, 138/400/42, C.N.C. to S.N.A., 31/12/37; Assistant Soil Erosion Officer to A.N.C., 31/12/37; NTS 9531, 138/400(69), Monthly Report: April 1936; and Assistant Soil Erosion Officer to A.N.C., 3/2/38. For resistance more generally see T.A., T.A.D.,

HKN 33, 42/0, Departmental Circular No. 11 of 1948; HKN 38, 43/15/3, C.N.C. to N.C., 4/4/51.

17 For a full account of this dispute see T.A., C.A.D., NTS 314, 12/55, Quotation from Minutes of Inquiry at N.C.'s Office, 18/11/49.

18 The file which covers this account is T.A., C.A.D., NTS 314, 12/55. Quotation from Minutes of Inquiry at N.C.s Office, 18/11/49.

19 T.A., C.A.D., NTS 314, 12/55, Informal Memo, Native Affairs Department, 1/12/49.

20 De Beer, "Groepsgebondenheid", 49.

21 S.A.I.R.R., *Establishment*, 2.

22 Chaskalson, "Rural Resistance"; and Delius, "Sebatakgomo".

23 Lucky Kekana interview, 3/4/90. The remainder of the paragraph is drawn from De Beer, "Groepsgebondenheid", 48-55.

24 Lucky Kekana interview, 3/4/90.

25 Hendricks, "Loose Planning", 319.

26 M. Horrell, *Visit to Bantu Areas of the Northern Transvaal June/July 1965* (Johannesburg: S.A.I.R.R., 1965), 13, 15.

27 Delius, "Sebatakgomo".

28 Sansom, "Leadership", 45.

29 Puka interview; and Tsebe interview.

30 T.A., C.A.D., NTS 6252, 10/313P, S.N.C. to S.N.A., 28/2/22; and T.A.D., MPT 195, 72/15, South African Police to Town Clerk, 8/5/39.

31 Pitje, "Traditional Systems: Part I", 55, 57, 59; and Sansom, "Leadership", 126.

32 Pitje, "Traditional Systems: Part I", 57-61; and Jackson, *The Langa*, 119.

33 Obed Kutumela, interviewed with John Kutumela, Hanna Schulze and I.H., Sekgakgapeng, 15/1/89.

34 Pitje, "Traditional Systems: Part I", 75. The spelling *kxoro* reflects an older orthography current at the time when Pitje wrote.

35 W. Eiselen, "The Suto-Chuana Tribes: Sub-Group II: The Bapedi (Transvaal Basotho)", an article to accompany photographs by A.M. Duggan-Cronin in A.M. Duggan-Cronin, *The Bantu Tribes of South Africa: Reproductions of Photographic Studies* Vol. II, Section II (Cambridge and Kimberley: Deighton, Bell and Alexander McGregor Memorial Museum, 1931), 44; and H. Scheub, "Oral Poetry as History", *New Literary History*, 3, 1987, 478, 484.

36 Tshwane Mvundlela and Ledile Kekana, interviewed by Motlalepula Mashao, Debra Nails and I.H., Mošate, Valtyn, 1/10/88.

37 Lucky Kekana interview, 9/4/90.

38 N.J. van Warmelo, *The Bakgatla ba ga Mosetlha*, Union of South Africa, Department of Native Affairs, Ethnological Publication No. 17 (Pretoria: Government Printer, 1944), 4.

39 Alpheus Ledwaba, interviewed by Madimetša Ledwaba and I.H., Moletlane, 7/9/88.

40 Alfred Lesiba Kekana interview, 29/3/90. Interview originally in English.

41 Both stories from Alfred Lesiba Kekana interview, 22/6/90. Originally narrated in Sindebele.

42 The word is from Pitje, "Traditional Systems: Part I", 69.

43 The word is from Barber, "Interpreting *Oríkì*.", 20.

44 H.A. Junod, *The Life of a South African Tribe: Social Life*, Vol. I (London: Macmillan, 1927), 21. See also Scully, "Phalaborwa", 39-40, 73-5.

45 Alpheus Ledwaba interview.

46 For comparative material on everyday storytelling see Labov, "The Transformation"; Polanyi, "Literary Complexity"; Popular Memory Group, "Popular Memory"; Linde, "Private Stories"; and Stempel, "Everyday Narrative".

47 Mönnig, *The Pedi*, 218-34.

48 Mönnig, *The Pedi*, 56; and Kuper, "The Social Structure", 115. See P. McAllister, "Inclusion and Exclusion in the Oral Transmission of Ritual Knowledge: A Xhosa Communicative Strategy", in Sienaert and Bell, *Catching Winged Words*, 43-68, and his "Political Aspects of Xhosa Beer Drink Oratory", *English in Africa*, 15, 1, 1988, 83-95. See also J.L. Comaroff, "Talking Politics: Oratory and Authority in a Tswana Chiefdom", in M. Bloch (ed.), *Political Language and Oratory in Traditional Societies* (London: Academic Press, 1975), 141-61; and Comaroff and Roberts, *Rules and Processes*.

49 P. Connerton, *How Societies Remember* (Cambridge: Cambridge University Press, 1989), 57. For a comparative discussion on ritual language see McAllister, "Inclusion and Exclusion".

50 Pitje, "Tradition Systems: Part I", 59.

51 Thabankoane Motlatla, Group interview with members of the Bakenberg Tribal Authority by I.H., Bakenberg, 27/7/88.

52 Chaclice Kekana, interviewed by Peter Lekgoathi, Tamaties, Zebediela District, 5/5/89.

53 Connerton, *How Societies Remember*, 12. For studies of time in oral history see Henige, *The Chronology*, 27-48; and Miller, "Introduction", 13-18.

54 Kuper, "The Social Structure", 146-7, and his "Symbolic Dimensions", 16.

55 Kuper, "The Social Structure", 72.

56 C. Hamilton, "Ideology and Oral Traditions: Listening to the Voices 'From Below'", *History in Africa*, 14, 1987, 67-86.

57 For an example of this procedure in Mapela see Jackson, "The Langa Ndebele Calendar", and his *The Langa*, 127-32. See also Mönnig, *The Pedi*, 159.

58 M. Mashishi, interviewed by Boyboy Maboya, Sekgakgapeng, 13/6/90, and his written account of Mashishi history in Dr Maboya's possession. For the Kekana account see Mahula Kekana interview. For more discussion on this issue see Chapter 5.

59 Connerton, *How Societies Remember*, Ch. 3.

60 Shiloti interview; and Naomi Teffo interview.

61 Point based on personal observation. For a comparative perspective on changes to central Transvaal Ndebele settlement patterns see Jansen van Vuuren, "Die Vestigingspatroon", Appendices.

62 De Beer, "Groepsgebondenheid", 455; and Alfred Lesiba Kekana interview, 22/6/90. For comparative discussions on this point see James, "Kinship", 96, 133-63; and Comaroff, *Body of Power*, 57.

63 Lucky Kekana interview, 9/4/90.

64 For a discussion on the effects of mass education on male youth culture, see Delius, "*Dikgomo di ile*".

65 Naomi Teffo interview. Interview originally in English. See also Rampula interview.

66 Lekalakala interview.

67 Puka interview.

68 Kgosana interview, 1/3/90.

69 Sansom, "Leadership", 126.

70 Lucky Kekana interview, 9/4/90.

71 Opland, *Xhosa Oral Poetry*, 246-7.

72 Coplan, "Eloquent Knowledge", and his *In Township Tonight!*, 17-21.

73 Delius, "*Dikgomo di ile*", 9. Molalakgori Kekana interview; and Madimetša Kekana interview, 28/11/87.

74 Connerton, *How Societies Remember*, 36-7. There are, of course, other aspects of landscape over and above its domestic architecture that play a role in oral history and memory. But, as these will be discussed in Chapter 8, the focus here is limited to the everyday domestic surroundings.

75 · Mahlangu interview.

Chapter 5
The Craft of Oral Historical Narrative

1   Miller, "Introduction", 18.

2   See, for example, Henige, *The Chronology*, Ch. 1; Miller, "Introduction"; and Tonkin, "Historical Discourse".

3   In trying to make my way through the vast amount of material in this area, I have found the work of Louis Mink to be most accessible and clear. I have used his "Philosophical Analysis"; "History and Fiction"; and "Narrative Form". I have also relied on Gallie, *Philosophy*; White, *Tropics*, and his "The Question of Narrative".

4   Havelock, *The Literate Revolution*, 122-50; and Ong, *Orality*, Ch. 3.

5   Ong, *Orality*, 140.

6   Havelock, *The Literate Revolution*, 137.

7   Lord, *The Singer*, Ch. 2; Scheub, *The Xhosa Ntsomi*, Ch. 5; Okpewho, *The Epic*, 161-2; Havelock, *The Literate Revolution*, 122-50; and Ong, *Orality*, 31-77, 139-55.

8   See, for example, Mbiti, *Akamba Stories*, 28; Finnegan, *Limba Stories*, 49-50; Moephuli, "Structure and Character", 80; Okpewho, *The Epic*, Ch. 5; and Makgamatha, "Characteristics", 152.

9   Finnegan, *Limba Stories*, 49.

10   Scheub, "A Review", 2-3.

11   Okpewho, *The Epic*, Chs 3-5.

12   Okpewho, *The Epic*, 31-2.

13   On this point see A. Roberts, "The Uses of Oral Sources for African History", *Oral History*, 4, 1, 1976, 49.

14   Scheub, "Oral Poetry"; and White, "Power". See also D.P. Biebuyck, *Hero and Chief: Epic Literature from the Banyanga Zaire Republic* (Berkeley: University of California Press, 1978), who also makes the point that epics are concerned with the institution of chiefship, 56.

15   On culture heroes, see Henige, *The Chronology*, 64. This assessment of oral traditions is based on a selection of Transvaal examples. They appear in Transvaal Native Affairs Department, *Short History of the Native Tribes of the Transvaal* (Pretoria: Government Printing and Stationery Office, 1905); D.R. Hunt, "An Account of the Bapedi", *Bantu Studies*, 5, 1931; Van Warmelo, *Transvaal Ndebele Texts*; Ziervogel, *A Grammar*; Scully, "Phalaborwa"; and A. Kuper, "Fourie and the Southern Transvaal Ndebele", *African Studies*, 37, 1, 1978. See also G. Nkonki, "The Traditional Prose Literature of the Ngqika", M.A. Dissertation, University of South Africa, 1968, 120-31.

16   Tonkin, "Historical Discourse", 469.

17   Henige, "The Chronology", Chs 1-2.

18   Scheub, *The Xhosa Ntsomi*, Chs 4-5.

19   This paragraph and subsequent account based on De Waal, "Die Verhouding"; Jackson, *The Ndebele*, 13-18; P. Delius and S. Trapido, "Inboekselings and Oorlams: The Creation and Transformation of a Servile Class", in B. Bozzoli (ed.), *Town and Countryside in the Transvaal: Capitalist Penetration and Popular Response* (Johannesburg: Ravan, 1983); J. Naidoo, "Was the Siege of Makapansgat a Massacre or a Trekker Victory?", in his collection of essays, *Tracking Down Historical Myths: Eight South African Cases* (Johannesburg: Ad Donker, 1989). Archival sources include T.A., T.A.D., SS R539/53-R734/54 which comprise the military despatches sent from the cave and T.A., T.A.D., A 787, Vol. 201, File 120, Makapanspoortmoord, the sources from which an Afrikaner historian, Gustav Preller, constructed his account of the siege. It appeared as a short story "Baanbrekers", in *Oorlogsoormag en Ander Sketse en Verhale* (Cape Town: Nasionale Pers, 1931).

20   J.M. Orpen, *Reminiscences of Life in South Africa from 1846 to the Present Day* (1908; Cape Town: Struik, 1964), 250.

21 .Details from De Waal, "Die Verhouding", 24; and Jackson, *The Ndebele*, 52.
22 This account of the murders and their locations, which is the one that is generally agreed upon and is included in most sources, is drawn from Preller, "Baanbrekers" and Naidoo, "Was the Siege".
23 T.A., T.A.D., SS 9, Supl. 44/54, Undated document headed "Verslag van den Ondergetekende van den Expedietie tegen Makapaan en Mapela". For a discussion of the oral tradition see Chapters 5 and 6.
24 T. Wangemann, a German missionary who visited the caves in 1868, reported the presence of water. His account appears in *Ein Reise-Jahr in Süd-Afrika* (Berlin: Missionshauses, 1868), 455-60. The account that there was no water derives from the military despatches of M.W. Pretorius, the leader of the Boer forces. See T.A., T.A.D., SS 7, R733/54, Verslag van den Verregting van de Commandant Generaal, 6/12/ 1854. In this report Pretorius claims that 733 people were shot down while trying to get to the stream outside the cave. Many subsequent commentators followed this line. See, for example, J.A.I. Agar-Hamilton, *The Native Policy of the Voortrekkers: An Essay in the History of the Interior of South Africa – 1836-1858* (Cape Town: Maskew Miller, n.d.), 164; and Anon., "Makapan's Poort", in *Annals of South Africa: South Africa Handbooks, No. 17* (London: no publisher, n.d.). This booklet comprises articles reproduced from the periodical *South Africa*.
25 This is the interpretation put forward by Naidoo, "Was the Siege", 128, and erroneously attributed to Dart, *Adventures*.
26 Molalakgori Madimetša Kekana interview.
27 T.A., T.A.D., SS 7, R733/54.
28 T.A., T.A.D., SS 7, R733/54.
29 T.A., T.A.D., SS 7, R733/54; and T.A., T.A.D., SS 9, Supl. 45/54, Undated document headed "Verslag van den Ondergetekende na de Gedane Expediesie tegen Makapaan en Mapela".
30 .The interviews were as follows: Madimetša Klaas Kekana, interviewed by Peter Kekana, Edwin Nyatlo and I.H., Mošate, Valtyn, 28/11/87; Mahula Patrick Somarso Kekana, interviewed by Peter Kekana, Edwin Nyatlo and I.H., Mošate, Valtyn, 12/ 12/87; Leka Thinta Mokhonoane, interviewed by Peter Kekana, Edwin Nyatlo and I.H., Mošate, Valtyn, 12/12/87; Mosoamadite Kekana interview, 19/3/88; Morongoa Kgosana, interviewed by Johanna Moima, Nico Mabusela and I.H., Mahwelereng, 19/3/88; Maleka interview; Molalakgori Kekana interview; Group interview of Nseki Bilankulu, Lesiba Digashu, Matlhaba Langa, Mmasehlaba Langa, Sekgoma Langa, Kgarebe Moshia, Thabankoane Motlatla, interviewed by I.H., Bakenberg, 27/7/88; Madimetša Kekana, interviewed by Motlalepula Mashao, Debra Nails and I.H., Mošate, Valtyn, 1/10/88; Mashao and Mvundlela interview; Bowale interview; Chaclice Kekana interview; Cecil Lesiba Kekana, interviewed by Job Kekana, Tim Couzens and I.H., Mahwelereng, 7/3/89; Zaba Maluleke, interviewed by I.H. on the farm Makapansgat, Potgietersrus district, 5/4/88; Moses Ledwaba and Matthews Hlanga interview; Fred Ledwaba interview; Alpheus Ledwaba interview; Kutumela interview, 15/1/89; Ramasela interview; Mahlangu interview, 13/3/90; and Lucky Kekana interview, 3/4/90.
31 See Mönnig, *The Pedi*, 126; and Cecil Lesiba Kekana interview.
32 This episode of sheep trading formed part of the oral accounts that were collected at J.M Orpen's behest somewhere between the 1860s and 1890s. Orpen, *Reminiscences*, 254-6.
33 Madimetša Kekana interview, 28/11/87. For the conventions used in representing narrative excerpts from interviews, the reader is referred to the Preface and a Note on the Text at the beginning of this book.
34 This episode comes up in Cecil Lesiba Kekana interview; Fred Ledwaba interview; Group interview at GaLedwaba; and Alpheus Ledwaba interview.

35 This is the interpretation given in Maluleke interview; and Lucky Kekana interview, 3/4/90.

36 Molalalakgori Kekana interview.

37 Mokhonoane interview.

38 Madimetša Kekana interview, 28/11/87.

39 Maluleke interview.

40 For examples of this deceit motif see Hunt, "An Account", 287; and Scully, "Phalaborwa", 107, 247.

41 This account appears in Madimetša Kekana interview, 28/11/87; Mahula Kekana interview; Molalakgori Kekana interview; Madimetša Kekana interview, 1/10/88; Mashao and Mvundlela interview; Kutumela interview, 15/1/89; and Lucky Kekana interview, 3/4/90.

42 Orpen, *Reminiscences*, 255-6.

43 Madimetša Kekana interview, 28/11/87.

44 Mahula Kekana interview.

45 Mahula Kekana interview.

46 Madimetša Kekana interview, 28/11/87; and Leka Thinta Mokhonoane interview, 12/12/87.

47 Leka Thinta Mokhonoane interview, 12/12/87.

48 This set of events was narrated to the missionary, Heese, in the 1890s. Gurr, *Daniel Heese*, 5-6.

49 For examples of this process see Scully, "Phalaborwa", 26, 39, 73, 76; and testimony of M. Mathware, collected in B. Head, *Serowe: Village of the Rain Wind* (London: Heinemann, 1981), 10. For a more general discussion of topographical reference and its relation to time see F. Harwood, "Myth, Memory, and the Oral Tradition: Cicero in the Trobriands", *American Anthropologist*, 78, 4, 1976.

50 Maluleke interview.

51 Molalakgori Kekana interview.

52 Moletsi Mahlangu interview, 13/3/90.

53 See anonymous testimony headed "A History of the Ndebele", in Ziervogel, *A Grammar*, 181. See also Maluleke interview and Madimetša Kekana interview, 28/11/87.

54 Kgosana interview, 19/3/88.

55 Molalakgori Kekana interview.

56 Molalakgori Kekana interview; and Kutumela interview, 15/1/89.

57 Madimetša Kekana interview, 28/11/87.

58 Maluleke interview; Maleka interview; Bowale interview; and Molalakgori Kekana interview.

59 For a map of the known extent of the Makapan cave system see R. Mason, *Cave of Hearths: Makapansgat Transvaal* (Johannesburg: Archaeological Research Unit, University of the Witwatersrand, 1988), 49.

60 Madimetša Kekana interview, 28/11/87.

61 This model is drawn from Scheub, "Oral Poetry".

Chapter 6
The Meaning of Oral Historical Narrative

1 While the discussion of this topic occurs throughout much of *The Xhosa Ntsomi*, it is concentrated in one section, 75-89.

2 The tradition can, of course, be read in other ways. See, for example, much of Jackson, *Allegories*; and Beidelman, *Moral Imagination*, 169-77.

3 Scheub, *The Xhosa Ntsomi*, 76.

4   Scheub, *The Xhosa Ntsomi*, 76.

5   Scheub, *The Xhosa Ntsomi*, 76-7.

6   For an extended discussion on the influence of context on interviews see E.M. McMahan, *Elite Oral History Discourse: A Study of Cooperation and Coherence* (Tuscaloo: University of Alabama Press, 1989).

7   On the role of imagined audiences in oral interviews see McMahan, *Elite Oral History*, 14, 90-1.

8   Schapera, *A Handbook*, 84-9.

9   Schapera, *A Handbook*, 71-2.

10 J.L. Comaroff, "Chiefship in a South African Homeland: A Case Study of the Tshidi Chiefdom of Bophuthatswana", *Journal of Southern African Studies*, 1, 1, 1974.

11 James, "Kinship", 44.

12 Jackson, *The Ndebele*, 59.

13 In addition, to give a wider sense of how people narrate this episode, I include two other accounts in Appendices 4 and 5. The latter is by a man called Mahula Kekana. The former is another account from Madimetša Kekana narrated on a different occasion from the one mentioned above.

14 These groups include those at Bakenberg, the chiefdom descended from Mokopane's ally, Mankopane, and those who at some time have lived near the cave. One such group now resides at GaLedwaba, and testimony from residents in this area was referred to in the previous chapter. Another such group are the workers presently resident on the farm where the cave is located. Zaba Maluleke, quoted in the previous chapter, is one such person.

15 Havelock, *The Literate Revolution*, 139.

16 Scully, "Phalaborwa", 167.

17 Molalakgori Kekana's version does not use the core cliché, 'My name is Klaas,' although the foreman does identify the kidnapped chief by this name when he uses the phrase, 'He is referring to Klaas.'

18 The point was made by Heckford, *A Lady Trader*, 289.

19 In his account Molalakgori Kekana maintains that the men and the child chief return to Chidi. However, by this stage the move to Sefakaola would already have occurred.

20 As regards the tribute that the migrants bring, it is worth commenting on the shoes that are included in their gifts. Apparently one of the most sought-after items by early migrants, shoes were highly prized. According to one informant, migrants would soak their shoes in salt water to swell the seams so that in walking the shoes made a noise. When seated at the chief's court, migrants could impress everybody by tapping their shoes noisily on the ground, something that bare feet cannot do very effectively. While the reference may simply be facetious or arbitrary, one can read the detail as further evidence of the migrants' apparently voluntary subordination to the chief, for in giving him shoes, they part with one of their most treasured items. Rampula interview. See also *B.M.B.*, 23-4, 1892, 601.

21 Cecil Lesiba Kekana interview. While the meaning of the Turfloop is not entirely clear, it most probably refers to the farm Turfspruit that lies close to the river.

22 P. Delius, "Migrant Labour and the Pedi, 1840-80", in S. Marks and A. Atmore (eds), *Economy and Society in Pre-Industrial South Africa* (London: Longman, 1980).

23 Gurr, *Daniel Heese*, 75.

24 De Beer, "Groepsgebondenheid", 43, 53.

25 Miller, "Introduction", 8.

26 T.A., T.A.D., SS 9, Supl. 45/54, "Verslag van den Ondergetekende na de Gedane Expediesie tegen Makapaan en Mapela".

27 Heckford, *A Lady Trader*, 289.

28 Baines, *The Gold Regions*, 67.

29 I am grateful to Philip Bonner for bringing this point to my attention.

30   For accounts of the history of the Mokopane chiefdom, see T.A., T.A.D., GOV 1088, PS
      50/8/1907; and Transvaal Native Affairs Department, *Short History*, 54-5. See also
      Coetzee, "Die Strewe", 315-21; and De Beer, "Groepsgebondenheid", 34-53. For
      material on other Transvaal Ndebele traditions, see Van Warmelo, *Transvaal Ndebele
      Texts*, 18-19; Ziervogel, *A Grammar*, 181-203; Kuper, "Fourie", 111; B. Schneider,
      "Paint, Pride and Politics: Aesthetic and Meaning in Transvaal Ndebele Wall Art", Ph. D.
      Thesis, University of the Witwatersrand, 1986, 197-206; and James, "Kinship", 38-46.
31   Transvaal Native Affairs Department, *Short History*, 54-5; and De Beer,
      "Groepsgebondenheid", 34-5.
32   For transcriptions of oral accounts of Mzilikazi's attack see Gurr, *Daniel Heese*, 5-6;
      and T.A., T.A.D., GOV 1088, PS 50/8/1907, History: Valtyn Makapaan (Mokopane).
      The latter document also contains details of the Pedi attack. For details of the Ndebele
      invasion see, Cobbing, "The Ndebele", 15-20, 40-1; and Delius, *The Land*, 19-24. See
      also David Livingstone's account. He passed through Mankopane's chiefdom in 1847
      and claimed that "The people are rich in cattle, and were never subject to
      Mosilikatze." Schapera, *Livingstone's Missionary Correspondence*, 97. From these
      accounts, it would seem that Mzilikazi's armies at times passed the area by and at
      other times attacked it. On the Pedi attack see Hunt, "An Account", 283-4; and Delius,
      The Land, 15.
33   For examples of such accounts see T.A., T.A.D., GOV 1088, PS 50/8/1907, History:
      Valtyn Makapaan (Mokopane). For a related case see Delius, *The Land*, 24.
34   For an example of such an account which deals with Mzilikazi's attack see Gurr,
      Daniel Heese, 5-6.
35   T.A., T.A.D., KPT 32, 2/8/2, Undated affidavit. Frans Nuku Kekana was the major
      spokesman for the polity and much of his testimony is collected in the Native
      Commissioner's archive for Potgietersrus (KPT). For an excellent example see T.A.,
      T.A.D., GOV 1088, PS 50/8/1907, Extracts of Minutes from Late Location
      Commission.
36   T.A., C.A.D., NTS 314, 12/55, Minutes of meeting at N.C.'s office, 5/9/49.
37   The references come from Mahula Kekana interview; and Kgosana interview, 19/3/
      88.

Chapter 7
Testimony into Text

1   For a good example see a popular account of the siege in a recent newspaper article,
     "The Massacre of Makapansgat", in *South*, 28/3-3/4/91.
2   The major despatches are T.A., T.A.D., SS 7, R733/54, Verslag van den Verregting
     van de Commandant Generaal, 6/12/1854; SS 9, Supl. 44/54, Undated document
     headed "Verslag van den Ondergetekende van den Expedietie tegen Makapaan en
     Mapela"; and SS 9, Supl. 45/54, Undated document headed "Verslag van den
     Ondergetekende na de Gedane Expediesie tegen Makapaan en Mapela".
3   These details come from the report contained in T.A., T.A.D., SS 9, Supl. 44/54. Many
     of the same details appear in the other two despatches mentioned in the note above.
4   Kgosana interview, 19/3/88.
5   The claim is made in T.A., T.A.D., SS 7, R733/54.
6   This report is contained in T.A., T.A.D., SS 9, Supl. 44/54.
7   The claims of burial are made in testimony collected from Willem Pretorius and J.J.H.
     Engelbrecht. Both are preserved in the Gustav Preller papers, T.A., T.A.D., A 787,
     Volume (hereafter V.) 201, File (hereafter F.) 120, 71-9 and 94-5. The first testimony is
     headed "Willem Pretorius", the second appears under the heading, "De Moord van
     Makapanspoort". The latter also appeared in *De Volkstem*, 25/2/05.

8 Testimony of Willem Pretorius in T.A., T.A.D., A 787, V. 201, F. 102, 72-9. My translation.

9 Testimony of J.H.H. Engelbrecht in T.A., T.A.D., A 787, V. 201, F. 102, 95.

10 This point is based on personal observation. During the course of this research I was often asked what my topic of study was. Almost invariably, as soon as the word "Makapansgat" was out, people would respond with this detail of Hermanus Potgieter's death or with the details of some other atrocity.

11 *The Friend of the Free State and Bloemfontein Gazette*, 23/12/1854. Hereafter referred to as *The Friend*.

12 Reproduced in *The Friend*, 21/7/1855.

13 For an account of the anti-slavery movement and its relation to British plans for confederation in the subcontinent, see W. Kistner, "The Anti-Slavery Agitation Against the Transvaal Republic, 1852-1868", *Archives Year Book for South African History*, Vol. II (Parow: Government Printer, 1952).

14 J.P.R. Wallis (ed.), *The Matabele Journals of Robert Moffat 1829-1860*, Vol. II (London: Chatto & Windus, 1945), 378-9.

15 Wallis, *The Matabele Journals*, 379.

16 Wangemann, *Ein Reise-Jahr*, 455-60. His description of the siege also appeared in *Die Transvaal'sche oder Süd-Afrikanische Republik, Ergänzungsheft No. 24 zu Petermann's "Geographischen Mittheilungen"* [The Transvaal or South African Republic, Supplement No. 24 to Petermann's "Geographical Communication"] (No place of publication: Justus Perthes, 1868), 20-1. Another German account from the same time appears in *Globus: Illustrirte Zeitschrift für Länder-und Völkerkunde* [Illustrated Periodical of Geography and Anthropology] (No place of publication: Bibliographischen Instituts, 1864), 155.

17 .On this point see Delius, *The Land*, 118-19.

18 Baines, *The Gold Regions*, 68.

19 Heckford, *A Lady Trader*, 289.

20 The details of Kruger's and Theal's accounts which are discussed below are as follows. P. Kruger, *The Memoirs of Paul Kruger: Four Times President of the South African Republic: Told by Himself*, Vol. I (London: T. Fisher Unwin, 1902), 46-58. Although not mentioned on the title page, the work was transcribed by H.C. Bredall and P. Grobler. G. M. Theal, *History of South Africa since September 1795*, Vol. IV (1889; London: S. Sonnenschein, 1908), 27-32.

21 Orpen, *Reminiscences*, 254.

22 For examples of such accounts see J. Noble, *South Africa: Past and Present* (London: Longman, 1877), 173, 173A, 173B; and Norris-Newman, *With the Boers*, 58-9.

23 M. Twain, *More Tramps Abroad* (London: Chatto & Windus, 1897), 471. It is, of course, not entirely clear that it is the Makapansgat siege to which Twain is referring. The cave is in fact about 300 km (190 miles) north of Johannesburg. Also, there have been similar incidents in other parts of the Transvaal. One such siege occurred in 1882 when the Boers, aided by the Pedi, surrounded the mountain capital of the Ndzundza Ndebele which lay between present-day Middelburg and Lydenburg, a point approximately 200 km (125 miles) north-east of Johannesburg. However, the Ndzundza did not shelter in caves as much as in rocky strongholds. For accounts of this see Schneider, "Paint", 200-4; James, "Kinship", 46; and P. Delius, "The Ndzundza Ndebele: Indenture and the Making of Ethnic Identity", in Bonner, *Holding Their Ground*, 231. While this could ostensibly be the event to which Twain was referring, the mention of the smoking probably means that it was of the Makapansgat episode of which he was told.

24 Twain, *More Tramps*, 472.

25 Anon., "Makapan's Poort". The dating of this piece is difficult. The booklet comprises .a number of articles reprinted from *South Africa*, a periodical that appeared after

Union in 1910. However, from the piece itself, it is clear that it was written during the South African War and it must then subsequently have been taken up by the periodical and thereafter reissued in booklet form.

26   Theal, *History of South Africa*, Vol. IV, 27-32.

27   For an example of an historical text that discusses the siege, see G.W. Stow, *The Native Races of South Africa: A History of the Intrusion of the Hottentots and Bantu into the Hunting Grounds of the Bushmen, the Aborigines of the Country* (London: S. Sonnenschein, 1905). Although not stated on the title page, the book was edited by Theal. Agar-Hamilton, *The Native Policy*, 163.

28   Dart, *Adventures*, 97.

29   Distant, *A Naturalist in the Transvaal*, 81-2. For another mention of the caves, see C.J. Alford, *Geological Features of the Transvaal, South Africa* (London: Edward Standford, 1891), 49-50.

30   R. Antonissen, *Die Afrikaanse Letterkunde van Aanvang tot Hede* (Cape Town: Nasou, n.d.), 39-53; and G. Dekker, *Afrikaanse Literatuurgeskiedenis* (Cape Town: Nasou, n.d.), 10-32. See also I. Hofmeyr, "Bulding a Nation from Words: Afrikaans Language, Literature and Ethnic Identity, 1902-1924", in S. Marks and S. Trapido (eds), *The Politics of Race, Class and Nationalism in Twentieth-Century South Africa* (London: Longman, 1987), 109.

31   D'Arbez (pseud. of J.F. van Oordt), *Paul Kruger en die Opkomst der Zuid-Afrikaansche Republiek* (Amsterdam: Hollandsch-Afrikaansch Uitgewers, 1898); W. Brouwer, *Paul Kruger* (Amsterdam: L.J. Veen, 1899); F.A. McKenzie, *Paul Kruger: His Life Story* (London: Bowden, 1899); D'Arbez, *Van Schaapwachter tot President: Het Leven van Paul Kruger* (Amsterdam: De Bussy, 1904); and Kruger, *The Memoirs*.

32   See, for example, Brouwer, *Paul Kruger*, 25; and D'Arbez, *Van Schaapwachter*, 47-9.

33   This accounts appears in *De Volkstem*, 22/9/1890.

34   Hofmeyr, "Building a Nation"; and I. Hofmeyr, "Popularizing History: The Case of Gustav Preller", *Journal of African History*, 29, 1988.

35   Testimony of C. Pienaar (which appeared in *De Volkstem*), collected in T.A., T.A.D., A 787, V. 201, F. 120, 119.

36   For other accounts see *De Volkstem*, 17/2/90 and 25/2/05.

37   For details of the story see G.S. Preller, *Geskiedenis van die Kruger-standbeeld* (Pretoria: Ossewa-Boekhandel, n.d.); and J.H. Breytenbach, *Die Geskiedenis van die Krugerstandbeeld* (Pretoria: Krugergenootskap, 1954).

38   Kruger, *The Memoirs*, 49-51.

39   Kruger, *The Memoirs*, 48-9.

40   Orpen, *Reminiscences*, 255. Another account reproduced in *Die Noord Transvaler*, 29/5/64 claims that it was M.W. Pretorius who retrieved Potgieter's body.

41   H.C. Bosman, "Makapan's Cave", in *Makapan's Cave and Other Stories*, ed. S. Gray (Harmondsworth: Penguin, 1987), 15-23.

42   In doing the Makapansgat relief, Van Wouw requested photographs of typical clothing and weapons of the time. While the circumstances are not clear, it seems that this request prompted government officials to arrange a re-enactment of the siege so that photographs could be taken (see Plates 30 and 31).

43   On the details of Kruger biographies, plays and novels, see P. de Klerk, "Die Geskiedskrywing oor Paul Kruger" [The Historiography of Paul Kruger], M.A. Dissertation, University of Potchefstroom, 1969, 24-68 and 69-118.

44   Hofmeyr, "Popularizing History", 527.

45   Dart, *Adventures*, 92; T.A., T.A.D., A 787, V. 201, F. 102, 63-4; and Preller, "Baanbrekers", 14-15 fn. 2.

46   Krikler, "Agrarian Class Struggle". See also T.A., T.A.D., SNA 47, NA 1569/02, S.W.J. Scholefield to "My dear Windham", 12/7/02, for African expectations of reclaiming

land after the war.

47 T.A., C.A.D., UOD 436, X6/52/128, Copy of proclamation, 1/19/40.

48 For a fuller discussion of Preller, see Hofmeyr, "Popularizing History".

49 *Die Brandwag*, 10/12/14 and 15/1/15

50 The term *melkgebruik*, which literally means 'milk use', has no English equivalent. It denotes an arrangement whereby one person tends another's cows and keeps the milk product as payment.

51 De Waal, "Die Verhouding", 25 and 134.

52 Preller, "Baanbrekers", 115-16. My translation.

53 See T.A., T.A.D., A 787, V. 201, F. 120, 176-84, newspaper cuttings and handwritten notes.

54 Preller, "Baanbrekers", 137-8.

55 N. Courtney Acutt, "Makapan se Gruweldade" (Makapan's Atrocities), *Die Huisgenoot*, 6/5/38. My translation.

56 See, for example, M. du Plessis to Preller, 8/2/15; and B. Gildenhuys to Preller, 22/2/15, both in T.A., T.A.D., A 787, V. 201, F. 120.

57 *Die Noord-Transvaler*, 7/2/64.

58 See, for example, J.A. Robbertse, "Kultuurorganisasies: Potgietersrust", in Combrink, *Eeufees*, 181-90.

59 For a discussion of this event see A. Grundlingh and H. Sapire, "From Feverish Festival to Repetitive Ritual? The Changing Fortunes of Great Trek Mythology in an Industrializing South Africa, 1938-1988", *South African Historical Journal*, 21, 1989.

60 T.A., C.A.D., UOD 424, X6/52/8, Undated press-clipping. My translation.

61 For details of declaration see T.A., C.A.D., UOD 424, X6/52/8.

62 For details of white interest in the caves see P.V. Tobias, "The Makapan Valley: A Report on an Expedition (of Science Students) from the University of the Witwatersrand to the Makapansgat Valley, June-July 1945", a typescript in the possession of Professor Tobias and his article, "A Page from History", *Natal Daily Mail*, 15/1/47. I am indebted to Professor Tobias for making this material, and his memories of the Makapansgat cave, available to me.

63 T.A., C.A.D., UOD 424, X6/52/8, Undated document headed "A Note on the Possibility of Early Human Occupation of Certain Caves on the Farm Makapansgat No. 1667, District Potgietersrust, Transvaal".

64 Madimetša Kekana interview, 1/10/88.

65 Maluleke interview.

66 Figures from C.L. van Riet Lowe (ed.), *The Monuments of South Africa* (Pretoria: Government Printer, 1941), 22.

67 T.A., C.A.D., UOD 434, X6/52/1.

68 T.A., T.A.D., HKN 58, 76/15/2, N.C. to C.N.C., 27/5/48.

69 *Die Noord Transvaler*, 8/5/64. My translation.

70 L. Rousseau, *The Dark Stream: The Story of Eugène N. Marais* (Johannesburg: Jonathan Ball, 1982), 200-99 for Marais' stay in the Waterberg, and 237-44 for information on Van Rooyen. The story appears in L. Rousseau (ed.), *Eugène N. Marais: Versamelde Werke*, Part I (Pretoria: Van Schaik, 1984), 364-9.

71 T.A., T.A.D., KPT 40, 3/1/2, J.J. van Rooyen to R.M., 31/3/41, and 1/12/41.

72 Preller, "Baanbrekers", 129.

73 It is interesting to note that Bosman, a keen observer of rural Transvaal Afrikaner society, satirises the fascination with reinterments in a story, "Unto Dust", which first appeared in 1949. H.C. Bosman, "Unto Dust", in *Makapan's Cave*, 37-41.

74 *Die Noord Transvaler*, 13/3/64; 29/5/64; and 5/6/64.

75 J.H. Meyer, "Die Ontstaan en Ontwikkeling van Potgietersrus as Dorp", in Combrink, *Eeufees*, 17-25.

76 "Die Grootpad na die Noorde: 'n Oorsig van die Landbou- en Nywerheids-ontwikkeling van Noord Transvaal", supplement to *Die Vaderland*, 12/10/59, 26.
77 T.A., T.A.D., A 787, V. 201, F. 120, 76, Testimony of Willem Pretorius; Madimetša Kekana interview, 28/11/87; and Orpen, *Reminiscences*, 255.
78 For details of this cross-over see Tobias, "The Makapan Valley", which tells how details of the siege reached Tobias via a farmer who in turn had learned about it from survivors of the siege who worked for him in the 1890s.
79 J.C. Scott, *Weapons of the Weak: Everyday Forms of Peasant Resistance* (New Haven: Yale University Press, 1985), xvii.

Chapter 8
History as Farce?

1 Points taken from Harwood, "Myth", 783-96. See also Biebuyck, *Hero and Chief*, 36-7.
2 H. Glassie, *Passing the Time in Ballymenone: Culture and History of an Ulster Community* (Philadelphia: University of Pennsylvania Press, 1982), 621 and 664. See also 621-65.
3 Lévi-Strauss, *The Savage Mind*, 16-22. See also R.P. Werbner, "The Political Economy of Bricolage", *Journal of Southern African Studies*, 13, 1, 1986, 151-6.
4 Testimony of M. Mathware, collected in Head, *Serowe*, 10; and Madimetša Kekana interview, 1/10/88.
5 T.A., T.A.D., GOV 1085, 50/8/1907/9, Location Commission History of Native Tribes: Valtijn Makapan, Minutes of Native Location Commission, Potgietersrust, 2/11/06.
6 T.A., T.A.D., KPT 45, 4/3/3, R. Courtney-Acutt to N.C., 1/5/33.
7 Cecil Lesiba Kekana interview.
8 Alfred Lesiba Kekana interview, 22/6/90.
9 De Beer, "Groepsgebondenheid", 455.
10 This point is based on teaching and conversing with students at the Mokopane College of Education.
11 Scheub, *The Xhosa Ntsomi*, 90-100. See also D.H. Gough, "Xhosa Narrative: An Analysis of the Production and Linguistic Properties of Discourse with Particular Reference to Iintsomi Texts", D. Phil Thesis, Rhodes University, 1986, 187-8. My thanks to Molly Bill for the latter reference.
12 Cecil Lesiba Kekana interview.
13 Mosoamadite Kekana interview.
14 Miller, "Introduction", 36.
15 Mahula Kekana interview. It may seem that the informant is confusing Pampata with Bambatha, the leader of an anti-colonial uprising in Natal early this century. However, Shaka was known to have a liaison with a woman, Pampata. For details see E.A. Ritter, *Shaka Zulu: The Rise of the Zulu Empire* (1955; London: Longman, 1971), 125-7.
16 Moletsi Mahlangu interview, 13/3/90.
17 T.A., T.A.D., GOV 1088, PS 50/8/1907, History Valtyn Makapaan (Mokopane).
18 Transvaal Native Affairs Department, *Short History*, 29. However, other Kgatla traditions, while mentioning interaction with the Kekana, do not specifically mention Maroelaskop. See, for example, Van Warmelo, *The Bakgatla*, 3-6.
19 Lucky Kekana interview, 3/4/90.
20 Madimetša Kekana interview, 1/10/88.
21 Cecil Lesiba Kekana interview.
22 Cecil Lesiba Kekana interview.
23 While nobody was prepared to go on record with this story, it was often told informally.
24 Madimetša Kekana interview, 28/11/87.

25 Coetzee, "Die Strewe", 297-8 based in turn on Van Warmelo, *Transvaal Ndebele*, 14. See also Leka Thinta Mokhonoane interview, 12/12/87 who gives the same explanation.
26 Lucky Kekana interview, 3/4/90.
27 T.A., C.A.D., UOD 423, X6/52/1.
28 T.A., T.A.D., HKN 58, 67/15/2, N.C. to C.N.C., 27/5/48.
29 *Die Noord Transvaler*, 8/5/64.
30 Lucky Kekana interview, 9/4/90.
31 Lucky Kekana interview, 9/4/90.
32 The spelling of the name, "Dingaan", is an Afrikanerised rendition of "Dingane".
33 Fred Ledwaba interview.
34 For a discussion of this point see Scully, "Phalaborwa", 66-7, 118-19.
35 Werbner, "The Political Economy", 151.
36 Connerton, *How Societies Remember*, 36-7.
37 Alpheus Ledwaba interview.
38 Cecil Lesiba Kekana interview.
39 Madimetša Kekana interview, 1/10/88.
40 See for example "Masasara", in P.E. Schwellnus, *Padišo III* (Pretoria: Northern Sotho Book Depot, n.d.), 24-6, reproduced in Appendix 1. Maibelo, "The Structure", 4, identifies this as a story that comes from oral historical tradition.
41 Maibelo, "The Structure", 4.

Conclusion

1 Posel, "Influx Control", and "The State"; and T. Lodge, *Black Politics in South Africa since 1945* (Johannesburg: Ravan Press, 1983), 263-73.
2 Government Notice 939 of 1953, *Government Gazette*, Vol. 172, No. 5065, 8/5/53. See also S.A.I.R.R., *Establishment*, 2-3.
3 For an overview of this legislation and its political implications see Dubow, "Holding 'A Just Balance'", and his *Racial Segregation*, 77-127; and Lacey, *Working for Boroko*, 84-115.
4 See for example Street, *Literacy in Theory*, Chs 1-2; and Finnegan, *Literacy and Orality*, 1-14.
5 For a comparative discussion on this point see A. Shuman, *Storytelling Rights: The Uses of Oral and Written Texts by Urban Adolescents* (Cambridge: Cambridge University Press, 1986), 183-200.
6 L. White, "Poetic Licence: Oral Poetry and History", in Barber and De Moraes Farias, *Discourse and its Disguises*, 37.
7 Barber, "Interpreting", 13.
8 S. Feierman, *Peasant Intellectuals: Anthropology and History in Tanzania* (Madison: University of Wisconsin Press, 1990), 21.
9 For a fuller version of this debate see D. Attwell, "Political Supervision: The Case of the 1990 History Workshop", *Pretexts*, 2, 1, 1990, and my reply contained in "Introduction", *Pretexts*, 2, 2, 1990.

BIBLIOGRAPHY

This bibliography has been divided into:

I   Manuscript Sources Cited
II   Newspapers and Periodicals Cited
III Official Publications Cited
IV   Other Works Cited
V   Interviews Cited

I   MANUSCRIPT SOURCES CITED

Official

The following unindexed archives – all in the Transvaal Archives, Transvaal Archives Depot, Pretoria – were consulted in full:

Chief Commissioner for the Northern Transvaal (HKN)
Commissioner for Potgietersrus (KPT)
Magistrate for Potgietersrus (LPT)

Sections of the following indexed archives in the Transvaal Archives, Transvaal Archives Depot, were used:

Commandant-General of the South African Republic (KG)
Governor General (GOV)
The Municipality of Potgietersrus (MPT) (Only limited sections of this archive could be consulted, as much of it falls into the closed period.)
Secretary of State of the South African Republic (SS)
State President of the South African Republic (SP)

Sections of the following indexed archives in the Transvaal Archives, Central Archives Depot, were used:

The Department of Native Affairs (NTS)
The Lands Department (LDE)
The Union Education Department (UOD)

Unofficial

Collections of papers

Gustav Preller Papers, A 787, held at the Transvaal Archives, Transvaal Archives Depot

Individual unpublished items

Tobias, P.V. "The Makapan Valley: A Report of an Expedition (of Science Students) from the University of the Witwatersrand to the Makapansgat Valley, June–July 1945". Typescript in the possession of Professor P.V. Tobias, Department of Anatomy, Medical School, University of the Witwatersrand.

Mashishi, M. Untitled document recounting history of Mashishi lineage. In the possession of Dr B. Maboya, Mahwelereng.

II NEWSPAPERS AND PERIODICALS CITED

This section refers to runs of newspapers and periodicals consulted. Where a single article from a newspaper or periodical has been used it appears in the section "Other Works Cited".

Berliner Missionsberichte, 1865–92
The Friend of the Free State and Bloemfontein Gazette, 1854–5
Die Noord Transvaler, 1964–5
De Volkstem, 1890 and 1905

III OFFICIAL PUBLICATIONS CITED

Development Bank of Southern Africa and the Lebowa Government.
   Lebowa Development Information: Section 4: Population and Settlement. Development Bank of Southern Africa: Sandton, n.d.
   Lebowa Development Information: Section 5: Labour and Employment. Development Bank of Southern Africa: Sandton, n.d.
Republic of South Africa, Department of Co-operation and Development, Ethnological Publication No. 54, A.O. Jackson, *The Ndebele of Langa.* Pretoria: Government Printer, n.d.
   Department of Bantu Administration and Development, Ethnological Publication No. 52, A.O. Jackson, "The Langa Ndebele Calendar and Annual Agricultural Ceremonies". The Ethnological Section (ed.), *Ethnological and Linguistic Studies in Honour of N.J. van Warmelo.* Pretoria: Government Printer, 1969.
   Government Gazette, 10, 662, Notice 1881, 6/12/63.
   Government Gazette, 11, 751, Notice 437, 26/3/64.
Transvaal Native Affairs Department. *Short History of the Native Tribes of the Transvaal.* Pretoria: Government Printing and Stationery Office, 1905.
Union of South Africa, Mines Department. Geological Survey. *The Geology of the Country Around Potgietersrust.* Pretoria: Government Printer, 1911.
   Minutes of Evidence of the Eastern Transvaal Native Land Commission, UG32-'18.
   Department of Native Affairs, Ethnological Publication No. 1, N.J. van Warmelo, *Transvaal Ndebele Texts.* Pretoria: Government Printer, 1930.
   Report of the Geodetic Work of the Trigonometrical Survey, 1933–38.
   Annual Reports of the Department of Native Affairs, 1936–60.
   Report of the Geodetic Work of the Trigonometrical Survey, 1939–53.

Union of South Africa, Department of Native Affairs, Ethnological Publication No. 17, N.J. van Warmelo, *The Bakgatla ba ga Mosetlha*. Pretoria: Government Printer, 1944.

IV   OTHER WORKS CITED

Agar-Hamilton, J.A.I. *The Native Policy of the Voortrekkers: An Essay in the History of the Interior of South Africa – 1836–1858*. Cape Town: Maskew Miller, n.d.

Alford, C.J. *Geological Features of the Transvaal, South Africa*. London: Edward Standford, 1891.

Ancelet, B.J. "'And This is No Damn Lie': Oral History in Story Form", *International Journal of Oral History*, 4, 2, 1983.

Andrzejewski, B.W. and G. Innes. "Reflections on African Oral Literature", *African Languages*, 1, 1975.

Anon. *Globus: Illustrirte Zeitschrift für Länder-und Völkekunde*. No place: Bibliographischen Instituts, 1864.

——— "Die Grootpad na die Noorde: 'n Oorsig van die Landbou en Nywerheids-ontwikkeling van Noord Transvaal", *Die Vaderland*, 12/10/59.

——— "Makapan's Poort", *Annals of South Africa: South Africa Handbooks, No. 17*. London: no publisher, n.d.

Antonissen, R. *Die Afrikaanse Letterkunde van Aanvang tot Hede*. Cape Town: Nasou, n.d.

Argyle, J. and E. Preston-Whyte (eds). *Social System and Tradition in Southern Africa: Essays in Honour of Eileen Krige*. Cape Town: Oxford University Press, 1978.

Armstrong, N. and L. Tennenhouse (eds). *Violence and Representation: Literature and the History of Violence*. London: Routledge & Kegan Paul, 1989.

Attwell, D. "The British Legacy in Anglophone African Literary Criticism", *English in Africa*, 11, 1, 1984.

——— "Political Supervision: The Case of the 1990 History Workshop", *Pretexts*, 2, 1, 1990.

Babalola, S.A. *The Content and Form of Yoruba Ijala*. London: Oxford University Press, 1966.

Baines, T. *The Gold Regions of South East Africa*. 1877; Bulawayo: Books of Rhodesia, 1968.

Bakhtin, M. *Rabelais and his World*. H. Iswolsky (tr.). Cambridge, Mass.: Massachusetts Institute of Technology Press, 1968.

Bank, L. "The Janus-Face of Rural Class Formation: An Economic and Political History of Traders in Qwaqwa 1960–1986". Paper presented to the History Workshop Conference, University of the Witwatersrand, Johannesburg, 6-10/2/90.

Barber, K. "Yoruba *Oriki* and Deconstructive Criticism", *Research in African Literatures*, 15, 4, 1984.

——— "Popular Arts in Africa", *African Studies Review*, 3, 30, 1987.

——— "Interpreting *Oríkì* as History and as Literature", in Barber and De Moraes Farias, *Discourse and its Disguises*, 1989.

——— "Introduction", in Barber and De Moraes Farias, *Discourse and its Disguises*, 1989.

——— "Power and Subversion in Yoruba Praise Poetry". Paper presented to the conference, "Power, Marginality and Oral Literature", School of Oriental and African Studies, University of London, 17-19/2/91.

——— *I Could Speak Until Tomorrow: Oriki, Women and the Past in a Yoruba Town*. Washington: Smithsonian Institution Press, 1991.

Barber, K. and P.F. de Moraes Farias (eds). *Discourse and its Disguises: The Interpretation of African Oral Texts*. Birmingham: Centre of West African Studies, University of Birmingham, 1989.

Bauman, R. *Story, Performance, and Event: Contextual Studies of Oral Narrative*. Cambridge: Cambridge University Press, 1986.

Beidelman, T. "Approaches to the Study of African Oral Literature", *Africa*, 42, 1972.

—— *Moral Imagination in Kaguru Modes of Thought.* Bloomington: Indiana University Press, 1986.

Beinart, W. "Introduction: The Politics of Colonial Conservation", *Journal of Southern African Studies,* 15, 2, 1989.

Ben-Amos, D. "Analytical Categories and Ethnic Genres", *Genre,* 2, 1969.

—— "Folklore in African Society", *Research in African Literatures,* 6, 2, 1975.

—— *Sweet Words: Storytelling Events in Benin.* Philadelphia: Institute for the Study of Human Issues, 1975.

—— "The Historical Folklore of Richard M. Dorson", *Journal of Folklore Research,* 26, 1, 1989.

Berry, J. *Spoken Art in West Africa.* London: University of London, 1961.

Bertaux, D. (ed.). *Biography and Society.* London: Sage, 1981.

Bettelheim, B. *The Uses of Enchantment: The Meaning and Importance of Fairy Tales.* Harmondsworth: Penguin, 1976.

Biebuyck, D.P. *Hero and Chief: Epic Literature from the Banyanga Zaire Republic.* Berkeley: University of California Press, 1978.

Bill, M.C. "The Structure and Function of the Song in the Tsonga Folktale", *African Studies,* 42, 1, 1983.

Bloch, M. (ed.). *Political Language and Oratory in Traditional Societies.* London: Academic Press, 1975.

Bonner, P., I. Hofmeyr, D. James and T. Lodge (eds). *Holding Their Ground: Class, Locality and Culture in 19th and 20th Century South Africa.* Johannesburg: Ravan/Witwatersrand University Press, 1989.

Bosman, H.C. "Makapan's Cave", in *Makapan's Cave and Other Stories,* ed. S. Gray. Harmondsworth: Penguin, 1987.

—— "Unto Dust", in *Makapan's Cave and Other Stories,* ed. S. Gray. Harmondsworth: Penguin, 1987.

Bozzoli, B. "Marxism, Feminism and South African Studies", *Journal of Southern African Studies,* 9, 2, 1983.

—— (ed.). *Town and Countryside in the Transvaal: Capitalist Penetration and Popular Response.* Johannesburg: Ravan, 1983.

—— (ed.). *Class, Community and Conflict: South African Perspectives.* Johannesburg: Ravan, 1987.

Bozzoli, B. and P. Delius. "Radical History and South African Society", *Radical History Review,* 46-7, 1990.

Breytenbach, J.H. *Die Geskiedenis van die Krugerstandbeeld.* Pretoria: Krugergenootskap, 1954.

Brouwer, W. *Paul Kruger.* Amsterdam: L.J. Veen, 1899.

Burke, P. and R. Porter (eds). *The Social History of Language.* Cambridge: Cambridge University Press, 1987.

Bynum, D. *The Daemon in the Wood: A Study of Oral Narrative Pattern.* Cambridge, Mass.: The Center for the Study of Oral Literature, Harvard University, 1978.

Canary, R.H. and H. Kozicki (eds). *The Writing of History: Literary Form and Historical Understanding.* Wisconsin: Wisconsin University Press, 1978.

Canonici, N.N. "Educational Aspects of Trickster Folktales", in Sienaert and Bell, *Catching Winged Words,* 1988.

—— *The Inganekwane Tradition.* Durban: Department of Zulu Language and Literature, University of Natal, 1987.

Chartier, R. (ed.). *The Culture of Print: Power and the Uses of Print in Early Modern Europe.* L.G. Cochrane (tr.). Cambridge: Polity Press, 1989.

—— "General Introduction: Print Culture", in Chartier, *The Culture of Print,* 1989.

—— "The Practical Impact of Writing", in Duby *et al.,* *A History of Private Life,* 1989.

Chaskalson, M. "Rural Resistance in the 1940s and 50s", *Africa Perspective: New Series*, 1, 5-6, 1987.

Chatwin, B. *The Songlines*. London: Jonathan Cape, 1987.

Clanchy, M.T. *From Memory to Written Record: England 1066–1307*. London: Edward Arnold, 1979.

Cobbing, J.R.D. "The Ndebele under the Khumalos: 1820–1896". D. Phil. Thesis, University of Lancaster, 1976.

Coetzee, C.J. "Die Strewe tot Etniese Konsolidasie en Nasionale Selfverwesenliking by die Ndebele in die Transvaal". Ph. D. Thesis, University of Potchefstroom, 1980.

Cohen, D. *Womunafu's Bunafu: A Study of Authority in a Nineteenth-century African Community*. Princeton: Princeton University Press, 1977.

Cohen R. (ed.). *New Directions in Literary History*. London: Routledge & Kegan Paul, 1974.

Cole, M.M. *South Africa*. London: Methuen, 1961.

Cole-Beuchat, P.D. "Notes on Some Folklore Forms in Tsonga and Ronga", *African Studies*, 17, 4, 1958.

Comaroff, J. *Body of Power Spirit of Resistance: The Culture of a South African People*. Chicago: University of Chicago Press, 1985.

Comaroff, J.L. "Chiefship in a South African Homeland: A Case Study of the Tshidi Chiefdom of Bophutatswana", *Journal of Southern African Studies*, 1, 1, 1974.

—— "Talking Politics: Oratory and Authority in a Tswana Chiefdom", in Bloch, *Political Language*, 1975.

Comaroff, J.L. and S. Roberts. *Rules and Processes: The Cultural Logic of Dispute*. Chicago: University of Chicago Press, 1981.

Combrink, A.J. (comp.). *Eeufees Potgietersrust Centenary 1854–1954*. Potgietersrust: The Central Centenary Committee, n.d.

Connerton, P. *How Societies Remember*. Cambridge: Cambridge University Press, 1989.

Cope, T. "Towards an Appreciation of Zulu Folktales as Literary Art", in Argyle and Preston-Whyte, *Social System and Tradition*, 1978.

—— "Literacy and the Oral Tradition: The Zulu Evidence", in Whitaker and Sienaert, *Oral Tradition and Literacy*, 1986.

Coplan, D. *In Township Tonight! South Africa's Black City Music and Theatre*. Johannesburg: Ravan, 1985.

—— "Eloquent Knowledge: Lesotho Migrants' Songs and the Anthropology of Experience", *American Ethnologist*, 14, 3, 1987.

Cosentino, D. *Defiant Maids and Stubborn Farmers: Tradition and Invention in Mende Story Performance*. Cambridge: Cambridge University Press, 1982.

Courtney Acutt, N. "Makapan se Gruweldade", *Die Huisgenoot*, 6/5/38.

Couzens, T. and L. White (eds). *Literature and Society in South Africa*. Cape Town: Maskew Miller Longman, 1984.

Cressy, D. *Literacy and the Social Order: Reading and Writing in Tudor and Stuart England*. Cambridge: Cambridge University Press, 1980.

Cronin, J. "'Even Under the Rine of Terror': Insurgent South African Poetry", *Research in African Literatures*, 19, 1, 1988.

D'Arbez (pseud. of J.F. van Oordt). *Paul Kruger en die Opkomst der Zuid-Afrikaansche Republiek*. Amsterdam: Hollandsch-Afrikaansch Uitgewers, 1898.

—— *Van Schaapwachter tot President: Het Leven van Paul Kruger*. Amsterdam: De Bussy, 1904.

Darnton, R. *The Great Cat Massacre and Other Episodes in French Cultural History*. New York: Basic Books, 1984.

Dart, R. *Adventures with the Missing Link*. London: Hamish Hamilton, 1959.

Davis, N.Z. "Printing and the People in Early Modern France", in Graff, *Literacy and Social Development*, 1981.

De Beer, F.C. "Groepsgebondenheid in die Familie- Opvolgings- en Erfsreg van die Noord-Ndebele". D. Phil. Thesis, University of Pretoria, 1986.

Dégh, L. *Folktales and Society: Storytelling in a Hungarian Peasant Community*. Bloomington: Indiana University Press, 1969.

Dekker, G. *Afrikaanse Literatuurgeskiedenis*. Cape Town: Nasou, n.d.

De Klerk, P. "Die Geskiedskrywing oor Paul Kruger". M.A. Dissertation, University of Potchefstroom, 1969.

Delius, P. "Migrant Labour and the Pedi: 1840–80", in Marks and Atmore, *Economy and Society*, 1980.

—— *The Land Belongs to Us: The Pedi Polity, the Boers and the British in the Nineteenth-Century Transvaal*. Johannesburg: Ravan, 1983.

—— "The Ndzundza Ndebele: Indenture and the Making of Ethnic Identity", in Bonner *et al.*, *Holding Their Ground*, 1989.

—— "Sebatakgomo: Migrant Organization and the Sekhukhuneland Revolt", *Journal of Southern African Studies*, 15, 4, 1989.

—— "*Dikgomo di ile* (The Cattle have gone): The Changing Context of Resistance in Sekhukhuneland 1950–1986". Paper presented to the History Workshop Conference, University of the Witwatersrand, Johannesburg, 6-10/2/1990.

Delius, P. and S. Trapido. "Inboekselings and Oorlams: The Creation and Transformation of a Servile Class", in Bozzoli, *Town and Countryside*, 1983.

Deng, F.M. *Dinka Folktales: African Stories from the Sudan*. London: Africana, 1974.

Derrida, J. *Of Grammatology*. G.C. Spivak (tr.). Baltimore: Johns Hopkins University Press, 1976.

De Villiers, A. (comp.). *A Rural Development Strategy for Lebowa*. Mankweng: University of the North, 1984.

—— "The Lebowa Economy", in De Villiers, *A Rural Development Strategy*, 1984.

De Waal, J.J. "Die Verhouding Tussen die Blankes en die Hoofmanne Mokopane en Mankopane in die Omgewing van Potgietersrus, 1836–1869". M.A. Dissertation, University of South Africa, 1978.

De Wet, C. "Betterment Planning in a Rural Village in Keiskammahoek, Ciskei", *Journal of Southern African Studies*, 15, 2, 1989.

Distant, W.L. *A Naturalist in the Transvaal*. London: Porter, 1892.

Doke, C. "The Basis of Bantu Literature", *Africa*, 18, 4, 1948.

Dorson, R. (ed.). *African Folklore*. Bloomington: Indiana University Press, 1972.

—— "Africa and the Folkorist", in Dorson, *African Folklore*, 1972.

Dray, W.H. "On the Nature and Role of Narrative in Historiography", *History and Theory*, 10, 2, 1971.

Dubow, S. "Holding 'A Just Balance between White and Black': The Native Affairs Department in South Africa c. 1920–33", *Journal of Southern African Studies*, 12, 2, 1986.

—— *Racial Segregation and the Origins of Apartheid in South Africa, 1919-36*. Basingstoke: Macmillan, 1989.

Duby, G., P. Veyne and M. Perrot (eds). *A History of Private Life: Passions of the Renaissance*. A. Goldhammer (tr.), Cambridge, Mass.: Belknap, 1989.

Duggan-Cronin, A.M. *The Bantu Tribes of South Africa: Reproductions of Photographic Studies*. 4 vols. Cambridge and Kimberley: Deighton Bell and Alexander McGregor Memorial Museum, 1931.

Dundes, A. (ed.). *The Study of Folklore*. Englewood Cliffs: Prentice Hall, 1965.

Dundes, A. "Metafolklore and Oral Literary Criticism", *The Monist*, 50, 1966.

Du Plooy, J. "Die Onstaan- en Vestigingsgeskiedenis van Potgietersrus 1852–1904". M.A. Dissertation, University of Potchefstroom, 1989.

Eiselin, W. "The Suto–Chuana Tribes: Sub-Group II: The Bapedi (Transvaal Basotho)", in

Duggan-Cronin, *The Bantu Tribes*, 1931.

Eisenstein, E. "The Advent of Printing and the Problem of the Renaissance", *Past and Present*, 45, 1969.

Engelbrecht, S.P. (ed.). *Paul Kruger's Amptelike Briewe 1851–1877*. Pretoria: Volkstem, 1925.

Erlmann, V. "Colonial Conquest and Popular Response in Northern Cameroun, 1881–1907", in Whitaker and Sienaert, *Oral Tradition and Literacy*, 1986.

Esterhuyse, C.J. "Die Ontwikkeling van die Noord-Sothoskryftaal". M.A. Dissertation, University of Pretoria, 1974.

Evans-Pritchard, E.E. (ed.). *The Zande Trickster*. London: Oxford University Press, 1967.

Fabian, J. *Language and Colonial Power: The Appropriation of Swahili in the Former Belgian Congo 1880–1938*. Cambridge: Cambridge University Press, 1986.

Faris, D.E. "Narrative Form and Oral History: Some Problems and Possibilities", *International Journal of Oral History*, 1, 3, 1980.

Feierman, S. *The Shambaa Kingdom: A History*. Madison: University of Wisconsin Press, 1974.

———*Peasant Intellectuals: Anthropology and History in Tanzania*. Madison: University of Wisconsin Press, 1990.

Finnegan, R. (tr. and ed.). *Limba Stories and Storytelling*. London: Oxford University Press, 1967.

———"A Note on Oral Tradition and Historiographical Evidence", *History and Theory*, 9, 2, 1971.

———*Oral Literature in Africa*. 1970; Nairobi: Oxford University Press, 1976.

———"Literacy and Literature", in Lloyd and Gay, *Universals in Human Thought*, 1981.

———*Literacy and Orality: Studies in the Technology of Communication*. Oxford: Basil Blackwell, 1988.

Foley, J. (ed.). *Oral Traditional Literature: A Festschrift for Albert Bates Lord*. Columbus: Slavica, 1981.

Fox-Genovese, E. "Literary Criticism and the Politics of New Historicism", in Veeser, *The New Historicism*, 1989.

Furet, F. and J. Ozouf. "Three Centuries of Cultural Cross-Fertilization: France", in Graff, *Literacy and Social Development*, 1981.

Gaitskell, D. "Devout Domesticity? A Century of African Women's Christianity in South Africa", in Walker, *Women and Gender in Southern Africa*, 1990.

Gallie, W. *Philosophy and the Historical Understanding*. London: Chatto & Windus, 1964.

Geertz, C. *Negara: The Theatre State in Nineteenth-century Bali*. Princeton: Princeton University Press, 1980.

Glassie, H. *Passing the Time in Ballymenone: Culture and History of an Ulster Community*. Philadelphia: University of Pennsylvania Press, 1982.

Godzich, W. and J. Kittay. *The Emergence of Prose*. Minneapolis: University of Minnesota Press, 1987.

Goldstein, K.S. "On the Application of the Concepts of Active and Inactive Traditions to the Study of Repertory", *Journal of American Folklore*, 84, 1971.

Goody, J. (ed.). *Literacy in Traditional Societies*. London: Cambridge University Press, 1968.

———"Restricted Literacy in Northern Ghana", in Goody, *Literacy in Traditional Societies*, 1968.

———*The Logic of Writing and the Organization of Society*. Cambridge: Cambridge University Press, 1986.

Goody, J. and I. Watt. "The Consequences of Literacy", *Comparative Studies in Society and History*, 5, 1962-3.

Gough, D. "Xhosa Narrative: An Analysis of the Production and Linguistic Properties of Discourse with Particular Reference to Iintsomi Texts". D. Phil. Thesis, Rhodes University, 1986.

Graff, H.J. *The Literacy Myth: Literacy and Social Structure in the Nineteenth Century*. New York: Academic Press, 1979.

—— (ed.). *Literacy and Social Development: A Reader*. Cambridge: Cambridge University Press, 1981.

—— "Introduction", in Graff, *Literacy and Social Development*, 1981.

Grele, R. *Envelopes of Sound: The Art of Oral History*. Chicago: Precedent, 1985.

Grillo, R. (ed.). *Social Anthropology and the Politics of Language*. London: Routledge, 1989.

—— "Anthropology, Language, Politics", in Grillo, *Social Anthropology and the Politics of Language*, 1989.

Groenewald, M. "Educating Attitudes: An Account of a Performance of Ndebele Iibongo", in Sienaert and Bell, *Catching Winged Words*, 1988.

Grundlingh, A. and H. Sapire. "From Feverish Festival to Repetitive Ritual? The Changing Fortunes of Great Trek Mythology in an Industrializing South Africa, 1938–1988", *South African Historical Journal*, 12, 1989.

Gunner, E. "A Dying Tradition? African Oral Literature in a Contemporary Context", *Social Dynamics*, 12, 2, 1986.

—— "The Word, the Book and the Zulu Church of Nazareth", in Whitaker and Sienaert, *Oral Tradition and Literacy*, 1986.

Gurr, P. *Daniel Heese: Ein Lebensbild aus der Mission in Makapanspoort in Nord-Transvaal*. Berlin: Berliner Evangelische Missionsgesellschaft, n.d.

Guy, J. "Gender Oppression in Southern Africa's Precapitalist Societies", in Walker, *Women and Gender in Southern Africa*, 1990.

Hamilton, C. "Ideology, Oral Tradition and the Struggle for Power in the Early Zulu Kingdom". M.A. Dissertation, University of the Witwatersrand, 1985.

—— "Ideology and Oral Traditions: Listening to the Voices 'From Below'", *History in Africa*, 14, 1987.

Hammond-Tooke, W.D. (ed.). *The Bantu-Speaking Peoples of Southern Africa*. London: Routledge & Kegan Paul, 1959.

Harries, C.L. *The Law and Custom of the Bapedi and Cognate Tribes*. Johannesburg: Hortors, 1929.

Harwood, F. "Myth, Memory, and the Oral Tradition: Cicero in the Trobriands", *American Anthropologist*, 78, 4, 1976.

Havelock, E.A. *The Literate Revolution in Greece and its Cultural Consequences*. Princeton: Princeton University Press, 1982.

Head, B. *Serowe: Village of the Rain Wind*. London: Heinemann, 1981.

Heath, S.B. "The Function and Uses of Literacy", *Journal of Communication*, 30, 1980.

Heckford, S. *A Lady Trader in the Transvaal*. London: Sampson Low, 1882.

Hendricks, F.T. "Loose Planning and Rapid Resettlement: The Politics of Conservation and Control in Transkei, South Africa, 1950–1970", *Journal of Southern African Studies*, 15, 2, 1989.

Henige, D.P. *The Chronology of Oral Tradition*. Oxford: Clarendon Press, 1974.

Herskovits, M.J. "The Study of African Oral Art", *Journal of American Folklore*, 74, 1961.

Herskovits, M.J. and F.S. Herskovits. *Dahomean Narrative: A Cross-Cultural Analysis*. Evanston: Northwestern University Press, 1958.

Hobsbawm, E. and T. Ranger (eds). *The Invention of Tradition*. Cambridge: Cambridge University Press, 1983.

Hodgson, J. "The Genius of Ntsikana: Traditional Images and the Process of Change in Early Xhosa Literature", in Couzens and White, *Literature and Society*, 1984.

—— "Fluid Assets and Fixed Investments: 160 Years of the Ntsikana Tradition", in Whitaker and Sienaert, *Oral Tradition and Literacy*, 1986.

Hofmeyr, I. "Building A Nation from Words: Afrikaans Language, Literature and Ethnic Identity, 1902–1924", in Marks and Trapido, *The Politics of Race*, 1987.

—— "Introduction: Exploring Experiential Testimony – A Selection of History Workshop Papers", *Social Dynamics*, 14, 2, 1988.

—— "Narrative and Oral History". Paper presented to the African Studies Institute Seminar, University of the Witwatersrand, Johannesburg, 16/5/88.

—— "Popularizing History: The Case of Gustav Preller", *Journal of African History*, 29, 1988.

—— "Turning Region in Narrative: English Storytelling in the Waterberg", in Bonner *et al.*, *Holding Their Ground*, 1989.

—— "Introduction", *Pretexts*, 2, 2, 1990.

—— "'Nterata'/'The Wire': Fences, Boundaries and Cultural Resistance in the Potgietersrus District", *International Annual of Oral History, 1990* (New York: Greenwood Press, 1992).

—— "Review Article: Feminist Literary Criticism in South Africa", *English in Africa*, 19, 1, 1992.

Horrell, M. *Visit to Bantu Areas of the Northern Transvaal June/July 1965*. Johannesburg: South African Institute of Race Relations, 1965.

Hunt, D.R. "An Account of the Bapedi", *Bantu Studies*, 5, 1931.

Hunt, L. (ed.). *The New Cultural History*. Berkeley: University of California Press, 1989.

Irwin, P. *Liptako Speaks: History from Oral Tradition in Africa*. Princeton: Princeton University Press, 1981.

Jackson, A.O. *The Ndebele of Langa*. (See under Official Publications – Republic of South Africa.)

—— "The Langa Ndebele Calendar". (See under Official Publications – Republic of South Africa.)

Jackson, M. *Allegories in the Wilderness: Ethics and Ambiguity in Kuranko Narratives*. Bloomington: Indiana University Press, 1982.

James, D. *The Road to Doornkop: A Case Study of Removal and Resistance*. Johannesburg: South African Institute of Race Relations, 1983.

—— "Kinship and Land in an Inter-Ethnic Community". M.A. Dissertation, University of the Witwatersrand, 1987.

—— "A Question of Ethnicity: Ndzundza Ndebele in a Lebowa Village", *Journal of Southern African Studies*, 16, 1, 1990.

Jansen van Vuuren, C. "Die Vestigingspatroon van die Suid-Ndebele". M.A. Dissertation, University of Pretoria, 1983.

Johnson, J.P. "Note on Some Stone-Walled Kraals in South Africa", *Man*, 36, 1912.

Johnson, R. (ed.). *Making Histories: Studies in History-Writing and Politics*. London: Hutchinson, 1982.

Jones, A.M. and H. Carter. "The Style of Tonga Historical Narrative", *African Language Studies*, 8, 1967.

Jordan, A.C. (tr.). *Tales from Southern Africa*. Berkeley: University of California Press, 1973.

—— *Towards an African Literature: The Emergence of Literary Form in Xhosa*. Berkeley: University of California Press, 1973.

Junod, H.A. *The Life of a South African Tribe*. 2 vols. London: Macmillan, 1927.

Kinsman, M. "'Beasts of Burden': The Subordination of Southern Tswana Women ca. 1800–1840", *Journal of Southern African Studies*, 10, 1, 1983.

Kistner, W. "The Anti-Slavery Agitation Against the Transvaal Republic, 1852–1868". *Archives Year Book for South African History*. 15th Year, Vol. II. Parow: Government Printer, 1952.

Krikler, J. "Agrarian Class Struggle and the South African War", *Social History*, 14, 2, 1989.

Kruger, P. *The Memoirs of Paul Kruger: Four Times President of the South African Republic: Told by Himself.* 2 vols. London: T. Fisher Unwin, 1902.

Kunene, D.P. *Thomas Mofolo and the Emergence of Written Sesotho Prose*. Johannesburg: Ravan, 1989.

Kuper, A. "The Social Structure of the Sotho-speaking Peoples of Southern Africa: Parts I and II", *Africa*, 45, 1-2, 1975.

——— "Fourie and the Southern Transvaal Ndebele", *African Studies*, 37, 1, 1978.

——— "Symbolic Dimensions of the Southern Bantu Homestead", *Africa*, 50, 1, 1980.

——— *South Africa and the Anthropologist*. London: Routledge & Kegan Paul, 1987.

Labov, W. *Language in the Inner City: Studies in Black English Vernacular*. Oxford: Basil Blackwell, 1977.

Lacey, M. *Working for Boroko: The Origins of a Coercive Labour System in South Africa*. Johannesburg: Ravan, 1980.

La Hausse, P. "Oral History and South African Historians", *Radical History Review*, 46-7, 1990.

LaPin, D. "Narrative as Precedent in Yoruba Oral Tradition", in Foley, *Oral Traditional Literature*, 1981.

Lestrade, G.P. "Domestic and Communal Life", in Schapera, *The Bantu-Speaking Tribes*, 1966.

——— "Traditional Literature", in Schapera, *The Bantu-Speaking Tribes*, 1966.

Letsoalo, E.M. "The Settlement System", in De Villiers, *A Rural Development Strategy*, 1984.

Lévi-Strauss, C. *The Savage Mind*. London: Weidenfeld & Nicolson, 1966.

Linde, C. "Private Stories in Public Discourse", *Poetics*, 15, 1986.

Lloyd, B. and J. Gay (eds). *Universals in Human Thought: Some African Evidence*. Cambridge: Cambridge University Press, 1981.

Lodge, T. *Black Politics in South Africa since 1945*. Johannesburg: Ravan Press, 1983.

Lord, A.B. *The Singer of Tales*. Cambridge, Mass.: Harvard University Press, 1964.

Loubser, J.H.N. "Ndebele Archaeology of the Pietersburg Area". M.A. Dissertation, University of the Witwatersrand, 1981.

Louch, A.R. "History as Narrative", *History and Theory*, 8, 1, 1969.

Mafeje, A. "The Role of the Bard in a Contemporary African Community", *Journal of African Languages*, 6, 3, 1967.

Maibelo, J.R. "The Structure, Content, Educational and Literary Value of the Padišo Series by Dr. P.E. Schwellnus". B.A. Hons Dissertation, University of the North, 1982.

Makgamatha, P.M. "Characteristics of the Northern Sotho Folktales: Their Form and Structure". M.A. Dissertation, University of South Africa, 1987.

Maponya, E.R. "The Use of Communication by the Northern Sotho Speaking Blacks in the Pietersburg Region". M.A. Dissertation, University of the North, 1984.

Marais, E. "Die Laaste Mapela-Moord", in Rousseau, *Eugène N. Marais*, 1982.

Marais, J.S. "Die Landbou-Potensiaal van Potgietersrust", in Combrink, *Eeufees Potgietersrust*, n.d.

Mare, G. *African Population Relocation in South Africa*. Johannesburg: South African Institute of Race Relations, 1980.

Marivate, C.D.T. "Tsonga Folktales: Form, Content and Delivery". 2 vols. M.A. Dissertation, University of South Africa, 1973.

Marks, S. and A. Atmore (eds). *Economy and Society in Pre-Industrial South Africa*. London: Longman, 1980.

Marks, S. and S. Trapido (eds). *The Politics of Race, Class and Nationalism in Twentieth-century South Africa*. London: Longman, 1987.

Mason, R. *Cave of Hearths: Makapansgat Transvaal*. Johannesburg: Archaeological Research Unit, University of the Witwatersrand, 1988.

Mbiti, J.S. (ed.). *Akamba Stories*. London: Oxford University Press, 1966.

McAllister, P. "Conservatism as Ideology of Resistance among Xhosa-speakers: The

Implications for Oral Tradition and Literacy", in Whitaker and Sienaert, *Oral Tradition and Literacy*, 1986.

—— "Inclusion and Exclusion in the Oral Transmission of Ritual Knowledge: A Xhosa Communicative Strategy", in Sienaert and Bell, *Catching Winged Words*, 1988.

—— "Political Aspects of Xhosa Beer Drink Oratory", *English in Africa*, 15, 1, 1988.

—— "Resistance to 'Betterment' in the Transkei: A Case Study from Willowvale District", *Journal of Southern African Studies*, 15, 2, 1989.

McKenzie, D.F. "The Sociology of a Text: Oral Culture, Literacy and Print in Early New Zealand", in Burke and Porter, *The Social History of Language*, 1987.

McKenzie, F.A. *Paul Kruger: His Life Story*. London: Bowden, 1899.

McMahan, E.M. *Elite Oral History Discourse: A Study of Cooperation and Coherence*. Tuscaloo: University of Alabama Press, 1989.

Meyer, J.H. "Die Onstaan en Ontwikkeling van Potgietersrust as Dorp", in Combrink, *Eeufees Potgietersrust*, n.d.

Miller, J.C. (ed.). *The African Past Speaks: Essays on Oral Tradition and History*. Folkestone: Dawson/Archon, 1980.

—— "Introduction: Listening for the African Past", in Miller, *The African Past Speaks*, 1980.

Mink, L.O. "Philosophical Analysis and Historical Understanding", *The Review of Metaphysics*, 21, 4, 1968.

—— "History and Fiction as Modes of Comprehension", in Cohen, *New Directions in Literary History*, 1974.

—— "Narrative Form as a Cognitive Instrument", in Canary and Kozicki, *The Writing of History*, 1978.

Moephuli, I.M. "Structure and Character in Cyclic Folktales in Southern Sotho". M.A. Dissertation, University of South Africa, 1979.

Mofokeng, S.M. "A Study of Folk Tales in Sotho". M.A. Dissertation, University of the Witwatersrand, 1951.

—— "The Development of Leading Figures in Animal Tales in Africa". D. Phil. Thesis, University of the Witwatersrand, 1954.

Mönnig, H.O. *The Pedi*. 1967; Pretoria: Van Schaik, 1988.

Naidoo, J. *Tracking Down Historical Myths: Eight South African Case Studies*. Johannesburg: Ad Donker, 1989.

Neethling, S.J. "Die Xhosa Iintsomi: 'n Strukturele Benadering". D. Phil. Thesis, University of Stellenbosch, 1979.

Nel, D. "Die Drama van Makapansgrot: Soos deur die Naturelle Vertel", *Die Huisgenoot*, 24/3/33.

Nkonki, G. "The Traditional Prose Literature of the Ngqika". M.A. Dissertation, University of South Africa, 1968.

Noble, J. *South Africa: Past and Present*. London: Longman, 1877.

Norris-Newman, C.L. *With the Boers in the Transvaal and Orange Free State in 1880–1*. 1882; Johannesburg: Africana Book Society, 1976.

Okpewho, I. *The Epic in Africa: Towards a Poetics of the Oral Performance*. New York: Columbia University Press, 1979.

Olson, D.R. "On the Language and Authority of Textbooks", *Journal of Communication*, 30, 1980.

Ong, W. *Orality and Literacy: The Technologizing of the Word*. London: Methuen, 1982.

Oosthuizen, M. "A Study of the Structure of the Zulu Folktale with Special Reference to the Stuart Collection". M.A. Dissertation, University of Natal, Durban, 1977.

Opland, J. *Xhosa Oral Poetry: Aspects of a Black South African Tradition*. Johannesburg: Ravan, 1983.

—— "The Transition from Oral to Written Literature in Xhosa, 1823–1909", in Whitaker and Sienaert, *Oral Tradition and Literacy*, 1986.

—— "The Bible in Front, the Musket Behind: Images of White Oppression in Xhosa Oral Poetry". Paper presented to the Fourth National Technological Literacy Conference, Washington, 3-5/2/89.

Orpen, J.M. *Reminiscences of Life in South Africa from 1846 to the Present Day*. 1908; Cape Town: Struik, 1964.

Parry, B. "Problems in Current Theories of Colonial Discourse", *Oxford Literary Review*, 9, 1-2, 1987.

Passerini, L. "Italian Working Class Culture between the Wars: Consensus to Fascism and Work Ideology", *International Journal of Oral History*, 1, 1, 1980.

Pitje, G.M. "Traditional Systems of Male Education among Pedi and Cognate Tribes: Parts I-III", *African Studies*, 9, 2-4, 1950.

Polanyi, L. "Literary Complexity in Everyday Storytelling", in Tannen, *Spoken and Written Language*, 1982.

Popular Memory Group. "Popular Memory: Theory, Politics, Method", in Johnson, *Making Histories*, 1982.

Portelli, A. "The Peculiarities of Oral History", *History Workshop Journal*, 12, 1981.

—— "'The Time of My Life': Functions of Time in Oral History", *International Journal of Oral History*, 2, 3, 1981.

Posel, D. "Influx Control and the Construction of Apartheid, 1948–1961". D. Phil. Thesis, Oxford University, 1987.

—— "The State and Policy-Making in Apartheid's Second Phase". Paper presented to the History Workshop Conference, University of the Witwatersrand, Johannesburg, 6-10/2/90.

Preller, G. *Oorlogsoormag en Ander Sketse en Verhale*. Cape Town: Nasionale Pers, 1931.

—— "Baanbrekers", in Preller, *Oorlogsoormag: en Ander Sketse*, 1931.

—— *Geskiedenis van die Kruger-standbeeld*. Pretoria: Ossewa-Boekhandel, n.d.

Prins, G. *The Hidden Hippopotamus: Reappraisal in African History: The Early Colonial Experience in Western Zambia*. Cambridge: Cambridge University Press, 1980.

Ranger, T. "The Invention of Tradition in Colonial Africa", in Hobsbawm and Ranger, *The Invention of Tradition*, 1983.

Rappoport, J. "Mythic Images, Historical Thought, and Printed Texts: The Páez and the Written Word", *Journal of Anthropological Research*, 43, 1987.

Ritchken, E. "Chiefs, Migrants, the State and Ethnicity: The Leihlo le Naga Migrant Workers Organisation 1978–1986". Paper presented to the History Workshop Conference, University of the Witwatersrand, Johannesburg, 6-10/2/1990.

Ritter, E.A. *Shaka Zulu: The Rise of the Zulu Empire*. 1955; London: Longman, 1971.

Robbertse, J.A. "Kultuurorganisasie: Potgietersrust", in Combrink, *Eeufees Potgietersrust*, n.d.

Roberts, A. "The Uses of Oral Sources for African History", *Oral History*, 4, 1, 1976.

Rosaldo, M.Z. and L. Lamphere (eds). *Women, Culture, and Society*. Stanford: Stanford University Press, 1974.

—— "Introduction", in Rosaldo and Lamphere, *Women, Culture, and Society*, 1975.

Rosaldo, R. "Doing Oral History", *Social Analysis*, 4, 1980.

—— *Ilongot Headhunting: 1883–1974: A Study in Society and History*. Stanford: Stanford University Press, 1980.

Rosseau, L. *The Dark Stream: The Story of Eugène N. Marais*. Johannesburg: Jonathan Ball, 1982.

—— (ed.). *Eugène N. Marais: Versamelde Werke*. 2 vols. Pretoria: Van Schaik, 1984.

Sansom, B. "Leadership and Authority in a Pedi Chiefdom". D. Phil. Thesis, University of Manchester, 1970.

Schapera, I. (ed.). *David Livingstone: Family Letters 1841–1856*. 2 vols. London: Chatto &

Windus, 1959.

—— (ed.). *Livingstone's Missionary Correspondence: 1841–1856*. London: Chatto & Windus, 1961.

—— (ed.). *The Bantu-Speaking Tribes of South Africa: An Ethnographical Survey*. 1937; Cape Town: Maskew Miller, 1966.

—— *A Handbook of Tswana Law and Custom*. London: Frank Cass, 1970.

Scheub, H. "Introduction", in Jordan, *Tales from Southern Africa*, 1973.

—— *The Xhosa Ntsomi*. Oxford: Oxford University Press, 1975.

—— "A Review of African Oral Traditions and Literature", *African Studies Review*, 28, 2-3, 1985.

—— "Oral Poetry as History", *New Literary History*, 3, 1987.

Schneider, B. "Paint, Pride and Politics: Aesthetic and Meaning in Transvaal Ndebele Wall Art". Ph. D. Thesis, University of the Witwatersrand, 1986.

Schwellnus, P. *Padišo III*. Pretoria: Northern Sotho Book Depot, n.d.

—— "*Masasara*", in Schwellnus, *Padišo III*, n.d.

—— *Padišo B*. Pretoria: Northern Sotho Book Depot, n.d.

Scott, J.C. *Weapons of the Weak: Everyday Forms of Peasant Resistance*. New Haven: Yale University Press, 1985.

Scully, R.T.K. "Phalaborwa Oral Traditions". Ph.D. Thesis, State University of New York at Binghamton, 1978.

Shreve, G.M. and O. Arewa. "Forms and Genre in African Folklore Classification: A Semiotic Perspective", *Research in African Literatures*, 11, 3, 1980.

Shuman, A. *Storytelling Rights: The Uses of Oral and Written Texts by Urban Adolescents*. Cambridge: Cambridge University Press, 1986.

Sienaert, E. and N. Bell (eds). *Catching Winged Words: Oral Tradition and Education*. Durban: Natal University Oral Documentation and Research Centre, 1988.

Sitas, A. "The Voice and Gesture in South Africa's Revolution: A Study of Worker Gatherings and Performance-Genres in Natal". Paper presented to the History Workshop Conference, University of the Witwatersrand, Johannesburg, 6-10/2/90.

South African Institute of Race Relations. *Establishment of the Bantu Authorities: First and Second Interim Report*. Johannesburg: S.A.I.R.R., 1959.

Stempel, W-D. "Everyday Narrative as Prototype", *Poetics*, 15, 1986.

Stock, B. *The Implications of Literacy: Written Language and Models of Interpretation in the Eleventh and Twelfth Centuries*. Princeton: Princeton University Press, 1983.

Stone, L. "Literacy and Education in England 1640–1900", *Past and Present*, 42, 1969.

Stow, G.W. *The Native Races of South Africa: A History of the Intrusion of the Hottentots and Bantu into the Hunting Grounds of the Bushmen, the Aborigines of the Country*. London: S. Sonnenschein, 1905.

Street, B. *Literacy in Theory and Practice*. Cambridge: Cambridge University Press, 1984.

—— (ed.). *Cross-Cultural Approaches to Literacy*. Forthcoming.

—— "Introduction", in Street, *Cross-Cultural Approaches to Literacy*, n.d.

Surplus People Project. *Forced Removal in South Africa: The Transvaal*. 5 vols. Cape Town: Surplus People Project, 1983.

Tannen, D. (ed.). *Spoken and Written Language: Exploring Orality and Literacy*. Norwood: Ablex, 1982.

Tedlock, D. *The Spoken Word and the Work of Interpretation*. Philadelphia: University of Pennsylvania Press, 1983.

Theal, G.M. *History of South Africa since September 1795*. 11 vols. 1889; London: S. Sonnenschein, 1908.

Thwaite, M. *From Primer to Pleasure: An Introduction to the History of Children's Books in England from the Invention of Printing to 1914 with an Outline of Some Developments in Other Countries*. 1963; London: The Library Association, 1972.

Thompson, S. *The Folktale*. 1946; New York: The Dryden Press, 1951.

Tobias, P.V. "A Page from History", *Natal Daily Mail*, 15/1/47.

Tonkin, E. "The Boundaries of History in Oral Performance", *History in Africa*, 9, 1982.

―――― "Steps to the Redefinition of 'Oral History': Examples from Africa", *Social History*, 7, 2, 1982.

―――― "Investigating Oral Tradition", *Journal of African History*, 27, 1986.

―――― "Historical Discourses: The Achievement of Sieh Jeto", *History in Africa*, 15, 1988.

Turner, V.W. *The Forest of Symbols: Aspects of Ndembu Rituals*. New York: Cornell University Press, 1967.

Twain, M. (pseud. of S. Clements). *More Tramps Abroad*. London: Chatto & Windus, 1897.

Vail, L. and L. White. "The Art of Being Ruled: Ndebele Praise Poetry", in Couzens and White, *Literature and Society*, 1984.

―――― *Power and the Praise Poem: Southern African Voices in History*. Charlottesville: University of Virginia Press, 1991.

Van der Merwe, D.W. "Die Geskiedenis van die Berlynse Sendinggenootskap in die Transvaal 1860–1900". M.A. Dissertation, University of South Africa, 1975.

Van Riet Lowe, C.L. (ed.). *The Monuments of South Africa*. Pretoria: Government Printer, 1941.

Van Warmelo, N.J. (comp.). *Anthropology of Southern African in Periodicals to 1950: An Analysis and Index*. Johannesburg: Witwatersrand University Press, 1977.

―――― *The Bakgatla ba ga Mosetlha*. (See under Official Publications – Union of South Africa.)

―――― "The Classification of Cultural Groups", in Hammond-Tooke, *The Bantu-Speaking Peoples*, 1959.

―――― *Transvaal Ndebele Texts*. (See under Official Publications – Union of South Africa.)

Veeser, H.A. (ed.). *The New Historicism*. New York: Routledge, 1989.

Velay-Vallantin, C. "Tales as a Mirror: Perrault in the Bibliothèque Bleue", in Chartier, *The Culture of Print*, 1989.

Von Sydow, C.W. "Folktale Studies and Philology: Some Points of View", in Dundes, *The Study of Folklore*, 1965.

Wagner, R. "The Zoutpansberg: The Dynamics of a Hunting Frontier, 1848–1867", in Marks and Atmore, *Economy and Society*, 1980.

Walker, C. (ed.). *Women and Gender in Southern Africa to 1945*. Cape Town: David Philip, 1990.

Wallis, J.P.R. (ed.). *The Matabele Journals of Robert Moffat 1829–1860*. 2 vols. London: Chatto & Windus, 1945.

Wangemann, T. *Ein Reise-Jahr in Süd-Afrika*. Berlin: Missionshauses, 1868.

―――― Account of Siege (untitled), in *Die Transvaal'sche öder Süd-Afrikanische Republik, Ergänzungheft No. 24 zu Petermann's "Geographischen Mittheilungen"*. No place: Gotha/Justus Perthes, 1868.

Wellington, J.H. *Southern Africa: A Geographical Survey*. 2 vols. Cambridge: Cambridge University Press, 1955.

Werbner, R.P. "The Political Economy of Bricolage", *Journal of Southern African Studies*, 13, 1, 1986.

Whitaker, R. and E. Sienaert (eds). *Oral Tradition and Literacy: Changing Visions of the World*. Durban: Natal University Oral Documentation and Research Centre, 1986.

White, A. "Hysteria and the End of Carnival: Festivity and Bourgeois Neurosis", in Armstrong and Tennenhouse, *Violence and Representation*, 1989.

White, H. *Tropics of Discourse: Essays in Cultural Criticism*. Baltimore: Johns Hopkins University Press, 1978.

―――― "The Question of Narrative in Contemporary Historical Theory", *History and Theory*, 23, 1, 1984.

White, L. "Review Article: Literature and History in Africa", *Journal of African History*, 21, 1980.

———"Power and Praise Poetry", *Journal of Southern African Studies*, 9, 1, 1982.

———"Poetic Licence: Oral Poetry and History", in Barber and De Moraes Farias, *Discourse and its Disguises*, 1989.

Wright, M. *German Missions in Tanganyika 1891–1941*. Oxford: Clarendon Press, 1971.

Yawitch, J. *Betterment: The Myth of Homeland Agriculture*. Johannesburg: South African Institute of Race Relations, 1982.

Ziervogel, D. *A Grammar of Northern Transvaal Ndebele*. Pretoria: Van Schaik, 1959.

V INTERVIEWS CITED

Unless otherwise stated, all interviews and transcripts are in the possession of the author.

Interviews on Oral Historical Storytelling

Group interview with members of the Bakenberg Tribal Authority: Nseki Bilankulu, Lesiba Digashu, Matlhaba Langa, Mmasehlaba Langa, Sekgoma Langa, Kgarebe Moshia, Thabankoane Motlatla, interviewed by Isabel Hofmeyr, Bakenburg, 27/7/88.

Hosea Bowale, interviewed by Peter Lekgoathi, Tamaties, Zebediela district, 5/5/89.

Alfred Lesiba Kekana, interviewed by Isabel Hofmeyr, Sekgakgapeng, 22/6/90.

Cecil Lesiba Kekana, interviewed by Job Kekana, Tim Couzens and Isabel Hofmeyr, Mahwelereng, 7/3/89.

Chaclice Kekana, interviewed by Peter Lekgoathi, Tamaties, Zebediela district, 5/5/89.

Job Patja Kekana, interviewed by Isabel Hofmeyr, Westdene, Johannesburg, 5/3/89.

Job Patja Kekana, interviewed by Isabel Hofmeyr, Westdene, Johannesburg, 7/6/90.

Lucky Mokgaetši Mokekolwane Kekana and Mantutule Joyce Mmushi, interviewed by Jacob Mthembu and Isabel Hofmeyr, Makapanspoort Mission, Potgietersrus district, 3/4/90.

Madimetša Klaas Kekana, interviewed by Peter Kekana, Edwin Nyatlo and Isabel Hofmeyr, Mošate, Valtyn, 28/11/87.

Madimetša Klaas Kekana, interviewed by Motlalepula Mashao, Debra Nails and Isabel Hofmeyr, Mošate, Valtyn, 1/10/88.

Mahula Patrick Somarso Kekana, interviewed by Peter Kekana, Edwin Nyatlo and Isabel Hofmeyr, Mošate, Valtyn, 12/12/87.

Mashishi, M., interviewed by Boyboy Maboya, Mahwelereng, 13/6/90. Interview in the possession of B. Maboya, Mahwelereng.

Molalakgori Kekana, interviewed by Felix Malunga, Sidney Maaka and Isabel Hofmeyr, Mahwelereng, 10/8/88.

Mosoamadite Kekana, interviewed by Johanna Moima and Isabel Hofmeyr, Valtyn, 19/3/88.

Obed Kutumela, interviewed by John Kutumela, Hanna Schulze and Isabel Hofmeyr, Sekgakgapeng, 15/1/89.

Obed Kutumela, interviewed by Anna Kiti Kutumela and Isabel Hofmeyr, Sekgakgapeng, 20/4/90.

Piet Lesiba Kekana and Obed Kutumela, interviewed by Anna Kiti Kutumela and Isabel Hofmeyr, Sekgakgapeng, 26/4/90.

Morongoa Kgosana, interviewed by Johannes Moima, Nico Mabusela and Isabel Hofmeyr, Mahwelereng, 19/3/88.

Alpheus Ledwaba, interviewed by Madimetša Ledwaba and Isabel Hofmeyr, Moletlane, 7/9/88.

Fred Ledwaba, interviewed by Madimetša Ledwaba and Isabel Hofmeyr, Lebowakgomo, 7/10/88.

Moses Ledwaba and Matthews Hlanga, interviewed by Amos Ledwaba, Madimetša Ledwaba and Isabel Hofmeyr, 8/9/88.

Zaba Maluleke, interviewed by Isabel Hofmeyr at the farm Makapansgat, Potgietersrus district, 5/4/88.

John Maselela Maleka, interviewed by Johanna Moima and Isabel Hofmeyr, Mahwelereng, 19/3/88.

Leka Thinta Mokhonoane, interviewed by Peter Kekana, Edwin Nyatlo and Isabel Hofmeyr, Mošate, Valtyn, 12/12/87.

Leka Thinta Mokhonoane and Mosoamadite Kekana, interviewed by Jane Letsebe-Matlou and Isabel Hofmeyr, Mošate, Valtyn, 10/11/89.

Tshwane Mvundlela and Ledile Kekana, interviewed by Motlalepula Mashao, Debra Nails and Isabel Hofmeyr, Mošate, Valtyn, 1/10/88.

Calvin Mogahlahla Puka, interviewed by Isabel Hofmeyr, Makapanspoort Mission, Potgietersrus district, 8/4/90.

Asaph Tsebe, interviewed by Jane Letsebe-Matlou and Isabel Hofmeyr, Mahwelereng, 10/11/89.

Interviews on Oral Storytelling

Alfred Lesiba Kekana, interviewed by Isabel Hofmeyr, Sekgakgapeng, 29/3/90.

Christina Raisitja Kekana, interviewed by Alfred Lesiba Kekana and Isabel Hofmeyr, Sekgakgapeng, 3/4/90.

Christina Raisitja Kekana and Mogotlane Kekana, interviewed by Alfred Lesiba Kekana and Isabel Hofmeyr, Sekgakgapeng, Valtyn, 6/4/90.

Grace Karolo Kekana, interviewed by Jacobeth Ramupudu and Isabel Hofmeyr, Mošate, Valtyn, 23/3/90.

Grace Karolo Kekana, interviewed by Jacobeth Ramupudu and Isabel Hofmeyr, Mošate, Valtyn, 20/4/90.

Lucky Mokgaetši Mokekolwane Kekana and Mantutule Joyce Mmushi, interviewed by

Jacob Mthembu and Isabel Hofmeyr, Makapanspoort Mission, Potgietersrus district, 9/4/90.

Ramasela Serosina Kekana, interviewed by Alfred Lesiba Kekana and Isabel Hofmeyr, Sekgakgapeng, 30/3/90.

Morongoa Kgosana, interviewed by Helen Maime and Isabel Hofmeyr, Mahwelereng, 1/3/90.

Makgabo Ramasela Langa, interviewed by Morongoa Kgosana and Isabel Hofmeyr, Mahwelereng, 7/3/90.

Mashishi, M., interviewed by B. Maboya, Mahwelereng, 13/6/90.

Mosiwa Martha Lekalakala, interviewed by Jacobeth Ramupudu and Isabel Hofmeyr, Makapanspoort Mission, Potgietersrus district, 13/3/90.

Sophie Legkoathi and Emily Mashishi, interviewed by Helen Maime and Isabel Hofmeyr, Mahwelereng, 7/3/90.

Moletsi Daniel Mahlangu, interviewed by Jacobeth Ramupudu and Isabel Hofmeyr, Makapanspoort Mission, Potgietersrus district, 13/3/90.

Moletsi Daniel Mahlangu, interviewed by Jacobeth Ramupudu and Isabel Hofmeyr, Makapanspoort Mission, Potgietersrus district, 20/3/90.

Helen Maime, interviewed by Isabel Hofmeyr, Mahwelereng, 23/6/90.

Dikgopana Rampula, interviewed by Isabel Hofmeyr, Mahwelereng, 30/4/90.

Priscilla Ramokone Rampula, interviewed by Anna Kiti Kutumela, Obed Kutumela and Isabel Hofmeyr, Sekgakgapeng, 20/4/90.

Fransina Ramasela Sema, interviewed by Rose Lephondo, Sarah Teffo and Isabel Hofmeyr, Masehlaneng, 15/3/90.

Madumelana Shiloti, interviewed by Ruth Khaas and Isabel Hofmeyr, Mahwelereng, 28/2/90.

Naomi Teffo, interviewed by Isabel Hofmeyr, Mahwelereng, 9/4/90.

Sarah Teffo, interviewed by Rose Lephondo and Isabel Hofmeyr, Mahwelereng, 6/3/90.

Dinah Raisibe Thabeta, interviewed by Anna Kiti Kutumela, Obed Kutumela and Isabel Hofmeyr, Sekgakgapeng, 20/4/90.

INDEX

African studies, 2,7
Afrikaner nationalism, 14, 70, 139; and
  cultural movements, 153-5; and
  Makapansgat story, 144-9; and
  monuments, 149-50; and oral history,
  145; relation to Ndebele oral
  tradition, 171; see also Preller, and
  Historiography
Agar-Hamilton, J.A.I., 144
Anthropology, 1, 2; and oral history, 2, 5
Ardrey, R., 20

Baines, T., 132, 142
Bakenberg, 19, 68, 70, 76, 82
Bantu Authorities Act, 18, 79, 82; effects
  on chieftaincy, 124; and literacy, 175-
  6; and rural societies, 80
Bantu Education, 52, 166
Bantu Self-Government Act of 1959, 79
Barber, K., 1, 2, 4, 5, 179; *I Could Speak
  Until Tomorrow*, 2; "Popular Arts in
  Africa", 5
Beidelman, T., 5
Beinart, W., 80
Ben-Amos, D., 29
Berlin Mission Society, 14, 19, 42, 47, 165;
  establishment in Northern Transvaal,
  44-7; and education, 49; and literacy,
  46, 49; relation to Transvaal
  Republic, 142; see also Lutheranism,
  and Makapanspoort mission station
Betterment, 11, 70, 79, 81-3, 166;
  consequences, 80; culling, 70, 81;

effect on chieftaincy, 124; history
  of, 80; impact on oral storytelling,
  80; impact on rural societies, 80;
  popular perception of effects, 99;
  see also Forced removals
Bill, M., 34
Bosman, H.C., 146; "Makapan's Cave",
  146
Botha, L., 149
Boundaries: African views of, 73; and
  beacons, 74; colonial views of, 72;
  gerrymandering, 73; and identity,
  73; and surveying methods, 73; see
  also Fencing
Brandwag, Die, 150
Breaker Morant, 47
Bricolage, 6, 15, 167
Bricoleur, 160
Bureaucracy, 14; and boundaries, 74;
  and control of land, 72; and
  correspondence, 62-7; language of,
  72; and literacy, 42, 67; and orality,
  14
Bynum, D., 35

Chatwin, B., 20
Chidi, see Pruissen
Chieftaincy, 14; and betterment, 81;
  decline of, 124; divisions in, 179;
  effects of fencing on, 71; as fulcrum
  of oral historical narrative, 123-36;
  historiography of, 133; and official
  correspondence, 62; in oral

323